GW00497673

RONAY'S

JUST A BITE

1989

Establishment research is conducted by a team of full-time professional inspectors, who are trained to achieve common standards of judgement with as much objectivity as this field allows. Their professional identities are not disclosed until they seek information from the management after paying their bills. The Guide is independent in its editorial selection and does not accept advertising, payment or hospitality from establishments covered.

Egon Ronay's Guides
City Wall House,
Basing View, Basingstoke,
Hampshire RG21 2AP

Editorial contribution *Rosemary Forgan*

Design and Illustrations *Indent Designers and Illustrators*
Cartoons *Peter Neame*
Cover Design *Spero Communications Design Ltd*
Marketing and Sponsorship Consultants *Spero Marketing Consultancy Ltd*

Cartography by *Geoprojects (UK) Ltd.* All road maps are based on the Ordnance Survey Maps, with the permission of the Controller of HM Stationery Office. Crown copyright reserved. Town plans by *Intermap P.S. Ltd*, Reading.

The contents of this book are believed correct at the time of printing. Nevertheless, the publisher can accept no responsibility for errors or omissions or changes in the details given.

Distributed in the United Kingdom by the Publishing Division of The Automobile Association, Fanum House, Basingstoke, Hampshire RG21 2EA and overseas by the British Tourist Authority, Thames Tower, Black's Road, London W6 9EL.

ISBN 0 86145 783 8

AA Ref 57451

Typeset and printed in Great Britain by William Clowes Limited, Beccles and London

CONTENTS

THE • ENTRIES

TOWN • MAPS

with plotted Guide entries to

MAPS

FOREWORD

Tea has been our national drink for over a hundred years, and is likely to remain so for the foreseeable future. It is the perfect accompaniment to a delicious teatime snack or light lunch, such as those served by the establishments recommended in the Just a Bite Guide. So once again Brooke Bond is delighted to be sponsoring this Guide, which shares a common philosophy with PG Tips – that of promoting high quality at reasonable prices.

PG Tips is Britain's favourite natural refreshment with 45 million cups being drunk each day. Morever, as a natural complement to today's healthier diets, PG is becoming even more popular with the young, many of whom actively search for it when out for a meal.

That's why the standard of tea available to the public with their meals out is of great importance to us, and we are again pleased to be associated with Egon Ronay's Guides, a name synonymous with excellence.

GERAINT R. DAVIES

H O·W T O U S E T H I S G U I D E

T Y P E S · O F · E S T A B L I S H M E N T

For this Guide the inspectors have a brief to look for establishments serving good snacks and light meals. These snacks could be anything from a scone and a sandwich to a slice of quiche, a salad, a hot main course or perhaps something in the sushi line or ditto with dim sum.

Establishments where the food is judged outstanding are
★   shown with a star.   ★

Q U I C K · R E F E R E N C E · L I S T S

If you are looking specifically for somewhere that serves afternoon tea, wholefood or vegetarian meals, is handy for the motorway, or where you can eat on Sundays, late at night or out of doors, then consult the quick reference lists at the beginning of the book before turning to the gazetteer entry for a full description.

P R I C E S

Prices are quoted for two typical items or for the cost of a set tea where applicable. These prices were valid at the time of inspection but may have risen since then. Minimum charges per person are usually indicated in the entry.

L I C E N S I N G · A N D · O P E N I N G · H O U R S

It is indicated if an establishment is unlicensed.

Opening hours given refer specifically to times when the snacks described are available. For example, a restaurant offering just a bite at lunchtime does not have its evening hours listed if there is only a full dinner menu, but reference may be made to this in the entry.

As far as possible it is indicated which dishes are served throughout opening hours and which form part of a special lunch, tea or other menu. Many establishments have flexible hours because of their small size or remote location, and it is thus safest to check opening times. In addition, recent changes in the licensing laws may mean that some establishments will extend their opening hours beyond the times we have indicated, but it is advisable to check first.

PARKING

Details of the nearest convenient parking are given.

ORDER • OF • LISTINGS

London entries appear first and are in alphabetical order by establishment name. Listings outside London are in alphabetical order by location within the regional divisions of England, Scotland, Wales, the Channel Islands and the Isle of Man.

MAP • REFERENCES

Entries contain references to the map section at the end of the Guide or to the town plans (see contents for the list and page numbers).

SYMBOLS

★

Outstanding food

A good cup of tea
(see also page 59)

Dairy Crest Cheese Symbol of Excellence
(see also page 72 for cheeseboards considered outstanding)

LVs

Luncheon Vouchers welcome
(see also page 88)

Credit

Credit cards accepted

P

Nearest convenient spot for car parking

Considered by the management as suitable for wheelchairs

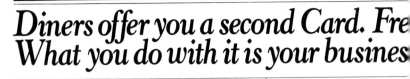

Diners offer you a second Card. Fre
What you do with it is your busines

This is an offer of two Diners Club cards for you.

One has Business Account marked on it. And that's exactly what it's for. The second card is for your personal expenses.

You get a two-part statement each month. One cheque settles both bills.

The second card doesn't cost you any extra.

Needless to say your Diners Club Cards are welcome at more than one million establishments around the World wherever you do business.

Only Diners Club offer two cards free. If you'd like to know how two cards are better than one, telephone 0252 513 500.

Diners means business
(and pleasure).

INTRODUCTION

There was a time when the choice available if you just wanted a quick snack or meal in this country was limited to take-away fish and chips or steak and kidney pie. That, thankfully, has all changed now, as a glance through the pages of this Guide easily demonstrates. As well as traditional English, Scottish and Welsh dishes, regional specialities are being increasingly offered from Cornwall to Cumbria. The range of establishments is extensive: sample the classic environment of a lofty London hotel for old-fashioned afternoon tea or a simple cottage tea room on the shores of a Scottish Loch. Both can offer that extra dimension that makes for a memorable eating experience.

ETHNIC CUISINE

Exciting, too, is the emergence of small and modestly-priced restaurants serving high-quality food from countries all round the world. In London alone, you can be transported into the culinary worlds of Thailand, Indonesia, Africa, the Caribbean, Turkey, the Middle East, America, Japan, Vietnam, Greece, Tibet and Switzer-land as well as the old stalwarts of France, Italy, India and China. Then there's Indonesian and Malaysian cooking *par excellence* at Munchy Munchy in Oxford, one of our three finalists for Just A Bite Restaurant of the Year; Middle Eastern cooking at Upstairs in Cambridge; Hungarian specialities at Meader's in Ross-on-Wye; Mexican dishes at Oat Cuisine in York; the excellent Indian vegetarian menu at Kalpna in Edinburgh or outstanding meat dishes at Black Chapati in Brighton; and northern European cuisine at the Flying Dutchman Hotel in St Peter Port, Guernsey. So now there is no excuse not to try something a bit different for a change, as these places are well within normal affordable limits.

HEALTHY AND UNHEALTHY

The joy of this Guide is that it encompasses many extremes, one of the most marked of which is the contrast between the numerous health food cafés and restaurants now springing up and capturing a willing clientele, and the wickedly fattening and unhealthy, but so delicious as to be quite irresistible, cakes, pastries and sweets which are lovingly home-made and charmingly served in our many delightful tea rooms, coffee shops and pâtisseries. Whether you wish to indulge yourself in a naughty treat or satisfy your tastebuds more virtuously with wholefood or vegetarian fare you will find here numerous excellent establishments to choose from.

PATIENCE

The only problem you might encounter with our smaller restaurants, cafés and tea rooms is that they are very popular and therefore often extremely busy, so do be patient if you have to wait for a table, or take the precaution of booking in advance if this is appropriate. Our inspectors have to exercise a great deal of patience in their work, as you will see from the feature on pages 47–49, 'An Inspector's Lot . . .'. I'm sure our proprietors would appreciate any easing of their frantic work rate!

SPECIAL INVESTIGATION

Our attention this year has been turned towards the service offered on cross-Channel routes by the various operators, and the eating facilities available within easy reach of both the English and Continental ports. See pages 29–40 for our interesting conclusions on the present standards of cross-Channel sea travel.

RESTAURANT
OF THE YEAR

3 Finalists

The award of Just a Bite Restaurant of the Year 1989 recognises all-round excellence in what an establishment sets out to do. A shortlist has been drawn up from the hundreds of entries in the Guide, and the three finalists are listed below and on pages 12–13. At the launch of the Guide the winner will be announced and be presented with a specially designed Wedgwood plaque.

MUNCHY MUNCHY
OXFORD
Restaurant of the Year Finalist

If they awarded a degree in Asian cooking at Oxford, Ethel Ow would surely graduate with major honours. Her cooking, inspired by Malaysia and Indonesia, is fast and full of flair, with herbs and spices and fresh fruit making delicate yet decisive contributions to a mouthwatering choice of dishes. Everything's splendid, so it's best to go in a group and sample the whole lot!

HANDSEL'S WINE BAR
EDINBURGH
Restaurant of the Year Finalist

The setting is an elegant Georgian house in the city centre, and since its opening in August 1986 Handsel's has proved a great success. Go-ahead owners David and Tina Thomson have the services of a very talented chef in 30-year-old Andrew Radford, whose menus provide customers with a daily-changing range of delightful and imaginative dishes based on the finest fresh produce.

WILTSHIRE KITCHEN
DEVIZES
Restaurant of the Year Finalist

It was a red-letter day for the citizens of Devizes when Ann Blunden opened the doors of her attractive corner restaurant nearly three years ago. Lunchtime brings lovely salads and quiches, along with ever-changing hot specials that are a real treat. At other times the sweet of tooth can gorge on gâteaux, revel in roulades or munch on monstrous meringues.

STARRED ENTRIES

THE FOLLOWING LIST HIGHLIGHTS ESTABLISHMENTS
WHERE THE FOOD IS JUDGED TO BE OF A PARTICULARLY
HIGH QUALITY. GAZETTEER ENTRIES FOR THESE PLACES
CARRY A STAR.

LONDON

Dorchester Hotel, Promenade,
W1
Granary, *W1*
Inn on the Park Lounge, *W1*
Inter-Continental Hotel,
Coffee House, *W1*
Justin de Blank, *W1*
Justin de Blank at General
Trading Company, *SW1*
Maison Bertaux, *W1*
Mandeer, *W1*
Pâtisserie Valerie, *W1*
The Savoy, Thames Foyer,
WC2
Tea Time, *SW4*
Topkapi, *W1*

ENGLAND

AMBLESIDE, Cumbria:
Rothay Manor
AMBLESIDE, Cumbria:
Sheila's Cottage
AVEBURY, Wiltshire: Stones
Restaurant
BILLINGSHURST, W Sussex:
Burdocks
BRIGHTON, E Sussex: Black
Chapati
BRIGHTON, E Sussex: Food
for Friends
BRIGHTON, E Sussex: The
Mock Turtle
BROADWAY, Hereford &
Worcester: Collin House Hotel
CHICHESTER, W Sussex:
Clinch's Salad House
COCKERMOUTH, Cumbria:
Quince & Medlar

CORSE LAWN,
Gloucestershire: Corse Lawn
House
DARTINGTON, Devon:
Cranks Health Food
Restaurant
DEVIZES, Wiltshire:
Wiltshire Kitchen
DUNSTER, Somerset: Tea
Shoppe
EASTBOURNE, E Sussex:
Byrons
ELLAND, W Yorkshire:
Berties Bistro
FROME, Somerset: Settle
HEREFORD, Hereford &
Worcester: Fat Tulip
IPSWICH, Suffolk: Orwell
House
KENDAL, Cumbria: The Moon
KEW, Surrey: Original Maids
of Honour
LUSTLEIGH, Devon:
Primrose Cottage
LYMPSTONE, Devon: River
House
LYNTON, Devon: Lee Cottage
LYONSHALL, Hereford &
Worcester: Church House
MARLBOROUGH, Wiltshire:
Polly
MELMERBY, Cumbria:
Village Bakery
OXFORD, Oxfordshire:
Munchy Munchy
PLUMTREE,
Nottinghamshire: Perkins Bar
Bistro
SHEFFIELD, S Yorkshire:
Just Cooking
STADDLE BRIDGE,
N Yorkshire: Cellar Bar at the
Tontine
TREBARWITH STRAND,
Cornwall: The Old Millfloor

Colbost
Inverness
Taynuilt
Cullipool
Crinan
Whitehouse
St Andrews
Edinburgh
Melmerby
Cockermouth
Ullswater
Whitby
Ambleside
Kendal
Staddle Bridge
Ballasalla
York
Elland
Sheffield
Caernarfon
Plumtree
Aberaeron
Lyonshall
Newport
Hereford
Broadway
Ipswich
Corse Lawn
Oxford
Avebury
Kew
London
Lynton
Devizes
Marlborough
Dunster
Frome
Billingshurst
Tunbridge Wells
Trebarwith
Strand
Lustleigh
Chichester
Brighton
Eastbourne
Worthing
Lympstone
Dartington

ANNEL
ANDS

Gorey
iour

TUNBRIDGE WELLS, Kent:
Downstairs at Thackeray's
ULLSWATER, Cumbria:
Sharrow Bay Country House
Hotel

WHITBY, N Yorkshire:
Magpie Café
WORTHING, W Sussex:
Fogarty's
YORK, N Yorkshire: Oat
Cuisine

SCOTLAND

COLBOST, Highland: Three
Chimneys
CRINAN, Strathclyde: Crinan
Coffee Shop
CULLIPOOL, Strathclyde:
Longhouse Buttery
EDINBURGH, Lothian:
Handsel's Wine Bar
EDINBURGH, Lothian:
Kalpna
EDINBURGH, Lothian: Laigh
Kitchen
INVERNESS, Highland:
Brookes Wine Bar
ST ANDREWS, Fife: Brambles
TAYNUILT, Strathclyde:
Shore Cottage
WHITEHOUSE, Strathclyde:
Old School Tea Room

WALES

ABERAERON, Dyfed: Hive on
the Quay
CAERNARFON, Gwynedd:
Bakestone
NEWPORT, Dyfed: Cnapan

CHANNEL ISLANDS

GOREY VILLAGE, Jersey:
Jersey Pottery Restaurant
ST SAVIOUR, Jersey:
Longueville Manor Hotel

ISLE OF MAN

BALLASALLA, Isle of Man: La
Rosette

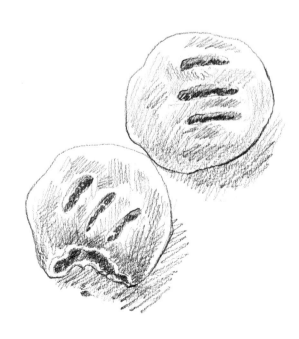

TEA. A QUESTION OF QUALITY.

*AT WHAT SPEED SHOULD A TEA BUSH GROW
TO ACQUIRE THE RICHEST FLAVOUR?*

Brooke Bond

PG
tips

A long time ago, Brooke Bond blenders established a golden rule: The bush that grows slowest grows the finest quality tea. Today, they know precisely where to find the

plantations producing these more flavoursome leaves. Their skill and intimate knowledge of tea is what makes PG Tips such a consistently good quality cup.

HOW MANY TEAS DO YOU NEED TO MAKE
A FINE QUALITY BLEND?

As many as twenty eight different teas are used to create PG Tips, because no single tea can produce that unique taste. Crops vary in quality from day to day and country to country and a great deal of skill is required of Brooke Bond blenders to balance the qualities of one leaf against another. Their skill and experience is evident in each day's blend of PG's famous flavour.

WHAT'S THE DIFFERENCE BETWEEN
A FINE QUALITY BLEND AND AN INFERIOR ONE:

Brooke Bond

PG
tips

A fine quality cup such as PG Tips is a skilful blend of many teas. Each leaf adds its own subtle shade of flavour, colour and brightness. Some leaves also infuse, or release their flavour, more quickly. Brooke Bond blenders sample as many as 500 different teas each week to produce the familiar PG taste. Small wonder that no other blend can boast such a famous flavour.

A boatful?

A ha

SH AMOUNT TO?

A cupful?

Brooke Bond

PG
tips

A tea drinking family uses the equivalent of the entire annual crop of a mature tea bush every fortnight! Fine tea is therefore rare and precious. Brooke Bond's long experience in growing and buying allows them to select the finest tea from each 'plucking' for their own blends. So ensuring that the famous taste of PG Tips is never compromised with lesser crops.

No wonder pg tips is britain's favourite tea.

TEA PLACE
OF THE YEAR

Tea has a very special affection in the hearts of the British, and the demand is once again on the increase. Afternoon tea in particular is a tradition that has latterly been revived, and this is the ninth year we are using the teapot symbol [🫖] to show establishments that serve a good cup of tea. The range of teas has grown considerably over those years, with exotic specialities like Darjeeling and Lapsang Souchong and a variety of teas scented with fruits and herbs.

Our **Tea Place of the Year** award is presented annually to a tea place in Britain that is judged to make and serve an outstanding cup of tea, along with a high quality range of cakes, pastries, scones, sandwiches and the like. This is our eighth quest, and, as usual, our team of regular inspectors have downed countless cups of tea and munched their way through a mountain of cakes and pastries before arriving at their conclusion. The **Tea Place of the Year 1989** award goes to:

SHORE COTTAGE
TAYNUILT • STRATHCLYDE

Lily McNaught rises with the lark – or maybe a little earlier – to bake the cakes, breads and scones that have made her 200-year-old cottage on the shore almost a national monument. She's been with us since our very first *Just A Bite Guide*, and there could be no worthier winner of our award – just a bite of her scones and lemon sponges, her shortbread and walnut cake will tell you why!

Another delivery of Britain's most famous bacon.

Crossing the Channel

Will it make you sick?

Despite industrial relations problems in the early summer of 1988, we took a chance on completing this selective survey into cross-Channel ferry and hovercraft services, facilities provided at the port terminals on either side of the Channel and our recommendations for places to stay overnight and to eat well for reasonable prices. Luckily, the decision to proceed was a good one, as only once was a picket line in evidence and this caused no particular problems. The setbacks that we did encounter could in no way be blamed on industrial action, but were unfortunately only too likely to be a regular feature of this kind of travel. On one ferry, our inspector, stuck in a non-moving queue waiting for uneatable food, sighed 'Roll on the Channel Tunnel!' and a chorus of voices echoed 'Hear, hear!'

This just about sums it up, except that you *can* be very lucky – but it's a bit like playing Russian roulette. P & O provided arguably the best boat, the *Pride of Dover*, and also the worst, the *Viking Venturer;* Brittany Ferries served up the best restaurant food fairly consistently but lost ground on the cafeteria; Sally Line were tops for punctuality and bottom for practically everything else; Hoverspeed crafts were the quickest but gave the roughest ride; and Sealink ships ranged from average to well below average, only beating the others for their duty-free facilities. Some ferries were spotless, others were quite disgustingly filthy. Most of the food was unacceptable.

On the plus side, however, we found some delightful restaurants in the Continental Channel ports which, if you are on a day trip, or just passing through, are well worth a visit. Many of these serve up expertly cooked, locally caught fresh fish at moderate prices in picturesque surroundings. (We have been unable to include opening times, however.) If you find that your ferry timings are awkward, we have also listed a few hotels in England and on the Continent for you to choose from. Some are modestly priced, but others are a little on the expensive side, so do check first.

Finally, our inspectors were asked to grade certain aspects of their trips. The results of these ratings can be found on page 40, and should enable you to make a reasoned choice based on your own priorities when crossing the Channel – speed, comfort, punctuality, good food and service or just a limitless supply of cheap duty-frees!

PLYMOUTH

A busy port for cross-channelling, with an abundance of hotels and restaurants; if you can, stay at either the **Holiday Inn** or the **Mayflower Post House Hotel.** Both, on the expensive side, are on the Hoe, overlooking the ferry terminal, although it's a long drive round by car. We can't find any good 'budget' eating places to recommend here, but it is still advisable to have some kind of meal in the town. **Chez Nous** is an excellent restaurant, but quite expensive – certainly don't leave it till you get to the ferry terminal as the facilities are barely passable, although an attempt is made at a cheap cooked breakfast for £1.85. A bureau de change and a newspaper stand are about the most useful services here.

BRITTANY FERRIES *TREGASTEL*

'She's not a bad old ship, but you can't turn a grandmother into a virgin.' So said the purser, on this atmospherically French ferry, on board which the aromas of fresh pâtisserie and coffee mingle in the **Café La Pergola** and **La Brioche D'Orée** restaurant. The boat left 20 minutes late with some 900 passengers, the majority French, and there was instantly a hubbub of activity among the crew. Obtaining a cup of coffee required some patience, but later at 11am there was breathing space when 173 of the French passengers repaired to the restaurant, for a first-sitting special lunch of red roast beef with a pepper sauce with pommes boulangère, asperges au lard and tomates farcies, all of which looked most impressive. Less so was the lunch for the rest of the passengers, delayed until 1.30pm, but the self-served hors d'oeuvres buffet of seafoods and salads, the leg of pork in orange sauce and the richly flavoured fish stew were worth trying, even if the vegetables left much to be desired and the beef was no longer red. The set price of £8.30 included pastries and cheese for afters, and the open fruit flans and prime Camembert and Brie were a delight. All in all, the experience, contributed to by the food, service, ambience and glorious weather, was a pleasantly memorable one.

ROSCOFF

The Bretons of the picturesque town of Roscoff were universally charming, and it is well worth a few hours looking round here. George Fabres cooks brochettes of chicken, pork, monkfish or oysters (in season) right before your eyes at **La Brocherie** in Rue Edouard-Corbière, or try **Chez Gaston** between the ferry and the town for a light meal. The sweet-toothed should head straight for the **Salon de Thé 'Marie Stuart'** for coupes glâcés, cakes and pastries. Hotels to seek out are the reasonably priced central **Hotel des Bains** and **Hotel Les Tamaris,** both overlooking the bay. Port facilities were virtually nil, and the bar was full of sweaty sailors!

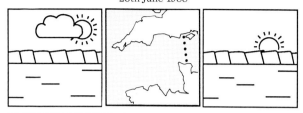

POOLE

Easily the most pleasant English port, Poole services only one ferry terminal which is within walking distance of the old town and the lovely quay. If you are booked on the early sailing, stay overnight at the **Antelope Hotel** in the High Street, or if that is full there is the more costly **Hospi-** **tality Inn** right on the quay itself. For quality snacks, walk up to the pedestrian shopping centre for **Inn à Nutshell**, or stay in the old town to sample Harry's fresh fish in the bar of the **Crown Hotel**. Tea, coffee and biscuits are all you will be able to get at the terminal itself.

BRITTANY FERRIES *COURNOUAILLE*

This prompt and efficiently run ferry carries the 'Les Routiers' label, which gives an indication of what to expect – a no-nonsense, good-value service. But don't forget that the ship is primarily a truck freighter of 33,000 tons and the frills are kept to a minimum, especially in the restaurant where tables are formica-topped, napkins are of the paper variety and the menu offers a choice only of main courses. That said, the food itself was freshly cooked and tasty and served with mineral water and a full litre of red wine on every table, with a coffee to follow. At £6 per head it represented excellent value. Soup and pâté courses were followed by roast pork with pineapple or roast lamb with onion sauce, served with fresh beans and pommes alumettes. Fruit tart to finish, with a wedge of Camembert. The cheaper cafeteria did not provide the same quality or choice of main dishes, but at least the croissants were baked on board and a passable breakfast could be had for about £2.60. After eating, recline in the comfortable lounge seats to watch the free film, or retire to a spotless cabin. The 4½-hour crossing time can thus be agreeably spent, and the passage through Poole Harbour provides some spectacular views.

CHERBOURG

The sprawling nature of the town and naval base are more reminiscent of Portsmouth than Poole, but there is some charm to be discovered in the 'old town', where you are more likely to find inexpensive fish restaurants, crêperies and cafés than on the waterfront. Our inspector's 'pick of the day' was the **Salon de Thé 'A Yuard'** on the Place de la Fontaine, which had a truly stunning variety of pastries, mer- ingues and tartelettes inside, and home-made ice cream cornets outside. Virtually adjacent is **Maresh**, offering a good cold buffet, but the hot dishes were disappointing. If you're staying in Cherbourg, three modest hotels are worth a look – the honeycomb-shaped **Hotel Chantereyne** and the **Hotel Mercure** on the waterfront, while closer to the town centre is the **Hotel Moderna**.

PORTSMOUTH

Here the ferry terminal, some distance from the town, seethes with private cars and commercial vehicles alike, and the very beginning of your trip is consequently likely to render you confused, angry and frustrated. Foot passengers don't get a better deal, either – the only long-stay car park costs £5 a day! To add insult to injury, the catering and bar facilities at the terminal are abysmal, so, if you want sustenance, take your own. If you have to stay overnight before your trip, Southsea is preferable to Portsmouth, with a choice of the **Crest Hotel**, the **Hospitality Inn** or the **Pendragon Hotel**. Here, also, you can get some decent vegetarian food at the **Country Kitchen** in Marmion Road during the day, or try the bustling evening atmosphere and good cooking at **Rosie's Vineyard** in Elm Grove. It just might help you to forget what's in store!

P & O *VIKING VENTURER*

Where do we begin? With the uncleanliness of the ship, the unfriendliness of the crew or the lateness of departure? Or how about our poor inspector's plaintive cry when considering that this may have been the first introduction to British catering for some French travellers – 'Pity our cousins!' He was 'almost at a loss to describe how dreadful the lunch (in the Carvery) was'; the tablecloth was stained and the flowers made of paper, but these trifles paled into insignificance when compared with the utterly disgraceful quality and presentation of the food itself. Oily tuna with raw onion, soggy pasta shells, tinned salads, tasteless beef in rapidly congealing packet gravy and saturated evil-tasting vegetables, all stone cold. Sweets and cheeses were no better, and at £5.95 the meal would have been totally unacceptable in a pub. Steer well clear! A reclining seat will cost you an extra £2.50 by day, but £5 at night. Our inspector was very relieved to get off.

LE HAVRE

You can almost fall off the ferry onto the waterfront, with its cafés and bars, and the frenetic fish market is just along the quay. The food in Le Havre is generally unremarkable, but for a pleasant snack and a quaffable glass of red or rosé wine go to **Le Moulin de la Galette**, where nearly 100 varieties of Breton-style pancakes cooked on a bakestone are the speciality. Fresh fish is the main *raison d'être* of seafront restaurants such as **Le Pied dans L'O**, more trendy in name than décor, and the **Hotel Monaco** which offers a reasonably priced *menu touristique*. You could stay here, too, or try the modest **Vikings** for accommodation. In the town, there is the **Hotel Marly**, or car drivers can motor on for 20 minutes to the **Hotel Ibis** at Le Bregne. Ferry terminal facilities are sadly lacking.

NEWHAVEN
19th June 1988

NEWHAVEN

If you drive straight through to the boat, you can easily miss the Sealink motorists' buffet, where the food is very basic, but not bad for all that, cooked to order and reasonably priced. Newspapers are available here too. As for Newhaven itself, sadly we cannot recommend any hotels or places to eat in the town – it is far better to go to Brighton, Lewes or Eastbourne. In all three there is a good choice of hotels, and some of our starred *Just A Bite* restaurants are to be found in both Brighton and Eastbourne. (Consult this Guide for details.)

SEALINK *VERSAILLES*

Desperately in need of refurbishment and extremely dirty, this large ship had various bars, a cinema, a snack bar and a buffet restaurant. The 'Euro Lounge' is available to those willing to cough up an extra £2 to get away from the crowds, but this, disappointingly, turned out to be a small, depressing and not very clean room full of reclining seats, only worth the money if you need a quiet place to sleep. Our inspector, having embarked at 10am English time, would have liked some breakfast, but it was 11am as far as the surly French staff were concerned and time for lunch. Unfortunately this was little consolation as the food was disgusting beyond description, and the restaurant itself was filthy. The most memorable item was the gâteau, but only for its horrendous chemical taste. The self-service café was no improvement, with uncleared tables, more filth, and even more inedible offerings. The return journey was delayed five hours with no advance warning, the *Chartres* being taken out of service and the *Versailles* substituted, but this gave our inspector the opportunity to go into Dieppe to buy some decent food for the return journey. At least the ship had been cleaned up a bit when our inspector reboarded, and she was able to enjoy her picnic on a well-worn and comfortable sofa by the forward windows of the spacious bar. Half an hour after docking back at Newhaven, motorists finally managed to drive off the ferry, no doubt extremely relieved to do so.

DIEPPE

Driving off the boat, which docks practically in the heart of town, you find yourself heading towards the Boulevard de Verdun, near to the shopping area and the seafront. The **Hotel L'Univers**, atmospheric and attractive, is situated here, and nearby is **A la Duchesse de Berry**, in Place du Puits Salé off the Grande Rue, a good pâtisserie and salon de thé, where cakes, teas and breakfasts are to be recommended. For restaurants you want the Quai Henry IV (on to which foot passengers walk directly from the ferry) – the **Restaurant de Newhaven** is typical, with decent service and dependable cooking emphasising fresh fish. Go for the set price tourist menus for good value. Port facilities are nil.

  # DIEPPE
21st June 1988

FOLKESTONE

With the check-in for cars both quick and efficient, and plenty of departure information being given out, Folkestone is not a bad launching-off point. The motorists' buffet at the Sealink terminal, however, is extremely basic and not worth bothering with, although toilet facilities cater well for the disabled and you can get last-minute insurance. In Folkestone itself, we can't recommend any budget eateries, but full restaurants include **La Tavernette** in Clifton Gardens for Italian cooking and **Paul's** in Bouverie Road West. The **Burlington Hotel** has pleasant sea views and offers modest accommodation.

SEALINK *HENGIST AND HORSA*

Hengist, which left Folkestone fifteen minutes late, was shabby and gave the impression of having been well used, but there was a good plan of the ship on display throughout. The car deck was filthy and smelly, but there was some compensation for this: motorists when checking in were issued with a ticket for free tea or coffee in the motorists' lounge (a facility unique to Sealink at the time of our inspections). There was no food available here, but the chance to avoid coach and school parties and enjoy tea, coffee or alcoholic drinks was greatly welcomed. In fact, on the return trip, on the *Horsa*, one Briton with his family was moved to congratulate Sealink in writing for supplying such an exclusive facility. 'Refreshers', the snack bar, served the same unappetising offerings as the check-in buffet – cheap and nasty microwaved burgers and pizzas, and tasteless hot drinks in paper cups. 'The Pantry' self-service restaurant strongly resembled a motorway café in both layout and quality of food. The hot dishes such as battered fish, stuffed bacon rolls and grilled gammon were at least freshly cooked, but the vegetables were a let-down. The staff were cheerful and helpful in spite of the depressing nature of their surroundings.

BOULOGNE

Drive off the ferry straight into town and the main shopping area, where there is a disconcerting number of English-style restaurants serving chips and hot dogs! Avoid these like the plague, and make a beeline for the pâtisserie and salon de thé **Lugand** in Rue Grande for excellent breakfasts, snacks and pastries at moderate prices. For something more substantial, walk or drive to Boulogne beach to find **La Plage** (tel. 21 31 4535) where the clientcle is primarily French and you must book at lunchtime. In the old town, there are several inexpensive restaurants on Rue de Lille, such as **Le Jardin de la Haute Ville.** Recommended hotels are the **Hotel Faidherbe** in Rue Faidherbe and the **Hotel Metropole** in Rue Thiers. Boulogne's terminal facilities are very poor.

DOVER
22nd June 1988

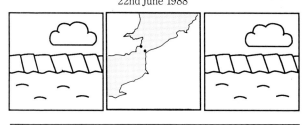

DOVER

The most popular departure point for English tourists because of the proximity to the French coast, Dover is consequently a bustling port. The perfect place, too, for a picket line when there is an NUS strike! Crossing this, nevertheless, proved quite painless for our inspector. The terminal facilities are extensive, including bank and bureau de change, and AA, RAC, P & O and Sealink desks. The simple buffet, predictably, was not up to much, so it is wise to eat before you get there, but unfortunately there is a dearth of good eating places in the town. Better still, then, to wait till you get to Calais. Both the **White Cliffs Hotel** and the **Dover Moat House** are handy for the ferry terminals and the hoverport, if you have chosen to travel by hovercraft (see page 39).

P & O *PRIDE OF DOVER* AND *PRIDE OF KENT*

Our inspector exclaimed of the *Pride of Dover* that 'if ever I cross the Channel again I shall travel on this ship'. Praise cannot be too high for the gleaming and fresh-smelling car decks, the practical layout of the ship and the stylish and spotless décor. Service was cheerful and efficient in the restaurant, and even the food, if not wonderful, was better value than our inspectors were becoming used to. English breakfasts were cooked to order, and a special children's breakfast was available. The ferry left on time and the public address announcements were regular and informative. Pleasant seating areas, one even screened off for non-smokers, made a welcome change. In the cafeteria, the food was attractively presented if unimaginative (chips with everything) and of a reasonable standard. The *Pride of Kent* is a smaller and older boat but still spotless and well laid out. Catering was disappointing in its lack of flair (and consequently lack of customers), which was a great shame as the facilities were good. There was a fifteen-minute delay in leaving Calais, too.

CALAIS

A free bus is provided for foot-passengers into the town, as the ferry docks are some way away from the centre. When you get there, a choice of two superb French restaurants awaits you. The stylish **Le Channel** on Boulevard de Résistance offers two excellent-value tourist menus, dependably cooked. Dress smartly, and book before-hand (tel. 21 34 4230), for you will be mixing with the well-heeled businessmen of Calais. More casual is **L'Assiette** in Place de Suèdes, and the owner will advise you on what to order. Again, you must book (tel. 21 34 1510), and it is a good place to try out a smattering of French. Your best bet for a hotel is the **Hotel Richelieu** in Rue Richelieu, with a pleasant park opposite. Port facilities are very basic.

CALAIS
23rd June 1988

RAMSGATE

Ramsgate has an attractive town quay area, but access to the ferry can be severely impeded by tourist coaches getting stuck in the narrow roads. At Sally Line's terminal, there is only a tiny kiosk selling sweets, newspapers, a few uninviting sandwiches and tea or coffee in the inevitable paper cups. If you fancy something more interesting at lunchtime or in the evening, go to **Sands**, a wine bar and restaurant in Cliff Street where the cooking is varied and tasty. The nearest hotels we can recommend are in Canterbury where there is a very good choice.

SALLY LINE *VIKING 2* AND *THE VIKING*

The best thing we can say about these boats is that they both ran perfectly to schedule. The worst thing about *Viking 2* was that, apart from a cafeteria, the Finlandia restaurant and two bars, there was an amazing lack of seating space, causing many of the passengers to have to stand or walk around for the duration of the 2½-hour crossing. Food, too, was dire – mass-produced and overcooked. Appearancewise, the smörgasbord selection was colourful and fairly attractive, but this was not matched by the taste. The hot dishes did not even look pleasant. Staff were smartly turned out but could be a little offhand when faced with schoolchildren and coach parties, something they should surely be used to. *The Viking* had more in the way of lounge areas, including a non-smoking one, as well as four cabins. Lorry drivers were given first refusal on these, but our inspector did manage to procure one. It was windowless and sported two bunk beds, a tiny corner table and chair and a handbasin. Incredibly, though, there was no towel! On enquiry, it was revealed that towels were not and never had been provided. Now angry and loudly complaining, our inspector was eventually given one.

DUNKIRK

After a fairly unpleasant trip, it is highly aggravating to discover that you have docked some 15km to the west of Dunkirk itself! Nearly halfway to Calais, in fact. So don't even consider visiting Dunkirk on foot on this route. When you eventually arrive in the town it is quite modern, and has excellent shopping facilities and some good restaurants. In Rue du Leughenaer is **La Mer du Nord**, and at the railway station you will find **Richelieu-Buffet de la Gâre** which is a simple restaurant adjoining both a more elaborate one and also a lively bar. An excellent selection of cakes and pastries is to be had at the **Pâtisserie Boutteau** in Rue Clemenceau in the centre of town. At the entrance to the port is the **Borel Hotel**, good for reasonably priced comfortable accommodation with all the trimmings. Terminal facilities consisted of an old portakabin toilet and waiting room.

HARWICH
20th June 1988

HARWICH

Less frenetic than some of the other Channel ports, Harwich still held a surprise in store for our inspector – in the shape of a 3¾-hour delay to the Sealink sailing. Passengers had already passed through Customs into the boarding area, where they were then virtual prisoners, with only the appalling 'Traveller's Fare' café available for refreshments. Sealink's public relations at this point were lamentable, too. Our inspector had to enquire about the reason for the delay, and eventually people were told that there was a meeting taking place on board the ship! It later transpired that a member of staff had been sacked for a serious offence, but by that time Sealink were claiming an 'industrial dispute' as the cause. They did, however, apologise and offer bed and breakfast in Holland, as well as free telephone calls, to those who had been most inconvenienced. If you have any time to spare in Harwich itself, rather than captive in the ferry terminal, try **The Ha'Penny Pier** restaurant on the pier for some good-value, dependable cooking, and you can stay overnight at the **Pier at Harwich** as well as dining extremely well if you can afford it.

SEALINK *ST NICHOLAS*

On board, things were not much of an improvement. Staff were smiling and friendly enough, but the food in the 'Tradewinds' à la carte restaurant was ghastly, fish and vegetables being overcooked and the soup, described as fresh, more probably from a tin. Sweet was a dreadful grasshopper pie, a minty version of the ubiquitous Mississippi mud pie. On the plus side, there was ample seating throughout although the boat was packed, but a charge of £2.50 was made to watch the film. The only other catering facility, the 'Carte Blanche Pantry', was just as bad as the restaurant, with stodgy quiche, overcooked beef, pale greasy chips and dry rhubarb crumble. Fresh milk was only available by the half-pint, so you couldn't have it with your tea. If you're travelling at night, ask for a first-class cabin with a window, as without windows they are uncomfortable and claustrophobic. At 6am our inspector was woken with a cup of tea, but again no milk!

HOOK OF HOLLAND

The main street houses a delightfully pretty little pâtisserie, with just three tables, offering fine cakes and pastries. It is called **Maurits Zomer**. For more substantial meals, though still inexpensive, make your way the short distance to **Petit Vis-Restaurant** in Strandweg 14 for masterful fish and meat dishes – especially good are the raw herrings served with a glass of ice-cold liqueur and the wonderful double pancakes to finish. Don't stay overnight here; travel on to Rotterdam or the Hague. At the terminal there's the self-service Restaurette which is quite easily missed if you're not looking.

HOOK OF HOLLAND
20th June 1988

FELIXSTOWE/DOVER

22nd June 1988

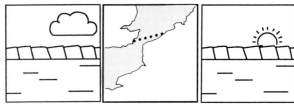

FELIXSTOWE

As you would expect of a large container port, Felixstowe is functional and devoid of character, but the terminal is better than most. After checking in, you can relax in a spacious and comfortable lounge area with a simple cafeteria, and cars are loaded quickly and efficiently. We can't recommend any restaurants in the town, but you can get good overnight accommodation at the **Brook Hotel** or the **Orwell Moat House**. (For Dover, see page 35.)

P & O *NORDIC FERRY* AND *REINE ASTRID*

The *Nordic Ferry* on first impressions from the car deck seemed drab in appearance, but the passenger areas were a pleasant surprise. Numerous lounges had comfortable seating, the cabins had tea and coffee-making facilities and the video lounge was free. The attractively decorated à la carte restaurant was reasonably priced but the standard of food only just passable, although the service was exemplary. 'Le Café du Jardin' was self-service with a small selection of basic foods. Pastries and salads were good, but the hot dishes very poor. Generally not a bad ferry, which is more than can be said for the *Reine Astrid*, which was small, filthy and late. Plenty of lounge space was available but the seats were badly stained. Some drunken English louts being thrown off (and rightly too) was the cause of the half-hour delay. Limited catering facilities were of a very low standard, some passengers sending back their stone-cold fish, but the video room was again free and some of the cabins surprisingly spacious and reasonably equipped.

ZEEBRUGGE and OSTEND

Zeebrugge is a tiny place, essentially a ferry port and fishing harbour, so you can look forward to eating some superb seafood. Try it al fresco outside a simple fish shop called **Bertje de Visser** in Tijokstraat about 1km from the ferry, or in total contrast there is a smart modern restaurant on Rederskaai called **Mon Manège a Toi**, which overlooks a long quay lined with large trawlers. The **Maritime**, Zeedijk 6, offers comfortable accommodation. At P & O's terminal there is a bright, modern check-in and quite attractive Jupiter cafeteria, which, sadly, only serves up food at the hamburger and baked beans level.

Ostend's seafront is choc-a-bloc with restaurants, and there is not an amusement arcade or greasy burger joint in sight! Fish is the highlight once more, and it is actually difficult to make a choice, but our inspector's eye was caught by **Korre** and **Belgica**, fairly close to each other on Visserskai. Small, intimate and friendly restaurants, they provide inexpensive, nicely prepared dishes. **Dewulf** in Kapellestraat is the place for real coffee and lovely cakes and pastries, and directly opposite the ferry terminal is the **Strand Hotel**, offering excellent and convenient accommodation. The terminal itself is primarily a 'trucker's stop', serving fry-ups.

ZEEBRUGGE/OSTEND

23rd June 1988

For a description of the port of Dover, see page 35.

DOVER–CALAIS HOVERSPEED *SWIFT*

Hovercrafts are perhaps the quickest, though definitely not the most comfortable, way of crossing the Channel, and cars are loaded and unloaded very swiftly, too. Be prepared to book well in advance for this reason, if you are taking your car. At Dover, foot-passengers fare quite well, with a clearly marked car park and easy access to the large and busy terminal, where facilities include newspapers and magazines on sale, a bureau de change, booking offices and a neatly laid out self-service café where drinks are served in proper cups. Hot and cold snacks on offer are of the usual dull and disappointing variety. Motorists check in and drive to a waiting area for loading, but when our inspector was there no information was forthcoming about how long the wait would be. Consequently, no-one felt any incentive to leave their cars to cross the rain-swept yard to the duty-free shop and café. On board the *Swift*, which was tatty and shabby, seating was cramped and due to limitations of space only cold drinks were available, as well as a very limited selection of duty-free goods. The 35-minute crossing was noisy and bumpy, but the hovercraft did leave and arrive on schedule.

BOULOGNE–DOVER HOVERSPEED *PRINCESS ANNE*

Again, foot passengers get the better end of the deal at Boulogne's hovercraft terminal, as car drivers have to walk from the loading area to the duty-free lounge. Basic facilities here are nonetheless reasonably decent. A bar–restaurant supplies tea, coffee and sandwiches at the bar, and main dishes at table, ranging from beef bourguignon and coquille St Jacques to chicken or sausage and chips. Motoring and car-hire services are also available. The hovercraft *Princess Anne* arrived late, and left even further behind schedule because they had decided to wait for 30 foot-passengers who were late checking in. Only a basic apology was given, and the final departure took place 40 minutes late. Our inspector thought this delay totally unnecessary, and the reason given quite unacceptable. The *Princess Anne* was also in need of refurbishment – seats were worn and torn, and some were actually broken. Facilities on board were exactly the same as on the *Swift*. In moderately rough conditions, the crossing was again loud and uncomfortable, and nerves were definitely frayed at the end of the trip. Not a relaxing way to travel, but it is quick.

For descriptions of the ports of Calais and Boulogne, see pages 35 and 34 respectively.

OUR RATINGS

Our inspectors were instructed to allocate marks on each journey for the following aspects:

1. Standard of English terminal eating facilities;
2. Standard of Continental port terminal eating facilities;
3. Ferry or hovercraft service:
   - a) standard of restaurant;
   - b) standard of cafeteria;
   - c) choice and prices in duty-free shop;
   - d) general comfort;
   - e) cleanliness of ship;
   - f) punctuality of sailings;
   - g) service on board.

From their gradings, we have drawn up the following 'league tables' to help you decide which port and/or service to opt for. In (1) and (2), remember that our grading may apply only to the terminal facilities of the particular carrier we used on that route. In (3), where more than one ship of a particular carrier has been used, we have taken an average over all of the boats. Punctuality is a crucial factor in the final grading, but then this may be one of the most important factors.

1. Standard of English terminal eating facilities

English Port	Rating out of 10
Newhaven	4
Dover	2
Felixstowe	2
Harwich	2
Plymouth	2
Poole	2
Folkestone	1
Portsmouth	1
Ramsgate	1

2. Standard of Continental port terminal eating facilities:

Continental Port	Rating out of 10
Hook of Holland	3
Ostend	3
Zeebrugge	3
Boulogne	2
Cherbourg	2
Roscoff	2
Calais	1
Dieppe	0
Dunkirk	0
Le Havre	0

3. Carrier comparison table (marks out of 100):

	P & O	Sealink	Brittany Ferries	Sally Line	Hoverspeed
Restaurant	36	17	55	35	–
Cafeteria	32	33	23	40	–
Duty-free	52	60	55	45	40
Comfort	53	48	50	35	40
Cleanliness	42	48	60	50	40
Punctuality	75	60	90	95	50
Service	45	47	53	70	50
Overall rating	48	45	55	53	44

"Would Madam like a little Gouda, Gouda or Gouda?"

*A*sk for Gouda and you'll be pleasantly surprised. In more ways than one. For, as well as young Gouda, there's the full flavoured mature in the black wax, and the delicately spiced Gouda with cumin seeds. Also keep an eye out for other Gouda specialities such as cream Gouda and Gouda with fine herbs. Together, they make Gouda the Dutch cheese that goes right across the board.

Dutch Cheese

DUTCH GOUDA. ROUND IN SHAPE, ROUND IN FLAVOUR.

OPEN·AIR·EATING

LONDON

Aspava, **W1**
L'Autre Wine Bar, **W1**
Balls Brothers, **EC2, EC4**
Blake's Wine & Food Bar,
WC2
Boos, **NW1**
Brasserie, **SW17**
La Brasserie, **SW3**
Bubbles Wine Bar, **W1**
Café Delancey, **NW1**
Café des Fleurs, **NW6**
Café Pélican, **WC2**
Café St Pierre Brasserie, **EC1**
The Café Society, **WC1**
Camden Brasserie, **NW1**
Charco's Wine Bar, **SW3**
Chequers, **NW1**
Cherry Orchard, **E2**
Cranks, **WC2**
Davy's Wine Vaults, **SE10**
Earth Exchange, **N6**
Efes Kebab House, **W1**
La Fin de la Chasse, **N16**
Granary, **W1**
Gyngleboy, **W2**
Hoults, **SW17**
Justin de Blank at General
Trading Company, **SW1**
Lou Pescadou, **SW5**
Macarthurs, **SW13**
Mélange, **WC2**
Meson Don Felipe, **SE1**
Meson Doña Ana, **W11**
Methuselah's, **SW1**
Mother Huffs, **NW3**
Nature's Garden, **SW11**
No 77 Wine Bar, **NW6**
Oliver's, **W14**
Ormes, **SW4**
Pasta Connection, **SW3**
Raw Deal, **W1**
Slenders, **EC4**
Tea Rooms des Artistes, **SW8**
Tiles Wine Bar, **SW1**
Verbanella Pasta Bar, **W1**
Villa Estense, **SW6**
Wilkins Natural Foods, **SW1**
Wine Gallery, **W11, SW3,
SW10**

ENGLAND

Aldeburgh, Suffolk:
Aldeburgh Festival Wine Bar
Alfriston, E Sussex: Drusillas
Thatched Barn
Alston, Cumbria: Brownside
Coach House
Alstonefield, Derbys: Old
Post Office Tea Rooms
Alton, Hants: Apple Crumble
Ambleside, Cumbria: Rothay
Manor
Ambleside, Cumbria:
Zeffirellis
Arundel, W Sussex: Belinda's
Tea Rooms
Ashtead, Surrey: Bart's
Avebury, Wilts: Stones
Restaurant
Aylesbury, Bucks: Seatons
Bakewell, Derbys: Green
Apple
Barden, N Yorks: Howgill
Lodge
Barnstaple, Devon: Lynwood
House
Bath, Avon: Bath Puppet
Theatre
Bath, Avon: Moon &
Sixpence
Bath, Avon: Number Five
Berkhamsted, Herts: Cook's
Delight
Berwick-upon-Tweed, Nthmb:
Scotsgate Wine Bar
Biddenden, Kent: Claris's Tea
Shop
Birmingham, W Mid: La
Galleria
Birmingham, W Mid: La
Santé
Bodiam, E Sussex: Knollys
Bolton Abbey, N Yorks:
Bolton Abbey Tea Cottage
Boot, Cumbria: Brook House
Restaurant
Bourton-on-the-Water, Glos:
Small Talk Tea Room
Brampton, Cumbria: Tarn
End

Brendon, Devon: *Rockford Cottage Tea Room*
Bridgnorth, Shrops: *Sophie's Tea Rooms*
Bridgwater, Somerset: *Nutmeg*
Brighton, E Sussex: *Black Chapati*
Brighton, E Sussex: *The Mock Turtle*
Bristol, Avon: *Arnolfini Café Bar*
Bristol, Avon: *Guild Café-Restaurant*
Bristol, Avon: *Rainbow Café*
Bristol, Avon: *Wild Oats II*
Broad Chalke, Wilts: *Cottage House*
Broadway, Hereford & Worcester: *Collin House Hotel*
Bury St Edmunds, Suffolk: *Beaumonts*
Caldbeck, Cumbria: *Priests Mill*
Canterbury, Kent: *Cogan House English Brasserie*
Canterbury, Kent: *Crotchets*
Canterbury, Kent: *Sweet Heart Pâtisserie*
Canterbury, Kent: *Il Vaticano Pasta Parlour*
Carlisle, Cumbria: *Hudson's Coffee Shop*
Cartmel, Cumbria: *Prior's Refectory Coffee Shop*
Castle Cary, Somerset: *Old Bakehouse*
Castle Combe, Wilts: *The Manor House*
Castleton, Derbys: *Rose Cottage Café*
Cerne Abbas, Dorset: *Singing Kettle*
Chatham, Kent: *Simson's*
Cheltenham, Glos: *Choirs Tea Rooms*
Cheltenham, Glos: *Langtry Pâtisserie & Tea Rooms*
Cheltenham, Glos: *The Retreat*
Chichester, W Sussex: *Chats Brasserie*
Chichester, W Sussex: *St Martin's Tea Rooms*
Chipping Campden, Glos: *Greenstocks*
Chipping Campden, Glos: *Kings Arms Hotel, Saddle Room*
Chipping Norton, Oxon: *Nutters*
Cirencester, Glos: *Brewery Coffee House*
Cirencester, Glos: *No. 1*
Cirencester, Glos: *Shepherds Wine Bar*
Clare, Suffolk: *Ship Stores*
Clawton, Devon: *Court Barn Country House Hotel*
Clifton Dykes, Cumbria: *Wetheriggs*
Collier Street, Kent: *Butcher's Mere*
Compton, Surrey: *Old Congregational Tea Shop*
Congleton, Ches: *Odd Fellows Wine Bar & Bistro*
Coniston, Cumbria: *Jumping Jenny at Brantwood*
Corse Lawn, Glos: *Corse Lawn House*
Coventry, W Mid: *Herbs*
Dartington, Devon: *Cranks Health Food Restaurant*
Dartmouth, Devon: *Spinning Wheel Café*
Dent, Cumbria: *Dent Crafts Centre*
Derby, Derbys: *Lettuce Leaf*
Devizes, Wilts: *Wiltshire Kitchen*
Dodd Wood, Cumbria: *Old Sawmill*
Dorchester, Dorset: *Potter In*
Dorrington, Shrops: *Country Friends*
Eton, Berks: *Eton Wine Bar*
Falmouth, Cornwall: *Pandora Inn*
Falmouth, Cornwall: *Secrets*
Froghall, Staffs: *The Wharf Eating House*
Frome, Somerset: *Settle*
Glastonbury, Somerset: *Ploughshares Café*
Glastonbury, Somerset: *Rainbow's End Café*
Grange-in-Borrowdale, Cumbria: *Grange Bridge Cottage*

Grantham, Lincs: *Knightingales*

Great Barton, Suffolk: *Craft at the Suffolk Barn*

Hadleigh, Suffolk: *Earlsburys, Janet's Coffee Shop*

Hatton, Warwicks: *Hatton Craft Centre*

Hawes, N Yorks: *Cockett's Hotel*

Heacham, Norfolk: *Miller's Cottage Tea Room*

Hereford, Hereford & Worcester: *Nutters*

Herstmonceux, E Sussex: *Praise the Lord*

High Lorton, Cumbria: *White Ash Barn*

Hope, Derbys: *Hopechest*

Hungerford, Berks: *Bear, Kennet Room*

Hungerford, Berks: *Behind the Green Door*

Huntingdon, Cambs: *Old Bridge Hotel Lounge*

Kendal, Cumbria: *Nutters*

Kendal, Cumbria: *Waterside Wholefoods*

Kingston, Surrey: *La La Pizza*

Lancaster, Lancs: *Libra*

Lavenham, Suffolk: *The Great House*

Leamington Spa, Warwicks: *Alastairs*

Leamington Spa, Warwicks: *Mallory Court*

Lewes, E Sussex: *Old Candlemaker's Café*

Lincoln, Lincs: *Wig & Mitre*

Low Laithe, N Yorks: *Carters, Knox Manor*

Luccombe Chine, I of W: *Dunnose Cottage*

Ludlow, Shrops: *Hardwicks*

Lustleigh, Devon: *Primrose Cottage*

Lynton, Devon: *Lee Cottage*

Lyonshall, Hereford & Worcester: *Church House*

Lytchett Minster, Dorset: *Slepe Cottage Tea Rooms*

Manchester, Gtr Mans: *Greens*

Matlock, Derbys: *Tall Trees*

Mentmore, Bedfordshire: *Stable Yard Craft Gallery & Tea Room*

Midsomer Norton, Avon: *Mrs Pickwick*

Milton Ernest, Bedfordshire: *The Strawberry Tree*

Minstead, Hants: *Honey Pot*

Newark, Notts: *Gannets*

Newcastle upon Tyne, Tyne & Wear: *Mather's*

Norwich, Norfolk: *Britons Arms Coffee House*

Offham, E Sussex: *Old Post House*

Painswick, Glos: *Cup House*

Painswick, Glos: *Painswick Hotel*

Penshurst, Kent: *Fir Tree House Tea Rooms*

Plumtree, Notts: *Perkins Bar Bistro*

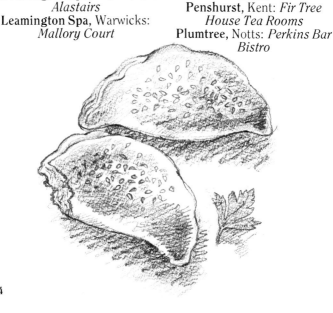

Polperro, Cornwall: *Captains Cabin*
Portsmouth (Southsea), Hants: *Rosie's Vineyard*
Reading, Berks: *Mama Mia*
Richmond, Surrey: *Wildefoods*
Romsey, Hants: *Cobweb Tea Rooms*
Romsey, Hants: *Latimer Coffee House*
Rottingdean, E Sussex: *Rottingdean Pâtisserie*
Rowlands Castle, Hants: *Coffee Pot*
Ryton-on-Dunsmore, Warwicks: *Ryton Gardens Café*
St Albans, Herts: *Kingsbury Mill Waffle House*
St Margaret's at Cliffe, Kent: *Roses*
St Mary's, Cornwall: *Tregarthens Hotel*
Salisbury, Wilts: *Michael Snell*
Sandwich, Kent: *Pinkies*
Selworthy, Somerset: *Periwinkle Cottage Tea Rooms*
Shipton, N Yorks: *Beningbrough Hall Restaurant*
Shoreham-by-Sea, W Sussex: *Cuckoo Clock*
Sidbury, Devon: *Old Bakery*
Skelwith Bridge, Cumbria: *Chesters*
South Molton, Devon: *Stumbles Wine Bar*
Spetisbury, Dorset: *Marigold Cottage*
Spilsby, Lincs: *Buttercross Restaurant*
Stamford, Lincs: *George of Stamford*
Stevenage, Herts: *De Friese Coffee Shop*
Stonham Aspal, Suffolk: *Stonham Barns*
Stratford-upon-Avon, Warwicks: *Slug & Lettuce*
Tarr Steps, Somerset: *Tarr Farm*
Taunton, Somerset: *Porters*

Tissington, Derbys: *Old School Tea Rooms*
Torquay, Devon: *The Mulberry Room*
Totnes, Devon: *Willow*
Trebarwith Strand, Cornwall: *House on the Strand*
Trebarwith Strand, Cornwall: *The Old Millfloor*
Tresco, Cornwall: *Island Hotel Restaurant*
Tunbridge Wells, Kent: *Downstairs at Thackeray's*
Tutbury, Staffs: *Cornmill Tea Room*
Ullswater, Cumbria: *Rampsbeck Hotel*
Upper Slaughter, Glos: *Lords of the Manor Hotel*
Wallingford, Oxon: *Annie's Tea Rooms*
Walton-on-the-Naze, Essex: *Naze Links Café*
Wansford-in-England, Cambs: *Haycock Hotel Lounge*
Wantage, Oxon: *Vale & Downland Museum Centre*
Wareham, Dorset: *Priory Hotel*
Warminster, Wilts: *Jenner's*
Warminster, Wilts: *Vincent's*
Waterperry, Oxon: *Waterperry Gardens Tea Shop*
Wells, Somerset: *Good Earth*
Westfield, E Sussex: *Casual Cuisine*
Willerby, Humb: *Cedars at Grange Park Hotel*
Williton, Somerset: *Blackmore's Bookshop Tea Room*
Williton, Somerset: *Orchard Mill*
Winchelsea, E Sussex: *Finches of Winchelsea*
Windermere, Cumbria: *Miller Howe Hotel*
Windsor, Berks: *Dôme*
Wirksworth, Derbys: *Crown Yard Kitchen*
Woodstock, Oxon: *Feathers Hotel, Garden Bar*
Wool, Dorset: *Rose Mullion Tea Room*

Woolpit, Suffolk: *The Bakery*
Wootton Common, I of W:
Lugleys Tea Gardens
Worcester, Hereford &
Worcester: *Natural Break*
Worthing, W Sussex:
Fogarty's
Worthing, W Sussex: *Mr
Pastry*
Yarm, Cleveland: *Coffee Shop*
York, N Yorks: *Bees Knees*
York, N Yorks: *Mulberry
Hall Coffee Shop*
York, N Yorks: *St Williams
College Restaurant*

SCOTLAND

Alloway, S'clyde: *Burns Byre
Restaurant*
Ardentinny, S'clyde:
Ardentinny Hotel Buttery
Arisaig, H'land: *Old Library
Lodge & Restaurant*
Colbost, H'land: *Three
Chimneys*
Crinan, S'clyde: *Crinan
Coffee Shop*
Dirleton, Loth: *Open Arms
Hotel*
Dryburgh Abbey, Bdrs:
Orchard Tearoom
Edinburgh, Loth: *Le Café
Noir*
Edinburgh, Loth: *Laigh
Kitchen*
Edinburgh, Loth: *Waterfront
Wine Bar*
Glenscorrodale, S'clyde:
*Glenscorrodale Farm
Tearoom*
Isle of Gigha, S'clyde: *Gigha
Hotel*
Kentallen of Appin, H'land:
Holly Tree
Kilchrenan, S'clyde:
Taychreggan Hotel
Kilfinan, S'clyde: *Kilfinan
Hotel*
Kincraig, H'land: *Boathouse
Restaurant*
Kyle of Lochalsh, H'land:
Highland Designworks
Moffat, D & G: *Rachel's
Pantry*

New Abbey, D & G: *Abbey
Cottage*
Newcastleton, Bdrs: *Copshaw
Kitchen*
Peebles, Bdrs: *Kailzie
Gardens Restaurant*
St Fillans, T'side: *Four
Seasons Hotel, Tarkon Bar*
Selkirk, Bdrs: *Philipburn
House Hotel*
Ullapool, H'land: *Ceilidh
Place*

WALES

Aberaeron, Dyfed: *Hive on
the Quay*
Bethesda, Gwynedd:
Mountain Kitchen
Cardiff, Sth Glamorgan: *Sage*
Cowbridge, Sth Glamorgan:
Off the Beeton Track
Eglwysfach, Dyfed: *Ty'n-y-
Cwm Tea Rooms*
Hay-on-Wye, Powys: *The
Granary*
Machynlleth, Powys: *Centre
for Alternative Technology*
Machynlleth, Powys: *Quarry
Shop*
Newport, Dyfed: *Cnapan*
Rhyd-y-Clafdy, Gwynedd: *Tu
Hwnt i'r Afon*
Wolf's Castle, Dyfed:
Wolfscastle Country Hotel

CHANNEL
ISLANDS

St Anne, Alderney: *Gossip*
St Peter Port, Guernsey:
Flying Dutchman Hotel
Gorey Village, Jersey: *Jersey
Pottery Restaurant*
St Brelade's Bay, Jersey:
*Hotel L'Horizon, Beech
Lounge*
St Saviour, Jersey:
Longueville Manor Hotel
Sark, Sark: *Stocks Buffet*

ISLE OF MAN

Douglas, Isle of Man:
L'Expérience

AN INSPECTOR'S LOT

BY ROSEMARY FORGAN

Our day started with breakfast in the café-restaurant of a well-known London department store. Arriving early (and never having met a fully-fledged Egon Ronay inspector before) I was on the lookout for an eighteen stone man, waddling – with great difficulty – up the escalator. I knew what years of tasting those 'yummy cakes' and 'good old-fashioned puddings', so seductively described in *Egon Ronay's PG Tips Just A Bite Guide*, had done to my waistline, and I assumed his had met with the same fate. I was therefore totally unprepared for the arrival of Mr X, a slim and healthy-looking young man who told me later he weighed the same as he had at the age of 17!

Somewhat disturbed by this I ordered a modest Continental breakfast while he opted for the full 'cholesterol corner' – bacon, eggs, sausage, the works – from a waitress who was blissfully unaware of the importance of this particular order.

One would expect the enthusiasm for food to have waned after nine years in the same job (which can mean eating out up to 15 times a week) but this was certainly not the case here. Mr X's face positively lit up as he recalled not just favourite restaurants but specific dishes he had really enjoyed.

It soon became clear, however, that our breakfast was not going to find a place amongst those cherished memories. My croissant had been chewy, a sure sign it had been reheated in the microwave, and much of the English breakfast remained uneaten. In order to be scrupulously fair, Mr X gave them a final chance by ordering a Danish pastry. It arrived stone-cold and tasted very dry. As we got ready to go, the lunch buffet was being set out, and sadly this clinched it. Overcooked beef, a drab grey-brown, and shiny square slices of ham (from a shiny square pig perhaps?). The custard topping on a pie had large cracks in it which suggested it was not very fresh. Without a word, we slipped away.

Unfortunately, the above experience is only too common. Amongst the files at the headquarters of Egon Ronay's Guides are the 'not recommended' reports, written after unsatisfactory inspections:

'Service is speedy,' begins one encouragingly, but continues, *'which is a shame because the wait between courses is the most enjoyable part of the evening . . .'.*

Unfortunately, the descriptions of bad food live on in the memory as clearly as the lyrical praise of the good. One can imagine only too easily 'a hot greasy smell that hits you as you walk in . . .' or 'tournedos bathed in a dishful of hot yellow oil', followed by 'lemon syllabub, watery and tasting of the fridge in which it must have stood for some time'.

One feels for the man who wrote, 'To think I fought through the wind and rain for *this* . . .' when describing a miserable hamburger joint. Another admitted, 'I could not bring myself to actually eat here. The tablecloths were filthy and stained (I think they get sent to the laundry once a month – whether they need it or not). The menu was unreadable because it was covered in mould. You could smell it 3 feet away.'

In addition to a steady diet of 'gristly hamburgers', 'country vegetable soup that turned out to be yesterday's left-overs stuck in a blender' and a quiche 'whose flavour was thankfully too weak to be offensive', the inspectors also endure 'surly, bad mannered and insolent service'. One who trekked miles found waitresses 'that seemed to have trouble carrying

more than one plate at a time and adding up'. To make matters worse: 'Though they spent a great deal of time in the kitchen, they had no idea what was on or off, creating more delays.' Another 'spent her time moaning loudly (and swearing) because she couldn't have the weekend off'!

Meanwhile, my day with Mr X had only just begun. After leaving the store (and what seemed all too short a walk along Brompton Road) astoundingly it was time for lunch! We visited an unpretentious Thai restaurant, Tui, around the corner from South Kensington Station. Mr X chose the dishes, and as we waited for the food to arrive he explained that by ordering the same dishes time and again a standard emerged against which new potential entries could be judged. For example in a Chinese restaurant he always ordered hot and sour soup and, where available, red bean pancakes. The inspectors also tend to order the complicated dishes, knowing that those will test the chef most fully. Poor spelling and carelessly written menus are usually warning signs that all may not be well within.

At Tui's we both enjoyed our mixed satay, accompanied by a good, hot crunchy peanut sauce. The only thing that distinguished us from the other diners was Mr X's insistence on tasting a forkful of the sauce on its own, the better to gauge its flavour. Next came lightly spiced chicken and a dish of transparent noodles and vegetables. The vegetables were a good colour and had a bite to them which complemented the slightly sticky texture of the fine noodles. By the time we had finished our sweets Mr X had made up his mind that the cooking here did warrant an entry in the Guide. The only drawback was that the proximity of tables occasionally meant unwelcome smoke drifting across from our neighbours.

After he had settled the bill, Mr X presented his card and asked to see the manager to clarify a few further points – hours of opening, speciality dishes and so on. This must be a heart-stopping moment for some restaurant owners or managers but here, to begin with at least, the staff seemed puzzled, rather than nervous or impressed, and it took some time to explain just what the Guide was all about! This seemed a rather charming reflection on the fact that the people here were too busy getting on with *their* job, of providing good food, to worry about such things.

By the time that had been sorted out, it was getting on for 2.30 and I was feeling extremely full. Mr X, however, had wisely paced himself for what lay ahead – another lunch!

This time it was the newly refurbished eaterie inside the Victoria and Albert Museum. Not many people have to face the daunting sight of a large portion of steak and kidney pie fifteen minutes after they have polished off a plate of noodles, Thai veg. and chicken, but such is the lot of an inspector! Allowances were made for the fact that we had arrived at the end of lunch, and I watched in amazement as Mr X tucked into celery soup and his pie. My pork terrine tasted too herby and my chocolate cake seemed dry, but I suspect this had more to do with my by-now jaded palate than the food itself. This is perhaps the difference between the professional and the enthusiastic amateur (well, I had been enthusiastic to begin with) and vindicates the organization's decision to employ professional inspectors instead of relying on reports sent in by members of the public. Eating out so often – and in such a wide variety of places – does mean inspectors have extremely high expectations and standards which can only be to the benefit of users of the Guides.

It is probably true that they are more drawn towards simple, wholesome food than say someone who perhaps eats out only once a month and for whom the mere thought of a rich cream and brandy truffled sauce is enough to get the gastric juices going. It can be a lonely job, as most of the inspections are carried out by one person dining alone, but this seems to make for a sounder judgement on what is being served up. I suspect that for many of us our (literally) gut reaction to a particular restaurant is coloured by the fact that that is where we celebrated a special anniversary (or had a dreadful row!).

Mr X said that most inspectors carried around quantities of paper napkins and even carrier bags in which to tip unwanted (and often inedible) left-overs without attracting too much attention. He recalled one occasion when, presented with an unpalatable mushroom soup, he delicately tipped the contents of the bowl out of the window – and to his horror saw it still congealed on the ivy when he drove past some weeks  later. A preferable fate, however, to the inspector who ordered a pasta salad: 'It was off – the pasta was slimy and it had the sickly sweet taste of gone-off mayonnaise and tuna fish – it had to be several days old. After one mouthful I spent the rest of the day worrying if I had salmonella poisoning.'

Happily it was a different story altogether at the Victoria and Albert. This was Mr X's second visit and, overall, his first positive impression had been confirmed, so he again asked to speak to the manager and/or chef. It was interesting to hear them talk with such genuine enthusiasm and pride in the fact that all dishes were freshly prepared and that the bread and cakes were genuinely home-baked. Herby terrine or no, they were obviously trying their best to produce quality food at an affordable price. By now it was four o'clock in the afternoon and all I could think of was a long walk (run even) to help digest all that food, but Mr X's day was far from over. Still looking fresh (and irritatingly slim) he was actually looking forward to a dinner inspection that evening.

Now that's what I call real stamina!

AN EGON RONAY'S GUIDE ONLY INCLUDES THE BEST.

LIGHT-DRY

CARTA BLANCA

RUM

Ron BACARDI Superior

BACARDI & CO., L.
Nassau, Bahamas

Coca-Cola

NOTHING FEELS LIKE BACARDI® AND COKE

SUNDAY · EATING

LONDON

Ajanta, W12
Aspava, W1
Athenaeum Hotel, Windsor
    Lounge, W1
Bill Stickers, W1
Le Bistroquet, NW1
Blake's Wine & Food Bar,
    WC2
Bloom's, E1, NW11
Brasserie, SW17
La Brasserie, SW3
British Museum Restaurant,
    WC1
Brown's Hotel Lounge, W1
Café des Fleurs, NW6
Café Pacifico, WC2
Café Pélican, WC2
Camden Brasserie, NW1
Carriages, SW1
Chequers, NW1
Chicago Pizza Pie Factory,
    W1
Chicago Rib Shack, SW7
Chuen Cheng Ku, W1
La Cloche, NW6
Cork & Bottle, WC2
Cranks, WC2
Daquise, SW7

Diwana Bhelpoori House,
    NW1, W2
Don Pepe, NW8
Dorchester Hotel,
    Promenade, W1
Dragon Gate, W1
Draycott's, SW3
Earth Exchange, N6
East West Restaurant, EC1
Ebury Wine Bar, SW1
Ed's Easy Diner, W1
L'Express Café, SW1
Fallen Angel, N1
Fifty-One Fifty-One, SW3
La Fin de la Chasse, N16
Gachon's, SE10
Gino's, W5
Goring Hotel Lounge,
    SW1
Govindas, W1
Green Cottage, NW3
Green's Champagne &
    Oyster Bar, SW1
Grill St Quentin, SW3
Gurkhas Tandoorí, W1
Harry Morgan's, NW8
Hoults, SW17
Hung Toa, W2
Hyatt Carlton Tower,
    Chinoiserie, SW1

*Hyde Park Hotel, Park
Room,* SW1
Ikkyu, W1
*Indian Veg. Bhel Poori
House,* N1
Inn on the Park Lounge, W1
*Inter-Continental Hotel,
Coffee House,* W1
Jade Garden, W1
Joe Allen, WC2
Julie's Bar, W11
Lantern, NW6
Lok Ho Fook, W1
Louis Pâtisserie, NW3
Macarthurs, SW13
*Maison Bouquillon, Le
Montmartre,* W2
*Maison Pechon Pâtisserie
Française,* W2
Manna, NW3
Marine Ices, NW3
Matono, W1
Maxie's, W7, SW1
Le Meridien Piccadilly, W1
Millward's, N16
Mother Huffs, NW3
Mulford's Wine Bar, W6
National Gallery Restaurant,
WC2
New Kam Tong, W2
New Shu Shan, WC2
No 77 Wine Bar, NW6
Oliver's, W14
Ormes, SW4
Paparazzi, W6
Pasta Underground, NW1
Le Petit Prince, NW5
Poons, WC2
*Portman Inter-Continental
Hotel, Portman Corner,* W1
Punters Pie, SW11
Raj Bhelpoori House, NW1
Rani, N3
Ravi Shankar, NW1
Redfords, NW11
The Ritz, Palm Court, W1
Rosemary Branch, N1
*Royal Lancaster Hotel
Lounge,* W2
Sabras, NW10
The Savoy, Thames Foyer,
WC2
*Sheraton Park Tower,
Rotunda Lounge,* SW1
Spices, N16

Suruchi, N1
Tea Rooms des Artistes, SW8
Tea Time, SW4
Tiger-under-the-Table,
NW11
Topkapi, W1
Tui, SW7
Tuk Tuk, N1
Tuxedo Junction, NW6
*Victoria & Albert Museum,
New Restaurant,* SW7
Villa Estense, SW6
*Village Delicatessen &
Coffee Shop,* W14
*Waldorf Hotel, Palm Court
Lounge,* WC2
Westbury Hotel Lounge, W1
Wholemeal Café, SW16
Wine Gallery, W11, SW10
Woodlands Restaurant, W1,
SW1 *& Wembley*

BATH

*Bath Puppet Theatre,
Canary, Moon & Sixpence,
Number Five, The Walrus &
the Carpenter*

BIRMINGHAM

*Bobby Browns in Town,
Chung Ying, Forbidden City,
New Happy Gathering*

BRIGHTON

*Allanjohn's, Black Chapati,
China Garden Restaurant,
Cripes!, Food for Friends, Pie
in the Sky, Ramada
Renaissance Hotel – Barts
Bar, Samsons*

BRISTOL

*Arnolfini Café Bar, Wild
Oats II*

CANTERBURY

*Cogan House English
Brasserie, Crotchets, Pizza
Place, Sweet Heart
Pâtisserie, Il Vaticano Pasta
Parlour*

CARDIFF
Champers, Riverside

EDINBURGH
Le Café Noir, Lune Town

GLASGOW
Joe's Garage

HARROGATE
Bettys

LIVERPOOL
Streets

MANCHESTER
Siam Orchid, Woo Sang, Yang Sing

OXFORD
Browns, Café M.O.M.A., Randolph Hotel Lounge

WARWICK
Bar Roussel, Charlotte's Tea Rooms, Piccolino's Pizzeria

YORK
Bettys, St Williams College Restaurant, Taylors Tea Rooms

WHY TIPO'S CO
EATING THEIR

165 PCS

DOE FUEL ECONOMY FIGURES FOR THE TIPO 1.6 DGT 30.4 MPG (9.3 L/100KM) URBAN CY
75 MPH. AND THE TIPO 1.4 DGT 33.2 MPG (8.5 L/100KM) URBAN CYCLE, 54.3 MPG (5.2
INFORMATION DIAL 100

MPETITORS ARE
HEARTS OUT.

Just compare what the Tipo gives you with what the competition offers.

No contest.

Only the Tipo gives you 100% galvanised steel on all exposed bodywork.

The Tipo is more economical, more aerodynamically efficient and gives you more interior width than any car in its class.

And the Tipo offers a wealth of standard equipment that leaves the others standing.

Yet, incredibly, the Tipo's competitors charge you more. But there's only one way to discover what a truly great car the Tipo really is.

Visit your nearest Fiat dealer and see one for yourself.

 EUROPE'S DRIVING FORCE

LATE · NIGHT · EATING

LONDON

Ajanta, W12
Almeida Theatre Wine Bar,
N1
Aspava, W1
Asuka, NW1
Athenaeum Hotel, Windsor
Lounge, W1
Baba Bhelpoori House, W2
Bentley's Wine Bar & Oyster
Bar, W1
Bill Stickers, W1
Le Bistroquet, NW1
Blake's Wine & Food Bar,
WC2
Brasserie, SW17
La Brasserie, SW3
Brasserie at L'Escargot, W1
Brown's Hotel Lounge, W1
Café Delancey, NW1
Café des Fleurs, NW6
Café Pacifico, WC2
Café Pastiche, SW6
Café Pélican, WC2
Café St Pierre Brasserie, EC1
Caffè Venezia, W1
Camden Brasserie, NW1
Carriages, SW1
Chequers, NW1
Chiang Mai, W1
Chicago Meatpackers, WC2
Chicago Pizza Pie Factory,
W1
Chicago Rib Shack, SW7
Chuen Cheng Ku, W1
La Cloche, NW6
Cork & Bottle, WC2
Cranks, WC2
Criterion Brasserie, W1
Diwana Bhelpoori House,
NW1, W2
Don Pepe, NW8
Dorchester Hotel,
Promenade, W1
Dragon Gate, W1
Ed's Easy Diner, W1
Efes Kebab House, W1
Fallen Angel, N1
La Fin de la Chasse, N16
Fino's Wine Cellar, W1
First Out, WC2

Geale's, W8
Gino's, W5
Goring Hotel Lounge, SW1
Green Cottage, NW3
Grill St Quentin, SW3
Gurkhas Tandoori, W1
Hung Toa, W2
Hyatt Carlton Tower,
Chinoiserie, SW1
Indian Veg. Bhel Poori
House, N1
Inn on the Park Lounge, W1
Inter-Continental Hotel,
Coffee House, W1
Jeeves Wine Cellar, W1
Joe Allen, WC2
Lantern, NW6
Lou Pescadou, SW5
Macarthurs, SW13
Manna, NW3
Matono, W1
Maxie's, SW1
Mélange, WC2
Le Meridien Piccadilly, W1
Meson Don Felipe, SE1
Meson Doña Ana, W11
Methuselah's, SW1
Le Metro, SW3
Millward's, N16
New Kam Tong, W2
New Shu Shan, WC2
No 77 Wine Bar, NW6
Odette's, NW1
Oliver's, W14
Ormes, SW4
Paparazzi, W6
Pasta Connection, SW3
Pasta Fino, W1
Pasta Underground, NW1
Le Petit Prince, NW5
Poons, WC2 (Leicester St &
Lisle St)
Portman Inter-Continental
Hotel, Portman Corner, W1
Punters Pie, SW11
Ravi Shankar, NW1
Royal Lancaster Hotel
Lounge, W2
The Savoy, Thames Foyer,
WC2
The Savoy, Upstairs, WC2
Shampers, W1

Soho Brasserie, **W1**
Spices, **N16**
Suruchi, **N1**
Tea Rooms des Artistes, **SW8**
Tiger-under-the-Table,
   NW11
Tiles Wine Bar, **SW1**
Topkapi, **W1**
Tui, **SW7**
Tuk Tuk, **N1**
Tuxedo Junction, **NW6**
Villa Estense, **SW6**
Volker Europa Wine Bar,
   WC2
Westbury Hotel Lounge, **W1**
Wine Gallery, **W11, SW3,**
   SW10

E N G L A N D

Atherstone, Warwicks:
   *Cloisters Wine Bar and
   Bistro*
Bakewell, Derbys: *Aitch's
   Wine Bar & Bistro*
Bath, Avon: *The Walrus &
   the Carpenter*
Birmingham, W Mid: *Chung
   Ying*
Birmingham, W Mid: *New
   Happy Gathering*
Bournemouth, Dorset:
   Superfish
Bradford, W Yorks: *Pizza
   Margherita*
Brighton, E Sussex: *Al
   Duomo*
Brighton, E Sussex: *China
   Garden Restaurant*
Brighton, E Sussex: *Cripes!*
Brighton, E Sussex: *Pie in
   the Sky*
Brighton, E Sussex: *Ramada
   Renaissance Hotel, Barts Bar*
Brighton, E Sussex: *Samsons*
Brighton (Hove), E Sussex:
   Twizzles
Bristol, Avon: *Cherries*
Bromley, Kent: *Hollywood
   Bowl*
Canterbury, Kent: *Crotchets*
Canterbury, Kent: *Pizza
   Place*
Canterbury, Kent: *Il Vaticano
   Pasta Parlour*

Chatham, Kent: *Simson's*
Cheam, Surrey: *Superfish*
Congleton, Ches: *Odd
   Fellows Wine Bar & Bistro*
East Molesey, Surrey:
   Hampton Court Brasserie
East Molesey, Surrey:
   Superfish
Eastleigh, Hants: *Piccolo
   Mondo*
Elland, W Yorks: *Berties
   Bistro*
Eton, Berks: *Eton Wine Bar*
Ewell, Surrey: *Superfish*
Gosforth, Tyne & Wear: *Girl
   on a Swing*
Kew, Surrey: *Pissarro's*
Kew, Surrey: *Wine &
   Mousaka*
King's Lynn, Norfolk:
   Antonio's Wine Bar
Kingston, Surrey: *La La
   Pizza*
Leamington Spa, Warwicks:
   Piccolino's
Leeds, W Yorks: *Salvo's*
Leeds, W Yorks:
   Strawberryfields Bistro
Lincoln, Lincs: *Troffs*
Lincoln, Lincs: *Wig & Mitre*
Liverpool, Merseyside:
   Everyman Bistro
Liverpool, Merseyside: *Streets*
Manchester, Gtr Mans:
   Brasserie St Pièrre
Manchester, Gtr Mans: *Siam
   Orchid*
Manchester, Gtr Mans: *Woo
   Sang*
Manchester, Gtr Mans: *Yang
   Sing*
Morden, Surrey: *Superfish*
Nottingham, Notts: *Pagoda*
Nottingham, Notts: *Ten*
Oxford, Oxon: *Browns*
Parkgate, Ches: *Chompers*
Richmond, Surrey: *Richmond
   Harvest*
Southampton, Hants: *La
   Margherita*
Stamford, Lincs: *George of
   Stamford*
Stratford-upon-Avon,
   Warwicks: *Pinocchio*
Tideswell, Derbys: *Poppies*
Tolworth, Surrey: *Superfish*

Tunbridge Wells, Kent: *Downstairs at Thackeray's*
Warwick, Warwicks: *Piccolino's Pizzeria*
Willerby, Humb: *Raffaele's*
Winchester, Hants: *Mr Pitkin's*
Windsor, Berks: *Angelo's Wine Bar*
Windsor, Berks: *Dôme*
Worthing, W Sussex: *River Kwai*
York, N Yorks: *Oat Cuisine*

SCOTLAND

Edinburgh, Loth: *Le Café Noir*
Edinburgh, Loth: *Kalpna*
Edinburgh, Loth: *Lune Town*
Edinburgh, Loth: *Waterfront Wine Bar*
Glasgow, S'clyde: *Café Gandolfi*
Glasgow, S'clyde: *Joe's Garage*
Inverness, H'land: *Brookes Wine Bar*

WALES

Cardiff, Sth Glamorgan: *La Brasserie*
Cardiff, Sth Glamorgan: *Champers*
Cardiff, Sth Glamorgan: *Le Monde*
Cardiff, Sth Glamorgan: *Riverside*
Swansea, West Glamorgan: *La Braseria*

ISLE OF MAN

Douglas, Isle of Man: *L'Expérience*

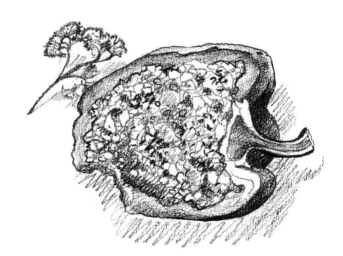

AFTERNOON·TEAS

LONDON

Athenaeum Hotel, Windsor
Lounge, W1
Brown's Hotel Lounge, W1
Dorchester Hotel,
Promenade, W1
Goring Hotel Lounge, SW1
Harrods Georgian
Restaurant & Terrace, SW1
Hyatt Carlton Tower,
Chinoiserie, SW1
Hyde Park Hotel, Park
Room, SW1
Inn on the Park Lounge, W1
Inter-Continental Hotel,
Coffee House, W1
Le Meridien Piccadilly, W1
Muffin Man, W8
Nanten, W1
Portman Inter-Continental
Hotel, Portman Corner, W1
The Ritz, Palm Court, W1
The Savoy, Thames Foyer,
WC2
Sheraton Park Tower,
Rotunda Lounge, SW1
Tea Time, SW4
Tiger-under-the-Table,
NW11
Waldorf Hotel, Palm Court
Lounge, WC2
Westbury Hotel Lounge, W1

ENGLAND

Alfriston, E Sussex: Drusillas
Thatched Barn
Alnwick, Nthmb: John
Blackmore's Restaurant
Alstonefield, Derbys: Old
Post Office Tea Rooms
Ambleside, Cumbria: Rothay
Manor
Ambleside, Cumbria: Sheila's
Cottage
Ashburton, Devon: Studio
Tea Shop
Ashford in the Water, Derbys:
Cottage Tea Room
Atherstone, Warwicks:
Muffins Salad Bar

Avebury, Wilts: Stones
Restaurant
Barden, N Yorks: Howgill
Lodge
Barnard Castle, Co. Durham:
Priors Restaurant
Bath, Avon: Canary
Beaminster, Dorset: Tea
Shoppe
Biddenden, Kent: Claris's Tea
Shop
Billingshurst, W Sussex:
Burdocks
Blanchland, Nthmb: White
Monk Tea Room
Bolton Abbey, N Yorks:
Bolton Abbey Tea Cottage
Bournemouth, Dorset:
Carlton Hotel Lounge
Bourton-on-the-Water, Glos:
Small Talk Tea Room
Brighton, E Sussex: The
Mock Turtle
Broad Chalke, Wilts: Cottage
House
Broadway, Hereford &
Worcester: Coffee Pot
Canterbury, Kent: Cogan
House English Brasserie
Canterbury, Kent: Sweet
Heart Pâtisserie
Carlisle, Cumbria: Hudson's
Coffee Shop
Castle Cary, Somerset: Old
Bakehouse
Castle Combe, Wilts: The
Manor House
Castle Hedingham, Essex:
Colne Valley Railway
Restaurant
Castleton, Derbys: Rose
Cottage Café
Cauldon Lowe, Staffs: Lindy's
Kitchen
Cerne Abbas, Dorset: Singing
Kettle
Cheddar, Somerset: Wishing
Well Tea Rooms
Cheltenham, Glos:
Promenade Pâtisserie
Chester, Ches: Chester
Grosvenor Library

Chipping Campden, Glos: *Greenstocks*

Cleveleys, Lancs: *Wholefood and Vegetarian Restaurant*

Collier Street, Kent: *Butcher's Mere*

Compton, Surrey: *Old Congregational Tea Shop*

Dartmouth, Devon: *Spinning Wheel Café*

Dorchester, Dorset: *Potter In*

Dunster, Somerset: *Tea Shoppe*

Eardisland, Hereford & Worcester: *Elms*

East Budleigh, Devon: *Grasshoppers*

Falmouth, Cornwall: *Pandora Inn*

Falmouth, Cornwall: *Secrets*

Froghall, Staffs: *The Wharf Eating House*

Frome, Somerset: *Settle*

Great Torrington, Devon: *Rebecca's*

Great Torrington, Devon: *Top of the Town*

Harrogate, N Yorks: *Bettys*

Hawes, N Yorks: *Cockett's Hotel*

Hawkshead, Cumbria: *Minstrels Gallery*

Henley-on-Thames, Oxon: *Copper Kettle*

Herstmonceux, E Sussex: *Praise the Lord*

Ilkley, W Yorks: *Bettys*

Kew, Surrey: *Original Maids of Honour*

Kirkbymoorside, N Yorks: *Hatters Castle Coffee Shop*

Lavenham, Suffolk: *The Great House*

Leamington Spa, Warwicks: *Mallory Court*

Leintwardine, Hereford & Worcester: *Selda Coffee & Crafts*

Low Laithe, N Yorks: *Carters, Knox Manor*

Luccombe Chine, I of W: *Dunnose Cottage*

Lustleigh, Devon: *Primrose Cottage*

Lynton, Devon: *Lee Cottage*

Lyonshall, Hereford & Worcester: *Church House*

Lytchett Minster, Dorset: *Slepe Cottage Tea Rooms*

Marlborough, Wilts: *Polly*

Marlow, Bucks: *Burgers*

Melmerby, Cumbria: *Village Bakery*

Midsomer Norton, Avon: *Mrs Pickwick*

Milton Ernest, Bedfordshire: *The Strawberry Tree*

Minstead, Hants: *Honey Pot*

Montacute, Somerset: *Montacute House Restaurant*

Mousehole, Cornwall: *Annie's*

New Romney, Kent: *Country Kitchen*

Newport, I of W: *God's Providence House*

Northallerton, N Yorks: *Bettys*

Offham, E Sussex: *Old Post House*

Oxford, Oxon: *Browns*

Oxford, Oxon: *Randolph Hotel Lounge*

Penshurst, Kent: *Fir Tree House Tea Rooms*

Poole, Dorset: *Inn à Nutshell*

Richmond, Surrey: *Wildefoods*

Romsey, Hants: *Cobweb Tea Rooms*

Rowlands Castle, Hants: *Coffee Pot*

Rye, E Sussex: *Swiss Pâtisserie*

St Michael's Mount, Cornwall: *Sail Loft*

Salisbury, Wilts: *Mainly Salads*

Salisbury, Wilts: *Michael Snell*

Sandwich, Kent: *Pinkies*

Selworthy, Somerset: *Periwinkle Cottage Tea Rooms*

Settle, N Yorks: *Car & Kitchen*

Sherborne, Dorset: *Church House Gallery*

Shoreham-by-Sea, W Sussex: *Cuckoo Clock*

Sidbury, Devon: *Old Bakery*

South Molton, Devon: *Corn Dolly*
Spetisbury, Dorset: *Marigold Cottage*
Spilsby, Lincs: *Buttercross Restaurant*
Stamford, Lincs: *George of Stamford*
Stamford, Lincs: *Mr Pips Coffee Shop & Restaurant*
Tewkesbury, Glos: *Wintor House*
Tissington, Derbys: *Old School Tea Rooms*
Torquay, Devon: *The Mulberry Room*
Trebarwith Strand, Cornwall: *The Old Millfloor*
Ullswater, Cumbria: *Sharrow Bay Country House Hotel Lounge*
Walberswick, Suffolk: *Potters Wheel*
Wallingford, Oxon: *Annie's Tea Rooms*
Wallingford, Oxon: *Lamb Coffee Shop*
Walton-on-the-Naze, Essex: *Naze Links Café*
Wareham, Dorset: *Priory Hotel*
Warminster, Wilts: *Jenner's*
Warwick, Warwicks: *Brethren's Kitchen*
Whitby, N Yorks: *Magpie Café*
Wimborne Minster, Dorset: *Quinneys*
Winchelsea, E Sussex: *Winchelsea Tea Room*
Windermere, Cumbria: *Miller Howe Hotel*
Windermere, Cumbria: *Victoria Cottage*

Woodstock, Oxon: *Feathers Hotel Lounge*
Wootton Bassett, Wilts: *Emms*
Worthing, W Sussex: *Fogarty's*
Worthing, W Sussex: *Mr Pastry*
York, N Yorks: *Bettys*
York, N Yorks: *Taylors Tea Rooms*

SCOTLAND

Dirleton, Loth: *Open Arms Hotel*
Dryburgh Abbey, Bdrs: *Orchard Tearoom*
Falkland, Fife: *Kind Kyttock's Kitchen*
Glasgow, S'clyde: *Joe's Garage*
Kentallen of Appin, H'land: *Holly Tree*
Ullapool, H'land: *Ceilidh Place*

WALES

Chepstow, Gwent: *Willow Tree*
Llanrwst, Gwynedd: *Tu-Hwnt-i'r-Bont*

CHANNEL ISLANDS

St Brelade's Bay, Jersey: *Hotel L'Horizon, Beech Lounge*
St Saviour, Jersey: *Longueville Manor Hotel*

The choice is yours.

At home you choose Flora for all the right reasons. You enjoy its light, delicate taste and you know it's made with pure sunflower oil, which is high in essential polyunsaturates, low in saturates, low in cholesterol.

Today you can also choose Flora when eating out because it's now available in portion packs at all the best restaurants in town.

WHOLEFOOD
AND
VEGETARIAN RESTAURANTS

LONDON

Baba Bhelpoori House, **W2**
Chequers, **NW1**
Cherry Orchard, **E2**
Country Life, **W1**
Cranks, **W1**, **WC2** (Adelaide
St & Great Newport St)
Cranks Health Food
Restaurant, **W1**
Dining Room, **SE1**
Diwana Bhelpoori House,
NW1, **W2**
Earth Exchange, **N6**
East West Restaurant, **EC1**
Fallen Angel, **N1**
First Out, **WC2**
Food for Thought, **WC2**
Govindas, **W1**
Indian Veg. Bhel Poori
House, **N1**

Justin de Blank at General
Trading Company, **SW1**
Mandeer, **W1**
Manna, **NW3**
Millward's, **N16**
Nature's Garden, **SW11**
Neal's Yard Bakery & Tea
Room, **WC2**
Raj Bhelpoori House, **NW1**
Rani, **N3**
Ravi Shankar, **NW1**
Raw Deal, **W1**
Sabras, **NW10**
Slenders, **EC4**
Spices, **N16**
Suruchi, **N1**
Wholemeal Café, **SW16**
Wilkins Natural Foods, **SW1**
Woodlands Restaurant, **W1**,
SW1 & Wembley

ENGLAND

Alton, Hants: *Apple Crumble*
Altrincham, Gtr Mans: *Nutcracker Vegetarian Restaurant*
Ambleside, Cumbria: *Zeffirellis*
Ashtead, Surrey: *Bart's*
Avebury, Wilts: *Stones Restaurant*
Barnard Castle, Co. Durham: *Priors Restaurant*
Berkhamsted, Herts: *Cook's Delight*
Birmingham, W Mid: *La Santé*
Bournemouth, Dorset: *Henry's*
Bournemouth, Dorset: *Salad Centre*
Bowness-on-Windermere, Cumbria: *Hedgerow*
Brighton, E Sussex: *Black Chapati*
Brighton, E Sussex: *Food for Friends*
Brighton, E Sussex: *Saxons*
Bristol, Avon: *Cherries*
Bristol, Avon: *Wild Oats II*
Bury St Edmunds, Suffolk: *Beaumonts*
Cambridge, Cambs: *Kings Pantry*
Cambridge, Cambs: *Nettles*
Castle Cary, Somerset: *Old Bakehouse*
Cauldon Lowe, Staffs: *Lindy's Kitchen*
Chatham, Kent: *Food for Living Eats*
Chichester, W Sussex: *St Martin's Tea Rooms*
Chipping Norton, Oxon: *Nutters*
Christchurch, Dorset: *Salads*
Cleveleys, Lancs: *Wholefood and Vegetarian Restaurant*
Cockermouth, Cumbria: *Quince & Medlar*
Coventry, W Mid: *Herbs*
Croydon, Surrey: *Hockneys*
Dartington, Devon: *Cranks Health Food Restaurant*
Derby, Derbys: *Lettuce Leaf*

Glastonbury, Somerset: *Ploughshares Café*
Glastonbury, Somerset: *Rainbow's End Café*
Gosforth, Tyne & Wear: *Girl on a Swing*
Grantham, Lincs: *Knightingales*
Hereford, Hereford & Worcester: *Marches*
Hereford, Hereford & Worcester: *Nutters*
Hythe, Kent: *Natural Break*
Ipswich, Suffolk: *Marno's*
Kendal, Cumbria: *Waterside Wholefoods*
Kidderminster, Hereford & Worcester: *Natural Break*
Lancaster, Lancs: *Libra*
Launceston, Cornwall: *The Greenhouse*
Ludlow, Shrops: *Hardwicks*
Ludlow, Shrops: *Olive Branch*
Manchester, Gtr Mans: *Greens*
Newport, I of W: *Full of Beans*
Norwich, Norfolk: *Café La Tienda*
Nottingham, Notts: *Ten*
Poole, Dorset: *Inn à Nutshell*
Portsmouth (Southsea), Hants: *Country Kitchen*
Richmond, Surrey: *Richmond Harvest*
Richmond, Surrey: *Wildefoods*
Ryton-on-Dunsmore, Warwicks: *Ryton Gardens Café*
Salisbury, Wilts: *Mainly Salads*
Shrewsbury, Shrops: *Delanys Vegetarian Restaurant* (Wyle Cop & St Alkmunds Square)
Shrewsbury, Shrops: *The Good Life*
Skipton, N Yorks: *Herbs*
Stratford-upon-Avon, Warwicks: *Café Natural*
Stroud, Glos: *Mother Nature*
Swindon, Wilts: *Acorn Wholefoods*
Tiverton, Devon: *Angel Foods*
Totnes, Devon: *Above Town Wholefood Eating House*

Totnes, Devon: *Willow*
Tunbridge Wells, Kent: *Pilgrims*
Ware, Herts: *Sunflowers*
Warminster, Wilts: *Jenner's*
Wells, Somerset: *Good Earth*
Worcester, Hereford & Worcester: *Natural Break*
Worthing, W Sussex: *Nature's Way Coffee Shop*
Yeovil, Somerset: *Trugs*
York, N Yorks: *Bees Knees*
York, N Yorks: *Oat Cuisine*
York, N Yorks: *Wholefood Trading Company*

SCOTLAND

Edinburgh, Loth: *Helios Fountain*

Edinburgh, Loth: *Hendersons Salad Table*
Edinburgh, Loth: *Kalpna*
Edinburgh, Loth: *Sunflower Country Kitchen*
Kyle of Lochalsh, H'land: *Highland Designworks*
Peebles, Bdrs: *Sunflower Coffee Shop*
St Andrews, Fife: *Brambles*
Ullapool, H'land: *Ceilidh Place*

WALES

Cardiff, Sth Glamorgan: *Sage*
Carmarthen, Dyfed: *Waverley Restaurant*
Machynlleth, Powys: *Centre for Alternative Technology*
Machynlleth, Powys: *Quarry Shop*

LONDON · BY · AREAS

BAYSWATER & NOTTING HILL

Baba Bhelpoori House, **W2**
Diwana Bhelpoori House (Westbourne Grove), **W2**
Geale's, **W8**
Gyngleboy, **W2**
Hung Toa, **W2**
Julie's Bar, **W11**
Maison Bouquillon, **W2**
Maison Pechon Pâtisserie Française, **W2**
New Kam Tong, **W2**
Royal Lancaster Hotel Lounge, **W2**
Wine Gallery (Westbourne Grove), **W11**

BLOOMSBURY

British Museum Restaurant, **WC1**
Café Society, **WC1**
Cranks (Tottenham Street), **W1**
Efes Kebab House, **W1**
Gurkhas Tandoori, **W1**
Ikkyu, **W1**
Jeeves Wine Cellar, **W1**
Mandeer, **W1**

CHELSEA & FULHAM

Café Pastiche, **SW6**
Charco's Wine Bar, **SW3**
Fifty-One Fifty-One, **SW3**
Hiders, **SW6**
Justin de Blank at General Trading Company, **SW1**
Lou Pescadou, **SW5**
Pasta Connection, **SW3**
Villa Estense, **SW6**
Wine Gallery (Hollywood Road), **SW10**

CITY

Balls Brothers (Cheapside), **EC2**
Balls Brothers (Moorgate), **EC2**
Balls Brothers, **EC4**
Bottlescrue, **EC1**
Café St Pierre Brasserie, **EC1**
East West Restaurant, **EC1**
Green House, **EC3**
Nosherie, **EC1**
Oasis in the City, **EC1**
Pavilion Wine Bar, **EC2**
Le Poulbot Pub, **EC2**
Slenders, **EC4**
Sweetings, **EC4**

COVENT GARDEN

Blake's Wine & Food Bar, **WC2**
Café Pacifico, **WC2**
Cranks (Adelaide Street), **WC2**
First Out, **WC2**
Food for Thought, **WC2**
Joe Allen, **WC2**
Mélange, **WC2**
Neal's Yard Bakery & Tea Room, **WC2**
The Savoy, Thames Foyer, **WC2**
The Savoy, Upstairs, **WC2**
Waldorf Hotel, Palm Court Lounge, **WC2**

EAST LONDON

Bloom's, **E1**
Cherry Orchard, **E2**
Faulkners, **E8**

KNIGHTSBRIDGE & KENSINGTON

La Brasserie, **SW3**
Chicago Rib Shack, **SW7**
Daquise, **SW7**
Draycott's, **SW3**
L'Express Café, **SW1**
Grill St Quentin, **SW3**
Harrods Dress & Upper Circles, **SW1**
Harrods Georgian Restaurant & Terrace, **SW1**
Hyatt Carlton Tower, Chinoiserie, **SW1**
Hyde Park Hotel, Park Room, **SW1**
Maxie's (Knightsbridge), **SW1**

Le Metro, **SW3**
Muffin Man, **W8**
*Sheraton Park Tower
Restaurant,* **SW1**
Tui, **SW7**
*Victoria & Albert Museum,
New Restaurant,* **SW7**
*Wine Gallery (Brompton
Road),* **SW5**

MAYFAIR & MARYLEBONE

Aspava, **W1**
*Athenaeum Hotel, Windsor
Lounge,* **W1**
L'Autre Wine Bar, **W1**
Brown's Hotel, Lounge, **W1**
Bubbles Wine Bar, **W1**
Caffe Venezia, **W1**
Chicago Pizza Pie Factory,
W1
*Dorchester Hotel,
Promenade,* **W1**
Fenwicks, Salad Express,
W1
*Fino's Wine Cellar (North
Row),* **W1**
Granary, **W1**
Ikeda, **W1**
Inn on the Park Lounge, **W1**
*Inter-Continental Hotel,
Coffee House,* **W1**
Justin de Blank, **W1**
Kitchen Yakitori, **W1**
Maison Sagne, **W1**
Nakamura, **W1**
Nanten, **W1**
*Portman Hotel, Portman
Corner,* **W1**
Raw Deal, **W1**
Topkapi, **W1**
Verbanella Pasta Bar, **W1**
Westbury Hotel Lounge, **W1**
*Woodlands Restaurant
(Marylebone Lane),* **W1**
Yumi, **W1**

NORTH & NORTH-WEST LONDON

Almeida Theatre Wine Bar,
N1
Asuka, **NW1**
Le Bistroquet, **NW1**
Bloom's, **NW11**

Boos, **NW1**
Café Delancey, **NW1**
Café des Fleurs, **NW6**
Camden Brasserie, **NW1**
Chequers, **NW1**
La Cloche, **NW6**
*Diwana Bhelpoori House
(Drummond Street),* **NW1**
Don Pepe, **NW8**
Earth Exchange, **N6**
Fallen Angel, **N1**
La Fin de la Chasse, **N16**
Green Cottage, **NW3**
Harry Morgan's, **NW8**
*Indian Veg. Bhel Poori
House,* **N1**
Lantern, **NW6**
Laurent, **NW2**
Louis' Pâtisserie, **NW3**
Manna, **NW3**
Marine Ices, **NW3**
Millward's, **N16**
Mother Huff's, **NW3**
No. 77 Wine Bar, **NW6**
Odette's, **NW1**
Pasta Underground, **NW1**
Le Petit Prince, **NW5**
Le Plat du Jour, **NW1**
Raj Bhelpoori House, **NW1**
Rani, **N3**
Ravi Shankar, **NW1**
Redfords, **NW11**
Rosemary Branch, **N1**
Sabras, **NW10**
Spices, **N16**
Suruchi, **NW3**
Tiger-under-the-Table,
NW11
Tuk Tuk, **N1**
Tuxedo Junction, **NW6**
Upper Street Fish Shop, **N1**
Woodlands (Wembley)

ST JAMES'S

Bentley's Wine & Oyster Bar,
W1
Country Life, **W1**
Criterion Brasserie, **W1**
*Fino's Wine Cellar (Swallow
Street),* **W1**
*Green's Champagne &
Oyster Bar,* **SW1**
Le Meridien Piccadilly, **W1**
The Ritz, Palm Court, **W1**
Simpson's Wine Bar, **W1**

SOHO & TRAFALGAR SQUARE

Bill Stickers, **W1**
Brasserie at L'Escargot, **W1**
Café Pélican, **WC2**
Chiang Mai, **W1**
Chicago Meatpackers, **WC2**
Chuen Cheng Ku, **W1**
Cork & Bottle, **WC2**
Cranks (Great Newport Street), **WC2**
Cranks Health Food Restaurant, **W1**
Dragon Gate, **W1**
Ed's Easy Diner, **W1**
Govindas, **W1**
Jade Garden, **W1**
Lok Ho Fook, **W1**
Maison Bertaux, **W1**
National Gallery Restaurant, **WC2**
New Shu Shan, **WC2**
Pasta Fino, **W1**
Pâtisserie Cappuccetto, **W1**
Pâtisserie Valerie, **W1**
Poons (Leicester Street), **WC2**
Poons (Lisle Street), **WC2**
Shampers, **W1**
Soho Brasserie, **W1**
Le Tire Bouchon, **W1**
Volker Europa Wine Bar, **WC2**
Woodlands (Panton Street), **SW1**

SOUTH-EAST LONDON

Bon Ton Roulet, **SE24**
Colonel Jasper's, **SE10**
Cuddeford's Wine Bar, **SE1**
Davy's Wine Vaults, **SE10**
Dining Room, **SE1**

Gachons, **SE10**
Meson Don Felipe, **SE1**
Skinkers, **SE1**

SOUTH-WEST LONDON

Brasserie, **SW17**
Hoults, **SW17**
Macarthurs, **SW13**
Nature's Garden, **SW11**
Ormes Wine Bar & Restaurant, **SW4**
Punters Pie, **SW11**
Tea Room des Artistes, **SW8**
Tea Time, **SW4**
Twenty Trinity Gardens, **SW9**
Wholemeal Vegetarian Restaurant, **SW16**

VICTORIA & WESTMINSTER

Carriages, **SW1**
Ebury Wine Bar, **SW1**
Goring Hotel Lounge, **SW1**
Methuselah's, **SW1**
Tapster, **SW1**
Tiles, **SW1**
Wilkins Natural Foods, **SW1**

WEST LONDON

Ajanta, **W12**
Gino's, **W5**
Linda's, **W9**
Maxie's (Boston Parade), **W7**
Meson Doña Ana, **W11**
Mulford's Wine Bar, **W6**
Old Heidelberg, **W4**
Oliver's, **W4**
Paparazzi, **W6**
Village Delicatessen & Coffee Shop, **W14**

Owen Meredith
1831–91

He may live without love – what is passion but pining?
But where is the man who can live without dining?
Lucile

Bennett Cerf

Good manners: The noise you don't make when you're
eating soup.
Laughing Stock (1945)

Marie Dressler

If ants are such busy workers, how come they find time
to go to all the picnics?
Cited by Cowan in *The Wit of Women*

P. B. Shelley
1792–1822

Though we eat little flesh and drink no wine.
Yet let's be merry: we'll have tea and toast:
Custards for supper, and an endless host
of syllabubs and jellies and mince pies,
And other such lady-like luxuries.
Letter to Maria Gisborne

The Dairy Crest Symbol of Excellence

DAIRY CREST

Symbol of Excellence

Wherever you see this sign, you will be entering an establishment where the quality and presentation of cheeses is excellent.

The Dairy Crest Symbol of Excellence is only awarded by the Egon Ronay's Guides' team of inspectors where they find a high standard of cheese available — whether presented on a cheeseboard or included in a meal or snack.

Now in its third year, the Award is an on-going sign of commitment from Britain's leading cheese manufacturer, Dairy Crest Foods, to the improvement of cheese quality, variety and presentation.

The Symbol is recognised nationally by caterers who strive to reach its high standards, and by the ever more discerning public who are seeking nothing but the best when eating in hotels, restaurants, pubs and cafes.

So, wherever you see the Egon Ronay's Guide Dairy Crest Symbol of Excellence, you will enjoy guaranteed quality of:

TASTE — through expert selection, handling and storage

VARIETY — through imaginative use of traditional, new and local cheeses

PRESENTATION — through the use of colour, texture and shape to give a mouth-watering display

INFORMATION — through the caterer's knowledge and understanding

Where you find English cheeses at their best, you will be sure to find Dairy Crest's own excellent cheeses, such as the famous Lymeswold range, the reduced-fat Tendale range and the full selection of England and Welsh traditional cheeses and prize-winning Cheddars and Stilton.

DAIRY CREST

OUTSTANDING CHEESEBOARDS

LONDON

Le Bistroquet, NW1
Cuddeford's Wine Bar, SE1
Gyngleboy, W2
Methuselah's, SW1
Le Metro, SW3
Pavilion Wine Bar, EC2
Le Tire Bouchon, W1

ENGLAND

Avebury, Wilts: *Stones Restaurant*
Berwick-upon-Tweed, Nthmb: *Scotsgate Wine Bar*
Canterbury, Kent: *Cogan House English Brasserie*
Chester, Ches: *Chester Grosvenor Library*
Corse Lawn, Glos: *Corse Lawn House*

Eastbourne, E Sussex: *Byrons*
Stevenage, Herts: *De Friese Coffee Shop*
Tresco, Cornwall: *Island Hotel Restaurant*

SCOTLAND

Glasgow, S'clyde: *De Quincey's/Brahms & Liszt*

WALES

Cowbridge, Sth Glamorgan: *Off the Beeton Track*
Llanberis, Gwynedd: *Y Bistro Bach*
Rhyd-y-Clafdy, Gwynedd: *Tu Hwnt i'r Afon*

WHERE TO EAT ON AND OFF MOTORWAYS

M1 LONDON·TO·LEEDS

LONDON

6 ST ALBANS — *4 miles* — **Kingsbury Mill Waffle House**

St Michael's Street. Take the **A405** towards St Albans and follow signs to the Verulamium Theatre.

Freshly-baked waffles with sweet or savoury toppings are served at this ancient mill dating from Elizabethan times.

8 HEMEL HEMPSTEAD — *3 miles* — **Gallery Coffee Shop**

Old Town Arts Centre, High Street. Take the **A4147**. At second roundabout turn right and follow the road for 1½ miles to the High Street. The Arts Centre is on the left.

Part of a bustling arts centre, this bright brasserie offers sandwiches, soup, pâté and imaginative main courses. Good home baking and sweets as well.

8 BERKHAMSTED — *7 miles* — **Cook's Delight**

360 High Street. Take the **A414** through Hemel Hempstead and then follow the **A41** to Berkhamsted which leads into the High Street.

Vegetarian and macrobiotic dishes with a Far Eastern flavour are the speciality at this little tea room behind a health food shop.

25 **DERBY** *8 miles* Lettuce Leaf

21 Friar Gate. Take the **A52** towards the town centre which runs into Friar Gate.

Consult the blackboard for the day's specials at this little wholefood restaurant – they could include things like celery hotpot and vegetables provençale.

26

31 Greyfriar Gate. Take the **A610** to the city centre and follow signs to the bus station.

Try the dim sum at this unpretentious Chinese restaurant at lunchtime, or full Cantonese cooking in the evening.

26 **NOTTINGHAM** *5 miles* The Q in the Corner at Ziggi's

3 Victoria Street. Take the **A610** to the city centre. At Canning Circus roundabout go straight into Derby Road which leads into Maid Marian Way. The road passes the shopping centre and then veers left into Fletcher Gate. At the end turn left into Victoria Street.

You enter this welcoming restaurant through a ladies' fashion shop, and a range of home baked cakes and pastries and savoury snacks awaits you inside.

26 **NOTTINGHAM** *5 miles* Ten

10 Commerce Square, off High Pavement. Take the **A610** to the city centre. At Canning Circus roundabout go straight on into Maid Marian Way. At Garners Hill Park turn left and then first right into High Pavement.

Delicious vegetarian and wholefood dishes are on offer here, from nut rissoles to savoury herb waffles and vegetable burgers.

29 **WARSOP** *8 miles* Goff's

4 Burns Lane. Take the **A617** into Mansfield and then the **A60** to Warsop. At the traffic lights turn right into Burns Lane.

Lunch is a treat here, with fresh ingredients and imaginative cooking. Try a bolognese pancake or creamed garlic mushroom salad.

33   SHEFFIELD   *5 miles*   Just Cooking

16 Carver Street. Take the **A630**, then **A57** into the city centre to Charter Square roundabout and Carver Street is near to Grosvenor Hotel.

The long lunchtime brings many delights here, typified by cheese and mushroom quiche or a lamb and apricot casserole bursting with flavour. Also delicious salads and sweets.

33   SHEFFIELD   *5 miles*   Toff's Restaurant & Coffee House

23 Matilda Street. Take the **A630**, then **A57** into the city centre. Follow signs for The Moor.

Summery surroundings in which to enjoy tea and cakes as well as tasty lunchtime dishes such as wholemeal quiche, mushroom tartlets and chicken casserole.

47   LEEDS   *1 mile*   Salvo's

115 Otley Road, Headingley. Follow the signs for the city centre and then follow the **A660** for about 3 miles.

A lively Italian restaurant serving huge pizzas, pasta, fresh fish and meat dishes with style and authentic flavour.

47   LEEDS   *1 mile*   Strawberryfields Bistro

159 Woodhouse Lane. Follow the signs for city centre and then take the **A69**, following signs to the University.

Burgers and pizzas are popular snack meals at this simply appointed bistro just out of the city centre, as are salads, vegetarian dishes and steaks.

LEEDS

LONDON

J U N C T

2   KEW   *1 mile*   Original Maids of Honour ★

288 Kew Road. Take the **A4**, then turn on to the **A307** and follow the signs to Kew Bridge towards Richmond.

Baking of the highest class has brought far-reaching fame to this marvellous tea shop. Cream slices, brandy snaps and the scrumptious Maids of Honour touch on a galaxy of delights.

J U N C T

6   ETON   *3 miles*   Eton Wine Bar

82 High Street. Take the **A355**, following signs for Eton.

Neat, friendly and informal, with a menu that shows imagination. Some typical delights include smoked salmon and spinach mousse and veal and almond casserole.

J U N C T

6   WINDSOR   *3 miles*   Dôme

5 Thames Street. Follow the dual carriageway into the town centre and head for the castle entrance. Dôme is opposite.

A lively and spacious café-bistro which is open all day for food with a distinctly French flavour, from croissants to main dishes.

J U N C T

10   WOKINGHAM   *3 miles*   Setters Bistro

49 Peach Street. Take the **A329(M)**, signposted to Wokingham, then follow the **A329**.

The blackboard tempts lunchtime visitors with tasty specials like leek and potato soup, chicken goulash and steak and kidney pie. Delicious sweets too.

J U N C T

11   READING   *4 miles*   Mama Mia

11 St Mary's Butts. Take **A33** into Reading and follow signs for Ramada Hotel.

Sound, reliable cooking make this town-centre restaurant a very popular and lively place. Pasta, pizzas and traditional meat dishes.

14 HUNGERFORD   *3 miles*   Bear, Kennet Room

41 Charnham Street. Follow **A338** into town centre. The Bear is on the left.

Snatch a snack or linger over a full meal at this traditional inn. Typical fare includes fish soup, stuffed aubergines, baked trout and terrine of summer fruit.

15 SWINDON   *4 miles*   Acorn Wholefoods

40 Havelock Street. Take the **A419** and follow signs into town centre. Havelock Street is about 50 yards past the Brunel shopping centre on the left.

A pretty self-service wholefood restaurant above a health food shop serving a good selection of fresh vegetarian and seafood dishes.

16 WOOTTON BASSETT   *2½ miles*   Emms

147 High Street. Take the **A3102** into the High Street.

Opposite the church, this smart café offers a wide range of home-made soups, savoury snacks and cakes all day long.

17 CASTLE COMBE   *8 miles*   Manor House Hotel

Follow the **A429** to Chippenham. From the town centre take the **A420** for 2 miles. Turn right onto the **B4039**.

Stop off for a proper old-fashioned English high tea, set tea or cream tea in this delightful 17th-century stone manor house.

19 BRISTOL   *6 miles*   Arnolfini Café-Bar

Narrow Quay, Prince Street. Take the **M32** and follow signs to city centre.

Old dockland warehouses are home for the arts complex of which this is a part. There's a varied menu, from seafood pancakes and lamb kebabs to curries, quiches and gooey sweets.

19   BRISTOL   *6 miles*   Guild Café-Restaurant

68 Park Street. Take the **M32** and follow signs to city centre. Park at Clifton Down multi-storey car park.

A nice feature of this first-floor café is a leafy outdoor area. The basic menu of home-made cakes, biscuits and cheese rolls is supplemented by lunchtime savouries and sweets.

22   CHEPSTOW   *2 miles*   Willow Tree

'The Back', Chepstow River Bank. Take the **A466** to the town centre and follow signs to the river bank.

Right down by the river is this 16th-century cottage with conservatory-style tea room, providing cakes, scones and savoury dishes such as casseroled pork.

32   CARDIFF   *5 miles*   Armless Dragon ★

97 Wyverne Road, Cathays. Take the **A470** to the town centre. Follow signs to Cathays Station.

A wide range of imaginative dishes is available in this restaurant, from kidneys in brandy to spicy chicken winglets, as well as delicious desserts.

32   CARDIFF   *5 miles*   Sage

Wellfield Court off Wellfield Road. Take the **A470** into the town centre. Follow signs to Roath. Take the Albany Road and turn left at the lights past the shopping centre.

A friendly atmosphere and some tasty cooking combine well in this wholefood and vegetarian restaurant, serving salads, main meals and home baking.

CARDIFF

BIRMINGHAM

6 OMBERSLEY   *4 miles*   Ombersley Gallery Tea Room

Church Terrace. Take the **A449** towards Kidderminster. Ombersley is signposted to the left.

Biscuits and scones, rhubarb flan and Genoa sponge are among the baked goodies, with pâtés and moussaka for savoury palates in this old-world tea room.

7 WORCESTER   *4 miles*   Natural Break

17 Mealcheapen Street. Take the **A44** into the town centre. On the High Street turn left into Mealcheapen Street.

One of a chain of self-service restaurants serving freshly cooked sweet and savoury items throughout the day.

9 CORSE LAWN   *7 miles*   Corse Lawn House ★

Nr Gloucester. Follow the **A438** through Tewkesbury and then the **B4211** to Corse Lawn.

The bar food here makes excellent use of best quality fresh produce, from pâté au cognac and crab terrine to salmon trout with lime and dill, with lovely sweets to follow.

11 CHELTENHAM   *4 miles*   Choirs Tea Rooms

5 Well Walk. Take the **A40** into the town centre. From the High Street turn right into Clarence Street. Well Walk is at the bottom.

A delightfully restored bow-windowed tea room offering a range of cakes with tea, sandwiches, pizzas, salads and soups.

11 CHELTENHAM   *4 miles*   Langtry Pâtisserie & Tea Rooms

56 High Street. Take **A40** into the town centre and follow the one-way system.

Locals and tourists make tracks for this Victorian tea shop to sample the delights of the bakehouse beyond the garden. Savoury snacks, too, and ice cream specialities.

JUNCT

| 11 | CHELTENHAM | *4 miles* | Retreat |

10 Suffolk Parade. Take the **A40** towards the town centre down Lansdown Road and Andover Road. This leads into Suffolk Road; Suffolk Parade is on the left.

Soup, quiche, taramasalata, wholewheat spaghetti, curried crab puffs and chilli with yoghurt are some of the items on the menu at this busy wine bar.

JUNCT

| 13 | PAINSWICK | *8 miles* | Cup House |

Bisley Street. Take the **A419** and follow signs to Stonehouse and Stroud. From Stroud take the **A46** into Painswick.

Home-made scones, slices and flapjacks go down a treat at teatime, while for lunch there's a simple choice of sandwiches and light snacks.

JUNCT

| 17 | BRISTOL | *6 miles* | Rainbow Café |

10 Waterloo Street, Clifton. Take the **A4018** to Clifton. Turn right off Princess Victoria Street in the town centre.

A haven of good healthy cooking, where excellent tea is served all day with cheese or fruit scones and scrumptious cakes.

JUNCT

| 20 | CLEVEDON | *2 miles* | Murrays |

91 Hill Road. Follow signs to the seafront. At the Pier, take the first right, then the first left and Hill Road is on the right.

Home baking is the speciality here. At tea time there are oven-warm scones and rich fruit cake, and savoury specials for lunch.

JUNCT

| 23 | BRIDGWATER | *4 miles* | Nutmeg |

8 Clare Street. Take the **A38**. Follow the signs to Bridgwater and take Clink Road. Clare Street is on the left just past the police station.

Cooked breakfasts give the day a good start at this popular café, and later offerings like cakes, sandwiches and a lunchtime hotpot keep up the good work.

| 25 | TAUNTON | *2 miles* | Castle Hotel, Bow Bar |

North Street. Take the **A358** and follow signs for town centre and then Wellington. Turn right before the Top Rank Club and right by the car park.

It is part of the Castle Hotel, but this tapestry-hung bar has its own entrance. Light lunches offer things like turkey sandwiches, noodles with seafood and minute steak.

| 25 | TAUNTON | *2 miles* | Porters |

49 East Reach. Following signs for the town centre, take the **A358** and then the **A38** which leads into East Reach.

A cheerful and leafy wine bar where you can have open sandwiches or more substantial dishes like trout with celery sauce or deep-fried Camembert.

| 27 | TIVERTON | *7 miles* | Angel Foods |

1 Angel Terrace. Take the dual carriageway to Tiverton and follow signs for the town centre. The café is opposite the library.

Tucked behind a shop, this tiny wholefood café offers wholesome imaginative snacks and a range of herbal teas.

| 30 | LYMPSTONE | *5 miles* | River House |

The Strand. Take the **A376** into the town centre.

With lovely views across the river Exe to Powderham Castle, this is a splendid spot to enjoy freshly cooked and flavoursome food, the emphasis being on fish.

EXETER

BIRMINGHAM

J
U
N
C
T

17 CONGLETON *7 miles* Odd Fellows Wine Bar & Bistro

20 Rood Hill. Take **A534** into the town centre. Turn left at first junction, left again at roundabout and then first right into Rood Hill.

The imaginative lunchtime and evening menu is matched by suitably skilful cooking, prime ingredients and colourful presentation. Herby salads are good, as are sweets such as home-made ice cream.

J
U
N
C
T

18 MIDDLEWICH *3 miles* Tempters

11 Wheelock Street. Take the **A54** and follow signs to the town centre which will lead you into Wheelock Street.

A restful split-level restaurant with starters like avocado with curried mayonnaise and main courses from honeyed lamb to plaice in white wine.

J
U
N
C
T

19 ALTRINCHAM *6 miles* Nutcracker Vegetarian Restaurant

43 Oxford Road. Take the **A556** through Bowden and then the **A56** to Altrincham. Turn right at Regent Road (just before overhead footbridge) and continue to the T-junction. Turn right, take left-hand fork and first left into Oxford Road.

A long-time local favourite, this pretty vegetarian restaurant has a counter display of good baking, with savoury items at lunchtime.

J
U
N
C
T

34 LANCASTER *2 miles* Libra

19 Brock Street. Follow signs for city centre. Turn left at the Town Hall into Dalton Square. Libra is on right.

Herb teas and delicious savoury bread flavoured with tomato and garlic are specialities at this friendly vegetarian restaurant.

J
U
N
C
T

37 KENDAL *6 miles* Corner Spot Eating House

2 Stramongate. Follow the **A684** into town centre.

At the foot of a cobbled hill at one end of the market place, this unpretentious first-floor café provides good honest fare through the day. Try one of the delicious cakes or enjoy a lunchtime snack like quiche or jacket potato.

37 KENDAL — 6 miles — The Moon ★

129 Highgate. Take the **A684** to Kendal and follow signs to the town centre. Highgate is 300 yards on the right after the start of the one-way system.

A deservedly popular restaurant abounding with warmth and character, and serving delicious food from smoked haddock and fennel cheese bake to lamb casserole.

37 KENDAL — 6 miles — Nutters

Yard 11, Stramongate. Follow the **A684** through the town centre. Nutters is opposite the New Road car park.

Savoury snacks at this old-beamed coffee shop could include smoked cod quiche, chicken and sweetcorn pie and filled jacket potatoes.

40 CLIFTON DYKES — 2 miles — Wetheriggs

Nr Penrith. Take the **A66** (heading for Penrith) and turn right onto the **A6** to Clifton Dykes.

Part of a craft and heritage centre, this café provides quiches, pizzas, soups, salads and some delicious home baking.

40 ULLSWATER — 5 miles — Sharrow Bay Country House Hotel Lounge ★

Pooley Bridge, nr Penrith. From the **A66** (heading towards Keswick) turn left onto the **A592** and then left again for Pooley Bridge.

Superb afternoon teas can be enjoyed here in an elegant setting with beautiful views. Sandwiches, scones, cakes and pastries to savour, but you must book.

43 CARLISLE — 2 miles — Hudson's Coffee Shop

Treasury Court, Fisher Street. Follow **A69** into town centre and towards the cathedral. The coffee shop is a 2 minute walk away.

Delightful little coffee shop where scones, caramel shortbread and chocolate slice make light bites with tea or coffee. Salads, a quiche and hot daily special at lunchtime.

CARLISLE

THE FIAT GUIDE
TO SUCCESSFUL
MOTORING

Fiat main and service dealers are strategically situated across the United Kingdom to offer comprehensive sales, servicing and repair facilities together with an abundant availability of spares and accessories.

At the time of going to press we have 344 dealerships, as shown in the list below, bringing the stylish Fiat range close to home and ensuring that you can easily contact us wherever you are.

To learn of any possible new appointments nearer to you please contact the Fiat Information Service, Dept ER88, Windsor, Berks SL4 3BA. Telephone: 01-897 0922.

★Denotes Service Only Dealer.

ENGLAND

AVON
BATH: **MOTOR SERVICES (BATH) LTD**
Locksbrook Rd. 0225 428000
BRISTOL: **AUTOTREND LTD**
724-726 Fishponds Rd. 0272 659491
BRISTOL: **BAWNS (BRISTOL) LTD**
168-176 Coronation Rd. 0272 631101
CLEVEDON: **JEFF BROWNS**
(CLEVEDON) Old Church Rd. 0272 871211
WESTON-SUPER-MARE:
JEFF BROWNS (LYMPSHAM)
Bridgewater Rd. 0934 72300/72696
★ THORNBURY BRISTOL: **SHIPPS OF**
THORNBURY
Midland Way. 0454 413130

BEDFORDSHIRE
BEDFORD: **OUSE VALLEY MOTORS**
9 Kingsway. 0234 64491
BIGGLESWADE: **OWEN GODFREY LTD**
91-119 Shortmead St. 0767 313357
BILLINGTON: **D & J AUTOS LTD**
The Garage, Leighton Buzzard Rd.
0525 383068
LUTON: **BLACKABY & PEARCE**
(LUTON) LTD
Poynters Rd. 0582 667742

BERKSHIRE
GORING-ON-THAMES: **COURTS GARAGE**
(GORING)
42 Wallingford Rd. 0491 872006
MAIDENHEAD: **SOUTH BERKSHIRE**
MOTOR CO. LTD
264-270 Windsor Rd. 0628 71628
NEWBURY: **BLACK AND WHITE**
GARAGE
Hermitage Rd, Cold Ash. 0635 200444
READING: **JACK HILL (READING) LTD**
Chatham Street Multi-Storey Car Park.
0734 582521
WINDSOR: **ANDREWS OF WINDSOR**
110 St Leonards Rd. 0753 866108

BUCKINGHAMSHIRE
★ AMERSHAM: **AMERSHAM MOTORS LTD**
Chesham Rd. 0494 722191
AYLESBURY: **AMERSHAM MOTORS**
Stoke Rd. 0296 81181
BEACONSFIELD: **MAURICE LEO LTD**
15 Gregories Rd. 04946 6171
BOURNE END: **CARCHOICE LTD**
Station Rd. 06285 22606

GERRARDS CROSS:
BURWOODS GARAGE LTD
Oxford Rd, Tatling End. 0753 885216
HIGH WYCOMBE: **DESBOROUGH**
MOTOR CO LTD
41 Desborough Ave. 0494 36331
MILTON KEYNES: **ELMDENE MOTORS LTD**
Townsend Thoresen Auto Centre, Unit 15,
Erica Rd. 0908 320355

CAMBRIDGESHIRE
CAMBRIDGE: **HOLLAND FIAT CENTRE**
315-349 Mill Rd. 0223 242222
MARCH: **CARL PORTER LTD**
Causeway Garage, The Causeway. 0354
53340/55956
PETERBOROUGH: **PETERBOROUGH**
AUTOS
Midland Rd. 0733 314431
St. IVES: **OUSE VALLEY MOTORS**
Station Rd. 0480 62641

CHESHIRE
ALTRINCHAM: **S. DAVIS**
(ALTRINCHAM) LTD
Dunham Rd. 061 928 4444
CHESTER: **COWIES OF CHESTER**
Mountview, Sealand Rd. 0244 374440
★ CONGLETON: **ROBIN HOOD GARAGE**
West Heath. 0260 273219
CREWE: **COPPENHALL GARAGE**
Cross Green. 0270 500437
MACCLESFIELD: **D.C. COOK**
London Rd. 0625 28866
NORTHWICH: **STATION ROAD GARAGE**
(NORTHWICH) LTD
Station Rd. 0606 49957
WARRINGTON: **WILLIAM MARTYN**
GARAGES LTD
Wilderspool Causeway. 0925 50417

CLEVELAND
MIDDLESBROUGH: **REG VARDY LTD**
Trunk Rd (Opp Brambles Farm). 0642 244651
STOCKTON-ON-TEES: **WENTANE**
MOTORS LTD
100 Yarm Lane. 0642 611544

CORNWALL
NEWQUAY: **TOWER OF NEWQUAY**
Tower Rd. 0637 872378/877332
TRURO: **W.H. COLLINS & SON**
(MOTORS) LTD
Kenwyn Mews. 0872 74334

CUMBRIA
BARROW-IN-FURNESS:
COUNTY PARK MOTORS
County Park Industrial Est., Park Rd.
0229 36888
CARLISLE: **GRIERSON & GRAHAM**
(CARLISLE) LTD
33 Church St, Caldewgate. 0228 25092
FLIMBY: **DOBIE'S GARAGE**
Risehow. 0900 812332
★ KENDAL: **CRAIGHILL & CO LTD**
113 Stricklandgate. 0539 20967/8
KESWICK: **KESWICK MOTOR CO LTD**
Lake Road Garage. Sales: 0596 72534

DEVON
BARNSTAPLE: **NORTH DEVON**
MOTOR CO Pottington Ind Est. 0271 76551
EXETER: **SIDWELL STREET MOTORS**
LTD 85-88 Sidwell St. 0392 54923
★ NEWTON ABBOT: **QUAY GARAGE**
The Avenue. 0626 52525/6
★ OKEHAMPTON: **F. J. GLASS & CO**
(1981) LTD
57 Exeter Rd. 0837 2255
PAIGNTON: **BABBACOMBE**
GARAGE LTD
Totnes Rd. 0803 556796
PLYMOUTH: **MUMFORDS OF**
PLYMOUTH Plymouth Pl. 0752 261511
SIDMOUTH: **CENTRAL GARAGE**
(SIDFORD) LTD
Crossways, Sidford. 03955 3595

DORSET
BOURNEMOUTH: **CAFFYNS PLC**
674-680 Wimborne Rd, Winton. 0202 5121
POOLE: **CAFFYNS PLC**
552-554 Ashley Rd, Parkstone. 0202 71539
WEYMOUTH: **OLDS**
172 Dorchester Rd. 0305 786311

CO DURHAM
CONSETT: **TRAVELWISE**
Delves La. 0207 502353
★ CROOK: **BROOKSIDE GARAGE LTD**
New Rd. 0388 762551
★ DARLINGTON: **E. WILLIAMSON**
(MOTORS) LTD
1-7 Woodland Rd. 0325 483251
★ SACRISTON: **HUNTER & CHATER**
Woodside Garage, Wilton Rd. 091 371 042

ESSEX
BASILDON: **H.W.S.**
Roundacre, Nethermayne. 0268 22261
BUCKHURST HILL: **MONTROE MOTORS**
Epping New Rd. 01-504 1171
CHELMSFORD: **M.M. AUTOS (CHELMSFORD)**
Colchester Rd. 0245 361731
COLCHESTER: **D. SALMON CARS LTD**
Sheepen Rd. 0206 563311
FRINTON-ON-SEA: **POLLENDINE MOTORS LTD**
132 Connaught Ave. 0255 679123/674341
HARLOW: **MOTORSALES (HARLOW) LTD**
Elizabeth Way, Burnt Mill. 0279 412161
HUTTON: **HUTTON GARAGES LTD**
661 Rayleigh Rd. 0277 210087
★ROMFORD: **McQUIRE MOTORS LTD**
299-307 Collier Row La. 0708 766806
SOUTHEND-ON-SEA: **BELLE VUE MOTORS LTD**
460-464 Southchurch Rd. 0207 64945
WESTCLIFF-ON-SEA: **H.W.S.**
684 London Rd. 0702 470000

GLOUCESTERSHIRE
CHELTENHAM: **DANEWAY MOTOR CO LTD** 84 Bath Rd. 0242 523879
STROUD: **PAGANHILL SERVICE STATION LTD** 105 Stratford Rd. 04536 4781
GLOUCESTER: **WARNERS MOTORS LTD**
Quedgeley Garage, Quedgeley.
0452 720107
★WOTTON-UNDER-EDGE: **WOTTON MOTOR CENTRE LTD**
Gloucester St. 0453 842240

GREATER MANCHESTER
ASHTON-UNDER-LYNE: **PREMIER MOTOR CO**
Manchester Rd, Mossley. 04575 67121
BOLTON: **D.C. COOK (BOLTON) LTD**
Kay St/Higher Bridge. 0204 362000
BURY: **BLACKFORD BRIDGE CAR SHOW LTD**
701 Manchester Rd, Blackford Bridge.
061-766 1346
LEIGH: **SMALLBROOK SERVICE STATION**
Smallbrook La. 0942 882201/891939
MANCHESTER: **D.C. COOK (MANCHESTER) LTD**
Midland Street Garage, Ashton Old Road.
061-273 4411
OLDHAM: **D.C. COOK (OLDHAM) LTD**
23-37 Lees Rd. 061-624 8046
ROCHDALE: **D.C. COOK (ROCHDALE) LTD**
Queensway. 0706 33222
STOCKPORT: **D.C. COOK (STOCKPORT) LTD**
West End Garage, Heaton La. 061-480 6661

HAMPSHIRE
ALDERSHOT: **CLEVELAND CARS LTD**
Ash St, Ash. 0252 334055
ANDOVER: **CLOVERLEAF CARS (ANDOVER)** Salisbury Rd. 0264 61166
BASINGSTOKE: **CLOVERLEAF CARS (BASINGSTOKE)**
London Rd (A30). 0256 55221
BITTERNE: **SEWARDS BITTERNE**
Bursledon Rd. 0703 422202
PORTSMOUTH: **CANNON GARAGES (PORTSMOUTH) LTD**
117 Copnor Rd. 0705 691621
RINGWOOD: **WELLS RINGWOOD**
Salisbury Rd. 04254 6111
SOUTHAMPTON: **SEWARDS**
Rushington Roundabout, Totton Bypass.
0703 861001
WINCHESTER: **GRAYSTONES**
12-14 City Rd. 0962 62244

HEREFORD & WORCESTER
EVESHAM: **BRIGHTS GARAGE**
3 Cheltenham Rd. 0386 2301
HEREFORD: **GODSELL'S (HEREFORD) LTD**
BATH St. 0432 274134
KIDDERMINSTER: **STANLEY GOODWIN MOTORS LTD**
Worcester Rd. 0562 820202

WORCESTER: **BOWLING GREEN GARAGE (POWICK) LTD**
Powick. 0905 830361
BROMSGROVE: **NEALE'S GARAGE (1985) LTD**
2-12 Station St. 0527 72071

HERTFORDSHIRE
CROXLEY GREEN: **CROXLEY GREEN MOTORS LTD**
185 Watford Rd. 0923 55511
HEMEL HEMPSTEAD: **SHAW & KILBURN LTD**
Two Waters Rd. 0442 51212
HERTFORD: **PAMSONS MOTORS HERTFORD** 80 Ware Rd. 0992 584147
HITCHIN: **SERVAL (HITCHIN) LTD**
Ickleford. 0462 54526
KNEBWORTH: **LISLES MOTOR REPAIRS LTD**
London Rd, Woolmer Green. 0438 811011
ST. ALBANS: **LAP GROUP**
2 Beech Rd. Marshalswick. 0727 50871

HUMBERSIDE
BRIDLINGTON: **JORDANS**
248 Quay Rd. 0262 670331
DRIFFIELD: **GEORGE WILLIAMSON (GARAGES) LTD**
82-84 Middle St., South. 0377 43130
★GRIMSBY: **ERIC C. BURTON & SONS LTD**
Station Garage, Wellowgate. 0472 355951
★GOOLE: **J. WARDLE & SONS LTD**
Boothferry Rd., Howden. 0430 430388
HULL: **AB MOTOR CO of HULL LTD**
96 Boothferry Rd. 0482 506976/54256
HULL: **JORDAN & JUBILEE GARAGE**
45-52 Witham. 0482 24131
SCUNTHORPE: **BRUMBY SERVICE GARAGE LTD**
The Fiat Centre, Normanby Rd.
0724 861191

ISLE OF WIGHT
SANDOWN: **HODGE & CHILDS LTD**
Station Ave. 0983 402552

KENT
ASHFORD: **ASHFORD MOTOR CO**
Chart Rd. 0233 22281
BECKENHAM: **BRUTONS OF BECKENHAM LTD**
181 Beckenham Rd. 01-650 3333
BEXLEYHEATH: **BELLWAY MOTORS KENT** 303/307 Broadway. 01-301 0420
BROMLEY: **THAMES**
96 Bromley Hill. 01-460 4646
DEAL: **CAMPBELLS OF DEAL LTD**
6 The Marina. 0304 363166
FARNBOROUGH: **FARNWAY SERVICE LTD** 2 Church Rd. 0689 50121
★GILLINGHAM: **AUTOYACHTS LTD**
171 Pier Rd. 0634 281333
★GRAVESEND: **MARTINS GARAGE**
50 Singlewell Rd. 0474 66148
★HAM STREET: **ANNINGS MARSH ROAD** Nr Ashford. 023 373 2275
HYTHE: **RAMPART GARAGE**
15-17 Rampart Rd. 0303 67088
MAIDSTONE: **MCS GEORGE STREET LTD** George St. 0622 677524/5/6
★MARGATE: **S & S MOTORS**
10-12 Park La. 0843 227778
ORPINGTON: **GODDINGTON SERVICE STATION** 318 Court Rd. 0689 20337
RAMSGATE: **S & S MOTORS LEVERPOINT LTD**
Willsons Rd. 0843 593465
★SITTINGBOURNE: **J G BURGESS & CO**
Ufton Lane Garage. 0795 23815
SWANLEY: **FOREMAN BROS LTD**
London Rd. 0322 68411
TUNBRIDGE WELLS: **G. E. TUNBRIDGE LTD** 319 St. John's Rd. 0892 511522

LANCASHIRE
BLACKBURN: **BARKERS**
King St. 0254 52981

BLACKPOOL: **DIXON AUTOMARKETS**
Rigby Rd. 0253 751212/401226
BURNLEY: **D. C. COOK (BURNLEY) LTD**
Parker St. Kingsway. 0282 58271
COLNE: **EAGLE SERVICE STATION**
Stonebridge Works, Windybank.
0282 863254
LANCASTER: **G & L CAR SERVICE LTD**
Wheatfield St. 0524 39957
PRESTON: **LOOKERS GROSVENOR MOTORS LTD**
306-310 Ribbleton La. 0772 792823
WIGAN: **WILLIAM MARTYN (WIGAN) LTD** Great George St. 0942 826390

LEICESTERSHIRE
★EARL SHILTON: **SWITHLAND MOTORS LTD**
42 Wood St. 0455 44111
LEICESTER: **TRINITY MOTORS (D. R. WATTAM) LTD**
47 Blackbird Rd. 0533 530137
★MARKET HARBOROUGH: **BADGER BROTHERS**
109 Main St., Lubenham. 0858 66984
MELTON MOWBRAY: **ROCKINGHAM CARS LTD**
Manor Garage, Mill St. 0664 60141
WIGSTON: **KILBY BRIDGE MOTORS LTD**
Kilby Bridge. 0533 881109/886264

LINCOLNSHIRE
★BOSTON: **LONDON ROAD GARAGE**
200 London Rd. 0205 55500
GRANTHAM: **WILLSONS OF GRANTHAM LTD**
Spittlegate Level. 0476 74117
LINCOLN: **MINSTER CARS**
316-322 Wragby Rd. 0522 34805
LOUTH: **BURTONS OF LOUTH**
Legbourne Rd. 0507 607555
★RIPPINGALE: **WILLSONS OF RIPPINGALE**
Windmill Garage, Bourne. 077 835777
SKEGNESS: **DRM MOTORS**
Beresford Ave. 0754 67131
SLEAFORD: **RALPH DEAR**
Greyless Garage, Grantham Rd. 05298 674

LONDON
LONDON E4: **ALLEN BRIGGS (MOTORS) LTD**
47-59 Chingford Mount Rd. 01-527 5004/5
LONDON E14: **NORTH CITY AUTOS**
255-259 East India Dock Rd. 01-538 2121
LONDON N7: **CONTINENTAL MOTOR CENTRE LTD**
Campdale Rd. 01-272 4762
LONDON N12: **LINDSAY BROTHERS LTD**
920 High Rd. 01-455 1022
LONDON N17: **BRUCE MOTOR GROUP**
127 Lordship La. 01-808 9291
★LONDON NW10: **MARN SERVICE CENTRE**
854 Coronation Rd. 01-965 7001/2/3/4
LONDON NW11: **PAMSONS MOTORS**
761/3 Finchley Rd. 01-458 5968/8384
LONDON SE9: **CLIFFORDS OF ELTHAM**
Well Hall Rd. 01-850 3834
LONDON SE18: **WOOLWICH MOTOR CO**
160-170 Powis St. 01-854 2550
LONDON SE19: **SG SMITH MOTORS LTD**
Crown Point Service Station, Beulah Hill.
01-670 6266
LONDON SE23: **PREMIER MOTORS (FOREST HILL) LTD**
163/167 Stanstead Rd. 01-291 1721
LONDON SW12: **BALHAM AUTOS**
147 Balham Hill SW12 9DL. 01-675 6744/5/6/7
★LONDON SW15: **AF TANN LTD**
51-57 Upper Richmond Rd. 01-870 8844
★LONDON SW19: **SPUR GARAGE LTD**
39 Hartfield Rd. 01-540 3325
LONDON W1: **FIAT MOTOR SALES LTD**
61-64 Baker St. 01-486 7555
LONDON W11: **RADBOURNE RACING LTD** 1a Clarendon Rd. 01-727 5066
LONDON W12: **MARN WEST LONDON**
370-376 Uxbridge Rd. 01-749 6058/9
★LONDON W13:
DICKENS & JOSE MOTORS LTD
145 Northfield Ave. 01-567 0430

THE FIAT GUIDE TO SUCCESSFUL MOTORING

MERSEYSIDE
BIRKENHEAD: **FIRS GARAGE (WIRRAL) LTD**
Claughton Firs, Oxton. 051-653 8555
FORMBY: **ALTAR AUTOS LTD**
Altar Rd. 07048 73342
HESWALL: **HARDINGS (HESWALL) AUTOS LTD** May Rd. 051-342 8471
∗SOUTHPORT: **MILNER & MARSHAL LTD** 89-91 Bath St. North. 0704 35535
ST. HELENS: **FORWARD AUTOS**
Gaskell St. 0744 21961
LIVERPOOL: **STANLEY MOTORS (LIVERPOOL) LTD**
243 East Prescot Rd. 051-228 9151
LIVERPOOL: **CROSBY PARK GARAGE LTD**
2 Coronation Rd, Crosby. 051-924 9101
LIVERPOOL: **LAMBERT AUTOS LTD**
Custom House, Brunswick Business Park.
051-708 8224

MIDDLESEX
HAMPTON HILL: **SUPREME AUTOS (HAMPTON HILL) LTD**
7-11 Windmill Rd. 01-979 9061/2
NORWOOD GREEN: **FIRST COUNTY GARAGES LTD**
Norwood Rd. 01-571 2151
WEMBLEY: **FIAT MOTOR SALES LTD**
372 Ealing Rd. 01-998 8811
WEST DRAYTON: **PRIORS**
127 Station Rd. 0895 444672
WHITTON: **SPEEDWELL GARAGE (WHITTON) LTD**
53/55 High St. 01-894 6893/4
WRAYSBURY: **CONCORDE GARAGE (WRAYSBURY)**
31 Windsor Rd. 078481 2927/2815

NORFOLK
KING'S LYNN: **DENNIS MARSHALL LTD**
Scania Way. 0533 771331
NORWICH: **POINTER MOTOR CO LTD**
Aylsham Rd. 0603 45345/6
∗NORWICH: **WOODLAND CAR SALES LTD** Salhouse Rd. 0603 70111
SCOLE: **DESIRA MOTOR CO LTD**
Diss Rd. 037 9740741
SHERINGHAM: **EARLGATE MOTORS LTD**
41 Cromer Rd. 0263 822782
GREAT YARMOUTH: **DESIRA MOTOR CO LTD** North Quay. 0493 844266

NORTHAMPTONSHIRE
CORBY: **ROCKINGHAM CARS LTD**
Rockingham Rd. 0536 68991
KETTERING: **GRADY BROTHERS (KETTERING) LTD**
Britannia Rd. 0536 513257
KILSBY (nr. Rugby): **HALFWAY GARAGE (1986) LTD**
Crick Cross Rds. 0788 822226
NORTHAMPTON: **MOTORVOGUE LTD**
74 Kingsthorpe Rd. 0604 714555
RUSHDEN: **ROCKINGHAM CARS LTD**
John St. 0933 57500

NORTHUMBERLAND
HEXHAM: **MATT CLARK LTD**
Tyne Mills. 0434 603013/603236
STAKEFORD: **T. LIDDELL & SON**
Milburn Terrace. 0670 815038

NOTTINGHAMSHIRE
NEWARK-ON-TRENT: **ELLIOTS GARAGE (NEWARK)** Sleaford Rd. 0636 703405
∗NOTTINGHAM: **TECNICO**
81-85 Talbot St. 0602 473547
RUDDINGTON: **JCS GARAGES LTD**
Manor Park Garage, Wilford Rd.
0602 844114/844164
SUTTON-IN-ASHFIELD: **J.J. LEADLEY LTD**
Downing St. 0623 515222
∗WORKSOP: **BARRATT MOTORS LTD**
7-15 Newcastle Ave. 0909 475124

OXFORDSHIRE
BANBURY: **WHITE HORSE GARAGE (BANBURY) LTD**
21-27 Broad St. 0295 50733
CARTERTON: **BRIZE NORTON GARAGES LTD**
Carterton Rd. 0993 844144
HENLEY-ON-THAMES: **BELL STREET MOTORS (HENLEY) LTD**
66 Bell St. 0491 573077
OXFORD: **J.D. BARCLAY LTD**
Botley Rd. 0865 722444
WANTAGE: **MELLORS OF CHALLOW LTD**
Farringdon Rd. 023 572751

SHROPSHIRE
∗LUDLOW: **PRL MOTORS**
Lower Galdeford Garage. 0584 4104
∗SHREWSBURY: **WAVERLEY GARAGE LTD**
Featherbed La, Harlescott. 0743 236951
TELFORD: **T.J. VICKERS & SONS**
Trench Rd, Trench. 0952 605301

SOMERSET
BRIDGEWATER: **STACEY'S MOTORS**
48 St John St. 0278 423312
MINEHEAD: **MINEHEAD AUTOS LTD**
37-39 Alcombe Rd. 0643 3379/3238
STREET: **RIZZUTI BROTHERS**
West End Garage. 0458 42996
TAUNTON: **COUNTY GARAGE (TAUNTON) LTD**
Priory Ave. 0823 337611
YEOVIL: **ABBEY HILL MOTOR SALES**
Boundary Rd. Lufton Trading Est. 0935 29115

STAFFORDSHIRE
CHASETOWN: **SPOT OF CHASETOWN**
Highfields Rd. 054 36 5544
NEWCASTLE-UNDER-LYME: **B.S. MARSON & SONS**
Deansgate Garage, Keele Rd. 0782 622141
STAFFORD: **BOSTONS OF MILFORD**
16 The Green, Milford. 0785 661226
STOKE-ON-TRENT: **PLATT'S GARAGE (LONGTON) LTD**
Lightwood Rd, Longton. 0782 319212/3/4
∗UTTOXETER: **SMITHFIELD ROAD GARAGE LTD**
Smithfield Rd. 08893 3838

SUFFOLK
BECCLES: **BRAND (MOTOR) ENGINEERS LTD**
Ringsfield Rd. 0502 716940
∗BURY ST. EDMUNDS: **DESIRA MOTOR CO.LTD** Mildenhall Rd. 0284 750001
IPSWICH: **STATION GARAGE**
Burrell Rd. 0473 690321
∗LEISTON: **AVENUE SERVICE STATION**
King George's Avenue. 0728 830654
NEEDHAM MARKET: **TURNER'S (NEEDHAM MARKET) LTD**
30 High St. 0449 721212

SURREY
CAMBERLEY: **MARN CAMBERLEY**
71 Frimley Rd. 0276 64672
CHEAM: **GODFREY'S (SUTTON & CHEAM) LTD**
50 Malden Rd. 01-644 8877
CROYDON: **THAMES**
115 Addiscombe Rd. 01-655 1100
ENGLEFIELD GREEN: **SAVAGE & SONS (MOTOR ENGINEERS) LTD**
Victoria St. 0784 39771
EPSOM: **H.F. EDWARDS & CO LTD**
4 Church St. 03727 44444
∗FARNHAM: **FRENSHAM ENGINEERING CO**
Shortfield, Frensham. 025125 3232
GUILDFORD: **ABC GUILDFORD**
Pilot Works, Walnut Tree Close. 04835 75251
KENLEY: **MARN KENLEY**
60 Godstone Rd. 01-660 4546

NEW MALDEN: **LAIDLER MOTOR CO LTD**
69 Kingstone Rd. 01-942 6075
REIGATE: **COLIN CRONK**
87/89 Bell St. 0737 223304
WALLINGTON: **BALHAM AUTOS (WALLINGTON)**
268 London Rd. 01-647 5527/8

EAST & WEST SUSSEX
BRIGHTON: **TILLEYS (SUSSEX) LTD**
100 Lewes Rd. 0273 603244
BURGESS HILL: **TILLEYS (SUSSEX) LTD**
Chandlers Garage, London Rd. 04446 43431
∗CHICHESTER: **TANGMERE GARAGE**
Tangmere-by-pass. 0243 782478
∗EAST GRINSTEAD: **FELBRIDGE GARAGE** Eastbourne Rd. 0342 24677
HORSHAM: **WILSON PURVES LTD**
Brighton Rd. 0403 61821/65637
HAILSHAM: **G.F. SHAW LTD**
Cowbeech. 0323 833321
∗ISFIELD: **ROSEHILL GARAGE**
Isfield, Nr Uckfield. 082575 313/445
PULBOROUGH: **FLEET GARAGE (FITTLEWORTH) LTD**
Fittleworth. 079 882 307/244
SHOREHAM-BY-SEA: **KEEN & BETTS (SHOREHAM) LTD**
Adur Garage, Brighton Rd. 0273 461333
ST LEONARDS-ON-SEA: **ST LEONARDS MOTORS LTD**
Church Wood Drive. 0424 53493
WADHURST: **EATON BROS.**
Forge Garage, Beech Hill. 089288 2126
WORTHING: **PDH (GARAGES) LTD**
Downlands Service Station,
Upper Brighton Rd. 0903 37487

TYNE & WEAR
GATESHEAD: **BENFIELD MOTORS LTD**
Lobley Hill Rd. 091-490 0292
NEWCASTLE-UPON-TYNE: **BENFIELD MOTORS LTD**
Railway St. 091-273 2131
SUNDERLAND: **REG VARDY LTD**
16-18 Villiers St. 091-510 0550
WHITLEY BAY: **WHITLEY LODGE MOTOR CO** Claremont Rd. 091-252 3347

WARWICKSHIRE
BALSALL COMMON: **CARSTINS LTD**
324 Station Rd. 0676 33145
NUNEATON: **RESEARCH GARAGE (NUNEATON) LTD**
Hunchwood Rd. 0203 382807
STRATFORD-UPON-AVON: **GM WYATT GARAGES (STRATFORD) LTD**
Western Rd. 0789 67159
WARWICK: **GRAYS GARAGE LTD**
Wharf St. 0926 496231

WEST MIDLANDS
∗BIRMINGHAM: **COLMORE DEPOT LTD**
35 Sutton New Rd, Erdington. 021-377 6533
BIRMINGHAM: **COLMORE DEPOT LTD**
979 Stratford Rd, Hall Green. 021-778 2323
∗CLENT: **HOLY CROSS GARAGE LTD**
Bromsgrove Rd. 0562 730557
COVENTRY: **SMITH & SONS MOTORS LTD** Roland Ave, Holbrooks. 0203 667778
HARBOURNE: **HARBOURNE AUTOMOBILES**
50-52 High St. 021-427 3235
MARSTON GREEN: **MARSTON GREEN GARAGE**
32 Station Rd. 021-779 5140
SOLIHULL: **TAMWORTH GARAGE LTD**
The Green, Tamworth in Arden. 056 442218
TIPTON: **CALDENE AUTOLAND**
Burnt Treet. 021-520 2411
WALSALL: **SPOT OF WALSALL**
44a Ward St. 0922 32911
∗WEST BROMWICH: **COLMORE DEPOT LTD** Birmingham Rd. 021-525 9408
WOLVERHAMPTON: **A N BLOXHAM LTD**
The Fiat Centre, Raby St. 0902 57116

WILTSHIRE
★CHIPPENHAM: **WADHAM STRINGER –
CHIPPENHAM**
21 New Rd. 0249 655757
SWINDON: **TARGET GARAGE LTD**
Elgin Drive. 0793 512685

YORKSHIRE
★BARNSLEY: **S.A. SNELL
(BARNSLEY) LTD**
436-440 Doncaster Rd. Stairfoot. 0226 731234
BRADFORD: **WEST YORKSHIRE MOTOR
GROUP** Keighley Rd. Frizinghall. 0274 490031
BRADFORD: **JCT 600**
The Italian Car Centre, Sticker La.
0274 667234
CASTLEFORD: **AIRE AUTOS LTD**
Lock La. 0977 515806
★DONCASTER: **R ROODHOUSE LTD**
York Rd. 0302 390444
★HALIFAX: **MAYFIELD GARAGE
(HALIFAX) LTD**
Queens Rd. 0422 330800
HARROGATE: **CROFT & BLACKBURN
LTD** Leeds Rd, Pannal. 0423 879236
HUDDERSFIELD: **WEST YORKSHIRE
MOTOR GROUP**
Lockwood Rd. 0484 537500
KEIGHLEY: **WEST YORKSHIRE
MOTOR GROUP**
Hardings Rd. 0535 603073/681121
LEEDS: **JCT 600 (LEEDS) LTD**
Spence La. 0532 431843
LEEDS: **WHITEHEAD & HINCH LTD**
South Broadgate La, Horsforth.
0532 585056
★MALTON: **BENTLEYS GARAGE**
Amotherby. 0653 3616
MIRFIELD: **THORNTON MOTORS
OF DEWSBURY LTD** Calder Garage,
117 Huddersfield Rd. 0924 498316
★NORTHALLERTON: **TIM SWALES
(CAR SALES) LTD**
Clock Lane Garage, Osmotherley.
060 983 263/666
ROTHERHAM: **DEREK G. PIKE & CO**
126 Fitzwilliam Rd. 0709 361666
RIPON: **RICHARD CHESTER LTD**
Dallamires La. 0765 4803
SCARBOROUGH: **MISKIN &
KNAGGS LTD** Manor Rd. 0723 364111/3
★SELBY: **PARKINSON'S GARAGE LTD**
Hambleton 0757 828181
SHEFFIELD: **GT CARS**
Suffolk Rd. 0742 721370/721378/722748
WAKEFIELD: **PICCADILLY WAKEFIELD
LTD** Bradford Rd. 0924 290220
YORK: **PICCADILLY AUTO CENTRE**
84 Piccadilly. 0904 34321

SCOTLAND
ABERDEEN: **CALLANDERS GARAGE
(AUTOPART) LTD**
870 Great Northern Rd. 0224 695573
AYR: **ROBERT McCALL LTD**
Galloway Ave. 0292 260416
BATHGATE: **J & A BROWNING LTD**
11 East Main St. 0501 40536
BRECHIN: **KAY'S AUTO CENTRE**
18 Clerk St. 03562 2561
★COATBRIDGE: **R J CROSS LTD**
206 Bank St. 0236 35774
DOLLAR: **STEWART BROTHERS**
28-34 Bridge St. 025 942233/4
★DUMBARTON: **DUNCAN McFARLANE
& SON** 96 Church St. 0389 63689
DUMFRIES: **CENTRAL CAR SALES**
77 Whitesands. 0387 61378
DUNDEE: **MACALPINE MOTORS**
Macalpine Rd. 0382 818004
DUNFERMLINE: **FLEAR & THOMSON LTD**
128-138 Pittencrieff St. 0383 722565/6
EDINBURGH: **CROALL & CROALL**
Glenogle Rd. 031 556 6404/9
EDINBURGH: **HAMILTON BROTHERS
(EDINBURGH) LTD**
162 St Johns Rd. 031 334 6248
FALKIRK: **ARNOLD CLARK
AUTOMOBILES LTD**
Falkirk Rd, Grangemouth. 0324 474766

★FORRES: **DICKSON MOTORS
(FORRES) LTD** Tytler St. 0309 72122/3
GLASGOW: **RITCHIES**
393 Shields Rd. 041 429 5611
GLASGOW: **PEAT ROAD MOTORS
(JORDAN HILL) LTD**
120 Whittingehame Drive,
Jordanhill. 041 357 1939
GOUROCK: **MANOR VEHICLE (TURIN)
LTD** 92 Manor Crescent. 0475 32356
HAWICK: **BORDER MOTOR CO**
12 Havelock St. 0450 73881
INVERNESS: **DONALD MACKENZIE LTD**
62 Seafield Rd. 0463 235777/8,
IRVINE: **HARRY FAIRBURN LTD**
Ayr Rd. 0294 72121
KILMARNOCK: **GEORGE BICKETT
& CO LTD**
67-79 Campbell St. Riccarton. 0563 22525/6
★LANARK: **J & J FERGUSON**
Wellgatehead. 0555 3106
LEVEN: **LINKS GARAGE (LEVEN)**
Scoonie Rd. 0333 27003
OBAN: **HAZELBANK MOTORS LTD**
Stevenson St. 0631 66476
PAISLEY: **HAMILTON BROS LTD**
Ralson Garage, 255 Glasgow Rd.
041 8829901
★PAISLEY: **LOCHFIELD GARAGE**
4-8 Lochfield Rd. 041 884 2281
PERTH: **MACALPINE OF PERTH**
St Leonards Bank. 0738 38511
PETERHEAD: **CLYNE AUTOS**
Seaview, St Fergus. 077 983 258
★PITSCOTTIE BY CUPER: **D.H.
PATTERSON MOTOR ENGINEERS**
Burnbank Garage. 033482 200
★RUTHERGLEN: **McKECHNIE
OF RUTHERGLEN**
77 Farmeloan Rd. 041 647 9722/5915
ST BOSWELLS: **ST BOSWELLS
GARAGE**
St Boswells. 08352 2259/3475
STIRLING: **HAMILTON BROTHERS LTD**
44 Causeway Head Rd. 0786 62426
TRANENT: **WILLIAM B COWAN LTD**
The Garage Elphinstone. 0875 610492

ORKNEY ISLES
KIRKWALL: **J & M SUTHERLAND**
Junction Rd. 0856 2158

SHETLAND ISLES
AITH: **AITH AUTOS LTD**
Aith By Bixter. 059 581 230
LERWICK: **AITH AUTOS LTD**
9 Blackhill Industrial Estate.
0595 3385/4450

WALES
ABERDARE: **WILSONS CAR SALES
(ABERDARE) LTD**
Canal Rd. Cwmbach. 0865 875577/883717
ABERGELE: **SLATERS EUROCARS LTD**
Marine Rd, Pensarn. 0745 822021/823387
ABERGAVENNY: **CLYTHIA MOTOR CO**
Merthyr Rd, Llanfoist. 0873 6888
ABERYSTWYTH: **EVANS BROS**
Royal Oak Garage, Llanfarian.
0970 61 2311/2
★BLACKWOOD: **A.J. STEVENS & SONS**
High Bank Garage, Fairview. 0443 831703
★BRIDGEND: **TS GRIMSHAW
(BRIDGEND) LTD**
Tremains Rd. 0656 652984
BUILTH WELLS: **PRYNNE'S SERVICE
STATION LTD** Garth. 059 12287
CARDIFF: **T.S. GRIMSHAW LTD**
Fiat House, 329 Cowbridge Road East.
0222 395322
CARDIGAN: **B.V. REES**
Abbey Garage, St Dogmaels. 0239 612025
CARMARTHEN: **WILLIAM DAVIES
& SONS**
Central Garage, St Catherine St.
0267 236284
CHEPSTOW: **TUTSHILL SERVICE
STATION**
Gloucester Rd. 02912 3304/70062

CWMBRAN: **C.K. MOTOR CO
(SOUTH WALES) LTD**
10/11 Court Road Industrial Estate.
06333 72711
KILGETTY: **STEPASIDE GARAGE LTD**
Camarthen Rd. 0834 813786
LLANISHEN CARDIFF: **YAPP'S
GARAGES LTD**
Fidlas Rd. 0222 751323
NEWPORT: **L.C. MOTORS**
121 Corporation Rd. 0633 212548/598892
PWLLHELI: **PULROSE MOTOR
SERVICES LTD**
Ala Rd. 0758 612827
SWANSEA: **MOORCROFT MOTORS LTD**
54 Sway Rd. Morriston. 0792 75271
★TONYREFAIL: **VALLEY MILL MOTORS**
Gilfach Rd. 0443 670742
WREXHAM: **N & G DICKENS LTD**
Border Service Station, Gresford.
097 883 6262

NORTHERN IRELAND
ARMAGH: **ARMAGH GARAGES LTD**
Portadown Rd. 0861 524252
BALLYMENA: **YOUNGS
(BROUGHSHANE) LTD**
11 Raceview Rd. Broughshane.
0266 861380/861497
BALLYMONEY: **MODEL CAR MART**
Model Rd. 026 56 63275
BANBRIDGE: **ANNAGH MOTORS
(BANBRIDGE) LTD**
51 Church St. 08206 24495
BANGOR: **JAMES THOMPSON**
135-141 Bryansburn Rd. 0247 463911
BELFAST: **BAIRD CARS**
7-9 Boucher Rd. 0232 247770
BELFAST: **B.A.S. (MOTORS) LTD**
45-47 Rosetta Rd. 0232 491049/491676
BELFAST: **DICK & CO (BELFAST) LTD**
43 Mallusk Rd, Newtownabbey.
0232 342511
BELFAST: **W.J. BELL & SON**
40-50 Townsend St. 0232 241394
★DOWNPATRICK: **DSC CARS**
10/12 Church Street, Downpatrick.
0396 612858/614322
DUNGANNON: **FRANCIS NEILL
MOTORS (DUNGANNON) LTD**
1 Ranfurley Rd. 086 87 22552
ENNISKILLEN: **T & T TOWN &
COUNTRY CARS LTD**
Sligo Rd. 0365 22440
LISBURN: **DORNAN'S SERVICE
STATION (LISBURN) LTD**
22 Market Pl. 08462 77412
★NEWRY: **N.W. KEHOE & SONS**
18 Patrick St. 0693 66500/63193
OMAGH: **GLENPARK MOTORS**
62 Gortin Rd. Co Tyrone. 0662 46521
PORTADOWN: **ANNAGH
MOTORS WORKS**
Mahon Industrial Estate, Mahon Rd.
0762 332552

CHANNEL ISLANDS
GUERNSEY: **GT CARS**
Les Banques Garages, St Sampsons. 0481
47838
JERSEY: **BEL ROYAL MOTOR WORKS
LTD** Bel Royal, St. Lawrence. 0534 22556

EUROPE'S DRIVING FORCE

LUNCHEON · VOUCHERS WELCOMED

LONDON

Aspava, **W1**
Balls Brothers, **EC2**
*Bentley's Wine Bar & Oyster
Bar,* **W1**
Bill Stickers, **W1**
Blake's Wine & Food Bar,
WC2
British Museum Restaurant,
WC1
Cherry Orchard, **E2**
Country Life, **W1**
Cranks, **W1, WC2** (Adelaide
St & Great Newport St)
*Cranks Health Food
Restaurant,* **W1**
Criterion Brasserie, **W1**
Daquise, **SW7**
Diwana Bhelpoori House,
NW1, W2
East West Restaurant, **EC1**
Ed's Easy Diner, **W1**
Efes Kebab House, **W1**
Fallen Angel, **N1**
Faulkners, **E8**
Fenwicks, Salad Express,
W1
Fino's Wine Cellar, **W1**
(North Row & Swallow St)
First Out, **WC2**
Food for Thought, **WC2**
Geale's, **W8**
Gino's, **W5**
Govindas, **W1**
Granary, **W1**
Gurkhas Tandoori, **W1**
*Indian Veg. Bhel Poori
House,* **N1**
Justin de Blank, **W1**
*Justin de Blank at General
Trading Company,* **SW1**
Lok Ho Fook, **W1**
Macarthurs, **SW13**
*Maison Bouquillon, Le
Montmartre,* **W2**
*Maison Pechon Pâtisserie
Française,* **W2**
Mandeer, **W1**
Marine Ices, **NW3**

Maxie's, **W7, SW1**
Millward's, **N16**
Muffin Man, **W8**
National Gallery Restaurant,
WC2
*Neal's Yard Bakery & Tea
Room,* **WC2**
New Shu Shan, **WC2**
Nosherie, **EC1**
Pâtisserie Valerie, **W1**
Pavilion Wine Bar, **EC2**
Raj Bhelpoori House, **NW1**
Ravi Shankar, **NW1**
Raw Deal, **W1**
Redfords, **NW11**
Slenders, **EC4**
Soho Brasserie, **W1**
Spices, **N16**
Le Tire Bouchon, **W1**
Tuxedo Junction, **NW6**
Verbanella Pasta Bar, **W1**
*Victoria & Albert Museum,
New Restaurant,* **SW7**
*Village Delicatessen &
Coffee Shop,* **W14**
Volker Europa Wine Bar,
WC2
Wilkins Natural Foods, **SW1**

ENGLAND

Aylesbury, Bucks: *Seatons*
Bath, Avon: *Canary*
Bexhill, E Sussex: *Trawlers*
Billericay, Essex: *Webber's
Wine Bar*
Birmingham, W Mid:
Forbidden City
Birmingham, W Mid: *La
Galleria*
Bournemouth, Dorset:
Henry's
Bournemouth, Dorset: *Salad
Centre*
Bradford, W Yorks: *Pizza
Margherita*
Bridgwater, Somerset:
Nutmeg

Brighton, E Sussex: *Food for Friends*
Bristol, Avon: *Rainbow Café*
Bristol, Avon: *Wild Oats II*
Bromley, Kent: *Hollywood Bowl*
Burnley, Lancs: *Butterfingers*
Cambridge, Cambs: *Kings Pantry*
Cambridge, Cambs: *Nettles*
Canterbury, Kent: *Crotchets*
Canterbury, Kent: *Pizza Place*
Canterbury, Kent: *Il Vaticano Pasta Parlour*
Carlisle, Cumbria: *Hudson's Coffee Shop*
Chatham, Kent: *Food for Living Eats*
Chatham, Kent: *Simson's*
Cheam, Surrey: *Superfish*
Cheltenham, Glos: *Langtry Pâtisserie & Tea Rooms*
Cheltenham, Glos: *Promenade Pâtisserie*
Cheltenham, Glos: *The Retreat*
Chichester, W Sussex: *Clinchs Salad House*

Chislehurst, Kent: *Mrs Bridges' Kitchen*
Christchurch, Dorset: *Salads*
Corse Lawn, Glos: *Corse Lawn House*
Croydon, Surrey: *Hockneys*
Dartington, Devon: *Cranks Health Food Restaurant*
Derby, Derbys: *Lettuce Leaf*
Dorchester, Dorset: *Potter In*
East Molesey, Surrey: *Superfish*
Eastbourne, E Sussex: *Qualisea*
Eastleigh, Hants: *Piccolo Mondo*
Ewell, Surrey: *Superfish*
Grays, Essex: *R. Mumford & Son*
Great Torrington, Devon: *Rebecca's*
Great Yarmouth, Norfolk: *Friends Bistro*
Harrogate, N Yorks: *Bettys*
Henley-on-Thames, Oxon: *Barnaby's Brasserie*
Hereford, Hereford & Worcester: *Marches*
Ilkley, W Yorks: *Bettys*
Ipswich, Suffolk: *Marno's*

Continued on page 90

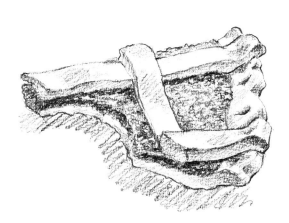

89

Kendal, Cumbria: *Corner Spot Eating House*
Kendal, Cumbria: *Nutters*
Kew, Surrey: *Wine & Mousaka*
Kidderminster, Hereford & Worcester: *Natural Break*
Kingston, Surrey: *La La Pizza*
Leamington Spa, Warwicks: *Regency Fare*
Leeds, W Yorks: *Strawberryfields Bistro*
Liverpool, Merseyside: *Everyman Bistro*
Lytham, Lancs: *Lytham Kitchen*
Manchester, Gtr Mans: *Woo Sang*
Manchester, Gtr Mans: *Yang Sing*
Market Harborough, Leics: *Taylors Fish Restaurant*
Marlow, Bucks: *Burgers*
Midsomer Norton, Avon: *Mrs Pickwick*
Morden, Surrey: *Superfish*
Newcastle upon Tyne, Tyne & Wear: *Mather's*
Newmarket, Suffolk: *Jane's Wine Bar*
Newport, I of W: *Full of Beans*
Northallerton, N Yorks: *Bettys*
Norwich, Norfolk: *Swelter's*
Norwich, Norfolk: *Waffle House*
Nottingham, Notts: *Pagoda*
Oxford, Oxon: *St Aldate's Church Coffee House*
Parkgate, Ches: *Chompers*
Poole, Dorset: *Inn à Nutshell*
Portsmouth (Southsea), Hants: *Country Kitchen*
Richmond, Surrey: *Richmond Harvest*
Salisbury, Wilts: *Mainly Salads*
Sheffield, S Yorks: *Toff's Restaurant & Coffee House*
Shoreham-by-Sea, W Sussex: *Cuckoo Clock*
Shrewsbury, Shrops: *Delanys Vegetarian Restaurant*

Shrewsbury, Shrops: *The Good Life*
Southampton, Hants: *La Margherita*
Stevenage, Herts: *De Friese Coffee Shop*
Stratford-upon-Avon, Warwicks: *Café Natural*
Stratford-upon-Avon, Warwicks: *Slug & Lettuce*
Stroud, Glos: *Mother Nature*
Swindon, Wilts: *Acorn Wholefoods*
Tolworth, Surrey: *Superfish*
Tunbridge Wells, Kent: *Delicious*
Ware, Herts: *Sunflowers*
Warwick, Warwicks: *Bar Roussel*
West Byfleet, Surrey: *Janes Upstairs*
Worcester, Hereford & Worcester: *Natural Break*
Worthing, W Sussex: *Nature's Way Coffee Shop*
Yeovil, Somerset: *Trugs*
York, N Yorks: *Bettys*
York, N Yorks: *Wholefood Trading Company*

SCOTLAND

Edinburgh, Loth: *Le Café Noir*
Edinburgh, Loth: *Hendersons Salad Table*
Edinburgh, Loth: *Sunflower Country Kitchen*
Falkirk, Central: *The Coffee Cabin*
Glasgow, S'clyde: *Smith's*
Glasgow, S'clyde: *Upstairs Café*

ISLE OF MAN

Douglas, Isle of Man: *L'Expérience*

Ogden Nash
1902–71

By undraped nymphs
I am not wooed;
I'd rather painters painted food . . .
'The Clean Platter' in *The Face is Familiar* (1954)

C. Herman Senn

Oh, I am a festive chafing dish,
I foam, and froth, and bubble,
I sing the song of meat and fish,
And save a deal of trouble.
Chafing Dish and Casserole Cookery (1908)

Jonathan Swift
1667–1745

Promises and pie-crust are made to be broken.
Polite Conversation

'Saki' (H. H. Munro)
1870–1916

I believe that I once considerably scandalised her
by declaring that clear soup was a more important
factor in life than a clear conscience.
The Blind Spot

JUST DESSERTS

Even when the meal is an informal one it is not complete without some
sort of sweet treat to round it off. When it comes to the sweet course
simplicity is the key to success; alternatively, if you are going to be
more adventurous with your cooking, then go for a dessert that can be
prepared in advance so that you can relax during the meal.

To offer inspiration, here is a selection of recipes contributed by chefs
from some of our starred entries. There are three special desserts that
you can prepare in advance, and a mouth-watering chocolate pudding
that is so simple to make. They are all temptingly sweet and
flavoursome, made with one of the most natural foods available to us –
sugar. In its many forms sugar provides us with a valuable source of
energy and, like any other foods, if it is not eaten to excess it can play an
excellent role in a healthy diet plan.

So follow our professional examples and treat everyone to a perfect
pudding!

KULFI
Kalpna, Edinburgh
Ajay Bhartdwaj

Serves 8-10

600 ml/1 pint milk
300 ml/½ pint whipping cream
300 ml/½ pint double cream
395 g/10 oz can sweetened
condensed milk

395 g/14 oz can evaporated milk
30 ml/2 tbsp sugar
5 ml/1 tsp ground cardamom
seeds
30 ml/2 tbsp chopped pistachio
nuts

Whisk all the ingredients, except the pistachio nuts, together
until thoroughly combined. If you like, do this in a large
liquidiser. Stir in the pistachio nuts. Pour the kulfi into a freezer
container and freeze until firm. To achieve the authentic shape
for the ice cream, the mixture should be frozen in paper cones. If
you do try this, prepare cones of greaseproof paper, making them
several layers thick. Lightly grease the insides of the cones with a
little oil to prevent the kulfi sticking. Support the cones in paper
cups while they are freezing. Allow the kulfi to stand at room
temperature for 5 minutes before serving.

APPLE JALOUSIE

Jersey Pottery, Gorey, Jersey
Franco Frezza

Serves 6-8

Pastry base
175 g/6 oz plain flour
pinch of salt
75 g/3 oz butter
50 g/2 oz sugar
1 egg yolk
few drops of vanilla essence

Filling
100 g/4 oz lemon curd
2-3 cooking apples,
  peeled, cored and sliced
50 g/2 oz sugar

25 g/1 oz raisins
50 g/2 oz blanched almonds,
  slivered

Topping
225 g/8 oz puff pastry,
  defrosted if frozen
45 ml/3 tbsp apricot jam,
  warmed and sieved
15 ml/1 tbsp boiling water
100 g/4 oz icing sugar
45 ml/3 tbsp warm water
50 g/2 oz flaked almonds, toasted
beaten egg to glaze

Place the flour and salt for the pastry base in a bowl. Rub in the butter, then mix in the sugar and bind the ingredients into a short dough with the egg yolk, adding a few drops of vanilla essence. Press together, wrap in cling film or foil and chill briefly, then roll out into an oblong measuring about 30.5 × 15 cm/ 12 × 6 in. Place the pastry on a baking tray, trim the edges and prick all over with a fork. Chill for 30 minutes, then bake at 190°C/375°F/Gas 5 for 10 minutes. Remove from the oven and increase the temperature to 220°C/425°F/Gas 7.

Spread the pastry base with the lemon curd, leaving a border of 1 cm/½ in all round the edge. Top the curd with the apples, sugar, raisins and slivered almonds.

Roll out the puff pastry large enough to cover the filling completely. Trim the edges, then fold the puff pastry loosely in half. Make slits in from the folded side to within 2.5 cm/1 in of the opposite edge, leaving a 5 cm/2 in border uncut at both ends. Dampen the edges of the pastry base, then lift the folded puff over one side of the filling. Unfold the pastry to cover the filling completely showing the pastry slats down the middle of the jalousie. Press the edges together well, trim off any excess puff pastry and brush with beaten egg. Bake for 20–25 minutes, until puffed and golden.

Mix the apricot jam and boiling water and spread over the cooked jalousie. Leave to cool. Mix the icing sugar and warm water to make a thin glâcé icing, then spread this thinly over the cold jalousie and top with the toasted flaked almonds. Cut into slices to serve.

HAZELNUT ROULADE

Sheila's Cottage, Ambleside
Stewart and Janice Greaves

Serves 6

175 g/6 oz shelled hazelnuts
4 eggs, separated
45 g/1½ oz brown soft sugar
2.5 ml/½ tsp ground mixed spice
300 ml/½ pint double cream
100 g/4 oz raspberries

Decoration
shelled hazelnuts
raspberries

Coarsely grind the nuts in a food processor or liquidiser. Line a
23 × 21.5 cm/12 × 8½ in Swiss roll tin with non-stick cooking
parchment and grease well. Preheat the oven to 200°C/400°F/
Gas 6. Whisk the egg yolks and sugar together until thick and
creamy. In a separate bowl, using a clean whisk, whisk the egg
whites until stiff. Using a large metal spoon, fold the egg yolk
mixture, ground nuts and spice into the whites. Pour the mixture
into the prepared tin and bake for 10–12 minutes, until evenly
browned on top. Have ready a clean tea towel topped with a piece
of greaseproof paper and sprinkle a little sugar over the
greaseproof paper. Turn the cooked roulade out on to the paper.
Carefully remove the lining paper. Leave until just cool. Whip the
cream and spread two-thirds over the cooled roulade. Top with
the raspberries and roll up. Decorate with the remaining cream,
piped into swirls down the length of the roulade, a few whole
hazelnuts and extra raspberries. Serve with a simple sauce of
raspberries, lightly poached with a sprinkling of sugar and
pûréed, then sieved to remove the seeds.

CHOCOLATE PUDDING
Byrons, Eastbourne
Simon and Marion Scrutton

Serves 6

100 g/4 oz unsalted butter
100 g/4 oz caster sugar
2 eggs (size 2), beaten
25 g/1 oz ground almonds
100 g/4 oz self-raising flour
50 g/2 oz cocoa
45 ml/3 tbsp sweet sherry

Chocolate sauce
225 g/8 oz plain dessert chocolate
50 g/2 oz butter
60 ml/4 tbsp golden syrup

Cream the butter and sugar together until smooth and light. Mix in the ground almonds. Sift the flour and cocoa together and mix into the pudding. Lastly mix in the eggs and sherry, and stir gently until the mixture is smooth. Turn into a buttered 1.1 litre/2 pint pudding basin or six individual moulds. Smooth the top with the back of a metal spoon and cover with buttered foil. Tie the foil down securely and steam the large pudding for 2 hours, or the small ones for 1½ hours. To make the chocolate sauce, break the chocolate into a basin and add the other ingredients. Place over a saucepan of hot water and stir occasionally until melted and combined. Do not allow the water to boil. Turn out the pudding and serve with chocolate sauce. To 'feather' the sauce, make some with half of the cream and reserve half, then add the rest of the cream for a lighter colour. Add drops of the darker sauce and 'draw out' with a skewer. Decorate the pudding with flaked almonds, orange zest and icing sugar.

ESTABLISHMENTS
BY COUNTIES

ENGLAND

AVON

Bath: *Bath Puppet Theatre, Canary, Moon & Sixpence, Number Five, Rossiter's, Tarts Restaurant, Theatre Vaults, The Walrus & the Carpenter*
Bristol: *Arnolfini Café Bar, Cherries, Guild Café-Restaurant, Rainbow Café, Wild Oats II*
Clevedon: *Murrays*
Midsomer Norton: *Mrs Pickwick*

BEDFORDSHIRE

Mentmore: *Stable Yard Craft Gallery & Tea Room*
Milton Ernest: *Strawberry Tree*

BERKSHIRE

Eton: *Eton Wine Bar*
Hungerford: *Bear, Kennet Room, Behind the Green Door*
Reading: *Mama Mia*
Windsor: *Angelo's Wine Bar, Dôme*
Wokingham: *Setters Bistro*

BUCKINGHAMSHIRE

Aylesbury: *Seatons*
Marlow: *Burgers*

CAMBRIDGESHIRE

Cambridge: *Kings Pantry, Nettles, Upstairs*
Ely: *Old Fire Engine House*
Huntingdon: *Old Bridge Hotel Lounge*

Wansford-in-England: *Haycock Hotel Lounge*

CHESHIRE

Bridgemere: *Bridgemere Garden World Coffee Shop*
Chester: *Chester Grosvenor Library*
Congleton: *Odd Fellows Wine Bar & Bistro*
Middlewich: *Tempters*
Parkgate: *Chompers*

CLEVELAND

Yarm: *Coffee Shop*

CORNWALL

Falmouth: *Pandora Inn, Secrets*
Launceston: *The Greenhouse*
Mawgan: *Yard Bistro*
Mousehole: *Annie's*
Polperro: *Captain's Cabin*
St Mary's: *Tregarthens Hotel*
St Michael's Mount: *Sail Loft*
Trebarwith Strand: *House on the Strand, Old Millfloor*
Tresco: *Island Hotel Restaurant*

CUMBRIA

Alston: *Brownside Coach House*
Ambleside: *Rothay Manor, Sheila's Cottage, Zeffirellis*
Boot: *Brook House Restaurant*
Bowness-on-Windermere: *Hedgerow*
Brampton: *Tarn End*
Caldbeck: *Priests Mill*
Carlisle: *Hudson's Coffee Shop*

Cartmel: *Prior's Refectory Coffee Shop, St Mary's Lodge*
Clifton Dykes: *Wetheriggs*
Cockermouth: *Quince & Medlar*
Coniston: *Jumping Jenny at Brantwood*
Dent: *Dent Crafts Centre*
Dodd Wood: *Old Sawmill*
Embleton: *Wythop Mill*
Grange-in-Borrowdale: *Grange Bridge Cottage*
Grange-over-Sands: *At Home*
Grasmere: *Baldry's*
Hawkshead: *Minstrels Gallery*
High Lorton: *White Ash Barn*
Kendal: *Corner Spot Eating House, Moon, Nutters, Waterside Wholefoods*
Keswick: *Bryson's Tea Room*
Melmerby: *Village Bakery*
Skelwith Bridge: *Chesters*
Ullswater: *Rampsbeck Hotel, Sharrow Bay Country House Hotel Lounge*
Ulverston: *Renaissance Bistro*
Windermere: *Miller Howe Hotel, Miller Howe Kaff, Victoria Cottage*

DERBYSHIRE

Alstonefield: *Old Post Office Tea Rooms*
Ashbourne: *Ashbourne Gingerbread Shop*
Ashford-in-the-Water: *Cottage Tea Room*
Bakewell: *Aitch's Wine Bar & Bistro, Green Apple*
Baslow: *Cavendish Hotel*
Calver Bridge: *Derbyshire Craft Centre Eating House*
Castleton: *Rose Cottage Café*
Derby: *Cutlers Bistro, Lettuce Leaf*
Hope: *Hopechest*
Matlock: *Strand Restaurant, Tall Trees*
Tideswell: *Poppies*
Tissington: *Old School Tea Rooms*
Wirksworth: *Crown Yard Bistro*

DEVON

Ashburton: *Studio Tea Shop*
Barnstaple: *Lynwood House*
Brendon: *Rockford Cottage Tea Room*
Clawton: *Court Barn Country House Hotel*
Dartington: *Cranks Health Food Restaurant*
Dartmouth: *Spinning Wheel Café*
East Budleigh: *Grasshoppers*
Great Torrington: *Rebecca's, Top of the Town*
Honiton: *Dominoes*
Lustleigh: *Primrose Cottage*
Lympstone: *River House*
Lynton: *Lee Cottage*
Sidbury: *Old Bakery*
South Molton: *Corn Dolly, Stumbles Wine Bar*
Tiverton: *Angel Foods*
Torquay: *The Mulberry Room*
Totnes: *Above Town Wholefood Eating House, Willow*

DORSET

Beaminster: *Tea Shoppe*
Bournemouth: *Carlton Hotel Lounge, Henry's, Salad Centre, Superfish*
Bridport: *Morgan's*
Cerne Abbas: *Singing Kettle*
Christchurch: *Salads*
Dorchester: *Potter In*
Lytchett Minster: *Slepe Cottage Tea Rooms*
Poole: *Inn à Nutshell*
Sherborne: *Church House Gallery*
Spetisbury: *Marigold Cottage*
Wareham: *Priory Hotel*
Wimborne Minster: *Quinneys*
Wool: *Rose Mullion Tea Room*

CO. DURHAM

Barnard Castle: *Market Place Teashop, Priors Restaurant*

ESSEX

Billericay: *Webber's Wine Bar*
Castle Hedingham: *Colne Valley Railway Restaurant*
Colchester: *Bistro Nine, Poppy's Tea Room*
Grays: *R. Mumford & Son*
Harwich: *Ha'Penny Pier*
Walton-on-the-Naze: *Naze Links Café*

GLOUCESTERSHIRE

Birdlip: *Kingshead House*
Bourton-on-the-Water: *Small Talk Tea Room*
Cheltenham: *Choirs Tea Rooms, Langtry's Pâtisserie & Tea Rooms, Promenade Pâtisserie, Retreat*
Chipping Campden: *Greenstocks, Kings Arms Hotel, Saddle Room*
Cirencester: *Brewery Coffee House, No. 1, Shepherds Wine Bar*
Corse Lawn: *Corse Lawn House*
Painswick: *Cup House, Painswick Hotel*
Stroud: *Mother Nature, Old Lady Tea Shop*
Upper Slaughter: *Lords of the Manor Hotel*

GREATER MANCHESTER

Altrincham: *Nutcracker Vegetarian Restaurant*
Manchester: *Brasserie St Pièrre, Greens, Siam Orchid, Woo Sang, Yang Sing*

HAMPSHIRE

Alton: *Apple Crumble*
Eastleigh: *Piccolo Mondo*
Minstead: *Honey Pot*
Portsmouth (Southsea): *Country Kitchen, Rosie's Vineyard*
Romsey: *Cobweb Tea Rooms, Latimer Coffee House*

Rowlands Castle: *Coffee Pot*
Southampton: *La Margherita*
Winchester: *Mr Pitkin's*

HEREFORD & WORCESTER

Broadway: *Coffee Pot, Collin House Hotel, Goblets*
Eardisland: *Elms*
Hereford: *Fat Tulip, Marches, Nutters*
Kidderminster: *Natural Break*
Ledbury: *Feathers Hotel*
Leintwardine: *Selda Coffee & Crafts*
Leominster: *Granary Coffee House*
Lyonshall: *Church House*
Ombersley: *Ombersley Gallery Tea Room*
Ross-on-Wye: *Meader's*
Worcester: *Natural Break*

HERTFORDSHIRE

Berkhamsted: *Cook's Delight*
Hemel Hempstead: *Gallery Coffee Shop*
St Albans: *Kingsbury Mill Waffle House*
Stevenage: *De Friese Coffee Shop*
Ware: *Sunflowers*

HUMBERSIDE

Grimsby: *Granary, Leon's*
Willerby: *Cedars at Grange Park Hotel, Raffaele's*

ISLE OF WIGHT

Luccombe Chine: *Dunnose Cottage*
Newport: *Full of Beans, God's Providence House*
Wootton Common: *Lugleys Tea Gardens*
Yarmouth: *Jireh House*

KENT

Biddenden: *Claris's Tea Shop*

Bromley: *Hollywood Bowl*
Canterbury: *Cogan House English Brasserie, Crotchets, Pizza Place, Sweet Heart Pâtisserie, Il Vaticano Pasta Parlour*
Chatham: *Food for Living Eats, Simson's, Where the Dickens*
Chislehurst: *Mrs Bridges' Kitchen*
Cliftonville: *Batchelor's Pâtisserie*
Collier Street: *Butcher's Mere*
Cranbrook: *Cranes*
Hythe: *Natural Break*
Lamberhurst: *The Down*
New Romney: *Country Kitchen*
Penshurst: *Fir Tree House Tea Rooms*
Ramsgate: *Sands*
Rochester: *Casa Lina*
St Margaret's at Cliffe: *Roses*
Sandwich: *Pinkies*
Tunbridge Wells: *Cheevers, Delicious, Downstairs at Thackeray's, Pilgrims*

LANCASHIRE

Burnley: *Butterfingers*
Cleveleys: *Wholefood & Vegetarian Restaurant*
Lancaster: *Libra*
Lytham: *Bennett's Bistro, Lytham Kitchen*
Poulton-le-Fylde: *Anna's Bistro*

LEICESTERSHIRE

Market Harborough: *Taylors Fish Restaurant*

LINCOLNSHIRE

Grantham: *Knightingales*
Lincoln: *Troffs, Whites, Wig & Mitre*
Spilsby: *Buttercross Restaurant*
Stamford: *George of Stamford, Mr Pips Coffee Shop & Restaurant*

MERSEYSIDE

Liverpool: *Everyman Bistro, Streets*

NORFOLK

Burnham Market: *Soul Kitchen*
Diss: *Weavers*
Great Yarmouth: *Friends Bistro*
Heacham: *Miller's Cottage Tea Room*
King's Lynn: *Antonio's Wine Bar*
Norwich: *Britons Arms Coffee House, Café La Tienda, Swelter's, Waffle House*
Swaffham: *Red Door*

NORTHUMBERLAND

Alnwick: *John Blackmore's Restaurant*
Berwick-upon-Tweed: *Funnywayt'Mekalivin, Kings Arms Hotel, Hideaway, Scotsgate Wine Bar*
Blanchland: *White Monk Tea Room*

NOTTINGHAMSHIRE

Newark: *Gannets*
Nottingham: *Pagoda, The Q in the Corner at Ziggi's, Shôgun, Ten*
Plumtree: *Perkins Bar Bistro*
Warsop: *Goff's*

OXFORDSHIRE

Blewbury: *Lantern Cottage*
Chipping Norton: *Nutters*
Henley-on-Thames: *Barnaby's Brasserie, Copper Kettle*
Oxford: *Browns, Café M.O.M.A., Heroes, Munchy Munchy, Randolph Hotel Lounge, St Aldate's Church Coffee House*

Wallingford: *Annie's Tea Rooms, Lamb Coffee Shop*
Wantage: *Vale & Downland Museum Centre*
Waterperry: *Waterperry Gardens Tea Shop*
Woodstock: *Brothertons Brasserie, Feathers Hotel Garden Bar & Lounge*

SHROPSHIRE

Bishop's Castle: *No 7*
Bridgnorth: *Sophie's Tea Rooms*
Dorrington: *Country Friends*
Ludlow: *Aragon's, Hardwicks, Olive Branch*
Oswestry: *Good Companion*
Shrewsbury: *Cornhouse, Delanys Vegetarian Restaurants, Good Life*

SOMERSET

Bridgwater: *Nutmeg*
Castle Cary: *Old Bakehouse, Tramps*
Cheddar: *Wishing Well Tea Rooms*
Dunster: *Tea Shoppe*
Frome: *Old Bath Arms, Settle*
Glastonbury: *Ploughshares Café, Rainbow's End Café*
Montacute: *Montacute House Restaurant*
Selworthy: *Periwinkle Cottage Tea Rooms*
Tarr Steps: *Tarr Farm*
Taunton: *Bow Bar, Porters*
Wells: *Cloister Restaurant, Good Earth*
Williton: *Blackmore's Bookshop Tea Room, Orchard Mill*
Yeovil: *Trugs*

STAFFORDSHIRE

Abbots Bromley: *Marsh Farm Tea Rooms*
Cauldon Lowe: *Lindy's Kitchen*
Froghall: *The Wharf Eating House*

Kinver: *Berkeley's Bistro*
Tutbury: *Cornmill Tea Room*

SUFFOLK

Aldeburgh: *Aldeburgh Festival Wine Bar*
Bury St Edmunds: *Beaumonts*
Clare: *Peppermill Restaurant, Ship Stores*
Felixstowe: *Hamiltons Tea Room*
Great Barton: *Craft at the Suffolk Barn*
Hadleigh: *Earlsbury's – Janet's Coffee Shop*
Ipswich: *Marno's, Mortimers Oyster Bar, Orwell House*
Lavenham: *The Great House*
Newmarket: *Jane's Wine Bar*
Stonham Aspal: *Stonham Barns*
Walberswick: *Potters Wheel*
Woodbridge: *The Wine Bar*
Woolpit: *The Bakery*

SURREY

Ashtead: *Bart's*
Cheam: *Superfish*
Compton: *Old Congregational Tea Shop*
Croydon: *Hockneys*
East Molesey: *Hampton Court Brasserie, Superfish*
Ewell: *Superfish*
Kew: *Original Maids of Honour, Pissarro's, Wine & Mousaka*
Kingston: *La La Pizza*
Morden: *Superfish*
Richmond: *Refectory, Richmond Harvest, Wildefoods*
Tolworth: *Superfish*
West Byfleet: *Janes Upstairs, Superfish*

EAST SUSSEX

Alfriston: *Drusillas Thatched Barn, Singing Kettle*
Bexhill: *Trawlers*
Bodiam: *Knollys*
Brighton: *Al Duomo, Allanjohn's, Black Chapati,*

China Garden Restaurant, Cripes!, Food for Friends, The Mock Turtle, Pie in the Sky, Ramada Renaissance Hotel, Barts Bar, Samsons, Saxons, Twizzles
Eastbourne: *Byrons, Qualisea*
Herstmonceux: *Praise the Lord*
Lewes: *Old Candlemaker's Café, Pattisson's Restaurant*
Offham: *Old Post House*
Ringmer: *Coffee House*
Rottingdean: *Rottingdean Pâtisserie*
Rye: *Swiss Pâtisserie*
Ticehurst: *Plantation Tea Company*
Westfield: *Casual Cuisine*
Winchelsea: *Finches of Winchelsea, Winchelsea Tea Room*

WEST SUSSEX

Arundel: *Belinda's Tea Rooms*
Billingshurst: *Burdocks*
Chichester: *Chats Brasserie, Clinchs Salad House, St Martin's Tea Rooms*
Shoreham-by-Sea: *Cuckoo Clock*
Tangmere: *River Kwai*
Worthing: *Fogarty's, Mr Pastry, Nature's Way Coffee Shop, River Kwai*

TYNE & WEAR

Gateshead: *Marks & Spencer Garden Restaurant*
Gosforth: *Girl on a Swing*
Newcastle-upon-Tyne: *Mather's*

WARWICKSHIRE

Alderminster: *Bridge House*
Atherstone: *Cloisters Wine Bar & Bistro, Muffins Salad Bar*
Hatton: *Hatton Craft Centre*
Kenilworth: *Ana's Bistro, George Rafters*

Leamington Spa: *Alastairs, Mallory Court, Piccolino's, Regency Fare, Ropers*
Ryton-on-Dunsmore: *Ryton Gardens Café*
Stratford-upon-Avon: *Café Natural, Pinocchio, Slug & Lettuce*
Studley: *Interesting Things*
Warwick: *Bar Roussel, Brethren's Kitchen, Charlotte's Tea Rooms, Piccolino's Pizzeria*

WEST MIDLANDS

Birmingham: *Bobby Browns in Town, Chung Ying, Forbidden City, La Galleria, New Happy Gathering, La Santé*
Coventry: *Herbs*
Solihull: *Bobby Browns*

WILTSHIRE

Avebury: *Stones Restaurant*
Bradford-on-Avon: *Corner Stones*
Broad Chalke: *Cottage House*
Castle Combe: *Manor House*
Devizes: *Wiltshire Kitchen*
Marlborough: *Polly*
Salisbury: *Just Brahms, Mainly Salads, Michael Snell*
Swindon: *Acorn Wholefoods*
Warminster: *Jenner's, Vincent's*
Wootton Bassett: *Emms*

NORTH YORKSHIRE

Barden: *Howgill Lodge*
Bolton Abbey: *Bolton Abbey Tea Cottage*
Harrogate: *Bettys, William & Victoria Downstairs, William & Victoria Restaurant*
Hawes: *Cockett's Hotel*
Kirkbymoorside: *Hatters Castle Coffee Shop*
Low Laithe: *Carters – Knox Manor*
Northallerton: *Bettys*
Pateley Bridge: *Willow*

Ripon: *Upper Loft*
Settle: *Car & Kitchen*
Shipton: *Beningbrough Hall*
Skipton: *Herbs*
Staddle Bridge: *Cellar Bar at the Tontine*
Whitby: *Magpie Café*
York: *Bees Knees, Bettys, Mulberry Hall Coffee Shop, Oat Cuisine, St Williams College Restaurant, Taylors Tea Rooms, Wholefood Trading Company*

SOUTH YORKSHIRE

Sheffield: *Just Cooking, Toff's Restaurant & Coffee House*

WEST YORKSHIRE

Bradford: *Pizza Margherita*
Elland: *Berties Bistro*
Haworth: *Weavers*
Horsforth: *Stuarts Wine Bar*
Ilkley: *Bettys*
Leeds: *Salvo's, Strawberryfields Bistro*

SCOTLAND

BORDERS

Dryburgh Abbey: *Orchard Tearoom*
Newcastleton: *Copshaw Kitchen*
Peebles: *Kailzie Gardens Restaurant, Sunflower Coffee Shop*
Selkirk: *Philipburn House Hotel*

CENTRAL

Balfron: *Coffee Mill*
Falkirk: *Coffee Cabin*

DUMFRIES & GALLOWAY

Dalbeattie: *Coffee & Things*
Dumfries: *Opus Salad Bar*
Moffat: *Rachel's Pantry*

New Abbey: *Abbey Cottage*
Stranraer: *L'Apéritif*

FIFE

Falkland: *Kind Kyttock's Kitchen*
St Andrews: *Brambles*

GRAMPIAN

Aboyne: *Alford House Restaurant*
Drybridge: *Old Monastery*

HIGHLAND

Arisaig: *Old Library Lodge & Restaurant*
Colbost: *Three Chimneys*
Dulnain Bridge: *Muckrach Lodge Hotel*
Inverness: *Brookes Wine Bar*
Kentallen of Appin: *Holly Tree*
Kincraig: *Boathouse Restaurant*
Kinlochbervie: *Kinlochbervie Hotel*
Kyle of Lochalsh: *Highland Designworks*
Strathcarron: *Carron Restaurant*
Tarbet: *Tigh-na-Mara Seafood Restaurant*
Ullapool: *Ceilidh Place*

LOTHIAN

Dirleton: *Open Arms Hotel*
Edinburgh: *Le Café Noir, Café Saint Jacques, Handsel's Wine Bar, Helios Fountain, Hendersons Salad Table, Kalpna, Laigh Kitchen, Lune Town, Sunflower, Waterfront Wine Bar*

ORKNEY

Stromness: *Hamnavoe Restaurant*

STRATHCLYDE

Alloway: *Burns Byre Restaurant*
Ardentinny: *Ardentinny Hotel Buttery*
Crinan: *Crinan Coffee Shop*
Cullipool: *Longhouse Buttery*
Dunoon: *Black's Tea Room*
Glasgow: *Belfry, Café Gandolfi, Joe's Garage, De Quincey's/Brahms & Liszt, Smith's, Ubiquitous Chip, Upstairs Café, Warehouse Café*
Glenscorrodale: *Glenscorrodale Farm Tearoom*
Hardgate: *Elle Coffee Shop*
Helensburgh: *Original Famous Coffee House*
Isle of Gigha: *Gigha Hotel*
Kilchrenan: *Taychreggan Hotel*
Kilfinan: *Kilfinan Hotel*
Lamlash: *Carraig Mhor*
Largs: *Green Shutter Tea Room*
Milngavie: *Famous Coffee House*
Taynuilt: *Shore Cottage*
Whitehouse: *Old School Tearoom*

TAYSIDE

Dundee: *Raffles Restaurant*
Dunkeld: *Tappit Hen*
Inchture: *Inchture Milk Bar*
Pitlochry: *Luggie Restaurant*
St Fillans: *Four Seasons Hotel – Tarkon Bar*

Carmarthen: *Waverley Restaurant*
Eglwysfach: *Ty'n-y-Cwn Tea Rooms*
Newport: *Cnapan*
Wolf's Castle: *Wolfscastle Country Hotel*

GWENT

Chepstow: *Willow Tree*

GWYNEDD

Bethesda: *Mountain Kitchen*
Caernarfon: *Bakestone*
Llanberis: *Y Bistro Bach*
Llanrwst: *Tu-Hwnt-i'r-Bont*
Rhyd-y-clafdy: *Tu Hwnt I'r Afon*

POWYS

Hay-on-Wye: *Granary, Lion's Corner House*
Machynlleth: *Centre for Alternative Technology, Quarry Shop*

SOUTH GLAMORGAN

Cardiff: *Armless Dragon, La Brasserie, Champers, Le Monde, Riverside, Sage*
Cowbridge: *Off the Beeton Track*

WEST GLAMORGAN

Swansea: *La Braseria*

WALES

CLWYD

Llanrhaeadr: *Lodge*

DYFED

Aberaeron: *Hive on the Quay*
Aberystwyth: *Connexion*

CHANNEL ISLANDS

ALDERNEY

St Anne: *Gossip*

GUERNSEY

St Peter Port: *Flying Dutchman Hotel*

103

JERSEY

Gorey Village: *Jersey Pottery Restaurant*
St Brelade's Bay: *Hotel L'Horizon, Beech Lounge*
St Saviour: *Longueville Manor Hotel*

SARK

Sark: *Stocks Buffet*

ISLE OF MAN

Ballasalla: *La Rosette*
Douglas: *L'Expérience*
Ramsey: *Harbour Bistro*

LONDON

Ajanta

12 Goldhawk Road W12
MAP 10 A4
01-743 5191
P street parking

Open 12–2.30 (Sun from 12.30) & 6–12
Closed 3 days Xmas

Chicken tikka masala £4.10 Prawn
muglai £3.10

First-class cooking and good value for
money raises this friendly Indian restaurant
near Shepherd's Bush out of the ordinary.
The menu relies on many traditional
specialities, with sauces that can be tem-
perate or fiery to suit any palate. Moist,
tender meat dishes, chicken tikka, kebabs
and pasandra are harmoniously served
with aromatic pilau rice and vegetables.
Traditional sweets complete your meal. *No
dogs.*

Credit Access, Amex, Visa

Almeida Theatre Wine Bar

1a Almeida Street N1
MAP 11 D1
01-226 0931
P street parking

Open 11–3 & 6–11
Closed Sun (except for special concerts)
& Bank Hols (when no theatre
production)

Cheesy corn soup 95p Baked marrow
& salad £3.35 ℗

It can get very busy on theatre nights, but
it all adds to the atmosphere at this friendly
wine bar. A good choice of wines by bottle
or glass accompanies everything from
wonderfully garlicky houmus to pork
chops in cider and apple sauce, huge
dressed salads, cheesy peanut pie and
stuffed peppers. A hearty appetite is
essential to do justice to the generous
portions. Chocolate mocha cake or apple
pie make a delicious finale. *No dogs.*

Aspava

18 Shepherd Street W1
MAP 12 B4
01-491 8739
P NCP in Carrington Street

Open noon–midnight
Closed 25 Dec

Shish kebab £4.35 Mixed meze £2.50

Aspava has recently expanded but the
menu remains the same, offering a popular
range of well-prepared items from houmus
to taramasalata and the house speciality of
mixed meze with hot and cold hors
d'oeuvre like aubergines and peppers with
creamy yoghurt. Main dishes created from
top-quality ingredients range from succulent shish kebab to braised knuckle of veal
and traditional moussaka. Children's portions. *Non-smoking area. No dogs.*

LVs

Asuka

209a Baker Street NW1
MAP 11 B2
01-486 5026
P NCP in Glentworth Street

Open 12–2.30 & 6–11
Closed Sat lunch, all Sun & Bank Hols

Assorted sushi rolls from £5.50 De-luxe
assorted sushi £12

Sited in a small arcade off a busy street,
the attractive Far Eastern setting of black
woodwork and Japanese lanterns creates
an elegant and intimate atmosphere. Here
you can watch your food being prepared
from a colourful range of fresh raw fish.
The selection varies from day to day
according to the availability of only the
very freshest fish. Try sushi made with
familiar salmon or sole or the more exotic
yellow tail or cuttlefish. Japanese green
tea is served. *No dogs.*

Credit Access, Amex, Diners, Visa

Athenaeum Hotel, Windsor Lounge

116 Piccadilly W1
MAP 12 B4
01-499 3464
P Brick Street car park

Open 24 hours

Smoked haddock & Gruyère omelette
£3.50   Afternoon tea £4.50 🍵

Elegance is the watchword here, with fern-filled urns, Grecian statues and tea from a silver pot. The all-day menu offers soup, club and steak sandwiches, rarebit, salads and smoked salmon. The set tea brings finger sandwiches and excellent oven-warm scones, dotted with sultanas and served with jam and thick yellow cream, plus a choice of pastries, moist Marsala and almond cake perhaps, or a crumbly cream-filled meringue. *No dogs.*

Credit Access, Amex, Diners, Visa

L'Autre Wine Bar

Shepherd Street W1
MAP 12 C4
01-499 4680
P NCP in Carrington Street

Open 12–3.30 & 5.30–11
Closed Sat, Sun, lunch Bank Hols & all
1 Jan & 25 & 26 Dec

Chicken & Brie in chilli sauce £5.25
Avocado & crispy bacon £2.50 🍷

Seafood dominates the menu at this lively little wine bar in the heart of Shepherd's Market. The selection includes Atlantic prawns with garlic mayonnaise, smoked Loch Fyne trout, spinach and mussel bake and a splendid seafood buffet. Flavoursome alternatives appear in the shape of Mexican enchiladas and burritos, Cumberland smoked sausages and oak-smoked ham. Interesting sweets and excellent French cheeses to finish. *No children. No dogs.*

Credit Access, Visa

N·E·W ENTRY *Baba Bhelpoori House*

29 Porchester Road W2
MAP 11 A3
01-221 7502
P NCP Porchester Road

Open 12–3 & 6–11
Closed Mon & 25 Dec

Bhajis £1.50   Gujerati style thali
£4.50

Caring owners and a homely, welcoming atmosphere make this brightly decorated Indian vegetarian restaurant a pleasure to visit. On offer are a variety of tasty snacks, made with fresh herbs and spices, that include crispy bhajis, vegetable curries based on potatoes or chick peas, dosas and samosas, plus traditional sweets such as shrikhand or lassi yoghurt drink. Try Gujerati style thali for a complete meal. *Minimum charge £3. No dogs.*

Credit Access, Visa

Balls Brothers

6 Cheapside EC2
MAP 10 D4
01-248 2708
P NCP Paternoster Row

Open 11.30–3 & 5–7.30
Closed Sat, Sun & Bank Hols

Roast beef sandwich £2.80   Cheese
platter £2.90 🍷

The large patio is a popular summer attraction at this city wine bar with inside eating space on the ground floor and basement. Dark panelling, antiques and wooden floors provide the traditional back-ground, and generously-filled sandwiches (smoked turkey mayonnaise, avocado and cream cheese, roast beef with horseradish) are the favourite snack. Good-quality Brie, Stilton and Cheddar, the occasional slice of moist fruit cake, and some excellent wines complete the picture. *No children.*

Credit Access, Amex, Diners, Visa

Balls Brothers

Moor House, Moorgate EC2
MAP 10 D4
01-628 3944
P NCP at London Wall

Open 11.30–2.30
Closed Sat, Sun & Bank Hols

Avocado with crabmeat £2.75   Sirloin
steak £6.50   ℰ

The oldest and largest branch of this
popular city wine bar chain differs from its
sisters in offering a small selection of
waitress-served meals in its basement
restaurant. From noon, starters such as
duck and orange pâté or gravad lax can be
followed by roast beef, steak or a daily
special like calf's liver with bacon. There's
an appetising cold buffet too, plus simple
sweets and good cheeses. Generously-filled
sandwiches available upstairs and down.

Credit Access, Amex, Diners, Visa   **LVs**

Balls Brothers

2 Old Change Court, St Paul's
Churchyard EC4
MAP 11 D3
01-248 8697
P Distaff Lane NCP

Open 11.30–3
Closed Sat, Sun & Bank Hols

Avocado & bacon sandwich £2.90
Cheese platter £3   ℰ

A recent facelift has brightened up the
decor at this ever-busy wine bar in a
modern precinct facing St. Paul's. Lavishly
filled sandwiches are always popular, with
choices like smoked turkey with celery and
apple, pastrami with mayonnaise and win-
ter-warming hot salt beef and grilled steak.
There is also a fine cheese platter featuring
Stilton, Brie, mature Cheddar and Dolce-
latte, some fruit and often a slice of fruit
cake. Patio. *No children. No dogs.*

Credit Access, Amex, Diners, Visa

Bentley's Wine Bar & Oyster Bar

11 Swallow Street W1
MAP 13 A3
01-734 0401
P NCP in Shaftesbury Avenue

Open 12–3 & 5.30–11
Closed Sun & Bank Hols

Fresh crab bisque £2.70   Seafood
strudel £3.95   ℰ

Best of all worlds in this seafood restaurant
accommodating most palates. A choice of
oysters and cold specialities upstairs, and
a varied seafood, meat and pasta menu in
the basement wine bar. Choose a baked
fish pie, seafood crêpe, clam bisque, pork
brochette with coconut or linguine with
bolognese sauce. Chef's daily specials
might include chicken in a mushroom
sauce. Soups, omelettes, salads and sandwiches abound. *Non-smoking area. No
dogs.*

Credit Access, Amex, Diners, Visa   **LVs**

Bill Stickers

18 Greek Street W1
MAP 13 B2
01-437 0582
P Soho Square

Open 12–3am (Fri & Sat till 6am & Sun
till midnight)
Closed 1 wk Xmas

Burger, chips & salad £5.50   Bangers
& mash £5.50

Don't be put off by the gimmick mock-
Victorian decor of this late-closing Soho
restaurant. It's worth enduring the naked
cherub for the menu of popular, tasty
dishes such as chilli con carne, bangers
and mash, nutty vegetarian burgers served
with salad and good garlic bread. Finish
with eclairs, apple pie or ice cream. Friendly
service by hussar-style waiters continues
into the small hours.

Credit Access, Amex, Diners, Visa   **LVs**

Le Bistroquet

273 Camden High Street NW1
MAP 11 B1
01-485 9607
P meter parking

Open noon–midnight (Sun till 11)
Closed 3 days Xmas

Aubergine mousse £2.50 Spicy
sausages with potato pûrée
£3.95 ☺ 🍵

The popularity of this bistro testifies to the
superb cooking here. The fixed price menu
for lunch and dinner represents excellent
value, while other choices include spinach
and cream cheese gâteau, sautéed steak
with excellent matchstick chips, and a
beautifully cooked fishcake accompanied
by fresh parsley sauce. Also available are
sandwiches, assiettes, salads and irresistible desserts. Excellent cheeses and fine
wines add the finishing touches. *No dogs.*

Credit Access, Amex, Visa

Blake's Wine & Food Bar

34 Wellington Street WC2
MAP 13 D2
01-836 5298
P NCP in Gerrard Street

Open 11.30–11 (Sun till 10.30)
Closed 25 & 26 Dec

Pasta palermo £4.10 Sandringham pie
£3.90 ☺

Three minutes' walk from the Royal Opera
House is this busy wine bar much fre-
quented by the young. Serve yourself with
quiches, meat pies and salads, or choose a
hot dish like lasagne, chicken casserole or
steak and kidney pie. Varieties of quiche
include bacon and mushroom, leek and
courgette and cheese and onion. Good
cheeses are complemented by decent wines
by the glass. Tea, coffee and cakes are
available all day. *No children. No dogs.*

Credit Access, Amex, Diners, Visa **LVs**

Bloom's

130 Golders Green Road NW11
MAP 9 B2
01-455 1338
Open 12–9.30
Closed Fri, Sat, 25 Dec & Jewish hols

90 Whitechapel High Street E1
MAP 10 D4
01-247 6001
Open 11.15–9.15 (Fri till 2.30)
Closed Sat, 25 Dec & Jewish hols

P street parking NW11/own car park E1
Chopped liver £1.90 Schnitzel £5.20

These two traditional and much-loved
kosher restaurants are still in full bloom.
Both have become institutions in the best
possible sense, serving huge portions of
traditional kosher food with bustle, noise
and verve. Try a hearty borscht, chopped
herring, the hot salt beef followed by halva,
apple strudel or lockshen pudding. Enjoy
the performance of the waiters too – they
are part of the entertainment! Children's
portions. *No dogs.*

Credit Access, Visa

Bon Ton Roulet

127 Dulwich Road, Herne Hill SE24
MAP 10 D6
01-733 8701
P street parking

Open 7pm–10.30pm
Closed Sun, Bank Hols, 1 wk Aug & 10
days Xmas

Smoked salmon & cucumber mousse
£1.80 Stuffed breast of chicken with
peanut butter sauce £5.95 ☺

A popular, informal restaurant which
would benefit from a little redecoration,
but the meals are well cooked and the
portions are generous. Choose from the
printed menu or the blackboard which lists
the soup and dish of the day. Starters
might be pear and Stilton or watercress
and kipper salad, and main courses include
beef masala, roast lamb with garlic sauce,
braised wood-pigeon and devilled turkey.
Excellent sweets such as mango and
brandy fool or lemon mousse. *No dogs.*

Boos

1 Glentworth Street, Marylebone Road NW1
MAP 11 B2
01-935 3827
P NCP in Glentworth Street

Open Wine Bar: 11.30–3 & 5.30–8
Fayre Exchange: 8.30–4.30, Sat 11–3
Closed Sat (except Fayre Exchange in summer), Sun, Bank Hols, 3 wks Sept & 2 wks Xmas

Smoked salmon & cream cheese sandwich £3.25   Waldorf salad £1.80 🕑

In the wine bar Michael and Judith Rose offer a stunning selection of wines, complemented by simple but enjoyable snacks ranging from soup, sandwiches and cheeses to home-cooked ham with salad, quiche and a daily hot special. Don't miss Michael's delicious cheesecake – especially the Amaretto-flavoured. Upstairs is Fayre Exchange, which offers snacks such as croissants, filled baguettes, fish chowder and salad. *Minimum charge (wine bar) £1.50. No children. No dogs.*

Credit Access, Amex, Diners

Bottlescrue

52 Bath House, Holborn Viaduct EC1
MAP 11 D3
01-248 2157
P NCP in Snow Hill

Open 11.30–3 & 5–8.30
Closed Sat, Sun, Bank Hols & 2–3 days Xmas

Mediterranean prawns £3.95   Poached salmon & salad £5.95 🕑

City businessmen frequent this relaxed wine bar situated virtually opposite Holborn Station. Every nook and cranny is filled with wine bottles, sawdust covers the floor and empty hogsheads serve as tables. The food is simple and wholesome – start with prawns or crab, go on to game pie or cold meats with salads, and conclude with treacle tart, chocolate mousse or fruit pie. Sandwiches are made with granary bread and plenty of fillings, like trout and cucumber.

Credit Access, Amex, Diners, Visa

Brasserie

11 Bellevue Road SW17
MAP 10 C6
01-767 6982
P street parking

Open 12–3 & 7–11
Closed 25 & 26 Dec

Seafood pasta £4.50   Lamb steak with rosemary £4.50 🕑

Imaginative cuisine and the bonus of fresh fish daily at this lively and informal bar/restaurant overlooking Wandsworth Common. Nouvelle-ish ideas dominate the menu: chilled vegetarian mousse with saffron sauce, or poached salmon with tomato and champagne hollandaise. Duck pâté is a tasty curtain-raiser to veal slices tossed with fresh limes and sorrel, or poached scallops with peppercorns. Chocolate roulade and crème brûlée to finish. Carefully-chosen wines. *No dogs.*

Credit Access, Visa

La Brasserie

272 Brompton Road SW3
MAP 12 B5
01-584 1668
P meter parking &

Open 8am–midnight (Sun from 10am)
Closed 25 & 26 Dec

Soup de poisson £2.90   Crêpe de volaille aux poireaux £5.80 🕑

A hint of Paris in South Kensington, with its lively, bustling atmosphere, pavement tables and first-class service. Daily specials, like flavourful moules marinière and veal escalope with asparagus, supplement the regular list of typically French dishes: perhaps onion soup or Roquefort salad followed by kidneys in Pernod, sole meunière or grilled steak. Excellent sweets from the trolley and a fine selection of French wines. *No dogs.*

Credit Access, Amex, Diners, Visa

Brasserie at L'Escargot

48 Greek Street W1
MAP 13 B2
01-437 2679
P NCP Gerrard Street

Open 12–3 & 5.30–11.15
(Sat from 6)
Closed Sat lunch, all Sun, Bank Hols
& 10 days Xmas

Warm spinach & Gruyère cheese tart
£3.95   Pasta with prawns, fennel &
mushrooms £5.95   🅴

Hugely popular with the young and fashionable, this lively, informal Soho brasserie
is just the place to star-gaze while enjoying
an elegant light bite. Seasonable vegetables
dressed with hazelnut oil, smoked lamb
served with spiced apricots and a delicious
filo pastry parcel filled with goat's cheese,
spinach and ratatouille typify the imaginative savoury range. Stylish sweets like
warm cherry and Kirsch pancake to finish.
No dogs.

Credit Access, Amex, Diners, Visa

N·E·W
ENTRY

British Museum Restaurant

Great Russell Street WC1
MAP 11 C3
01-636 1555
P YMCA NCP

Open 10.30–4.15, Sun 2.30–5.15
Closed 1 Jan, 24, 25 & 26 Dec

Chicken breasts in white wine £3.95
Lemon roulade 95p

Replicas of the Elgin marbles extend a
museum motif into this self-service museum restaurant. Justin de Blank in style,
the food is generally good, ranging from
cold platters, salads and sandwiches to
appetising ham and rare beef, ricotta and
leek strudel and tuna and egg pancakes.
Top and tail a light spinach roulade with a
flavoursome seafood chowder and almondy
pear slice. Pastries galore, cheesecake,
lemon roulade and scones satisfy the sweet
tooth. *No smoking. No dogs.*

LVs

Brown's Hotel Lounge

Albermarle & Dover Street W1
MAP 13 A3
01-493 6020
P NCP in Carrington Street

Open 9am–12.30am

Set afternoon tea £8.95   Club sandwich
£7   🍵

Smooth, professional service adds to the
comfort at this delightfully traditional
lounge with its oak panelling, soft lamplight and deep, inviting armchairs. From 3
to 6 drop in for a faultless afternoon tea of
toasted scones, dainty sandwiches and
featherlight pastries, or try an elegant light
lunch featuring splendid sandwiches and
seasonal delights such as summer salad,
soup, smoked salmon with fresh crab, and
raspberries with clotted dream. *No dogs.*

Credit Access, Amex, Diners, Visa

Bubbles Wine Bar

41 North Audley Street W1
MAP 11 B3
01-499 0600
P NCP under Marriott Hotel   ♿

Open 11–3 & 5.30–10.30
Closed Sat eve, all Sun & Bank Hols

Steak sandwich £5.50   Pork fillet with
honey & ginger £6.80   🅴

On the ground floor of this wine bar, the
speciality dishes are charcoal grills,
whereas downstairs in the bistro the choice
ranges from steak sandwiches and Lincolnshire sausages with home-made dill
pickle to pork fillet with honey and ginger.
Meat is the main attraction, but there is a
vegetable pâté if you prefer. Desserts
include pavlova and chocolate marquise.
Excellent selection of wines by the glass or
bottle. *No dogs.*

Credit Access, Amex, Diners, Visa

Café Delancey

3 Delancey Street NW1
MAP 11 C1
01-387 1985
P meter parking &

Open 9.30am–11.30pm
Closed Sun, 1 Jan & 25 & 26 Dec

Delancey breakfast £3.40   Steak
sandwich £4.95 ⊖

Pavement tables in summer, friendly staff
and a full menu available all day evokes a
truly Continental atmosphere at this smart
café. Glance through the newspapers
provided while you wait for your
choice – perhaps perfectly cooked trout
fillet in filo pastry followed by poached
chicken breast with rosti, calf's liver and
bacon or one of the daily specials. Delicious
French desserts or cheeses round things
off. *No dogs.*

Credit Access, Visa

Café des Fleurs

N·E·W ENTRY

280 West End Lane NW6
MAP 9 B2
01-435 5290
P street parking

Open 10.15am–11.45pm
Closed 25 & 26 Dec

Marinated herrings in soured cream
£1.70   Calf's liver £5.50 ⊖

Charcoal-grilled meats and fish predomi-
nate at this adeptly run brasserie. Eat
alfresco in summer or at spaciously arranged tables in the split level interior.
Sauté of chicken livers or a delicious
tomato and rosemary soup can be followed
with spatchcock chicken with herbs
(grilled). Occasionally there are specials –
tagliatelle with tuna, vegetarian leek gratin
or fresh tuna fish. A long sideboard dazzles
with delectable desserts. Traditional Sunday lunch. *No dogs.*

Credit Access, Visa

Café Pacifico

5 Langley Street WC2
MAP 13 C2
01-379 7728
P NCP in St Martin's Lane

Open 11.30am–11.45pm (Sun 12–
10.45)
Closed Bank Hols & 1 wk Xmas

Nachos sonora £2.25   Chimichanga del
mar £5.80

The original Mexican cantina-style restaurant is so popular it now has branches in
Amsterdam and Paris serving many varieties of tacos (filled corn tortilla pancakes),
enchilladas (unfried cheesy pancakes), vibrant chilli and the old favourites – subtly
spiced, cool, guacamole and corn chips.
New on the menu are fajitas – chicken or
beef strips on a sizzling skillet. There are
tequila-based concoctions to sooth any
burning throats. Children's portions. *No
dogs.*

Credit Access, Visa

Café Pastiche

307 Lillie Road SW6
MAP 10 B5
01-385 1130
P street parking

Open 11-30–2.30 & 5.30–11
Closed Sun & Bank Hols

Chicken livers with sour cream £1.75
Cream of vegetable & orange soup £1.60

Run in friendly, relaxed fashion, this cosy
restaurant and basement wine bar offers a
tempting variety of carefully prepared,
imaginative dishes. Hearty soups, deliciously sauced pasta and garlic mushrooms
are all favourite light bites, while more
substantial offerings include lamb steak
served with an apricot, marjoram and wine
sauce and a lovely fresh jacket potato. To
finish, perhaps rich chocolate cheesecake
or refreshing blackcurrant sorbet.

Credit Access, Visa

Café Pélican

45 St Martin's Lane WC2
MAP 13 C3
01-379 0309
P NCP Bedford Bury Avenue &

Open 11am–2am (Sun till 11.30pm)
Closed Good Fri & 1 wk Xmas

Continental breakfast £4.95 Grilled
steak £8.95 ℮

In summer – English weather permitting –
you can sit and eat Continental style on
the pavement here. Inside it is very French
too. There's excellent coffee to accompany
the delicious light snacks, available all day,
like warm and tasty brioche and a splendid
croque monsieur with a good crisp salad.
Sweet things such as a very enjoyable
mixed fruit tart and wonderful looking
meringues are displayed on the bar
counter. More substantial meals are available too. *No dogs.*

Credit Access, Amex, Diners, Visa

Café St Pierre Brasserie

29 Clerkenwell Green EC1
MAP 11 D2
01-251 6606
P meter parking

Open 12–3 & 5.30–11
Closed Sat, Sun & Bank Hols

Rich chicken liver pâté £1.45 Breast
of chicken with pink peppercorn sauce
£3.95 ℮

Capable cooking in pleasant surroundings
keeps this smart brasserie busy – especially
at lunchtimes, when booking is advised.
Blackboard specials supplement the short
set menu and always include a dish of the
day (perhaps lamb chops in caraway seed
sauce) and a fish choice such as seafood
pasta. Deep-fried Camembert and grilled
sardines are typical starters, and look out
for the lovely, light raspberry mousse
among desserts. *No dogs.*

Credit Access, Amex, Diners, Visa

N·E·W ENTRY The Café Society

32 Procter Street, Red Lion Square WC1
MAP 11 D3
01-242 6691
P street parking

Open 8–8
Closed Sat, Sun, Bank Hols & 2 wks
Aug

Goose pâté £3.10 Chocolate mousse
£2.50

There's a delightful continental feel to this
little brasserie/café – pavement tables,
daily newspapers, fresh flowers and Gallic
waiters. From early morning you can have
a traditional English or continental breakfast or magnificent potato pancakes topped
with fried eggs. Snacks encompass light
fluffy omelettes, crisp salads and interesting sandwiches. Desserts include all the
classics from chocolate mousse to a tart
tatin. Excellent espresso and cappucino.
No dogs.

Credit Access, Amex, Visa

Caffé Venezia

15 New Burlington Street W1
MAP 13 A2
01-439 2378
P NCP in Kingly Street &

Open 12–3 & 5.30–11.30
Closed Sun & 25 & 26 Dec

Cappelletti del lucchese £4 Apricot
sorbet £1.85 ℮

Pasta dishes in imaginative combinations
can be found at this bright, spacious Italian
restaurant. Try green and white noodles
with fresh mussels or the excellent gnocchi
richly sauced with duck and tomatoes. The
fish, too, is first rate, especially the simpler
offerings like grilled red mullet or skewered
Mediterranean prawns, while more elaborate dishes include veal with artichokes
and bacon-wrapped quail. Traditional starters and sweets; enjoyable espresso. *No
dogs.*

Credit Access, Amex, Diners, Visa

Camden Brasserie

216 Camden High Street NW1
MAP 11 C1
01-482 2114
P street parking

Open 12–3 & 6.30–11.30 (Sun
6–10.30)
Closed Bank Hols (lunchtimes)
& 1 wk Xmas

Merguez sausages £2.30   Lamb
brochette £6   ⊖

The menu here is short and uncomplicated
but all dishes are well prepared and
enjoyable. In addition, daily 'specials' are
offered, such as mushroom soup or fresh
trout. The brasserie specialises in charcoal-
grilled dishes of lamb, beef and fish,
supplemented with well-cooked pasta,
large portions of vegetables and good
coffee. Dessert of the day might be a rich,
fluffy chocolate mousse. In fine weather it
is possible to sit outside. Children's portions. *No dogs.*

Carriages

43 Buckingham Palace Road SW1
MAP 12 C4
01-834 8871
P meter parking

Open 11.30–11
Closed Sat & Sun (in winter), Bank Hols
& 4 days Xmas

Smoked salmon and scrambled eggs
£6.25   Pork fillet stuffed with spinach
£6.25   ⊖

A popular establishment on two floors,
now open throughout the day for light
bites and main meals. Shrimp bisque or
tacos with chilli might precede chicken
and grapefruit salad, venison escalope with
green peppercorns, a juicy steak or hamburger. Finish with cheese or minty chocolate mousse. Drop in for afternoon tea in
summer. *Minimum lunchtime charge £4.
No children upstairs at lunchtime. No
dogs.*

Credit Access, Amex, Diners, Visa

Charco's Wine Bar

1 Bray Place, off Anderson Street SW3
MAP 12 B5
01-584 0765
P meter parking

Open 12–3 & 5.30–10.30
Closed Sun, Bank Hols & 3 days Xmas

Salmon & spinach tartlet £2.75   White
chocolate mousse £2.50   ⊖

The cold buffet laid out on crisp, white
clothed tables at lunchtime (and served
from the kitchen in the evenings), boasts
good looking ham, moist salmon with
excellent mayonnaise and crisp fresh
salads. On the regular menu are starters
like clam chowder or goujons of plaice,
and main courses such as suprême of
chicken and a pasta dish of the day. The
desserts, too, perhaps strawberry flan or
crème brûlée, make a fine finish. Children's
portions. Open air eating in summer.

Credit Visa

Chequers

18 Chalk Farm Road NW1
MAP 9 C3
01-485 1696
P street parking   ♿

Open 10am–12.30am
Closed 25 Dec

Selection of 3 dishes £2.95   Cheesecake £1.20

A chess players' haunt, this modest little
café has a simple formula: lentil soup
(winter only), a choice of eight hot dishes,
and eight salads, along with a small
selection of sweets. You eat well and
healthily. Select three dishes, or opt for
the open buffet and eat as much as you
wish. The hot dishes, with an Egyptian
bias, might be parsley-garnished potatoes
with a buttery, herby sauce, mushrooms
with celery or pasta with tomato and fresh
mint. *Unlicensed. No smoking. No dogs.*

Credit Access, Amex

Cherry Orchard

241 Globe Road E2
MAP 9 D3
01-980 6678
P street parking &

Open 12–10.30
Closed Sun, Mon, Bank Hols, 1 wk Aug

Mushroom ravioli £3.95   Apple, pear &
date crumble £1.45   🍵

A Buddhist co-operative runs this relaxed and informal vegetarian restaurant. Their appetising selection of dishes spans home-made soup (try minty pea), colourful salads, filled baked potatoes and hot daily specials like cauliflower boulangère or chilli kidney beans. Sweets include moist apple, pear and date crumble and there's a good variety of teas to enjoy with wholesome cakes such as vegan fruit or banana munch. Garden. *Unlicensed (bring your own). No smoking. No dogs.*

Credit Access, Visa   **LVs**

Chiang Mai

48 Frith Street W1
MAP 13 B2
01-437 7444
P Soho Square

Open 12–3 & 6–11.30
Closed Sun & Bank Hols

Hot & sour beef salad £3.75   Roast pork
with noodles £3.95

Fresh ingredients are skilfully handled and enhanced by subtle spicing and flavouring at this spruce Thai restaurant in the heart of Soho. For a truly authentic taste of their national cuisine, don't miss the quite superb chicken curry with coconut cream. Other choices range from popular satay with peanut sauce to exotic fried beef with kaffir lime leaves and chillies, and there is a good variety of rice, noodle and vegetarian dishes. *No smoking. No dogs.*

Credit Access, Amex, Visa

N·E·W ENTRY   Chicago Meatpackers

96 Charing Cross Road WC2
MAP 13 C1
01-379 3277
P Cambridge Circus NCP

Open 11.45–11.30, Sat 12–11
Closed Sun & 25 & 31 Dec

Applewood smoked ribs £5.50
Hamburger £3.75

A bright and lively establishment where the quirky decor features a plastic cow sporting illuminated cuts (shoulder, rump, etc), two model railways running overhead and enamel plaques depicting the eponymous Chicago meatpackers. The menu is, inevitably, a meat-lover's delight, offering decently cooked hamburgers and steaks as the mainstay, all served with good fresh salad garnish. Pecan pie for afters. Children's menu. *Non-smoking area. No dogs.*

Chicago Pizza Pie Factory

17 Hanover Square W1
MAP 11 C3
01-629 2669
P meter parking

Open 11.45–11.30, Sun 12–10.30
Closed 24, 25, 26 & 31 Dec

Stuffed mushrooms £2   Cheese,
mushroom & peperoni
pizza (for 2) £6.85

Now over ten years old, Bob Payton's roomy basement restaurant still attracts a huge following for its famous deep-dish pizzas and lively atmosphere imported straight from Chicago. Top your pizza with everything from cheese and peperoni to olives and anchovies, accompanied by a salad and garlic bread. Stuffed mushrooms are the favourite starter, and there's cheesecake for afters. *Non-smoking area. No dogs.*

Chicago Rib Shack

1 Raphael Street, Knightsbridge Green
SW7
MAP 12 B4
01-581 5595
P NCP Raphael Street &

Open 11.45–11.30, Sun 12–11
Closed 3 days Xmas

Rack of ribs £5.95   Onion loaf £2.45

Be prepared to wait at the fine oak bar or admire the stained glass windows before tackling a rack of spicy barbecued ribs at Bob Payton's bustling restaurant, where the emphasis is on quality, fun food. Alternatives include barbecued beef in a baguette plus salads and some super side orders like a huge onion loaf and crispy potato skins. If there's room finish with pecan pie or cheesecake, or simply mop-up with the hot towels provided. *Non-smoking area. No dogs.*

Chuen Cheng Ku

17 Wardour Street W1
MAP 13 B2
01-437 1398
P Swiss Centre NCP

Open dim sum 11–6 (full menu 11am–midnight, Sun till 11.30)
Closed 24 & 25 Dec

Steamed prawn dumplings £1.10
Steamed minced pork dumplings £1.10

A vast, bright and bustling Chinese restaurant where dim sum are pushed around on heated trolleys by reasonably helpful waitresses. The choice is extensive, and the steamed varieties are especially successful, including rice flour rolls, minced pork and shrimp dumplings or tripe in black bean and chilli sauce. Try noodles for a change – fried, braised, or in soup, and there's a delicious hot custard tart to finish. *No dogs.*

Credit Access, Amex, Diners, Visa

La Cloche

304 Kilburn High Road NW6
MAP 9 B3
01-328 0302
P street parking &

Open 12–3 & 7–12
Closed 25 & 26 Dec

Deep fried Gouda £1.85   Hot seafood
salad £4.25   🕑

The dull exterior can be rather off-putting, but inside this former butcher's shop oozes charm. The short, imaginative menu includes starters such as fresh salmon marinated in lime and dill on a bed of cracked wheat followed by, say, calf's liver with hot avocado sauce, delicious vegetable pancake, duck en croûte or a daily special (roast beef for Sunday lunch). Sweets are naughty-but-nice. *No dogs.*

Credit Access, Visa

Colonel Jasper's

161 Greenwich High Road SE10
MAP 10 D5
01-853 0585
P own car park

Open 12–2.30 & 5.30–10 (Sat 7–10)
Closed Sat lunch, all Sun, Bank Hols &
Xmas

Beefsteak, kidney & mushroom pie £3.95
Treacle tart with clotted cream £1.95
🕑

Sawdust-strewn floors, wooden tables between partitions, and candles burning in wine bottles set the scene here. The food is robust: a dish of prawns or salmon mousse for starters; beef steaks or juicy lamb, charcoal-grilled with garlic butter or a blackboard 'special' like spare ribs in ginger sauce for the main course. Chocolate mousse, treacle tart or fresh fruit could complete your meal. Children's portions. *No dogs.*

Credit Access, Amex, Diners, Visa

Cork & Bottle

44 Cranbourn Street WC2
MAP 13 C2
01-734 7807
P Swiss Centre NCP

Open 11–3 & 5.30–11 (Sun 12–2 & 7–10.30)
Closed 1 Jan & 25 & 26 Dec

Spicy chicken salad £5.25
Prawn & avocado salad £2.75   ℰ

Don Hewittson's crowded wine bar owes its popularity as much to its food and carefully chosen wine list as to its central location. The glass counter is packed with hot daily specials such as delicious braised ham and cheese pie and Toulouse sausage casserole. Cold dishes might include spicy ham and chicken salad, marinated mushrooms and roast meats together with excellent salads. Loch Fyne langoustines are occasionally available. *No children. No dogs.*

Credit Access, Amex, Diners, Visa

Country Life

1 Heddon Street W1
MAP 13 A3
01-434 2922
P meter parking

Open 11–2.30 (Fri till 2)
Closed Sat, Sun, Bank Hols & 1 wk Aug

Mushroom mountains £2.40   Tofu cheesecake 59p

Tucked away in the basement of a wholefood shop just off Regent Street, this vegan self-service restaurant is run on strict Seventh Day Adventist principles. A choice from some 20 different salads can accompany main dishes like potato and vegetable pie with cashew nut cream sauce, tofu spinach quiche or wholewheat spaghetti with tomato sauce. Round things off with fresh fruit salad or banana and date pudding. *Minimum charge £2.40. Unlicensed. No smoking. No dogs.*

LVs

Cranks

N·E·W
ENTRY

3 Adelaide Street WC2
MAP 13 C3
01-379 5919
P meter parking

Open Ground floor 10am–11pm; Downstairs 12–2.30 & 7–11
Closed Sun, 1 Jan & 25, 26 Dec

Mushroom stroganoff £2.80   Trifle £1.60   ℰ ♠

A recent addition to the Cranks' empire is this airy restaurant offering traditional buffet service at ground floor level and a new fixed-price alternative downstairs. Typically healthy and wholesome dishes range from sweet pepper and mushroom soup to vegetables in satay sauce and wholemeal potato, cheese and onion pie. Lots of super salads, of course. To finish, try the light, moist carrot cake. *Non-smoking area. No dogs.*

Credit Access, Visa   LVs

Cranks

17 Great Newport Street WC2
MAP 13 C2
01-836 5226
P NCP in St Martin's Lane

Open 8am–8.30pm (Sat from 10.30), also Sun 10–5

Savoury bake of the day £1.90   Banana & cashew cake 75p

Close to Leicester Square tube station, the newest Cranks offers the familiar formula of carefully prepared wholefood and vegetarian dishes to suit any time of day. Early birds can breakfast on creamy muesli, poached or scrambled eggs, filled rolls and scones, while later on, the excellent salads, soup and hot savouries like crunchy cauliflower and almond quiche appear. Sweet treats range from moist cashew nut and banana bread to tofu cheesecake and fruit trifle. *Non-smoking area. No dogs.*

LVs

Cranks

9 Tottenham Street W1
MAP 11 C2
01-631 3912
P meter parking

Open 8am–8pm (Sat from 9)
Closed Sun & Bank Hols

Hot daily savoury £2.80   Carrot cake
85p

Join the inevitable queues at the self-service counter of this roomy, pine-furnished vegetarian restaurant, for an appetising choice of snacks available throughout the day. Delicious sweet treats like moist honey, prune and spice cake or date slice are nice at any time, while from 11am the choice widens to include crunchy salads, vegetable lasagne or crumble, mushroom stroganoff and pleasant puds such as boozy fruit trifle. *Non-smoking area. No dogs.*

LVs

Cranks Health Food Restaurant

8 Marshall Street W1
MAP 13 A2
01-437 9431
P NCP at rear

Open Buffet: 8–7 (Sat from 9); Wine & Dine: 6.30–11
Closed Sun & Bank Hols

Homity pie £1.80   Honey, prune & spice cake 75p 🍵

The original of the Cranks empire differs from its sisters in that its all-day self-service buffet extends to wine and dine candlelit evenings. During the day, imaginative salads piled high in earthenware bowls still draw the crowds, along with flavourful soups and appetising savouries like pasta sauced with walnuts and mushrooms or wholewheat vegetable fricassée. Lighter bites include filled rolls and a vast array of cakes and sweets. *Non-smoking area. No dogs.*

Credit Access, Amex, Diners, Visa   LVs

Criterion Brasserie

222 Piccadilly W1
MAP 13 B3
01-839 7133
P NCP in Brewer Street &

Open 12–3 (Sun from 12.30) & 6–11 (Sun from 7)
Closed 25 Dec

Poire d'avocat au four £2.95   Tranche de gigot d'agneau grillée aux herbes £5.95 🅔

An elegant brasserie in Piccadilly Circus with mirrors, marbled walls and an ornate mosaic ceiling, offering a short bar menu from Roquefort cheese salad with spring onion, shellfish and mushroom soup or chicken pâté to pizzas. In the restaurant, you can have a full French meal, starting with baked snails or fish soup, and going on to pork with peppered cheese sauce, chicken cordon bleu or grilled lamb with herbs. Afternoon teas on weekdays. *No dogs.*

Credit Access, Amex, Diners, Visa   LVs

Cuddeford's Wine Bar

20 Duke Street Hill SE1
MAP 10 D4
01-403 1681
P Snowfields NCP

Open 11.30–3 & 5.30–8.30
Closed Sat, Sun & Bank Hols

Steak & kidney pie £5.20   Smoked turkey salad £3.90 🅔

Built into the brick-lined arches of London Bridge Station, this candlelit wine bar is especially popular at lunchtime, when the short regular menu of familiar favourites is supplemented by imaginative daily specials such as rack of lamb with redcurrant and red wine sauce or poached salmon with watercress mayonnaise. In the evening, only pâtés and prime cheeses are available. *No children under seven. No dogs.*

Credit Access, Amex, Diners, Visa

Daquise

20 Thurloe Street SW7
MAP 12 A5
01-589 6117
P meter parking

Open 10am–11pm
Closed 25 Dec

Stuffed cabbage £2.50   Meatballs £3.20

Daquise is a well-loved institution and standards remain consistently high. There are coffee and cakes in the morning and a full lunch menu from midday, which ranges through Continental and Polish special-ities: soups, a popular black sausage, stuffed cabbage, meatballs, sweet-cured herring, or Hungarian goulash to ome-lettes and salads. There are assorted specials: forest mushrooms perhaps or a Russian betok. Staff help those unfamiliar with the dishes. *No dogs.*

LVs

Davy's Wine Vaults

165 Greenwich High Road SE10
MAP 10 D5
01-858 7204
P own car park &

Open 12–2.30 & 5.30–10 (Sat from 7)
Closed Sun & Bank Hols

Ham off the bone £3.75   Sherry trifle
£1.75

Similar to its neighbouring sister restaur-ant, this low-ceilinged wine bar has candle-lit tables, wooden partitions and a terrace. Typical snacks from the menu might be smoked salmon, toasted 'fingers' covered with anchovy or Stilton, or a speciality like ham off the bone. For larger appetites there is a choice of pies: steak and oyster, pork and celery, chicken and chestnut or well-seasoned vegetarian. Leave room for treacle tart with clotted cream or the sherry-soaked trifle. *No dogs.*

Credit Access, Amex, Diners, Visa

Prices given are as at the time of our research and thus may change.

Dining Room

Winchester Walk, London Bridge SE1
MAP 10 D4
01-407 0337
P meter parking

Open 12.30–2.30 & 7–10
Closed Sat lunch, Sun, Mon & Bank Hols

Oyster, mushroom & bean sprout chop suey £4.75   Poached pear with carob sauce £2

Tucked away behind Southwark Cathedral and near the vegetable market, it can be difficult to find this basement restaurant set as it is down a narrow passage. The blackboard menu changes each week and offers a unique selection of mainly organic dishes and organic wines. Try the cream of cabbage soup with potato, or the leek, spinach and egg fritters with an endive and raddichio salad. Finish off with Greek yoghurt, honey and nuts for a wonderfully healthy meal. *No dogs.*

Diwana Bhelpoori House

114 Drummond Street NW1
MAP 11 C2
01-388 4867
P meter parking
Open 12–10
Closed Mon & 25 Dec

121 Drummond Street NW1
Map 11 C2
01-387 5556
P meter parking
Open noon-midnight
Closed 25 Dec

50 Westbourne Grove W2
Map 11 A3
01-221 0721
P street parking
Open 12–3 & 6–11, Sat & Sun 12–11
Closed Mon & 25 Dec

Annapurna thali £3.90   De luxe dosa
£2.90

These modest vegetarian restaurants offer menus of capably prepared Indian snacks and meals with a subtle use of herbs and spices. A newcomer to this cuisine should try a thali (set meal) like the house speciality which features a spicy lentil soup, rice, two vegetable curries, golden brown onion bhajis, raita, mango pickle and chapatis or pooris. Among other dishes are Madras dosas, crispy rice pancakes with vegetables and coconut chutney or aloo poori stuffed with potatoes and yoghurt and sweet and sour sauces, a dish from the Bombay area. To finish, try the kulfi, or Indian ice cream of milk flavoured with nuts and herbs, or the gulab jamun, spongy milk bon-bons in syrup. There are various teas and coffees and cold drinks like sweet lassi or a mango milkshake. Excellent value for money. *Unlicensed but bring your own wine. No dogs.*

Credit Access, Diners, Visa   LVs

N·E·W
ENTRY   ## Don Pepe

99 Frampton Street NW8
MAP 11 A2
01-262 3834
P street parking

Open noon–midnight
Closed 25 & 26 Dec

Seafood salad £1.50   Spanish omelette
80p

For a truly authentic taste of Spain, head for this chaotic tapas bar. You may have to jostle with the regulars to make your selection, but everyone is very friendly and helpful. Pick out a variety of dishes if you want to make a meal, or just a couple to enjoy with drinks. The simplest preparations work best – like tender octopus cooked in olive oil and pimento, grilled red peppers, fresh clams, or a classic tortilla, and the tripe will make many a convert. *No dogs.*

Credit Access, Amex, Diners, Visa

---

*Our inspectors never book in
the name of Egon Ronay's Guides.*

*They disclose their identity only
if they are considering an establishment for
inclusion in the next edition of the Guide.*

Dorchester Hotel, Promenade

Park Lane W1
MAP 12 B4
01-629 8888
P NCP in Audley Square &

Open 9am–1am

Minute steak on toast £12.50
Fillets of smoked trout £8.60
Afternoon tea £9 Gâteau £3

★ Faultless food matches the impeccable surroundings at this most elegant of hotel lounges. Arrive for afternoon tea and smartly attired, effortlessly efficient waiters will serve you freshly cut finger sandwiches of salmon, egg, cucumber or ham, wonderful oven-warm scones and dainty pastries – all to the soothing strains of music from the baby grand. Breakfast brings a basket of assorted breads and croissants, while for an elegant lunch or supper the choice includes Cornish crab soup, smoked trout fillets and a platter of cold roast beef. Seasonal berries and English cheeses round things off beautifully. *Minimum charge £5 (3–6). No dogs.* ★

Credit Access, Amex, Diners, Visa

N·E·W
ENTRY   *Dragon Gate*

7 Gerrard Street W1
MAP 13 C2
01-734 5154
P street parking

Open 12–11.30
Closed 25 Dec

Spicy eggplant £3.50   Sauté prawn with spicy sauce £5.90

A plain, neutral decor is the background for enjoying the food at London's original Szechuan restaurant. The menu offers a wide range of dishes like shrimps with hot garlic sauce, a pungent, well-flavoured spicy chicken and baked pork chops with chilli and salt. Lightly steamed Chinese greens with oyster sauce are a delightful vegetable, and well-made red pancakes a pleasing dessert. *No dogs.*

Credit Access, Amex, Diners, Visa

Draycott's

114 Draycott Avenue SW3
MAP 12 B5
01-584 5359
P meter parking

Open 12.30–2.45, 6–10.30 (Mon–Fri),
Sun 11.30–3

Closed 1 Jan & 3 days Xmas

Parma ham with fresh figs £3.25
Chicken & asparagus mille-feuille £6.75

Within walking distance of Sloane Square, this fashionable watering hole is a popular venue for Sunday brunch and elegant lunches. Sole and salmon terrine with watercress sauce, vichyssoise and tomato mousse with Parma ham are typical starters, while main courses might include rack of lamb, pork en croûte with apple stuffing and fillet steak béarnaise. Strawberry and nectarine tart, perhaps, or cheeses to finish. Filled croissants and baguettes are the only evening choice.

Credit Access, Amex, Diners, Visa

Earth Exchange

213 Archway Road N6
MAP 9 C2
01-340 6407
P street parking

Open 12–10
Closed Tues, Wed & Bank Hols

Fruit & nut curry £3.70   Strawberry
tofu cheesecake £1.10

In the basement of a craft centre and wholefood shop complex you will find this simple restaurant, furnished with pine tables, where self-service operates for the vegetarian food. All is prepared from organically grown produce, and the choice includes salads and hot dishes like aubergine and mushroom chilli or vegetable lasagne. There is always a vegan option, and sweets such as apple crumble, tofu cheesecake and carob cake round off the meal. *Non-smoking area. No dogs.*

East West Restaurant

188 Old Street EC1
MAP 9 D3
01-608 0300
P meter parking

Open 11–10 (Sat & Sun till 3)
Closed Bank Hols & 10 days Xmas

Salad bowl £1.90   Pear trifle £1.25

Japanese cooking is the big influence at this informal self-service restaurant run on strict macrobiotic lines. You can eat cheaply and well here – the daily-changing set meals are particularly good value. Choose from a selection that includes seaweed-wrapped sushi rolls, salads, miso soup and delicious ginger-glazed broccoli and cauliflower. Baked apples and couscous cake are typically wholesome sweets. *No smoking. No dogs.*

LVs

Ebury Wine Bar

139 Ebury Street SW1
MAP 12 B5
01-730 5447
P NCP in Semley Place

Open 12–2.45 & 6–10.30 (Sun till 10)
Closed 25 & 26 Dec

Cream of asparagus soup £1.60
Entrecôte steak £6.95   🅑

A favourite rendezvous for over 25 years this comfortable, friendly wine bar offers fine wines and food of consistently excellent quality. Imaginative starters like marinated mushrooms with red peppers and goat's cheese precede prime steaks and cutlets or an elaborate daily special such as spinach-stuffed boned quails with a honey and soy sauce. Sweets include hazelnut torte with raspberries. *Minimum charge £5.*

Credit Access, Amex, Diners, Visa

N·E·W
ENTRY   *Ed's Easy Diner*

12 Moor Street W1
MAP 13 C2
01-439 1955
P NCP Cambridge Circus

Open 11.30am–midnight (till 1am
Fri & Sat)
Closed 2 days Xmas

Original hamburger £2.65   Club
sandwich £2.95

Fashionably '50s in style, with its multi-coloured neon, glitzy decor and collection of Dime Selector jukeboxes providing the right music, this 21-seater diner is a fun place to enjoy first-class burgers. Extras to bulk out your 5oz of beef include grilled onions, chilli, melted cheese and guacamole, while alternative snacks range from lavishly loaded, egg bread roll sandwiches to smashing fries and sticky pecan pie. *No dogs.*

LVs

Efes Kebab House

80 Great Titchfield Street W1
MAP 11 C3
01-636 1953
P NCP Clipstone Street &

Open 12–11.30
Closed Sun, 1 Jan & 25 Dec

Diced lamb & onion kebab £4.15
Baklava £1

Named after the ancient Roman capital of Asia (Ephesus), this large, extremely popular Turkish restaurant specialises in succulent lamb and chicken kebabs cooked over an open charcoal grill. Start your meal with a selection of delicious mezes – everything from houmus, taramasalata and stuffed vine leaves to chicken in walnut sauce and fried filo pastry with egg and cheese filling. Turkish coffee and authentically sticky sweets to finish. Service can be a little too casual. Book. *No dogs.*

Credit Access, Amex, Visa **LVs**

L'Express Café

Joseph, 16 Sloane Street SW1
MAP 12 B4
01-235 9869
P NCP Cadogan Square

Open 9.30–6 (Wed till 6.30)
Closed Bank Hols

Club sandwich £5.95   Goats cheese salad £6.50 🍵

A popular, stylish haunt for Knightsbridge shoppers, this café – with friendly, efficient staff – is beneath the exclusive Joseph shop. The day starts with morning coffee and brioche, followed at lunchtime by such delicacies as quails' eggs and asparagus with a crisp endive salad, lightly poached salmon or spicy chicken tikka. There are assorted pastries and fancies to be enjoyed with excellent espresso coffee. *Minimum lunchtime charge £5.50. No dogs.*

Credit Access, Amex, Diners, Visa

Fallen Angel

65 Graham Street N1
MAP 11 D1
01-253 3996
P street parking

Open 11.30am–midnight,
Sun 12–11.30

Red dragon pie £2.90   Mushroom pastry with ragout sauce £3

Well conceived, delicious vegetarian dishes are available at this lively café, formerly a pub, near the Angel tube. Lentil and fresh coconut excels among the commendable soups. Main courses include mushroom and watercress gougère, leek and butterbean bake and chick pea Malay served with pasta, bean and leaf salads. Home-baked pastries feature devil's food cake and ginger and pear gâteau. This is a fun place, with a lively, mainly gay clientele. Cabaret on Friday and Saturday nights.

Credit Access, Visa **LVs**

Faulkners

424 Kingsland Road E8
MAP 9 D3
01-254 6152
P street parking

Open 12–2 & 5–10 (Fri from 4.15), Sat 11.30–10
Closed Sun, Bank Hols (except Good Fri) & 10 days Xmas

Cod fillet & chips £4.30   Haddock fillet & chips £4.50

Take a healthy appetite to this popular fish and chip restaurant. Huge portions of piping hot haddock – golden brown outside, deliciously moist within – come garnished with lemon wedges and accompanied by crisp, perfectly cooked chips. Other traditional favourites include fillet of plaice, cod and skate, while for a treat there's rainbow trout and Dover sole. Apple pie and custard for afters. *Minimum charge £1.75. Unlicensed. Non-smoking area. No dogs.*

LVs

Fenwicks, Salad Express

63 New Bond Street W1
MAP 11 C3
01-629 9161
P NCP Hanover Square

Open 9.30–5.30 (Thurs till 7)
Closed Sun & most Bank Hols

Open sandwich of cottage cheese & nuts
£2.35   Smoked trout salad £2.75   ℮

Flagging shoppers can recharge their batteries at this bright, popular salad bar in the basement of this West End store. Delicious cakes, pastries and croissants accompany tea or coffee, while the self-service counter has an attractive display of fresh, imaginative salads – perhaps bean, pasta and potato – colourful open sandwiches and filled jacket potatoes. Consult the blackboard for the day's soup and hot special. *Unlicensed. No smoking area. No dogs.*

LVs

N·E·W
ENTRY   ## Fifty-One Fifty-One

Chelsea Cloisters, Sloane Avenue SW3
MAP 12 B5
01-730 5151
P own car park

Open 11–3

Deep fried shrimps £3.95   Warm duck salad £6.75

On entering, spirits are immediately lifted by the bright, white decor and the Cajun music; head for the cocktail bar area near the entrance of this lively restaurant for American snacks *par excellence*. These include deep-fried aubergine filled with crab and topped with hollandaise, escargots baked in puff pastry with buffalo mozzarella and wild mushrooms, blackened shrimps with mustard sauce, or oysters served on the half shell. Valet parking, too! *No dogs.*

Credit Access, Amex, Diners, Visa

N·E·W
ENTRY   ## La Fin de la Chasse

176 Stoke Newington Church Street
N16
MAP 9 D2
01-254 5975
P street parking

Open 7pm–11pm, Sun 12.30–2.30
Closed Mon, Bank Hols, 2 wks Easter,
2 wks Aug, 1 wk Xmas (except 31st Dec)

Scallops with white butter sauce £2.40
Veal liver with mustard sauce £6.90

Booking is essential at this long, narrow restaurant owing to the great popularity of the imaginative and well prepared dishes on offer. Daily specials are chalked up on a blackboard to supplement the regular menu, which features starters like charlotte of scallops, home smoked duck and smoked salmon mousse with cognac. Main courses include roast chicken with pine kernels on fresh leaf spinach, lamb ragout with red wine and garlic and a vegetarian dish. Interesting desserts. *No dogs.*

Credit Access, Amex, Visa

Fino's Wine Cellar

19 Swallow Street W1
MAP 13 A3
01-734 2049
P NCP in Brewer Street

Open 11.30–3 & 5.30–11
Closed Sun & Bank Hols

Paella £3.40   Gâteau £1.85   ℮

Dim red lighting, risqué artwork and latin waiters add to the rakish charms of this brick-vaulted wine bar in the cellars of an old Edwardian building. Excellent sandwiches filled with everything from hot salt beef to cheese and chutney, plus salads based on, say, seafood or game pie, are always popular, while more substantial fare ranges from a hearty blackboard special like shepherd's pie to paella, pasta and burgers with chips. *No children. No dogs.*

Credit Access, Amex, Diners, Visa   **LVs**

Fino's Wine Cellar

12 North Row W1
MAP 11 B3
01-491 7261
P NCP at Marble Arch

Open 11.30–2.30 & 6.30–10.30
Closed Sat eve, all Sun & Bank Hols

Veal scaloppine alla fino £5.40   Crème
caramel £1.80   🍴

Low-ceilinged rooms and winding stairs
add to the atmospheric charms of this
popular wine bar on two floors. The cellar
offers light dishes like lasagne and chicken
pie: go upstairs for waitress service or
more substantial offerings such as hot salt
beef, calf's liver with sage or pan-fried veal
topped with cheese and asparagus. Stick
to fresh fruit or crème caramel for dessert.
Sandwiches available in both bars. *No
dogs.*

Credit Access, Amex, Diners, Visa   **LVs**

First Out

52 St Giles High Street WC2
MAP 13 C1
01-240 8042
P Central YMCA NCP

Open 11am–midnight
Closed Sun & Bank Hols

Vegetable hotpot £1.80   Marron glacé
dome £1.30

A youthful crowd gathers to catch up on
the latest gossip over tea, coffee and cakes
at this popular and noisy vegetarian restaurant in the shadow of Centre Point.
From midday until they run out, there's
more substantial fare in the shape of hearty
soups, wholemeal flans (aduki bean or leek
with a creamy wine sauce), quiches and
salads such as spicy chick pea or bulgar
wheat. Simple sweets include cheesecake,
pear flan and a fruit pie. *No dogs.*

LVs

Food for Thought

31 Neal Street WC2
MAP 13 C1
01-836 0239
P NCP in Shelton Street

Open 12–8
Closed Sat, Sun, Bank Hols & 2 wks
Xmas

Shepherdess pie £1.60   Strawberry &
chocolate scrunch £1.20   🍴 🍵

High creativity but low prices keep the
customers happy at this delightful little
basement vegetarian restaurant. The imaginative self-service selection changes
daily, but expect a tasty soup like sweetcorn and walnut, fresh, imaginative salads,
a choice of hot savouries (cauliflower and
mange-tout fondue, creamy watercress and
red pepper quiche), and lovely sweets such
as strawberry chocolate scrunch. Snack
on flapjacks and coconut cake at any time.
Unlicensed. No smoking. No dogs.

LVs

Gachon's

269 Creek Road, Greenwich SE10
MAP 10 D5
01-853 4461
P street parking

Open 12–2.30 & 6.30–10.30
Closed Sun & Tues eves, all Mon, Bank
Hols & 3 wks Jan

Lamb in redcurrant sauce £8.25   Terrine
of chicken livers £1.65

Though looking a trifle uncared for, this
small friendly bistro offers sound and
enjoyable cooking. Stuffed mushrooms
and rich onion soup are popular starters.
Daily specials supplement the regular
menu and may include a magnificent beef
bourguignon, chicken chasseur and a
vegetable-filled pancake. Crème brûlée,
mousse and gâteaux round things off. Tea,
coffee and assorted pastries are an extra
attraction on Saturday and Sunday afternoons. *No dogs.*

Credit Access, Diners, Visa

Geale's

2 Farmer Street W8
MAP 10 B4
01-727 7969
P street parking &

Open 12–3 & 6–11
Closed Sun, Mon (& Tues after Bank
Hols), 3 wks Aug & 2 wks Xmas

Fresh haddock £3.50   Deep fried shark
£3.50

The menu is marked up on a huge
blackboard at this very popular fish and
chip restaurant with its yellow-clothed
tables and very decent white wine list.
Nothing has changed here for years; the
fish is still delivered daily and includes
everything from cod to Torbay sole and
from haddock to black tipped shark from
the Seychelles. The portions are splendid,
the batter crisp and the chips are hand-cut.
There are a few simple starters and
puddings. *No dogs.*

Credit Access **LVs**

Gino's

70 The Mall, Ealing W5
MAP 10 A4
01-567 5237
P street parking

Open 12–3 & 7–11.30 (Fri & Sat till
midnight)
Closed Sun lunch & Bank Hols

Spaghetti alla mafia £3.30   Pollo alla
crema £5.40   ☺

A very Italian place which is so popular
that you often have to wait at the bar.
There is a varied menu of traditional Italian
pizza and pasta dishes (from spaghetti
carbonara to scaloppina al limone) plus
daily specials such as spicy Italian sausage,
grilled calf's liver, tortellini alla Parma or
fresh mussels. Sweets include zuppa Ing-
lese (a trifle with Italian meringue) and
chocolate gâteau. The atmosphere is lively,
so be warned! *No dogs.*

LVs

Goring Hotel Lounge

15 Beeston Place, Grosvenor
Gardens SW1
MAP 12 C5
01-834 8211
P NCP in Buckingham Palace Road

Open 10am–midnight

Hors d'oeuvre of seafood £5.50
Afternoon tea £5   ☺ ♣

Sink back into a comfortable leather
armchair and enjoy the timeless ritual of
afternoon tea in this civilised hotel lounge.
Excellent sandwiches, oven-warm scones
and the lightest of pastries are served from
the trolley, while throughout the day an
appealing selection of snacks include soup,
croque-monsieur, Welsh rarebit, a platter
of cold meats and colourful open sandwiches. Home-made ice creams and fruit
sorbets to finish. *No dogs.*

Credit Access, Amex, Diners, Visa

Govindas

9 Soho Street W1
MAP 13 B1
01-437 3662
P meter parking

Open 8.30–11 (Sun 12–4)
Closed 25 & 26 Dec & Jan 1

Govinda thali £4.90   Fruit trifle £1.20

Despite the difficulties of keeping to the
strict Krishna rules of food preparation,
the food here is remarkably varied. The
day starts with home-baked filled rolls and
sandwiches, muesli, yoghurt, fruit, and
simple cakes. From noon there are hot
savouries: lasagne, pizza, bean pot or
delicious subji (vegetables and herbs
cooked in their own juices) along with
salads and tasty olive bread. *Minimum
charge £2. Unlicensed. No smoking. No
dogs.*

Credit Access, Amex, Diners **LVs**

Granary

39 Albemarle Street W1
MAP 13 A3
01-493 2978
P street parking

Open 11.30–8 (Sat till 2.30)

Closed Sun & Bank Hols

Avocado stuffed with prawns, spinach & cheese £5.50   Beef burgundy £5.50   Cauliflower & aubergine lasagne £5.25   Seafood pasta £5.50

★ The surroundings in the Shah family's counter-service restaurant are modest; quarry tiled floor, some bare brick walls and pavement tables, but the extensive selection of consistently superb home-made dishes taste as good as they look. Service is swift and caring. Tender beef stroganoff on a bed of tasty rice has a flavoursome sauce topped with yoghurt. Other hot dishes are lamb, lemon and mint casserole and paella and pan-fried cod. Rare roast beef is an excellent cold choice. The puddings are splendid – delicious lemon sponge with plenty of apple and blackcurrant hot from the oven is a typical example. *Minimum lunchtime charge £3. No dogs.* ★

LVs

Green Cottage

9 New College Parade, Finchley Road
NW3
MAP 9 B3
01-722 5305
P street parking

Open 12–11.30
Closed 25 & 26 Dec

Wun tun soup £1.25   Roast pork & rice £2.50

Traditional Cantonese roast meats, appetisingly displayed in the window, are the ideal choice for just-a-biters at this popular, pleasantly modern Chinese restaurant. A combination of golden-brown roast duck, Char siu (roast marinated fillet of pork) and crispy belly pork, served on rice, makes for a substantial and well-priced meal. Popular alternatives include sweet and sour prawns and fried beef in oyster sauce. *No dogs.*

Green House

16 Royal Exchange EC3
MAP 10 D4
01-236 7077
P NCP in Broad Street

Open 11.30–3 & 5–7.30
Closed Sat, Sun & Bank Hols

Italian sausages £3   Smoked salmon £2.50

Next to the Bank of England, set into the walls of the Royal Exchange, right in the heart of the city, the intimate atmosphere is enhanced with mahogany wall panelling and marble bar. Appropriately, champagne is offered with accompanying snacks: dressed crab, plump prawns, pâté, ham or rare roast beef, quails' eggs and game pie. Seating is limited to just a few places, and the menu is also short and sweet. *No children. No dogs.*

Green's Champagne & Oyster Bar

36 Duke Street SW1
MAP 12 C4
01-930 4566
P NCP in Cavendish Hotel

Open 11.30–3 & 5.30–10.45
Closed Sun eve & Bank Hols

Salmon fish cakes £8.50   Six
oysters £9   🕾

At this stylish, mahogany panelled wine
bar in St James's you can be sure of
enjoying succulent seafood. For a special
treat, sit in the intimate booths and be
tempted by fresh lobster, salmon and
plump oysters. For the more budget
conscious there's a choice of dishes like
smoked salmon with scrambled eggs,
kipper pâté or for meat eaters steak
sandwiches. The wines have been scrupulously chosen and reasonably priced. The
Soave Classico is outstanding. *No dogs.*

Credit Access, Amex, Diners, Visa

Grill St Quentin

136 Brompton Road SW3
MAP 12 B4
01-581 8377
P NCP in Montpelier Street

Open noon–midnight (Sun till 11.30)

Green salad with grilled goat's cheese
£3.50   Veal chop £9.50   🕾

Concealed lighting in the low ceiling and
pale lemon walls with mirrors create a
light, bright look around the closely
packed tables. Care has gone into the
simple menu based on dependable cooking,
and the grills include steaks, rack of lamb,
breast of chicken and duck served with
chips. Start with gazpacho, smoked
salmon, fish pâté or spinach soup. Conclude with fruit tart, chocolate mousse or
floating islands in crême Anglaise. *No
dogs.*

Credit Access, Amex, Diners, Visa

Gurkhas Tandoori

23 Warren Street W1
MAP 11 C2
01-388 1640
P street parking

Open 12–3 & 6–12
Closed 25 & 26 Dec

Karang sekuwa £2.95   Lamb karahi
£3.25

Nepalese artefacts decorate this tiny, popular restaurant where it is necessary to
book at peak times. The authentic food
makes good use of fresh herbs and spices.
You might choose freshly fried onion
bhaji, tender chicken tikka in a well
flavoured masala sauce or lean lamb in an
excellent sauce with fresh ginger, and
freshly baked nan bread. Among the
vegetable dishes is a vanta tarkari –
chopped aubergine with fresh coriander
and other fragrant spices. *No dogs.*

Credit Access, Amex, Diners, Visa   **LVs**

Gyngleboy

27 Spring Street W2
MAP 11 A3
01-723 3351
P meter parking

Open 11–3 & 5.30–9
Closed Sat, Sun, Bank Hols, 1 Jan & 25,
26 Dec

Soup & bread £1.80   Beef bourguignon
£6.95   🕾

A traditional, studiously Dickensian wine
bar two minutes walk from Paddington
Station, and consequently very handy if
you have a long wait for your train.
Intimate candlelit tables and sawdust-
covered floors are the setting for enjoying
the cold meat or fish salads and sandwiches, game pie and a good selection of
cheeses. Puddings include apple pie and
seasonal fruits, and there is a good
selection of wines by the glass or bottle.
No dogs.

Credit Access, Amex, Diners, Visa

Harrods Dress & Upper Circles

Knightsbridge SW1
MAP 12 B4
01-730 1234
P own car park in Brompton Place

Open 9–5.45, Wed 9.30–6.45
Closed Sun & most Bank Hols

Prawn open sandwich £1.80   Treacle
& walnut pie £1.10

Located on different floors but offering a
similar selection of excellent snacks, these
two self-service restaurants provide a
welcome oasis for flagging shoppers. A
choice of savouries might include elegant
open sandwiches (the smoked salmon and
cream cheese is particularly good), freshly
made salads and quiches, with tandoori
chicken adding a touch of spice. Good
breads and top-notch pâtisserie (like the
lovely moist, dark chocolate gâteau) complete the picture. *No dogs.*

Credit Access, Amex, Diners, Visa

Harrods Georgian Restaurant & Terrace

Knightsbridge SW1
MAP 12 B4
01-730 1234
P own car park in Brompton Place   &

Open Restaurant: 9–11 & 3.45–5.30;
Terrace: 3.30–5.30
Closed Sun & most Bank Hols

Full English breakfast £6.25   Grand
buffet tea £5.75   ❤

A splendid display of cakes and pastries,
including caramel éclairs, mille-feuilles and
fruit tartlets greet you at the elegant
Georgian restaurant. Breakfasts are available in the mornings, and there's a carvery
set lunch between 12 and 2.30pm. For a
more informal atmosphere, the adjoining
Terrace offers tasty finger sandwiches as
well as a limitless choice of desserts.
*Minimum charge (restaurant) £3.95
(mornings) and £5.75 (afternoons). Non-
smoking area. No dogs.*

Credit Access, Amex, Diners, Visa

*Prices given are as at the time of our research
and thus may change.*

Harry Morgan's

31 St John's Wood High Street NW8
MAP 11 B1
01-722 1869
P side streets

Open 12–3 & 6–10, Sun 12–10
Closed Fri eve & 1 wk Xmas

Plate of salt beef £5.25   Lockshen
pudding £1.50

The local Jewish community flock to this
much-loved, little changed, restaurant to
enjoy chicken noodle soup, classic gefilta
fish, and arguably the best salt beef in
town. Pickled cucumbers, chopped liver
and omelettes are lighter alternatives,
whilst heartier appetites can plump for
veal escalope, stewed meat balls and roast
chicken. End your meal with the wonderful
vermicelli-based lockshen pudding. *No
dogs.*

Hiders

755 Fulham Road SW6
MAP 10 B5
01-736 2331
P street parking

Open 12.30–2.30
Closed Sat lunch, all Sun, Bank Hols
& 1 wk Xmas

Boiled silverside of beef with dumplings
£6.25   Arbroath smokies £3.75 ⊟

Huge mirrors, paintings and luxurious drapes provide the stylish background for an elegant light lunch selected from the evening carte or simpler fortnightly-changing menu. Rich onion soup or rondel of salmon topped with a walnut and prune crust might precede classic calf's liver with sage or splendid silverside of beef accompanied by horseradish dumplings and gorgeous gravy. Lovely sweets, too, like purée of raspberries with sherry zabaglione. *No dogs.*

Credit Access, Visa

Hoults

20 Bellevue Road, Wandsworth Common
SW17
MAP 10 C6
01-767 1858
P street parking

Open 12.30–2.45 & 6.30–10.45
Closed 1 wk Xmas

Spicy chicken with yoghurt £2.95
Steak & kidney pie £5.50 ⊟

Relaxed and easy-going, this popular wine bar has a sunny terrace overlooking leafy Wandsworth Common for alfresco eating. The monthly-changing menu offers competently prepared, brasserie-style favourites such as deep-fried Cambozola with gooseberry preserve, veal Marsala, roast rack of lamb and grilled lemon sole. Simple home-made sweets (apple pie, crème brûlée) and an interesting selection of wines by the glass. *No dogs.*

Credit Access, Amex, Visa

Hung Toa

54 Queensway W2
MAP 11 A3
01-727 6017
P NCP Queensway

Open 12–11
Closed 25 & 26 Dec

Soup £1.10   Roast crispy pork £4.40

A mouthwatering window display of magnificent roast meats attracts a steady stream of customers through the doors of this bustling Cantonese restaurant. Succulent, crispy duck or pork, served on a generous bed of rice with soya sauce, make magnificent eating – or choose one of the substantial one-plate rice and noodle dishes if your preference is less carnivorous. Also on the menu are various soups, beef and chicken dishes. Greater attention to decor and service would be welcome. *No dogs.*

Hyatt Carlton Tower, Chinoiserie

2 Cadogan Place SW1
MAP 12 B4
01-235 5411
P NCP in Cadogan Place &

Open 8am–midnight (till 1am Fri & Sat)

Western cobb salad £7.20   Set
afternoon tea £7.50 ◆

One of the classiest settings in town for a light meal or snack, this sumptuously elegant hotel lounge has the smart, attentive staff and stylish menu to match. Continental breakfast starts the day, followed from 11am by the main choice: delicious sandwiches and salads, soups, perhaps a featherlight quiche or prawn risotto, with seasonal berries among desserts. Mouthwatering cakes accompany afternoon tea. *Minimum charge of £5 from 12 to 7. No dogs.*

Credit Access, Amex, Diners, Visa

Hyde Park Hotel, Park Room

66 Knightsbridge SW1
MAP 12 B4
01-235 2000
P Motcomb Street NCP &

Open 7–10.30, 12.30–2.30 & 4–6 (Sun 8–11 & 4–6)

Danish pastry £1.30 Afternoon tea £8.50 ⊞ 🍵

A marvellous setting for enjoying all the trappings of a grand occasion created by this lovely Edwardian hotel. The room looks out over Hyde Park itself, and is particularly smart with pretty china and crisp table linen. Over a dozen quality teas can be sipped with smoked salmon sandwiches, scones, meringues and pastries. At lunchtime try the splendid buffet. Italian cuisine is featured in the evenings. *Non-smoking area. No dogs.*

Credit Access, Amex, Diners, Visa

Ikeda

30 Brook Street W1
MAP 11 B3
01-629 2730
P meter parking

Open 12.30–2.30
Closed Sat, Sun, Bank Hols & 10 days Xmas

Buta shoga-yaki £9.50 Sashimi lunch £11

Booking is essential at this very friendly yet tiny Japanese restaurant where Just-a-Biters will find the set menu lunches a good value introduction to Japanese dishes. Priced by the main course, the lunch also includes an appetiser, soup, home-made pickles, and fresh fruit. For the adventurous, the sashimi lunch (raw fish) is recommended, but there are also chicken and sirloin steak or tempura (prawns and vegetables deep-fried in light batter). *No dogs.*

Credit Access, Amex, Diners, Visa

Ikkyu

67 Tottenham Court Road W1
MAP 11 C2
01-636 9280
P street parking

Open 12.30–2.30 & 6–10.30 (Sun from 7)
Closed Sun lunch, all Sat & 8 days Xmas

Yakitori £6.75 Sukiyaki £8.95

You must book at this bustling, down-to-earth basement Japanese restaurant. Single diners are seated at the sushi bar, and there are booth-style tables for more intimate eating. The cooking is basic, honest and skilful, and the staff will help you choose from the varied menu. Some dishes are served in the pot and there are rice dishes and a selection of raw fish for sushi and sashimi. Try the yakitori or bean-curd steak with flaked bonito. *No dogs.*

Credit Access, Amex, Diners, Visa

Indian Veg. Bhel Poori House

N·E·W ENTRY

92 Chapel Market N1
MAP 11 D1
01-837 4607
P street parking

Open 12–3 & 6–11
Closed 25 Dec

Vegetable biryani £2.90 Gujerati thali £3.50

The attractive new Bhel Poori House has quickly established a strong following. The menu gives careful descriptions of dishes – lightly fried samosas filled with spicy vegetables and a tangy tomato relish or a choice of well prepared thali dishes. At weekends a buffet lunch features five different curries and two rice dishes and the invitation to eat as much as you like. There is a short list of traditional Indian desserts. *No dogs.*

Credit Access, Amex, Diners, Visa **LVs**

Inn on the Park Lounge

Hamilton Place, Park Lane W1
MAP 12 B4
01-499 0888
P own car park &

Open 9am–2am (Sun till 1am)

Complete tea £7.50   Croque
monsieur £5   Executive salad
£8.50   French pastry £1.50
🕒 🍵

★ Sink back into a plush, comfortable couch at this sumptuous panelled lounge decorated with magnificent plants and fresh flower arrangements and let your appetite be beguiled by a most delectable selection of elegant snacks. Breakfast here is a feast of seasonal fruits, juices, hot blueberry muffins, croissants and Danish pastries served until 11.30, while from midday the menu features such delights as Parma ham, smoked salmon and baby lobster, chicken pancakes, first-class club sandwiches and grilled lamb cutlets. Faultless cakes and pastries and generously filled sandwiches accompany morning coffee and the three set afternoon teas (served from 3–6). Impeccable service. *No dogs.* ★

Credit Access, Amex, Diners, Visa

Inter-Continental Hotel, Coffee House

1 Hamilton Place W1
MAP 12 B4
01-409 3131
P own car park &

Open 7am–midnight (Sat 2am)

Kedgeree £4.90   Calf's liver with
rösti potatoes £6.70   Tuna &
prawn salad £7.30   Hot waffle &
rum pot £4   🕒 🍵

★ From breakfast through lunch, afternoon tea and dinner, the Coffee House at this modern hotel offers some outstandingly memorable dishes. Breakfast is a buffet of wide choice, offering both the expected and the exciting. Available until a civilised 11am its delights include French cinnamon toast, kedgeree or a celebration champagne breakfast that becomes a celebration in itself. You can select a mix and match lunch from another extensive and beautifully displayed buffet or choose from an à la carte menu of imagination and style. Pastries and desserts are superb and the afternoon tea is justly popular. Children's menu. *No dogs.* ★

Credit Access, Amex, Diners, Visa

Jade Garden

15 Wardour Street W1
MAP 13 B3
01-439 7851
P Swiss Centre NCP

Open dim sum 12–5
Closed 3 days Xmas

Fried mixed vegetable dumplings £1.10
Split pea pudding £1.10

Some of the best dim sum around – beautifully fresh, always piping hot – attracts a constant stream of hungry customers to this long-established Chinese restaurant. Of particular note are the delicious crispy mixed vegetable dumplings, moist paper-wrapped prawns, chicken feet with black bean sauce and consistently excellent glutinous rice wrapped in lotus leaves. To finish, try the lotus paste buns or split pea pudding. *No dogs.*

Credit Access, Amex, Diners, Visa

Jeeves Wine Cellar

139 Whitfield Street W1
MAP 11 C2
01-387 1952
P meter parking

Open 11.30am–midnight
Closed Sun, Bank Hols & 1 wk Xmas

Chilli con carne £3.95   Lasagne £3.50
🅰

Popular with local business people, this lively basement wine bar offers enjoyable light snacks in an informal atmosphere. An appetising cold table displays home-cooked ham, fresh roast turkey, pâté, savoury pies and colourful salads, while the hot choice includes daily-changing specials like moussaka and chicken Oriental. There are vegetarian dishes, too, plus simple sweets (fruit salad, gâteau) and cheeses to finish. *No dogs.*

Credit Access, Amex, Diners, Visa

Joe Allen

13 Exeter Street WC2
MAP 13 D2
01-836 0651
P street parking

Open midday–1am (Sun till midnight)
Closed 25 & 26 Dec

Chicken fillet brochette £6   Fish of the day £6.50

Booking is essential at this lively American-style restaurant which remains as fashionable as ever. The extensive blackboard menu makes choice difficult, but there are excellent salads, favourites like Southern fried chicken and barbecued spare ribs, and daily specials from calf's liver with onions to tender veal in a mushroom sauce. Pecan pie is a popular sweet and there is also a selection of cakes. Service is appropriately slick. *No dogs.*

Julie's Bar

137 Portland Road W11
MAP 10 B4
01-727 7985
P street parking

Open 12–2.45, 4–6 & 7–10.45 (Sun 4.30–6, 7–10)
Closed 4 days Easter & 4 days Xmas

Sausage & mash £4.95   Norfolk treacle tart £1.95   🅰

Stained glass windows, wooden pews and labyrinthine rooms add to the charms of this character wine bar. Daily-changing lunch and evening menus offer much to tempt the tastebuds, from celery and Stilton soup or fried goat's cheese among starters, to such delicious main courses as cold poached salmon and guinea fowl in a creamy lime sauce. Delectable puddings include cherry cream choux buns and apricot and blackcurrant tart. Afternoon teas also available. No children in the evenings.

Justin de Blank

54 Duke Street W1
MAP 11 B3
01-629 3174
P Selfridges car park

Open 8.30–3.15 (Sat till 2)
& 4.15–9

Closed Sat eve, all Sun & Bank
Hols

Stuffed aubergine £3.75
Vegetable lasagne £3.75 Pork
medallions £4.10 Praline mousse
£1.80 🍵 🐚

★ A lively restaurant where an impressive choice of
carefully prepared hot and cold dishes is displayed on
the counter. Interesting, well-presented options such
as apple and celery soup, broccoli quiche and sweet
and sour pork accompany super dishes for vegetarians – the sweetcorn and potato cakes with fresh
vegetables and careful seasoning are a good example,
plus the filo pastry parcels filled with spinach,
mushrooms and cheese. Equally tempting are the
crisp salads, such as pasta and fruit, and the cold
meats, terrines, pâtés and roulades. Lightly textured
and packed with flavour blackcurrant cheesecake
makes a fine finish; alternatively sample the apple
crumble, orange mousse or delicious fruit brûlée.
Non-smoking area. No dogs.

Credit Access, Visa **LVs**

Justin de Blank at General Trading Company

144 Sloane Street SW1
MAP 12 B5
01-730 6400
P NCP in Cadogan Place

Open 9–5.30 (Sat till 1.45)

Closed Sun, Bank Hols & 2–3
wks Xmas

Cream of turnip soup £1.85
Spinach roulade £4.35 Banana
brûlée £1.85 Lemon crunch cake
85p 🍵

★ Like the store above it, this restaurant displays high
quality and good taste. It is attractively decorated
with terracotta floor tiles, rough hewn beams on the
walls, round tables and bentwood chairs. A most
charming feature is the conservatory where you can
sit to eat your choice of three healthy and substantial
set breakfasts whilst you read the newspapers
provided. The blackboard menu offers a light lunch
of soups, imaginative salads, and snacks such as
mushroom mousse and cold roast beef. The puddings
are divine and, like everything else, the cakes and
biscuits are fresh and baked on the premises. Try the
delicious Afghan biscuits (packed tight with chocolate and nuts), the date and coconut cake, or the
banana bread.

LVs

Kitchen Yakitori

12 Lancashire Court, New Bond
Street W1
MAP 11 C3
01-629 9984
P NCP in Hanover Square

Open 12–2.30
Closed Sun, Bank Hols & 10 days Xmas

Sashimi lunch £8 Yazizakana lunch £5

Set lunchtime menus at this tiny, teeming
Japanese restaurant are a wonderful introduction to Japanese cooking. A scruffy
courtyard bodes a very basic but clean
interior and the ingredients are excellent.
Select one of a dozen lunches including
tonkatsu (pork), natto (fermented soya
beans), ebi-frai (king prawns) or a rice dish
katsu-ju (pork). All are served with soya
bean soup, Japanese pickles, rice, fresh
fruit and Japanese tea. For the adventurous, eel dishes are the chef's speciality. *No
dogs.*

Lantern

23 Malvern Road NW6
MAP 9 B3
01-624 1796
P street parking

Open 12–3 & 7–midnight (Sun noon–
11)
Closed 25 & 26 Dec

Lamb's kidneys Florentine £4.25
Choux de crabes £1.85 ⊖

A simple formula and consistent standards
make Lantern and its sister restaurant, La
Cloche, popular choices. The menu and
decor are simple, the atmosphere informal
and the service prompt. Old favourites on
the menu include tagliatelle with meat or
vegetarian topping, chicken and asparagus
pancakes, cream of spinach soup with a
hint of lemon, well-made salmon cake with
anchovy sauce and a good filling portion
of duck en croûte. Traditional Sunday
lunch. *No dogs.*

Credit Access, Visa

Laurent

428 Finchley Road NW2
MAP 9 B2
01-794 3603
P street parking

Open 12–2 & 6–11
Closed Sun eve, Bank Hols & 3 wks Aug

Brique à l'oeuf £2 Couscous complet
£7

Laurent Farrugia's simple little café-style
restaurant has become a magnet to lovers
of authentic Tunisian couscous. Apart
from the starter of brique à l'oeuf (egg in a
crisp pancake), he offers just three choices:
basic vegetable couscous, couscous with
lamb and vegetables and royal couscous –
vegetables, lamb and a mixed grill served
with couscous. Finish with crêpe suzette,
sorbet and a cup of mint tea or Turkish
coffee. Children's portions. *No dogs.*

Credit Access, Visa

Lindas

4 Fernhead Road W9
MAP 9 B3
01-969 9387
P street parking

Open 12–2 & 6–10.15
Closed Sat lunch, all Sun, Bank Hols
& 2 wks annual holiday

Chicken with ginger £1.50 Spring rolls
£1.50

Linda Blaney and her English husband
Robin run this bright, modest little restaurant specialising in Vietnamese cooking, in
cheerful, informal fashion. Try their subtly
flavoured beef with rice stick soup, beautifully light spring rolls, spicy spare ribs or
a special mixed omelette. First-timers to
this delicate cuisine will find the set meals
good value and an excellent introduction.
*Minimum charge £5 in the evening. No
dogs.*

Credit Access, Diners, Visa

Lok Ho Fook

4 Gerrard Street W1
MAP 13 C2
01-437 2001
P NCP in Cambridge Circus

Open Dim sum 12–6; Full menu
12–2am
Closed 2 days Xmas

Har kau 95p   Sweet & sour wun tun £1

Situated at the pedestrianised end of Gerrard Street is this large and bustling Chinese restaurant, where you can sample good-quality dim sum such as deep-fried crab meat balls, paper-wrapped prawns and spring rolls. Delicately steamed beef siu mai or mie kai (rice in lotus leaves with meaty filling) are other alternatives, or you could opt for either a one-plate noodle or rice dish. No dogs.

Credit Access, Amex, Diners, Visa   LVs

Lou Pescadou

241 Old Brompton Road SW5
MAP 12 A5
01-370 1057
P meter parking

Open 12–3 & 7–12
Closed 10 days Xmas & all Aug

Soupe de poissons £3.80   Pizza fruits de
mer £4.80

Ring the bell to enter this bustling bistro-style restaurant with its closely-packed tables and bright Mediterranean scenes on rough white walls. Seafood is something of a speciality, the choice ranging from mussels to monkfish, mullet, oysters, clams and langoustines, and there are also steaks and a few daily dishes. Pizzas, pasta, omelettes and salads provide enjoyable light meals; traditional French sweets or cheeses to finish. No booking. No dogs.

Credit Access, Amex, Diners, Visa   LVs

Louis' Pâtisserie

12 Finchley Road NW3
/32 Heath Street NW3
MAP 9 B3/MAP 9 B2
01-722 8100/01-435 9908
P street parking   & (Finchley Rd)

Open Finchley Road: 9–6;
Heath Street: 9.30–6 (Mon from 10)
Closed 25 & 26 Dec

Sausage roll 60p   Baked cheesecake £1

These traditional pâtisseries of long standing continue to offer much that will tempt the sweet toothed with their delectable array of cakes, pastries and biscuits. There are a few savoury offerings (sausage rolls and croissants), but many deliciously sweet things – chestnut slice is an irresistible medley of layered sponge and cream with piped chestnut pûree, cheesecake is of the crumbly baked variety and the choice seems endless. Unlicensed. Non-smoking area. No dogs.

Macarthurs

147 Church Road SW13
MAP 10 A5
01-748 3630
P street parking

Open 12.30–2.30 & 6–11.30, Sat
12.30–midnight, Sun 12.30–11.30
Closed 1 Jan & 25, 26 & 31 Dec

Bacon burger £3.15   Chocolate brownie
£1.30

A cheerful, American-style diner with glass doors opening on to the pavement when it's fine. Juicy coarse ground hamburgers come in 13 different varieties here, from the more sophisticated blue cheese mushrooms in white wine sauce to tot-sized for the kids. Add a baked potato and a crisp salad, or opt for a tasty alternative like spicy spare ribs or vegetarian lasagne. Sinful sweets (pecan pie, devil's food cake) to finish. No dogs.

Credit Access, Amex, Diners, Visa   LVs

Maison Bertaux

28 Greek Street W1
Map 13 C2
01-437 6007
P NCP in Gerrard Place

Open 9–6

Closed Sun, Mon, Bank Hols
& following day & 4 wks July–Aug

Cheese tarts 60p   Fresh fruit tarts
£1.60   Danish pastries 70p
Florentines 90p

★ Almost unchanged since it opened in 1871 (apart from when M Vignaud's bakery moved from the basement to the upper floors three decades ago), this paragon of pâtisseries has been a Soho landmark for generations. The indispensable Mme Vignaud and her loyal staff care for customers. Order downstairs and then go up to enjoy your good pot of tea and such sweet delights as the gâteaux, pastries, fruit tarts, éclairs, almondines, florentines, cheesecake and mont blancs, or chocolate truffles that are second to none. If you prefer savoury items, choose cheese-filled croissants, tarts and individual quiches. *Unlicensed. Non-smoking area. No dogs.* ★

Credit Visa

Maison Bouquillon, Le Montmartre

45 Moscow Road W2
MAP 11 A3
01-727 4897
P meter parking

Open 8.30am–9.30pm
Closed 25 & 26 Dec

Beef Wellington £4.75   Chicken Kiev
£2.75

The cabinet display of excellent home baking almost fills this simply appointed little pâtisserie, whose tables are packed with happy customers throughout its long opening hours. Join them in a selection that includes rich chocolate gâteau, éclairs, Danish pastries and shiny-topped fruit flans, all delicious with a first-class brew. For savoury-tooths, the range is from cheese croissants to lunchtime salmon coulibiac.

LVs

Maison Pechon Pâtisserie Française

127 Queensway W2
MAP 11 A3
01-229 0746
P meter parking

Open 8–5 (Sun from 9)
Closed Bank Hols

Vegetable moussaka £2.20   Strawberry
tart 75p

Go through to the rear of the pâtisserie into the simple tea room where the choice of cakes and rolls is almost overwhelming. Danish pastries, éclairs, fruit tarts and slices, cheesecakes, meringues and macaroons are just some, and there are also savoury delights like sausage rolls, filled baguettes and quiches. At lunchtime, hot dishes appear – lasagne, veal escalope, omelettes or vegetable moussaka. Cakes and pastries can be taken out as well when you leave. *No dogs.*

Credit Access, Visa   LVs

Maison Sagne

105 Marylebone High Street W1
MAP 11 B2
01-935 6240
P NCP in Moxon Street &

Open 9–5 (Sat till 12.30)
Closed Sun & Bank Hols

Asparagus omelette £2.50   Mont blanc
90p

Pâtisserie 'par excellence' is the most fitting epithet for this bastion of exquisite pastries. Since 1921 hot brioches, croissants and flaky sausage rolls have come from the pristine kitchens to satisfy the most discerning breakfaster. Trompe l'oeil walls, white clad waiters and a window burgeoning with éclairs, walnut and caramel tarts, hazelnut meringues and macaroons are part of the timeless setting. Omelettes and ravioli are among the concessions to traditional lunchtime fare. *Unlicensed. No smoking. No dogs.*

Mandeer

21 Hanway Place, Tottenham
Court Road W1
MAP 11 C3
01-323 0660
P NCP under Central YMCA

Open 12–3 & 6–10.15

Closed Sun, Bank Hols & 1 wk
Xmas

Samosas £1.30   Patra £1.75
Mandeer deluxe thali £8.50
Tofu special £3.75 🫖

A series of elegant arches leads you down to the basement restaurant, where the atmosphere is tinted with incense and spices. Terracotta tiling, low overhanging table lamps and spacious tables create a very aesthetic environment for enjoying the beautiful Indian vegetarian cooking. Unspiced dishes are available, and special pans are used for these to preserve their distinctive taste. The extensive menu ranges from starters like samosas, bhajis, puris and dosas to more complicated main courses such as dried yellow peas in special sweet and sour sauce and onions, served with fine Indian vermicelli and green chutney and topped with yoghurt. Set meals (thalis) are excellent value. Good Indian desserts. *No smoking. No dogs.*

LVs

Manna

4 Erskine Road NW3
MAP 11 B1
01-722 8028
P street parking &

Open 6.30pm–11.30pm
Closed 4 days Xmas

Leek & cauliflower Dijonnaise £4.40
Mango mousse £1.75

A distinctive red-railed portico frames the doorway to this much-loved restaurant offering straightforward, enjoyable vegetarian fare. Mushrooms aïoli, stuffed tacos and crisp, colourful salads make light snacks or starters, while for something more substantial there are savoury flans (try zucchini and spring onion) and daily specials like courgette and celery Dijonnaise or layered red cabbage and potato. Pleasant sweets such as banana and butterscotch slice to finish. *Non-smoking area. No dogs.*

Marine Ices

8 Haverstock Hill NW3
MAP 9 C3
01-485 3132
P street parking

Open Restaurant: 12–2.45 & 6–10.15 (Sat 12–10.15); Ice Cream Parlour: 10.30am–10.45pm, Sun & Bank Hols 11.30–8
Closed Restaurant: Sun, Bank Hols & 3 wks Aug; Ice Cream Parlour: Good Fri, Jan 1 & 25 & 26 Dec

Penne al salmone £3.50   Coppa Stefana £2.50

The restaurant section of this well-known ice cream parlour offers a wide choice of Italian fare from antipasti and pizzas to six-way 'mix-and-match' pasta with sauces as well as various chicken, veal and liver dishes or salads. Of course, there are delectable ice creams to choose from for dessert, like coppa tiramisu – a serving of both coffee and hazelnut ice cream with a tiramisu topping. They also serve excellent espresso coffee. *Minimum charge (Rest.) £3.75. No dogs.*

LVs

We publish annually
so make sure you use the current edition.

Maxie's

7 Boston Parade, Boston Road W7
MAP 10 A5
01-567 9708
P street parking

Open 11.30–3 & 5.30–11, Sun 7–10.30
Closed Bank Hol Mons, 1 Jan & 25 & 26 Dec & Chinese New Year

Sweet & sour spare ribs £4.50   Prawns in black bean sauce £5.20

Chinese cooking is the speciality of this wine bar furnished with an abundance of greenery, marble-topped tables and classical background music. The menu ranges widely, from hot and sour soup, spring rolls and beef satay to griddle-sizzled prawns and chicken in black bean and chilli sauce. Vegetable and noodle dishes are also served, and there are toffee apples or bananas to finish. *No children. No dogs.*

Credit Access, Amex, Diners, Visa   **LVs**

Maxie's

143 Knightsbridge SW1
MAP 12 B4
01-225 2553
P NCP opposite Harrods   &

Open 12–11
Closed 4 days Xmas

Steamed scallops in shells £4.90
Chicken satay £3.70

Similarly dependable Chinese dishes are provided at this popular, dimly lit basement wine bar. The deliciously crispy shredded duck is full of flavour, as is the aromatic Mongolian lamb served with plum sauce. Lighter bites include wun tun soup, prawn toasts, deep-fried aubergine, mussels in black bean sauce, and a variety of stir-fried dishes, and there are toffee apples and bananas to finish. *No dogs.*

Credit Access, Amex, Diners, Visa   **LVs**

Mélange

59 Endell Street WC2
MAP 13 C1
01-240 8077
P Drury Lane NCP

Open 12–11.30 (Sat from 6)
Closed Sun, Bank Hols & 10 days Xmas

Mussel soup £2.40   Grilled steak with
Burgundy butter £6.90   🝙

Booking is essential at peak times for this
informal restaurant where the walls are
painted with skyscapes and the tables have
paper and crayons for budding artists. The
French menu is short but imaginative, with
choices like mussel soup, tender chicken
in a curry-flavoured mayonnaise and
perfectly grilled steak with burgundy
butter. Delicious vegetables accompany,
and there are appealing sweets and excellent coffee to finish. *No dogs.*

Credit Access, Amex, Diners, Visa

Le Meridien Piccadilly

Piccadilly W1
MAP 13 B3
01-734 8000
P valet parking   &

Open 10am–1am

Set afternoon tea £7.25   Smoked
salmon & scrambled egg toasted
sandwich £4   🝙

The chandeliers and deep, comfortable
armchairs create a wonderfully opulent
atmosphere in which to enjoy afternoon
tea. Scones come with little pots of jam
and double clotted cream; the finger
sandwiches are freshly made and the cakes
include an excellent strawberry tartlet in
crisp pastry, a good light textured chocolate mousse slice and subtly spiced custard
tart. An all-day snack menu includes hot
muffins and smoked salmon sandwiches.
Minimum charge £4 between 3–6.

Credit Access, Amex, Diners, Visa

N·E·W ENTRY   Meson Don Felipe

53 The Cut SE1
MAP 12 D4
01-928 3237
P meter parking   &

Open 12–3 & 5.30–11
Closed Sat lunch, all Sun & Bank Hols

Spicy Spanish sausages £1.65   Fried
potatoes in hot tomato sauce £1.50   🝙

Within sight of the Old Vic and close to
the South Bank arts complex, this friendly
Spanish tapas bar is ideal for pre- or post-
theatre snacks. The appetising and largely
authentic selection ranges from fried sardines and garlicky mushrooms to squid in
ink sauce and tuna-stuffed eggs, while a
blackboard offers more substantial fare
like beef in red wine and paella. Live
flamenco music at night. *Non-smoking
area. No children. No dogs.*

Credit Access, Visa

N·E·W ENTRY   Meson Doña Ana

37 Kensington Park Road W11
MAP 10 B4
01-243 0666
P street parking

Open 12–3 & 5.30–11
Closed Sun, Bank Hols, 1 wk Easter, 2
wks Aug & 10 days Xmas

Chorizo Castellana £1.65   Paella £3.50

Sit up at the bar and enjoy one or two
tapas with your aperitif at this traditional
Spanish meson, or choose several of the
tempting varieties on offer to make a tasty
sit-down meal. Typical delights range from
moist tortilla (delicious cold) and spicy
chorizo sausage to squid cooked in ink
and substantial daily specials such as paella
and lamb chops in wine sauce. Live
flamenco music at night. *No dogs.*

Credit Access, Visa

Methuselah's

29 Victoria Street, Nr Parliament
Square SW1
MAP 12 C4
01-222 3550
P NCP in Rochester Row

Open Brasserie: 9am–11pm; Wine Bar:
11–3 & 5.30–11
Closed Sat, Sun, Bank Hols & 1 wk
Xmas

Lancashire hotpot £5.95   Cheese & ham
pie with salad £4.95   🄴

This wine bar and brasserie is so close to
the Houses of Parliament that it even has
a division bell. Salads, cold meats, quiches,
pâtés and French cheeses are available in
the basement wine bar. On the ground
floor start with coffee and croissants, move
on to lunch grills, home-made soups or a
special such as chicken tandoori, with
pavlova or chocolate roulade to follow, or
just take tea with scones or pastries.
*Minimum lunchtime charge £6. No
children. No dogs.*

Credit Access, Amex, Diners, Visa

Le Metro

28 Basil Street SW3
MAP 12 B4
01-589 6286
P NCP in Pavilion Road 🚻

Open 7.30am–11pm (Sat from 2.30)
Closed Sun & most Bank Hols

Warm salad of chicken livers £2.40
Fillet of lamb with Dijon mustard sauce
£6.70   🄴

Sophistication is the watchword in this
busy basement wine bar beneath the
Capital Hotel, with soft yellow lighting and
carved polished wood furniture. The authentic French dishes are superbly cooked
and artistically presented, and are accompanied by excellent wines by the glass.
Main courses include trout Grenoblaise
and succulent fillet of lamb Dijonnaise.
Vegetables are crisp and delicious and
sweets are equally special from fruit salad
to strawberry tart. Excellent cheeseboard.

Credit Access, Visa

Millward's

97 Stoke Newington Church Street N16
MAP 9 D2
01-254 1025
P street parking

Open noon–midnight
Closed 1 wk Xmas

Spinach in sour cream sauce £4.75
Sherry trifle £1.50

Chris Millward caters imaginatively and
well for both vegans and vegetarians at his
pretty corner restaurant. The short regular
menu offers appetising starters like spiced
lentil pâté, houmus and aubergines provençale, with perhaps creamed mushroom
and green peppercorn pie, Oriental-style
cauliflower or leek and cream cheese-filled
pancakes to follow. Additional blackboard
specials are available from noon–5pm, and
indulgent sweets include apricot cream
and sherry trifle. *No dogs.*

Credit Access, Visa   **LVs**

Mother Huffs

12 Heath Street NW3
MAP 9 B2
01-435 3714
P street parking

Open 12–3
Closed Good Fri, 1 Jan & 25 & 26 Dec

Salmon fish cakes £4.25   Bread
& butter pudding £1.35   🄴

Tucked away off a courtyard, where tables
are set in summer, this rustic little attic
restaurant offers simple, satisfying fare.
Follow home-made soup with, perhaps,
steak and kidney pie, hearty lamb casserole
or deliciously moist fresh salmon and
spinach flan (served with buttery new
potatoes and dressed salad). Pleasant
sweets like chocolate roulade or lemon
meringue pie to finish. More elaborate
evening meals and a traditional lunchtime
Sunday roast. *Minimum charge £3.50.*

Credit Amex, Visa

Muffin Man

12 Wright's Lane W8
MAP 12 A4
01-937 6652
P meter parking

Open 8.15–6.30
Closed Sun & Bank Hols

Muffin Man tea £2.70   Ham, chicken & avocado double sandwich £2.75 🍷

The place to come for excellent breakfasts, with porridge, creamed eggs with ham and home-made marmalade. There are light lunches, such as Muffin Man rarebit, or tuna and spring onion salad, and the splendid original Muffin Man sandwich, stuffed with chicken, bacon, lettuce, tomato, cucumber and mayonnaise. A wide choice of teas, cakes, breads and scones is offered. Very popular, it can be crowded. Children's portions. *Unlicensed. Non-smoking area. No dogs.*

LVs

Mulford's Wine Bar

127 Shepherd's Bush Road W6
MAP 10 B5
01-603 2229
P meter parking

Open 12–2.30 & 6–10.30 (Sat from 6.30), Sun 7–10
Closed Bank Hols & 8 days Xmas

Chicken in tarragon & orange £4.50
Ham & watercress terrine £2.10

Lovely dried flower displays and lots of old photographs decorate this simple pleasant wine bar, but service can be rather inattentive. The blackboard menu offers choices like almond soup with lemon and croutons, mushrooms à la grecque, king prawn mayonnaise, a well made watercress and tomato roulade, crab and tomato quiche or an interesting chicken au fromage. Sweets can include butterscotch and biscuit cake, or chocolate chip cheesecake. It's wise to book at lunchtime.

Credit Access, Amex, Visa

Nakamura

31 Marylebone Lane W1
MAP 11 B3
01-935 2931
P NCP behind Debenhams

Open 12–2.30
Closed Sat, Sun & Bank Hols

Chicken teriyaki lunch £7   Pork deep fried lunch £6.50

Stylish simplicity is the hallmark of this very friendly little Japanese restaurant. On the ground floor you can watch the chef preparing the set sushi or raw fish lunch, which can include salmon, tuna, yellowtail and prawns. Other reasonably priced set lunches give you an excellent introduction to Japanese food. Each lunch is served with an appetiser, well-flavoured soya bean soup, rice, pickles and fresh fruit, to accompany main dishes like grilled fish or tempura with a light crisp batter. *No dogs.*

Credit Access, Amex, Diners, Visa

Nanten

6 Blandford Street W1
MAP 11 B3
01-935 6319
P meter parking

Open 12.30–2.30 & 6.30–10
Closed Sat lunch, all Sun, Bank Hols & 1 wk Xmas

Ramen £3.50   Yakitori lunch £7.20
🍷

Sit at the bar overlooking the grill and savour a set yakitori (Japanese kebabs) lunch. A cold appetiser – bean shoots with vinegar – is followed by a clear fragrant soup. Next, gently grilled kebabs of ox heart, beef, chicken wing, liver or gizzard in a piquant sauce. Thinly sliced beef with ginger continues the feast which ends lightly with fresh fruit and fragrant tea. Evening menu broadens to include the popular ramen – Chinese-style noodles in broth. Book. *No dogs.*

Credit Access, Amex, Diners, Visa

National Gallery Restaurant

Trafalgar Square WC2
MAP 13 C3
01-930 5210
P NCP Orange Street &

Open 10-5
Closed 1 Jan, Good Fri & 25 & 26 Dec

Spinach roulade £2   Chinese pork
casserole £3.95 ⊖

In the airy halls below the Gallery is this peaceful self-service restaurant where cold dishes such as coronation chicken and spinach roulade are served all day with a choice of six colourful salads. Hot dishes, like interesting soups or beef and olive casserole, are available from noon to 3pm. There are tempting sweets and home-made biscuits, cakes and pastries for morning coffee or tea. The queue can get long so arrive early for lunch. *Non-smoking area. No dogs.*

LVs

N·E·W
ENTRY
Nature's Garden

62 Lavender Hill SW11
MAP 10 C6
01-223 4618
P street parking

Open 9-6
Closed Sun

Crispy tofu with salad £1.45   Lemon
cake 55p ⊖

Eva Tang, who hails from Hong Kong, has recently left her accountancy job to run this modest concern in Lavender Hill. Health foods are sold on one side, and a few pine tables fill the other, where you can partake of the home-made treats from wholemeal bread, yoghurt, boiled eggs and muesli at breakfast time to cakes with tea and coffee. Lunchtime brings lentil mushroom layer, quiches, pizzas, salads, houmus, apple crumble and fruit compôte. *Unlicensed. No smoking. No dogs.*

Neal's Yard Bakery & Tea Room

6 Neal's Yard, Covent Garden WC2
MAP 13 C1
01-836 5199
P meter parking

Open 10.30-7.30 (Wed till 5, Sat till 4.30)
Closed Sun, Bank Hols & 10 days Xmas

Chilli & sweetcorn £1.40   Fresh fruit
trifle £1.40 ✿

The staff take turns to cook and serve at this tiny cooperative-run tea room, and the display case features a constantly changing range of wholefood goodies. Hot dishes such as minestrone, Caribbean casserole and vegetable bake appear from noon, while at other times you can snack on cheese scones, crunchy salads, vegetable pasties and delicious cakes like honey and malt sponge. Good selection of speciality teas. *Unlicensed. Non-smoking area. No dogs.*

LVs

New Kam Tong

59 Queensway W2
MAP 11 A3
01-229 6065
P NCP in Queensway

Open dim sum 12-5.45 (full menu
noon-midnight)

Dim sum from £1.15   Set lunch from
£7.20

Informal and functional, this lively restaurant serves full meals from midday to midnight and dim sum from noon to 5.45. Ideal for the business or family lunch, among the swiftly served dim sum are mixed meat croquettes, glutinous rice in lotus leaves, prawn dumplings and excellent prawn cheung. Chicken feet and duck's webs are served in a tasty black bean sauce and spare ribs are highly recommended. You can linger to enjoy the endless supply of tea. *No dogs.*

Credit Amex

New Shu Shan

36 Cranbourn Street WC2
MAP 13 C2
01-836 7501
P St Martin's Lane NCP

Open noon–midnight
Closed 25 & 26 Dec

Szechuan chicken £3.80   Sizzling
prawns with garlic sauce £5.80 🍵

Careful cooking and fine flavours distinguish the wide range of Cantonese and Szechuan dishes (the latter appear on the menu in red) offered at this delightful little family-run Chinese restaurant. Try the excellent hot and sour soup followed by tender lemon chicken and delicious braised bean curd served with crisply cooked vegetables. Red bean paste pancakes make the perfect finish. *Minimum charge £5 after 6pm. No dogs.*

Credit Access, Amex, Diners, Visa   **LVs**

No 77 Wine Bar

77 Mill Lane NW6
MAP 9 B2
01-435 7787
P street parking &

Open 12–3 & 6–11 (Thurs–Sat till 12 &
Sun 7–10.30)
Closed Bank Hols

Hamburger & Sun Valley salad £5.45
Banoffi pie £2.10 🐞

Natural wood, attractive prints and plenty of fresh flowers add to the pleasing ambience at this popular, informal wine bar. Consult the blackboard for the day's straight-forward, capably prepared selection – perhaps home-made soup, pâté or taramasalata followed by cheesy spinach and potato pie, king prawns with garlic mayonnaise, a juicy steak or quiche with salad. Puddings are good, particularly banoffi pie and flavoursome fresh peach and apple crumble. *Non-smoking area.*

Credit Access, Visa

Nosherie

12 Greville Street, Hatton Garden EC1
MAP 11 D2
01-242 1591
P NCP in St Cross Street

Open 8–5
Closed Sat, Sun, Bank Hols & all Jewish
Hols

Salt beef plate £3.65   Chicken liver salad
£2.95

Old-style standards have been drawing the faithful from the nearby diamond trade, in Hatton Garden, for years. Behind the take-away area, just-a-biters can sit at the long counter to enjoy good old fashioned Jewish fare (not Kosher), which might include chopped liver, chopped herring, nicely seasoned chicken soup, salt beef, enormous helpings of liver, onion and chips and other perennial favourites. Leave room for blintzes or spotted dick. *Minimum lunchtime charge £2.55. No dogs.*

LVs

N·E·W ENTRY   Oasis in the City

144 Clerkenwell Road EC1
MAP 11 D2
01-837 7373
P meter parking

Open 11–7
Closed Sat, Sun & Bank Hols

Salad niçoise £3.95   Salmon &
asparagus roll £7.50 🐞

Aimed primarily at a business clientele, this cheerful corner restaurant decorated in pretty pastel shades offers a nicely varied menu. Calf's liver and wild mushroom pâté or deep-fried Camembert could precede braised monkfish, Chinese crispy duck or a juicy fillet steak. There's a different special every day (osso buco on Tuesdays), and enjoyable sweets like rich chocolate gâteau to finish. Friendly and efficient service. *No dogs.*

Credit Access, Visa

Odette's

130 Regent's Park Road NW1
MAP 11 B1
01-586 8766
P street parking

Open 12.30–2.30 & 7–11
Closed Sun, Bank Hols & 10 days Xmas

Smokie & leek gratinée £4.15   Toulouse
sausages with apple purée & potatoes
£3.95   🅱

Both restaurant and wine bar facilities are
on offer here, with the latter being ideal
for the just-a-biter. The menu changes
each season, and the dishes cover a range
from deep-fried Camembert with gooseberry preserve, chicken and calf's liver pâté
or potted smokies to start, to main dishes
such as tuna fish bake, vegetarian moussaka or lamb ragout. Follow this up with
rice pudding, fruit brûlée, apricot tart or
chocolate truffle cake. *No dogs.*

Credit Access, Amex, Diners, Visa

Old Heidelburg

220 Chiswick High Road W8
MAP 10 A5
01-994 6621
P street parking

Open 9.30–5.30
Closed Sun & Bank Hols

Cream cheesecake £1.20   Chocolate
gâteau 90p

The tempting pâtisserie display draws
customers to both eat here and take away.
There are savoury snacks for lunch and
dinner, but just-a-biters should head for
the sweet things; for such delights as
large, fruity florentines, light and delicate
cheesecakes, nicely created mandarin gâteau, gooseberry torte and Bakewell tart.
All these delicious offerings are baked on
the premises by Mr Kaufmann who once
produced pâtisserie for the royal family at
Buckingham Palace. *Non-smoking area.*

Credit Access, Diners, Visa

Oliver's

10 Russell Gardens W14
MAP 10 B4
01-603 7645
P street parking

Open 12–11
Closed 25 & 26 Dec

Calf's liver £7.50   Strawberries in
Pernod £1.50 🐦

Virtually a West London institution, this
bustling bistro offers a wide selection of
fresh, thoughtfully prepared food. Lunchtime opens with a home-made soup –
possibly watercress – hot ratatouille or
cold poached salmon. Calf's liver provençal
and osso buco are popular choices from
the meat dominated main courses. Poultry
fans should try the pigeon in Pernod.
Extended evening menu. Simple sweets,
good coffee. Traditional Sunday lunch.
Patio. *Minimum charge £4.50 from 6pm.*
Unlicensed (bring your own). No dogs.

Ormes

67 Abbeville Road SW4
MAP 10 C6
01-673 2568
P street parking

Open 12–2.30 & 6.30–11, Sun 12–2
& 7–10.30
Closed 3 days Xmas

Asparagus tartlets £2.10   Chocolate
& hazelnut meringue £1.95   🅱

Relax amidst candlelit Victoriana at this
established wine bar south of Clapham
Common. Bistro-style fare served at old
sewing machine tables in a warren of rooms
employs fresh ingredients with honest
results. Starters encompass taramasalata,
deep-fried Camembert and a daily soup.
Lamb wellington, calf's liver with sage
butter, monkfish kebab or a vegetarian
chilli and cabbage timbale follow. Plans for
refurbishment will generally enhance the
setting. Pavement seating. *No dogs.*

Credit Access, Amex, Diners, Visa

Paparazzi

158 Fulham Palace Road W6
MAP 10 B5
01-741 5037
P street parking

Open noon–midnight, Sun 12–11
Closed 3 days at Xmas

Fine liver pâté £1.95   Spinach fettucine
£3.65   ☺

Freshly made pasta is carefully cooked and enjoyable at this stylish restaurant on several pine-floored levels. Try a vegetarian version (perhaps green peppers with capers and olives) as a change from such classic sauces as bolognese, vongole and carbonara, or go for a meaty special like escalope milanese. Appealing starters include baked bread sticks spread with anchovy paste, tomatoes and melted mozzarella. *Non-smoking area. No dogs.*

Credit Access, Amex, Diners, Visa

Pasta Connection

25 Elystan Street SW3
MAP 12 B5
01-584 5248
P street parking

Open 12.30–2.30 & 7–11.15
Closed Sat lunch, Sun & Bank Hols

Lasagne £2.85   Paellard di vitello £5.65

In summer there are tables on the pavement outside this cheerful Italian eatery. In the pleasant interior the Italian waiters serve you with good, well-seasoned, stock-based minestrone with fresh vegetables, various antipasti including carpaccio and pasta dishes like freshly made lasagne verde, grills of steak and veal and daily special sauced dishes such as entrecote chasseur. Finish with tiramisu – a sort of South Italian trifle.

Credit Access, Visa

Pasta Fino

27 Frith Street W1
MAP 13 B2
01-439 8900
P NCP Cambridge Circus

Open 12–11.30
Closed Sun, Bank Hols & 1 wk Xmas

Ravioli filled with spinach & ricotta
cheese £4.15   Selection of salami
& ham £2.50

Freshly cooked in the kitchen upstairs, multi-coloured and multi-shaped pasta with a sauce of your choosing is the basis of a meal at this informal Italian restaurant in the heart of Soho. The sauce you choose determines the price of your meal – but it is always good value for money. Vongole is a generous helping of tasty, herby tomato sauce with plenty of baby clams, or there is pollo – chicken with peppers and cream. *No dogs.*

Credit Access, Visa

Pasta Underground

214 Camden High Street NW1
MAP 11 C1
01-482 0010
P meter parking

Open 12–3 & 6–11 (till 11.30 Fri &
Sat), also Sun 12–10.30
Closed 25 & 26 Dec

Spaghetti al pesto £3.50   Chocolate
terrine £1.95

A lively, bustling basement restaurant with an upstairs bar and shop selling freshly made pasta. Let marinated goat's cheese salad or bresaola whet your appetite before tucking into delicious spaghetti with sliced potatoes and superbly authentic pesto, spinach ravioli or a meaty main course such as saltimbocca, calf's liver with sage and onion or spicy chicken brochette. Light, refreshing sweets and good coffee to finish. Cheerful young staff. *No dogs.*

Pâtisserie Cappuccetto

8 Moor Street, Cambridge Circus W1
MAP 13 C2
01-437 9472
P NCP Gerrard Street

Open 7.30am–8pm
Closed Sun & Bank Hols

Strawberry tartlette £1   Black Forest
gâteau £1.10

From early morning a stream of people
come to enjoy snacks from the exceedingly
tempting display at this friendly establishment. On the savoury side choose from
flaky croissants (plain, savoury or sweet),
or quiches and pizzas, which are all made
on the premises. For those with a sweet
tooth delectable pastries including lovely
mille-feuilles with good fondant icing,
strawberry tarts, éclairs, cream slices and
an assortment of gâteaux will prove irresistible. *Unlicensed. Non-smoking area.
No dogs.*

Pâtisserie Valerie

44 Old Compton Street W1
MAP 13 B2
01-437 3466
P Dean Street NCP

Open 8.30–7

Closed Sun & Bank Hols

Cheese croissant 65p   Strawberry
tart £1.40   White chocolate &
rum gâteau £1.45   Mille feuille
£1.10

★ The Scalzo family are in charge at this splendid Soho
pâtisserie which has been going strong for over 40
years. Sit at the refectory tables to tuck into the
delights displayed in the window which are designed
to overpower even the most dedicated diet-watchers. ★
Saturday sees the widest choice when there are over
30 varieties of delicious, delicate pastries to enjoy
with excellent loose leaf tea. It would be a crime to
miss such treats as chocolate truffle mousse, and, in
season, blueberry or loganberry tarts or the outstanding wild strawberry tart of exquisite pastry filled with
strawberry preserve and crême chantilly, liberally
studded with wild strawberries. *Unlicensed. No
dogs.*

LVs

Pavilion Wine Bar

Finsbury Circus Gardens EC2
MAP 10 D4
01-628 8224
P meter parking

Open 11.30–3 & 5.30–8
Closed Sat, Sun & Bank Hols

Smoked chicken pasta £4   Sweet
& sour pork £4.75 ©

Exceptional wines complement the delicious food offered at this popular, informal
wine bar overlooking the bowling green at
Finsbury Circus Gardens. Try moist, flavoursome pâté followed by smoked chicken
and mushroom fettucine for a lovely light
lunch, or choose an appetising hot dish
such as sweet and sour pork. Salads are
fresh and attractive and there are fine
French cheeses to finish. Slightly restricted
choice in the evening. *No children. No
dogs.*

Credit Access, Amex, Visa **LVs**

Le Petit Prince

5 Holmes Road NW5
MAP 9 C3
01-267 0752
P street parking

Open 12–2.30 & 7–11.30 (Sat till 11.45
& Sun till 11.15)
Closed Sat, Sun & Mon lunches, all
Bank Hols & 4 days Easter, 2 wks Aug &
1 wk Xmas

Vegetarian couscous £3.30   Braised
chicken couscous £4.50

Book to ensure a table at this colourful
and informal restaurant specialising in
North African cuisine. Couscous dominates the menu, a substantial feast consisting of a platter of steamed durum wheat
and a bowl of vegetable broth, to which
you add your choice of meat – lamb cutlets
and kebabs, braised chicken, meatballs or
spicy merguez sausages – served with a
hot chilli sauce. Simple, enjoyable starters
and sweets for diners with stamina. Don't
miss the peppermint tea. *No dogs.*

Plat du Jour

19 Hampstead Road NW1
MAP 11 C2
01-387 9644
P NCP Euston Centre   &

Open 11.30–8
Closed Sat, Sun & Bank Hols

Quiche & salad £2.85   Frangipan £1.65

Two ambitious young Italian restaurateurs
have taken over this popular bistro-style
wine bar, although their menu remains
predominantly French in flavour. A blackboard lists the day's dishes – perhaps
nettle soup followed by a couple of hot
main courses like chicken escalope or
richly sauced beef goulash, or various
salads with prawns, cheese or pâté. Finish
with an appealing sweet such as nutty,
moist almond cake, plus good French and
Italian cheeses.

Credit Access, Amex, Diners, Visa

Poons

4 Leicester Street WC2
MAP 13 B3
01-437 1528
P Swiss Centre NCP   &

Open 12–11.30
Closed Sun & 3 days Xmas

Stewed spice beef hotpot £3   Special
wind-dried food mix £2.90

Rise above the sometimes surly service and
enjoy fine Cantonese cooking. Wind-dried
dishes, the traditional Chinese way of
preserving food for winter, is the winning
feature – wind-dried duck exemplifies the
richly enhanced flavour. Original fried
oyster with crispy pork is one of the hot-
pots – virtually complete meals based on
tasty rice served in a cooking pot. Dumpling soup of light chicken broth is an
enjoyable starter. The sweets are limited –
stick to the orange wedges. *No dogs.*

Poons

27 Lisle Street WC2
MAP 13 C2
01-437 4549
P Swiss Centre NCP

Open 12–11.30
Closed Mon

Mixed barbecue £2.70   Wind-dried duck
£3.30

Authentic Cantonese in simple surroundings for those disheartened with Western-
ised counterfeits. Friendly staff advise on
dishes best approached in adventurous
mood. Wind-dried mixed food is the speciality perfectly complemented by fish and
green vegetable rice. Stewed chicken with
sausage exemplifies the quality cooking.
Try the original fried oyster with crispy
pork or unusual oil soaked squid. Best to
book. *Minimum charge £2 after 6pm.
Unlicensed. No dogs.*

Portman Inter-Continental Hotel, Portman Corner

22 Portman Square W1
MAP 11 B3
01-486 5844
P NCP in Portman Street

Open 11am–midnight

Salmon in lime cream sauce £7.50
Afternoon tea £7 🍵

Elegant snacks are the hallmark of this smart hotel. Try baked avocado with a poached egg and dill cream sauce, feta cheese quiche or consommé, or go for one of the equally imaginative sandwiches – perhaps pastrami on rye or a croissant filled with warm ham, cheese and tomatoes. Tasty alternatives include pasta, plough- man's and roast beef salad, while afternoon tea is a feast of dainty sandwiches, light scones and pastries. *Non-smoking area. No dogs.*

Credit Access, Amex, Diners, Visa

Le Poulbot Pub

45 Cheapside EC2
MAP 10 D4
01-236 4379
P NCP in Ave Maria Lane

Open 8–10.30 & 12–3
Closed Sat, Sun & Bank Hols

Omelette £3   Dish of the day from £5
🍵

A smart brasserie above the Roux brothers' elegant and comfortable basement restaur- ant, which has a very French flavour in both decor and cuisine. Delicious pâtisserie accompanies morning coffee, and at lunch- time there is an interesting menu compris- ing typically Gallic dishes such as pâté with herbs, omelettes and entrecôte béarnaise. Daily specials might be poulet fermière or navarin of lamb. Choose from apple tart, peach flan or chocolate gâteau for dessert. *No dogs.*

Punters Pie

183 Lavender Hill SW11
MAP 10 C6
01-228 2660
P street parking

Open 12–3 & 6–11.30 (Sun from 7)
Closed 1 wk Xmas

Parson's pie £3.95   Chocolate mousse
pie £1.95

Home-made pies are the mainstay of this cheerful, informal restaurant. Choose classic steak and kidney or go for mildly curried chicken, smoked fish or vegetables in cheese and parsley sauce. You can even order chocolate mousse pie enriched with orange liqueur as a splendid finale and, for the truly hungry, there are tasty starters such as tuna dip with crudités and wonder- ful garlic bread. Book. *No smoking. No dogs.*

Credit Access, Amex, Diners, Visa

Raj Bhelpoori House

19 Camden High Street NW1
MAP 11 C1
01-388 6663
P meter parking

Open 12–11.30
Closed 25 Dec

Raj thali £4.15   Kulfi 85p

Authentic vegetarian dishes from South India are the speciality of this neat, modest restaurant. Order the Raj thali for an introduction to the cuisine, comprising sauced mixed vegetables, rice, soft pan- cakes, refreshing raita and rich, custard- like shrikhand for dessert. Alternatives, enhanced by fresh herbs and spices, include samosas, vegetable kebabs and dosas (ground black lentil or semolina pancakes), with a variety of different fillings. *Unli- censed – bring your own. No dogs.*

Credit Access, Amex, Diners, Visa **LVs**

Rani

3 Long Lane N3
MAP 9 B1
01-349 4386
P street parking

Open 12.30-2 & 6-10.30
Closed Tues lunch & all Mon

Undhia £2.95   Thali £4.95

The menu explains the dishes in this simple, bright Indian vegetarian restaurant with a welcoming atmosphere. Try the special thali – a complete three course meal with well flavoured dal, rice, two mixed vegetable curries, hot, delicious onion bhajis, chapatis, raita and poppadom, and a choice of desserts. There are also various Indian snacks and other dishes and a special daily curry. *Minimum evening charge of £4. No children. No dogs.*

Credit Access, Visa

Ravi Shankar

135 Drummond Street NW1
MAP 11 C2
01-388 6458
P street parking   &

Open 12-11

Mysore thali £3.95   Masala dosa £2.90

South Indian vegetarian food is prepared with care, and spicing is sure in this simply furnished little place just off the Euston Road. The menu takes in starters and snacks (samosas, pooris, ground black lentil fritters); main course dosas, idli sambhar and vegetables with paratha; aubergine and okra bhajis; and sweets include rich, milky kulfi. There are also two versions of the traditional set meals or thali. Satisfying dishes and very reasonable prices. *No dogs.*

Credit Access, Amex, Diners, Visa   LVs

Raw Deal

65 York Street W1
MAP 11 B2
01-262 4841
P meter parking

Open 10am-10pm (Sat till 11)
Closed Sun, Bank Hols

Vegetable curry & rice £3.10   Mince pie 95p

Something of an institution after 20 years-plus of bringing wholesome vegetarian fare to the masses, this modest little corner restaurant remains as popular as ever. Table-sharing is a necessity at lunchtime, when soup, super salads and hot savouries like black-eyed bean casserole or potato and mushroom bake make their popular appearance, with perhaps delicious apricot crumble and home-made yoghurt for afters. *Unlicensed (but bring your own). Non-smoking area.*

LVs

Redfords

N·E·W
ENTRY

126 Golders Green Road NW11
MAP 9 B2
01-455 2789
P street parking

Open 12-2.30 (Sun till 3) & 5.30-10
Closed Jewish holidays

Chopped herring £1.50   Haddock fillet & chips £5.75

For a fish and chip restaurant with a difference, head for this vibrant restaurant in the heart of Golders Green. Side by side with more familiar items like haddock, cod, plaice and Dover sole, you'll find a sprinkling of traditional (not kosher) Jewish dishes like chopped herring and borsch soup. Freshly-made salads are offered as a tasty main course alternative. Helpings are enormous, but if you're feeling really self indulgent, finish with a lovely baked apple. *Minimum charge £3.50. No dogs.*

Credit Access, Amex, Visa   LVs

The Ritz, Palm Court

Piccadilly W1
MAP 12 C4
01-493 8181
P NCP in Arlington Square &

Open 9am–10.30pm

Set afternoon tea £10.50 🍵

With its splendid marble fountain, gilt chandelier and elegant Louis XIV chairs, this is surely London's most opulent setting for afternoon tea (two sittings, booking essential – as are jacket and tie for gentlemen). Dainty finger sandwiches, a light scone with jam and cream, delicious pastries and gâteaux form the choice at tea-time, and well-filled sandwiches are available at other times. *Minimum charge £9.25 between 3.30–5.30. No dogs.*

Credit Access, Amex, Diners, Visa

Rosemary Branch

N·E·W ENTRY

2 Shepperton Road N1
MAP 9 D3
01-226 4433
P street parking

Open 12–3 & 7–11

Moules marinière £3.50   Grilled trout £5

A small intimate café within a spacious pub, where upstairs there are fringe theatre productions, is the setting for some enjoyable and generous light snacks – imaginative and well-cooked to suit all tastes. You might choose from a vegetarian soup, fresh moules marinière, sautéed chicken liver salad, tacos with vegetables, grilled salmon with hash brown potatoes, salads, beefburgers or a steak and mushroom sandwich. To finish, a selection of simple sweets.

Royal Lancaster Hotel Lounge

Lancaster Terrace W2
MAP 11 A3
01-262 6737
P own car park

Open 7am–midnight

Afternoon tea £5.75   Vegeburger £3.95

Light snacks and sandwiches are served through the day in the quiet, pleasant lounge of this large hotel very near Hyde Park and central London. In the afternoon you can enjoy a traditional afternoon tea with freshly cut finger sandwiches, and light, well-baked scones with Devonshire clotted cream and a selection of jams in pots. At other times, light snacks are available in the shape of pastries and well-filled club sandwiches. *No dogs.*

Credit Access, Amex, Diners, Visa

Sabras

263 High Road, Willesden Green NW10
MAP 9 A3
01-459 0340
P street parking &

Open 12.30–3 & 6–10, Sat & Sun 12.30–10
Closed Mon, 2 wks Aug & 2 wks Xmas

Deluxe thali £7   Masala dhosa £3.50

The Desai family run their popular vegetarian restaurant very efficiently. The menu offers mainly South Indian dishes: a selection of spicy savouries (a tasty vegetable samosa – a lentil ball with onion, and dhokala – a delicious mix of yoghurt, lentils and spices), and other interesting dishes like the crisp pancake filled with vegetables, nuts, raisins and coconut. There are thalis – a complete set meal – and very good Indian sweets too. *Non-smoking area. No dogs.*

Credit Access, Visa

The Savoy, Thames Foyer

The Strand WC2
MAP 13 D3
01-836 4343
P own car park &

Open 9am–11pm

Afternoon tea £8.25   Smoked
salmon sandwich £4.10   Grilled
minute steak £7.50   Fruit-filled
Danish pastries £1.60

★ Afternoon tea in the elegant chandelier-hung room
of this grand hotel, accompanied by piano or harp
music, is a special experience. Tea consists of good-
sized finger sandwiches in brown or white bread with
a range of fillings, freshly baked light scones with
good jam and thick clotted cream and an excellent
choice of pastries, like tarts with fresh strawberries
and small éclairs, and excellent speciality teas. Tea is
served between 3.30 and 5.30, but at other times
tasty snacks are on offer, including sandwiches,
chicken liver parfait with raisins, grilled minute steak
on toast with tomato flavoured béarnaise. Impeccable
service. *No dogs.* ★

Credit Access, Amex, Diners, Visa

The Savoy, Upstairs

Strand WC2
MAP 13 D3
01-836 4343
P Adelphi Garage

Open noon–midnight (Sat from 5pm)
Closed Sun

Broccoli & pine kernel quiche £4.50
Smoked Scottish salmon £8.25

From its position on the first floor, this
elegant wine bar overlooks the hotel foyer.
Seafood dominates the short menu – try
the creamy red mullet and French bean
soup, crab, avocado and mango salad and
poached salmon – while alternatives might
include smoked turkey with spiced peaches
or hot roast sirloin of beef and potato
salad. To finish, try the excellent bread
and butter pudding.   Quality wines by the
glass. *No dogs.*

Credit Access, Amex, Diners, Visa

Shampers

4 Kingly Street W1
MAP 13 A2
01-437 1692
P NCP Kingly Street &

Open 11–3 & 5.30–11
Closed Sat eve, all Sun, Bank Hols
& 3 days Xmas

Ham & cheese pie £3.75   Lamb &
aubergine casserole £4.95

Don Hewitson's vibrant wine bar on the
fringes of Soho is a mecca for media folk
who appreciate its match of excellent wines
with imaginative food. To start, perhaps
creamy smoked trout mousse followed by
rich lamb and aubergine casserole or a
lighter dish of tagliatelle with leek and
Stilton sauce. Save on the calories with
oriental vegetarian salad, or add to them
with toffee and banana pie. Service is swift
and efficient. *No dogs.*

Credit Access, Amex, Diners, Visa

Sheraton Park Tower, Rotunda Lounge

Knightsbridge SW1
MAP 12 B4
01-235 8050
P NCP in building &

Open 12-8

Set afternoon tea £4.25   Smoked
salmon Danish open sandwich £4.50
🍵

Try this attractive circular lounge, in the
centre of a modern hotel with striking
decor, for a light snack from Danish open
sandwiches with smoked salmon, salami
or pâté to a delicious set afternoon tea.
This consists of finger sandwiches, light
fruit scones, cakes and pastries, one of
which is always hot – such as apple strudel
or pear tart. The much larger restaurant
overlooking Knightsbridge has a more
elaborate menu. *No dogs.*

Credit Access, Amex, Diners, Visa

Simpson's Wine Bar

Piccadilly W1
MAP 13 B3
01-734 2002
P meter parking

Open 9-5.15
Closed Sun & Bank Hols (except 1 Jan)

Quiche & salad £3.10   Fruit bavarois
£1.50 🍵

A discerning clientele frequents this dis-
creet little wine bar tucked away upstairs
in Simpson's store. Excellent tea accompanies delicious pastries, scones and fruit
tarts throughout the day, while at lunchtime the elegant choice includes open
sandwiches, an imaginative soup (perhaps
broccoli and Stilton), ham and cheese-
filled croissants and a couple of daily
specials such as steak and kidney pie or
vegetarian pasta. Try the silky-smooth,
lemony bavarois for dessert. *No dogs.*

Credit Access, Amex, Diners, Visa

Skinkers

42 Tooley Street SE1
MAP 10 D4
01-407 9189
P Snowfields NCP &

Open 11.30-2.45 & 5.30-8
Closed Sat, Sun & Bank Hols

Smoked salmon trout mousse £2.75
Charcoal-grilled sirloin of beef £5.90 🍴

Polished mahogany tables are dotted
amongst the stacks of wine cases in this
dark, intimate and cool cellar wine bar
underneath London Bridge station. The
menu is short and traditional, supplemented by blackboard specials ranging
from seafood platter, Parma ham with
melon, oak smoked salmon or prime
Scotch beef. Simple sweets are based on
seasonal fruits, and the cheeses are popular
here. Soup and sandwiches at the bar. Cold
food only in the evenings. *No dogs.*

Credit Access, Amex, Diners, Visa

Slenders

41 Cathedral Place, Paternoster
Square EC4
MAP 11 D3
01-236 5974
P Paternoster Square NCP

Open 7-6.15
Closed Sat, Sun & Bank Hols

Vegetable moussaka £2.70   Banana &
hazelnut cake 40p 🍴 🍵

Lunchtime queues testify to the continuing
popularity of this pine-furnished vegetarian restaurant. Appetising daily hot dishes
such as chilli bean and brown rice bake or
chunky vegetable casserole appear from
around 11am, while the self-service
counter offers filled rolls, quiche and
excellent salads. Delicious sweet treats
such as fluffy lemon meringue pie and
some fine teas round things off most
enjoyably. *Minimum lunchtime charge
£2. Unlicensed. Non-smoking area.*

LVs

Soho Brasserie

23 Old Compton Street W1
MAP 13 B2
01-439 3758
P NCP Shaftesbury Avenue

Open 10am–11.30pm
Closed Sun & Bank Hols

Shrimps cooked in cider £3.45
Pan-fried monkfish with garlic £8.35
🐟

Media and pop glitterati flock to this bustling, informal brasserie where American chef David Schwartz continues to delight with his imaginative cooking based on top-notch produce. A warm salad of wild mushrooms, grilled salmon with chive butter and lime and a perfectly light omelette typify his skilled touch, or you can tuck into a steak sandwich, grilled hamburger or herby sausages. A silky-smooth chocolate mousse can round things off. *No dogs.*

Credit Access, Amex, Diners, Visa **LVs**

N·E·W ENTRY Spices

30 Stoke Newington Church Street N16
MAP 9 D2
01-254 0528
P street parking &

Open 12.30–11.45
Closed Bank Hols

Mattar panir £3.95   Pakoras £1.65

Smartly decorated in burgundy, this newly re-opened Indian restaurant offers a good range of soundly prepared vegetarian dishes. Cashew nut fritters or lentil purée balls served with yoghurt and tamarind sauce might start your meal, followed perhaps by kofta curry, black lentil and rice flour pancakes, or home-made Indian cheese cooked with coriander. Greater use of fresh herbs and spices would be welcomed. *Non-smoking area. No dogs.*

Credit Access, Amex, Diners, Visa **LVs**

Suruchi

18 Theberton Street N1
MAP 11 D1
01-359 8033
P meter parking

Open 12–2.45 & 6–11
Closed 25 & 26 Dec

Dahi poori £1.30   Masala dosa £2.95

Book to ensure a table at this very popular, very relaxed Indian vegetarian restaurant. Among familiar favourites on the menu – including pooris, dosas and Gujerati-style complete meals – are less familiar offerings such as khati, a simple vegetable kebab, and dahi vada – lightly spiced fritters made from black pea flour and served with sweet and sour sauce and yoghurt. The good choice of sweets include rich, milky rasmalai. *Unlicensed. No dogs.*

Credit Amex, Visa

Sweetings

39 Queen Victoria Street EC4
MAP 10 D4
01-248 3062
P NCP Upper Thames Street

Open 11.30–3
Closed Sat, Sun & Bank Hols

Lobster soup £1.90   Salmon fish cakes
£5 🍴

An Edwardian mosaic stone floor and an old fashioned brass doorplate complement the traditional, unfussy fish dishes available at this much-loved City institution. Potted shrimp, dressed crab and jellied eels are ideal for a light lunch while lobster soup and salmon fish cakes, supplemented by a few specials like mussels, help fill hungrier stomachs. Favourite puddings like spotted dick or baked jam roll add the finishing touch or choose the good, creamy Stilton instead. *No dogs.*

Tapster

3 Brewers Green, Buckingham Gate
SW1
MAP 12 C4
01-222 0561
P meter parking

Open 11.30–3 & 5.30–8.30
Closed Sat, Sun & Bank Hols

Scotch salmon £5.50   Smoked turkey
breast & avocado £4.25   🍵

A traditional, candlelit basement wine bar
popular with office workers at lunchtime.
The small restaurant on a slightly raised
level serves soup, cold dishes and hot daily
specials like poached salmon. Otherwise
you might choose cold beef, ham or a game
pie with salad and hot new potatoes,
followed by apple pie or delicious chocolate
mousse. Sandwiches with a variety of
fillings are available in the bar area. *No
children. No dogs.*

Credit Access, Amex, Diners, Visa

N·E·W ENTRY   Tea Rooms des Artistes

697 Wandsworth Road SW8
MAP 10 C6
01-720 4028
P street parking

Open 11–11 (Mon from 7pm), Sun 12–
10.30

Vegetable lasagne £3.25   Banana
butterscotch flan £1.75   🍵

Popular for its live jazz music and art
exhibitions, this former 16th-century barn
is often crowded and always a treat. Choose
from the enormous variety of dishes at the
display counter. Alternatively, specials are
chalked on a blackboard and might include
smoked salmon and mushroom pasta,
vegetable moussaka or a choice of good
quality salads. Sweets are delicious: banana
butterscotch flan or maybe raspberry and
yoghurt tart. *No children in evenings.
No dogs.*

Credit Visa

Tea Time

21 The Pavement, Clapham
Common SW4
MAP 10 C6
01-622 4944
P street parking

Open 10–5.30 (Sat from 11, Sun
from 12)

Closed 1 wk Xmas

Scrambled eggs & smoked salmon
£3.25   Egg mayonnaise & cress
sandwich £1.45   Hot buttered
muffin 55p   Raspberry & sherry
trifle £1.50

 Overlooking the Common, these charming tea rooms
on two floors have a tempting window display of
goodies home-baked by local ladies. There are three
menus: until noon there are breakfast dishes like
delicious, silky-smooth scrambled eggs with smoked
salmon; from noon, wonderful sandwiches in various
breads or toasts and a lunchtime hotpot. From 2pm
come tea-time traditionals – crumpets, muffins,
scones, toasted tea cakes and set teas. Available
throughout the day are locally baked delights like
carrot or ginger cake, excellent coffee & walnut cake,
tangy lemon tarts, éclairs and pots of very good tea.
Unlicensed. Non-smoking area. No dogs.

Tiger-under-the-Table

**634 Finchley Road, Golders Green
NW11
MAP 9 B2
01-458 8273
P   street parking**

Open   12–3 & 6–11.15, Sat & Sun 12–
11.15
Closed   1 wk Xmas

Mee Goreng £3   Sweetcorn chowder
£1.60

The restaurant is cool and silvery but the
Singaporean food is vibrant and fiery.
Among the starters are satay, delicious
filled pancakes and soups. The main
courses include seafood, meat and vegetarian dishes. Chicken in fragrant coconut
gravy is highly recommended. Dishes are
served with rice, noodles or roti jala
(pancake strips). Set lunches and dinners
at weekends. On Sunday take your pick
from a table-load of dishes. *No dogs.*

Credit   Access, Amex, Diners, Visa

Tiles Wine Bar

**36 Buckingham Palace Road SW1
MAP 12 C5
01-834 7761
P   meter parking**

Open   12–3 & 5.30–11
Closed   Sat, Sun & Bank Hols

Chicken liver, port & green peppercorn
pâté £2.95   Steak & mushroom
vol-au-vent £5.75   🅿

The menu's short but full of imaginative
ideas at this delightful little wine bar.
Delicious starters like creamy cauliflower
and pink peppercorn soup lead on to
succulent main dishes such as grilled lamb
steak with fresh rosemary sauce. Other
tempting offerings might include pork stir-
fry with mange-touts and bean sprouts,
and a warm duck, orange and pine nut
salad. Look out for the strawberry gâteau
among the desserts.

Credit   Access, Amex, Diners, Visa

*Any person using our name
to obtain free hospitality is a fraud.*

*Proprietors, please inform
Egon Ronay's Guides and the police.*

Le Tire Bouchon

**6 Upper James Street W1
MAP 13 A2
01-437 5348
P   NCP in Brewer Street**

Open   8.30am–9.30pm
Closed   Sat, Sun & Bank Hols

Navarin d'agneau printanier £5.50
Filet de cabillaud boulangère £5.25   🅿

The decor of the split-level restaurant
creates an attractive setting in which to
enjoy dishes from the simple but appetising
menu. In the mornings there are croissants,
eggs and coffee, then from 11am throughout opening hours you can choose a hot
dish of the day, which might be soupe de
poissons, côte de boeuf rotie aux echalots,
lamb or escalope. To finish there are
French cheeses or a small selection of
simple sweets. *No dogs.*

Credit   Access, Amex, Visa   **LVs**

Topkapi

25 Marylebone High Street W1
MAP 11 B2
01-486 1872
P NCP in Moxon Street

Open noon–midnight

Closed 25 & 26 Dec

Stuffed aubergine £2   Smoked cod roe pâté £2   Grilled lamb kidneys £6.25   Turkish mixed grill £6.50

★ Named after the ancient Ottoman palace in Istanbul, this dimly lit restaurant hung with decorative brass trays provides a plush haven 12 hours every day in which to enjoy exceptionally fine, authentic Turkish cooking. Excellent raw materials, enhanced by fresh herbs and spices, are carefully prepared to produce such tempting dishes as stuffed vine leaves, hot soft cheese pastries and delicious taramasalata served with freshly baked pitta bread among starters, with succulent kebabs, grills or specials like oven-roasted lamb or truly authentic moussaka to follow. Vegetarian specials are available. Crisp, fresh salads accompany and to finish there's sticky baklava and excellent Turkish coffee. *No dogs.*

Credit Access, Amex, Diners, Visa

Tui

19 Exhibition Road SW7
MAP 12 A5
01-584 8359
P street parking

Open 12–2.30 & 6.30–11, Sun 12.30–3 & 7–10.30
Closed 3 days Xmas

Chicken red curry £4.25   Crab claws £8.35

A light, bright, cheerful restaurant with a relaxed atmosphere and uncluttered decor. There is no separate lunch menu, but a selection can be made from an interesting and varied à la carte menu. Try a combined choice of two or three dishes. Both menu and staff are helpful in explaining what the traditional Thai dishes are, such as satay – barbecued beef with peanut sauce served with cucumber salad. The dishes are carefully cooked and the flavours excellent. Thai ginger tea is served. *No dogs.*

Credit Access, Amex, Diners, Visa

Tuk Tuk

*N·E·W
ENTRY*

330 Upper Street N1
MAP 11 D1
01-226 0837
P meter parking

Open 12–3 & 6–11.30
Closed 25 & 26 Dec

Nua yang (grilled finely sliced steak with hot sauce & green salad) £3.50   Kao ohls mor din (rice & chicken cooked & served in a claypot) £3.50

There's excellent, inexpensive Thai food in this stylish little place near Islington Green. Sample the freshly made, spicy deep-fried fish and bean patties and satay from the variety of starters. Main courses come with rice. Mussaman is a lovely mild, meat curry with sweet potatoes; kao pahd ta le is rice fried with seafood and there are interesting vegetarian choices too. The sweet choices are simple. Children's portions. *No dogs.*

Credit Access, Amex, Visa

Tuxedo Junction

190 Broadhurst Gardens NW6
MAP 9 B3
01-625 5616
P street parking

Open 12–3 & 6–12, Sat & Sun noon–midnight
Closed 1 wk Xmas

Guacamole £1.95   Chicken creole £4.95

New larger-than-life owner Joe Toledano plans to spruce up the decor but retain the popular American–Mexican style food on offer here. The large choice of starters ranges from deep-fried potato skins and guacamole to crudités and nachos. Main courses include burgers, burritos, freshly made chicken Maryland with an exploded frankfurter, trout and T-bone steaks. Among the desserts is a sinfully tempting Kahlua cheesecake. *No dogs.*

Credit Access, Amex, Diners, Visa   **LVs**

Twenty Trinity Gardens

20 Trinity Gardens SW9
MAP 10 C6
01-733 8838
P street parking

Open 12.30–2.30
Closed Sat lunch, all Sun, Bank Hols & 1 wk Xmas

Noisettes of lamb with apricot sauce £7.25   Muesli meringues with honey & cream £2.25

At lunchtime you can choose a single dish from the set two or three course menus at this attractive, stylish restaurant. Starters include smoked haddock mousse, cod chowder, vegetable terrine or goat's cheese on garlic toast. Main courses offer lamb's liver in orange sauce, rabbit in Meaux mustard and cold salmon. Sweets are tempting: lime cream in mango sauce and delicious yoghurt. Interesting wine list. Full evening meals. *Non-smoking area. No dogs.*

Credit Access, Visa

Upper Street Fish Shop

324 Upper Street N1
MAP 11 D1
01-359 1401
P street parking

Open 12–2 (Sat till 3) & 5.30–10
Closed Mon lunch, all Sun, Bank Hols & wk following & 2 wks Xmas

Haddock & chips £3.80   Poached halibut with herb sauce £6   🍵

Olga Conway's effervescent personality dominates this bustling, upmarket fish restaurant. Traditional cod, plaice and haddock (served with real chips), are supplemented by daily specials including native oysters (in season) and poached dishes such as lemon sole or halibut in a fresh herb sauce. Homely sweets like enjoyable Bakewell tart or jam roly-poly to finish. *Minimum charge £4. Unlicensed – but bring your own. No dogs.*

Verbanella Pasta Bar

15 Blandford Street W1
MAP 11 B3
01-935 8896
P street parking

Open 12–3 & 6–10.30 (12–10 in summer)
Closed Sun & Bank Hols

Tagliatelle alla carbonara £3.50   Fruit brûlée £1.70

Decorated in the bright colours of the Italian tricolour, this popular little restaurant with pavement tables offers simple starters including good minestrone and salads and traditional Italian pasta dishes like tronette al pesto with above average home-made pesto and freshly cooked noodles, and special dishes of the day such as osso buco milanese. There are a few simple sweets too, including ice creams and fruit salads. *No dogs.*

Credit Access, Amex, Diners, Visa   **LVs**

Victoria & Albert Museum, New Restaurant

Cromwell Road SW7
MAP 12 A5
01-581 2159
P meter parking &

Open 10–5, Sun 2.30–5.30
Closed 1 Jan, Good Fri, May Day Bank
Hol & 25 & 26 Dec

Cream of spinach & watercress soup 90p
Barnsley chop in port & wine sauce £2.65
🍵

After the museum why not visit this airy
self-service restaurant? The main section
is furnished with attractive solid beech
tables and chairs, while the splendid
Painted Room is decorated with trompe
l'oeuil fascination. Dishes change daily
according to what's fresh and all are tasty
and cooked to a high standard. A variety
of salads and meat and fish dishes are
offered. There are lavish cakes and pastries, or simpler ones if you prefer. *Non-
smoking area. No dogs.*

LVs

Villa Estense

642 King's Road SW6
MAP 12 A6
01-731 4247
P street parking

Open 12.30–2.30 & 7–11.30
Closed Sun eve, Bank Hols & 4 days
Xmas

Tagliatelle carbonara £3.80 Escalope of
veal in mushroom & cream sauce £4.70

Excellent home-made pasta is the favourite
choice at this smart, bright Italian restaurant. Try the tagliatelle carbonara or perhaps penne all' arrabbiata with a garlicky
tomato, black olive and parsley sauce. A
lengthy list of pizzas includes lavish
pescatore with clams, prawns, squid and
anchovies, while veal, fish and chicken
dishes provide appetising alternatives.
There are also crisp salads and simple
sweets. Patio. *No dogs.*

Credit Access, Amex, Visa

Village Delicatessen & Coffee Shop

61 Blythe Road W14
MAP 10 B5
01–602 1954
P street parking

Open 9.30–4, Sun 10–2
Closed Bank Hols

Chicken & avocado bake £2.95
Vegetarian chilli £2.25

A short walk from the Olympia Exhibition
Halls takes you to this intimate basement
coffee shop, where a blackboard lists the
tasty wholesome dishes, like a delicious
roulé and spinach pancake in Gruyère and
mushroom sauce served with a beautifully
fresh green salad. Other choices range
from soup, taramasalata, houmus and pâté
for starters to quiches, jacket potatoes and
lamb provençale. Interesting sweets such
as pineapple shortcake or chocolate and
rum gâteau. *No dogs.*

LVs

Volker Europa Wine Bar

18 Orange Street WC2
MAP 13 B3
01-930 8849
P NCP in Whitcombe Street

Open 12–3 & 5.30–11
Closed Sat, Sun, Bank Hols & 1 wk
Xmas

German pea soup £2 Grilled German
sausages £3.80 🍵

Volker Kunz knows all his regulars by
name at this atmospheric cellar wine bar –
and also finds time to cook, and serve wine.
Simple, tasty snacks based on good fresh
ingredients include delicious smoked sausages and hearty German pea soup with
frankfurters, as well as sandwiches, cold
meat salads and filled jacket potatoes. Hot
baby rum babas are a favourite finale, and
there is a choice of over 25 different
champagnes available by the glass.

Credit Access, Amex, Diners, Visa **LVs**

Waldorf Hotel, Palm Court Lounge

Aldwych WC2
MAP 13 D2
01-836 2400
P NCP in Drury Lane

Open 7–6.30

Set afternoon tea £8.95   Buffet
breakfast £8.50   🍷

Coolly elegant in cream, soft green and
marble, the perennially appealing Palm
Court Lounge is open throughout the day
for some thoroughly tempting snacks.
Breakfast can start as early as 7am, while
light lunches (from 11.30) include delicious sandwiches, plus the New York
Waldorf salad and its London counterpart.
Afternoon tea itself (3.30–6.30) brings
scones, toasted muffins and a choice of
cakes, pastries and dainty sandwiches.
Smooth, if unhurried, service. *No dogs.*

Credit Access, Amex, Diners, Visa

Westbury Hotel Lounge

New Bond Street W1
MAP 13 A3
01-629 7755
P NCP in Burlington Street   ♿

Open 8.30am–11pm

Full afternoon tea £9   Clubhouse
sandwich £7   🍷

A luxurious retreat from the hustle and
bustle of Mayfair's Bond Street, this
handsome lounge sports fine pine panelling, plush chairs and an open fireplace.
Light breakfasts are followed by morning
coffee and a lunchtime buffet, but the real
highlight is afternoon tea. Beautifully
served finger sandwiches, toasted scones
or teacakes with clotted cream and jams
and a small selection of pastries accompany
an excellent pot of loose-leaf tea. Sandwiches available in the evening. *No dogs.*

Credit Access, Amex, Diners, Visa

Wholemeal Café

1 Shrubbery Road SW16
MAP 10 C6
01-769 2423
P street parking

Open 12–10
Closed 1 wk Xmas

Spinach & mushroom lasagne £2.80
Fruit crumble £1.10

Ever popular, this cheerful pine furnished
café continues to offer good snacks at
reasonable prices. Order at the counter
where you will find a soup – perhaps onion
and sunflower or sherry and potato – and
a choice of inventive salads (like mushroom
and avocado or broccoli and red pepper),
quiche and two daily hot dishes – chick
pea and coriander casserole or mushroom
and tomato cheese bake, perhaps. Finish
with fruit crumble, fruit salad or home-
made biscuits. *No smoking. No dogs.*

Wilkins Natural Foods

61 Marsham Street SW1
MAP 12 C5
01-222 4038
P meter parking

Open 8–5
Closed Sat, Sun & Bank Hols

Hot daily savoury £1.59   Date slice 56p

There is a simple but pleasing selection of
dishes at this counter-service wholefood
restaurant. From early morning there are
scones, yoghurt and cakes on offer, to be
followed a short time later by a few
imaginative salads. At midday hot dishes
like macaroni and mixed vegetable pie in a
cheesy sauce or chilli bean stew, samosas,
pizzas and filled baps appear. Try the fruit
bake or creamy tiramisu for dessert.
Unlicensed. No smoking. No dogs.

LVs

Wine Gallery

294 Westbourne Grove W11
MAP 9 B4
01-229 1877
P meter parking
Open 12–3 & 6–12
Closed 25 & 26 Dec

232 Brompton Road SW3
MAP 12 B5
01-584 3493
P meter parking
Open 12–3 & 6–12
Closed Sat eve, all Sun & 25 & 26 Dec

49 Hollywood Road SW10
MAP 12 A6
01-325 7572
P meter parking
Open 12–3 & 6–12
Closed 25 & 26 Dec

Fish pâté with spinach & herb sauce
£2.80   Mozzarella & turkey croquettes
£4.20 ⊖

Three attractive wine bars whose walls – as the name implies – are hung with fine contemporary paintings for sale. Arrive early to ensure a table at mealtimes, then make your choice from the varied and imaginative menu (the same at all three branches). Dishes such as flavoursome duck terrine with onion marmalade, smoked chicken, melon and avocado salad or freshwater fish pâté with spinach and herb sauce all make elegantly enjoyable snacks or starters. More substantial dishes range from beef bourguignon, vegetable curry and spare ribs with barbecue sauce to tasty cod fishcakes served with lobster sauce and crisp, golden chips or homely sausage, beans and mash. There's a short but excellent selection of both wines and desserts (note the rich, smooth chocolate mousse), and service is well-meaning and friendly. *No dogs.*

Credit Access, Visa

Woodlands Restaurant

77 Marylebone Lane W1
MAP 11 B3
01-486 3862
P NCP in Moxon Street
Open 12–3 & 6–11
Closed 25 Dec

37 Panton Street SW1
MAP 13 B3
01-839 7258
P meter parking
Open 12–3 & 6–11
Closed 25 & 26 Dec

402a High Road, Wembley
MAP 9 A3
01-902 9869
P street parking
Open 12–3 & 6–11
Closed 25 Dec

Onion rava masala £3.95   Chapatis with kurma £3.95

Part of a large chain, these three restaurants serve expertly cooked Southern Indian vegetarian food. Fresh herbs and spices create clean, distinctive and subtle flavours. Thalis, the set meals, are a good introduction to this type of food and staff are happy to offer explanations. A selection of starters as snacks could include potato bonda, potato stuffed patties, dahi vada, refreshingly spiced yoghurt with lentil doughnuts, or cashew nut pakoda – cashew nuts coated in crunchy lentil batter. There are nine dosa (pancake) dishes ranging from the plain rice and lentil dosa to the accomplished rava masala dosa, a cream of wheat pancake filled with onions, potatoes, nuts and spices. More unusually, uthappam are lentil pizzas topped with cabbage, tomatoes or coconut. Kurma, mixed vegetable curry, is an excellent rice dish. Delicious desserts, especially gulab jaman. *Minimum charge £4. No dogs.*

Credit Access, Amex, Diners, Visa

Yumi

110 George Street W1
MAP 11 B3
01-935 8320
P NCP Portman Hotel

Open 12–2.30 & 6–10.45
Closed Sat lunch, all Sun, Bank Hols,
1 wk Aug & 10 days Xmas

Red tuna sushi £1.50   Shake maki £3

Sit up at the bar to watch your sushi being skilfully prepared at this charmingly run Japanese restaurant, or eat the same dishes in the little restaurant downstairs. Fish is particularly well represented on the comprehensive list of excellent sushi; a beautifully fresh medley of salmon, turbot, tuna, mackerel and king prawns is highly recommendable. Delicious, too, are the popular hand rolls, including cucumber and egg. *No dogs.*

Credit Access, Amex, Diners, Visa

ENGLAND

ABBOTS BROMLEY   *Marsh Farm Tea Rooms*

Uttoxeter Road
MAP 5 B1 *Staffordshire*
Burton on Trent (0283) 840323
P own car park

Open 3–6
Closed Fri & end Oct–Easter Sun

Ham salad £1.90   Sherry trifle 60p

These tea rooms form part of a working farm, and Mrs Hollins uses fresh, untreated milk from her cows and free range eggs to noticeably delicious effect. Moist home-cooked meats – ham, beef and chicken – plus salmon and cheese are served as wholemeal sandwiches or with a green salad. Sweet delights include apple tarts, gâteaux and light sponges with home-made jams – like the aromatic damson which graces the fruit scones. Please phone first during the week. *Unlicensed. No dogs.*

ALDEBURGH   *N·E·W ENTRY*   *Aldeburgh Festival Wine Bar*

High Street
MAP 6 F2 *Suffolk*
Aldeburgh (072 885) 3743
P street parking

Open 11–5
Closed Mon

Ham ploughman's £2.15   Treacle & nut pie £1

Tucked behind the Festival box office, this modest little wine bar makes an excellent choice for a light snack. From the menu available throughout opening hours, enjoy a flavoursome vegetable soup, then tuck into a tasty ploughman's of home-cooked gammon or go for a seafood salad (perhaps local crab in season) or a hot daily special like lasagne or chicken liver sauté. Round off your meal with treacle and nut pie or chocolate mousse. *No children before 3pm.*

ALDERMINSTER   *N·E·W ENTRY*   *Bridge House*

Nr Stratford-upon-Avon
MAP 5 B2 *Warwickshire*
Stratford-upon-Avon (078 987) 521
P street parking

Open 2–6
Closed Mon, most Bank Hols & end Oct–Easter

Set afternoon tea £2.75   Salmon sandwich 95p

Five miles south of Stratford, right on the A34, is this delightful cottage tea room backing onto open fields full of sheep. Inside, high-backed chairs and stylish dressers combine with pretty fabrics and patchwork tablecloths to provide a most relaxed setting to enjoy a selection of delicious cakes and scones and a good refreshing cup of tea served in elegant white china. Try the Hollywood cake, beautifully moist with chocolate, biscuits and raisins, or the lovely coffee sponge. *No dogs.*

ALFRISTON   *Drusillas Thatched Barn*

Drusillas Corner
MAP 6 E4 *East Sussex*
Alfriston (0323) 870234
P own car park &

Open 10.30–5
Closed 1 Jan, 25 & 26 Dec & limited opening Nov–Mar

Soup with soda bread £1.65   Tipsy Sussex cake £1.45

Part of a complex which also includes a zoo, gardens and English wine centre, this spacious barn makes an attractive setting for coffee and cream teas. Serve yourself from the counter display of delicious cakes and bread baked on the premises. At lunchtime, there's Sussex vegetable broth, honey roast ham, roast chicken, savoury flans and ploughman's, with fruit crumble to finish. Garden and patio. *Non-smoking area. No dogs.*

Credit Access, Amex, Visa

ALFRISTON   *Singing Kettle*

6 Waterloo Square, Nr Polegate
MAP 6 E4 *East Sussex*
Alfriston (0323) 870723
P street parking

Open 10–5 (till 6 in summer)
Closed Mon (except Bank Hols), 25
& 26 Dec & early Jan–mid Feb

Ploughman's lunch £1.60   Scone tea
£1.35

The building is as old as the Mary Rose,
and the tea shop it houses is the longest
running in town. Geoffrey and Betty Carey
will adorn your lace-clothed table with pots
of tea and pile high your plate with cakes
like a Genoese iced lemon sponge, featherlight scones, a rich, moist ginger slice,
fruit cake or shortbread. A simple lunch of
rarebits, soups or sandwiches is available
from noon until two. It's a popular place,
so be prepared for a squeeze. *Unlicensed.*

ALNWICK   N·E·W   *John Blackmore's Restaurant*
                    ENTRY

1 Dorothy Forster Court, Narrowgate
MAP 4 D1 *Northumberland*
Alnwick (0665) 604465
P Polegate car park

Open 10.30–3 (till 5 in summer)
Closed Sun, Mon, 25 & 26 Dec, all Jan

Cold pheasant & chicken £2.50   Rich
chocolate mousse & blackcurrant sauce
£1.10 🫖

A charming restaurant in an 18th-century
town house where everything is carefully
prepared by John Blackmore. Try his
flavoursome chicken and carrot soup
followed by quiche and salad, a filled jacket
potato, tasty open sandwich or the day's
hot special. Sweets include freshly baked
fruit gâteau, while scones are popular
teatime treats. More elaborate evening
meals Thursday, Friday and Saturday. *No
smoking. No dogs.*

Credit Access, Amex, Visa

ALSTON   *Brownside Coach House*

MAP 3 C2 *Cumbria*
Alston (0498) 81263
P own car park &

Open 10–6
Closed Tues & Oct–Easter

Cumberland sausage £2.65
Rum butter & apricot tartlet 90p

Fine views and honest home-cooked fare
are on offer at Margery Graham's converted
coachhouse. Bacon and egg pie, sandwiches and baked potatoes are available all
day, while scones and fresh cream sponges
accompany morning coffee and afternoon
tea. Lunchtime brings treats like Cumberland sausages, smoked trout and pork
chops in creamy mustard sauce, with
home-made ice cream or popular toffee
and banana flan to finish. *Unlicensed. No
dogs.*

ALSTONEFIELD   *Old Post Office Tea Rooms*

Nr Ashbourne
MAP 5 B1 *Derbyshire*
Alstonefield (033 527) 201
P own car park

Open 10–12.15 & 2–5.30
Closed Wed, Fri & mid March–mid
November

Cream tea £1.70   Sandwich tea £2.50
🫖

Doubling as the village stores and post
office in a picturesque village, this delightful establishment also has two attractive
little tea rooms. Mrs Allen provides a
simple but extremely enjoyable selection
of light snacks, ranging from an egg to
superb honey roast ham sandwiches. There
are freshly-baked scones with delicious
locally-made jam and very tempting cakes
– chocolate fudge and lemon or raspberry
Bakewell tarts. *Unlicensed. Non-smoking
area. No dogs.*

ALTON

Apple Crumble

5 Normandy Street
MAP 5 C3 *Hampshire*
Alton (0420) 541176
P Orchard Lane car park

Open 9–4 (Sun 12–5)
Closed 1 Jan & 25, 26 Dec

Nut & cheese vegetable crumble £2.20
Pavlova £1.20 🥄

Old mahogany shopfittings run along one side of this wholefood vegetarian teashop and takeaway. Baking is done by the owners and local women, and includes flapjacks, scones, biscuits and sponge cakes. For the savoury palate, there are quiches, sandwiches, hot dishes like a well-flavoured tomato and vegetable brown rice risotto, or crispy mushroom layer. Devon apple cake and – of course – apple crumble, are among the puddings. *Unlicensed. No smoking.*

ALTRINCHAM   *Nutcracker Vegetarian Restaurant*

43 Oxford Road
MAP 3 C4 *Greater Manchester*
061-928 4399
P street parking

Open 10–4.45 (Wed till 2)
Closed Sun & Bank Hols

Spinach & pancake layer £2.25
Passandra £2.25 🥄

In a quiet side street Wendy Hatton and David Allen run their charming self-service vegetarian restaurant. The goodies include soup of the day, various quiches, baked potatoes, filled rolls, mixed salads and a hot dish of the day like vegetable pie sprinkled with sesame seeds. The sweets are very tempting (cheesecake, florentines and fresh fruit salad), and can be enjoyed with a good selection of speciality teas. *Children's portions. Non-smoking area. No dogs.*

AMBLESIDE   *Rothay Manor*

Rothay Bridge
MAP 3 C3 *Cumbria*
Ambleside (053 94) 33605
P own car park &

Open 12.30–2 & 3.30–5.30

Closed Early Jan–mid Feb

Home-made soup & roll £1
Buffet £4.50   Raspberry &
apple pie £1.65   Set afternoon
tea £4 🄟 🥄

★ Time your visit for the afternoon and you will be able to enjoy the splendid set tea in the inviting twin lounges of this pleasant hotel. Antique coffee tables combine well with ample armchairs and settees. Help yourself from a tempting display to moist banana bread or bara brith, apple sponge, brandy snaps, rich fruit cake and fresh cream gâteau, balancing the calorie intake with savoury bouchées, quiche and excellent home-cooked ham in sandwiches. At lunchtime, there is an appetising set-price buffet of cold cuts and salads, or just choose soup followed by cheese or a fruit pie. Home-baked biscuits accompany morning coffee. Lunch on Sundays is a traditional set meal. Garden and patio. *No dogs.* ★

Credit Access, Amex, Diners, Visa

AMBLESIDE

Sheila's Cottage

The Slack
MAP 3 C3 *Cumbria*
Ambleside (053 94) 33079
P King Street car park

Open 10.30–5.30

Closed Sun & all Jan

Salmon terrine £4.95   Smoked salmon & avocado roulade £5
Westmorland walnut & raisin tart £1.60   Lemon ice cream £1.50

★ Superb food, friendly, efficient service and a warm, bustling atmosphere help make this charming restaurant such a continuing delight. Lunchtime is especially popular (do book), when tempting savouries like herby Stilton pâté, marinated local herrings and sugar-baked ham with blackberry chutney can be followed by such luscious desserts as apricot strudel, sticky toffee pudding and brown bread ice cream. Mornings bring wonderful cakes and pastries – try richly delicious sachertorte – to enjoy with Swiss drinking chocolate topped with Jersey cream, while at teatime there's lovely lemon bread with lemon cheese, muffins and spicy bara brith. *Minimum lunchtime charge £3. Non-smoking area. No dogs.* ★

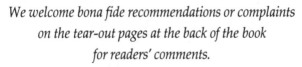

We welcome bona fide recommendations or complaints on the tear-out pages at the back of the book for readers' comments.

They are followed up by our professional team, but do complain to the management on the spot.

AMBLESIDE

Zeffirellis

Compston Road
MAP 3 C3 *Cumbria*
Ambleside (053 94) 33845
P car park behind

Open Café: 10–5.30; Pizzeria: 12–2.30 & 5–9.45
Closed Café: Thurs in winter & 25 & 26 Dec; Pizzeria: Mon, Thurs, Fri lunch & all Tues & Wed in winter

Fresh pasta with Stilton & mushroom sauce £3.95   Pizza funghi £2.95

Part of a shopping and cinema complex, both pizzeria and café offer imaginative and tasty vegetarian and wholefood dishes. Japanese Art Deco is the style of the pizzeria, where you can feast on wheatmeal and sesame seed pizzas topped with, perhaps, aubergines, courgettes, pine kernels and olives, or freshly made pasta with a choice of sauces. Downstairs, the Garden Room Café offers savoury snacks such as lentil and vegetable soup, and some good home baking. *No smoking. No dogs.*

Credit Access, Visa

ARUNDEL

N·E·W ENTRY

Belinda's Tea Rooms

13 Tarrant Street
MAP 6 D4 *West Sussex*
Arundel (0903) 882977
P Crown Yard car park

Open 10–5
Closed Mon (Oct–Jul) 4 wks Xmas

Steak & kidney pudding £2.95   Passion cake £1.25

Dark beams hung with shining brass and copperware, fresh flowers on polished wooden tables and pretty porcelain plates set the scene at Phyllis and Brendon McCartains' delightful tea shop, built as a barn in 1560. At lunchtime, tuck into fried plaice or the day's roast, followed by a homely steamed sponge. Teatime brings freshly cut sandwiches, light scones and tempting sweet treats such as moist passion cake. Garden and patio. *Non-smoking area. No dogs.*

ASHBOURNE

Ashbourne Gingerbread Shop

26 St John Street
MAP 5 B1 *Derbyshire*
Ashbourne (0335) 43227
P street parking

Open 8–5
Closed Sun (except 6 weeks July & Aug), 1 Jan & 25 & 26 Dec

Buck rarebit £1.35   Bakewell pudding £1.05

Delicately flavoured gingerbread men (available plain or chocolate coated) are the stars of the show at this characterful old beamed coffee shop run by the same family of bakers for over 100 years. Other sweet treats include prettily decorated fancy cakes, apple strudel, vanilla cheesecake, lemon torte and Black Forest gâteau, while on the savoury side there's a simple choice of open sandwiches (maybe turkey or prawn), and toasted snacks. *Unlicensed. No dogs.*

ASHBURTON

Studio Tea Shop

Kingsbridge Lane
MAP 8 C2 *Devon*
Ashburton (0364) 53258
P town centre car park

Open 9–6
Closed Sun, 1 Jan & 25 & 26 Dec

Beef stew & dumplings £1.65
Chocolate cake 70p   🍷 ☕

Admire Raymond Hunt's paintings in his first-floor gallery while you wait for a table (there are only four) in Mrs Hunt's spotless tea room below. The menu is sensibly short, the quality high: super home-baked cakes (try the apple, date and walnut), deliciously crumbly scones, freshly made sandwiches and a choice of ploughman's. There is always a popular home-made soup, too, plus an appetising daily hot special like sausage pie or a quiche. *Unlicensed.*

ASHFORD IN THE WATER

Cottage Tea Room

Fennel Street, Nr Bakewell
MAP 4 D4 *Derbyshire*
Bakewell (062 981) 2488
P Fennel Street car park   ♿

Open 10.30–12 & 2.30–5.30 (till 5 in winter)
Closed Tues, 1 Jan, Good Fri, 25 & 26 Dec & 1 wk Oct

Dark chocolate cake 50p   Savoury scone tea £1.65   🍷

A warm welcome and some delicious home baking await visitors to Betty and Bill Watkins' delightful village tea room. Morning coffee sees shortbread and lovely cakes like date and walnut or dark chocolate, while buttered currant loaf, cheese and herb scones, spicy farmhouse cake and freshly baked bread feature in the choice of set teas – all accompanied by an excellent brew. *Minimum charge £1.50 after 2.30. Unlicensed. No smoking. No dogs.*

ASHTEAD

34 The Street
MAP 6 D3 Surrey
Ashtead (037 22) 75491
P Peace Memorial Hall car park

Open 12–2 & 6–10.30
Closed Sat lunch, all Sun & Mon, Good
Fri & 25 & 26 Dec

Spiced chick peas with rice £2.25   Plum
crumble £1.15   🍲

Bart's

Cool and clever decor of wicker and
stainless steel sets the scene for this
wholefood vegetarian restaurant at one
end of the main shopping street. The short
lunch menu starts with soup and might be
followed by almond risotto or chilli bean
casserole. Well-prepared dishes also include flans, soups (tomato and lentil),
cheese and hazelnut pâté, buckwheat roast
or lasagne seasoned with walnuts and
sunflower seeds. Crumbles and home-made
ice cream. *Unlicensed. Non-smoking
area. No dogs.*

ATHERSTONE

66 Long Street
MAP 5 B1 Warwickshire
Atherstone (0827) 717293
P town-centre car parks

Open 12–2 & 7–11
Closed Sun

Beef stroganoff £6 Lasagne with salad &
jacket potato £2.95   ⊖

Cloisters Wine Bar and Bistro

Pictures of film stars adorn this unassuming wine bar/bistro, which offers imaginative and enjoyable cooking. Starters
include soup, stuffed mushrooms, fresh
herrings or pâté, and main courses might
be tuna in cucumber sauce, lamb and
courgette bake, smoked haddock pasta,
meat balls in chilli sauce or Mexican
chicken. Seasonal sweets range from summer pudding and speciality ice creams to
bread and butter pudding and jam roly-
poly. Lighter lunchtime snacks. *No dogs.*

Credit Access, Visa

*Prices given are as at the time of our research
and thus may change.*

ATHERSTONE

5 Market Street
MAP 5 B1 Warwickshire
Atherstone (0827) 715638
P market square

Open 9–5 (Thurs till 2)
Closed Sun, 2 days Xmas

Cauliflower & sweetcorn au gratin £2
Beefburger & salad £1

Muffins Salad Bar

Simple snacks, main meals and sound
home baking are the order of the day at
this unassuming little café. Toasted sandwiches, salads and filled jacket potatoes
provide light savoury bites, while the
hungry can tuck into nourishing soup
followed by a juicy burger, lamb casserole
or a vegetarian special – like their ever-
popular cauliflower and sweetcorn au
gratin. The apple pie, made with light,
buttery pastry, is first rate, and there's a
set cream tea in the afternoon. *No dogs.*

AVEBURY   *Stones Restaurant*

Marlborough
MAP 5 B3 *Wiltshire*
Avebury (06723) 514
P village car park &

Open 10–6 (Nov–Easter till 5)

Closed Mon–Fri Nov–Easter & 1
Jan & 25 & 26 Dec

Macaroni casserole with fromage
frais £2.40   Gougère filled with
baby mushrooms & corn £1.50
Rum & Cognac truffle cake £1.50
Cream tea £2   ⊖

★ Queueing at weekends with people who have travelled
from London just to sample Hilary Howard's inventive and refreshing vegetarian fare is not uncommon.
Home-made bread and scones vie for space with
gingerbread men at a self-service counter groaning
with salutary salads to accompany flans of perhaps
smoked cheese and chervil. Vegetables and herbs are
grown in the garden and organic cheeses, Wiltshire
unsalted butter, and fromage frais are freshly
delivered. Gooseberry champagne adds a lunchtime
sparkle to the 'Megaliths' daily specials or a 'Mason's
Lunch' of organic cheeses. Body replenished, repair
the soul with views over Avebury manor by the
ancient stone circles. Children's portions. *Non-
smoking area.* ★

AYLESBURY   *Seatons*

5 Market Square
MAP 5 C2 *Buckinghamshire*
Aylesbury (0296) 27582
P Buckingham Street car park

Open 12–2.30 & 7–10
Closed Mon eve, all Sun & 5 days Xmas

Roast beef & horseradish open sandwich
£3.25   Baked avocado £3.75   ⊖

Right in the town centre, this lively,
welcoming wine bar gets especially busy at
lunchtimes. Regulars flock for the imaginative and enjoyable food that ranges from
colourful open sandwiches and salad platters to main meals such as plaice with
mussels in tarragon cream sauce, vegetable
couscous or a daily special like creamy
almond chicken. Sweets such as apple,
date and pineapple crumble or a simple
fresh fruit salad make a satisfying finale.
No dogs.

Credit Access, Amex, Diners, Visa   **LVs**

BAKEWELL   *Aitch's Wine Bar & Bistro*

4 Buxton Road
MAP 4 D4 *Derbyshire*
Bakewell (062 981) 3895
P town-centre car parks &

Open 11.30–2.30 & 7–11
Closed Sun (Sept–April), 1 Jan & 25 Dec

Pickled Scottish salmon £2.75   Potted
Stilton in port & wine £2   ⊖

The generous dishes are carefully prepared
to order at this informal, friendly place,
but newspapers and periodicals are provided to while away any waiting time. The
short menu is varied and imaginative; the
dishes well flavoured, properly seasoned
and very satisfying. The Mediterranean
fish soup is pleasingly peppery and the
moussaka authentic with tasty lamb and a
thick creamy béchamel. Other specials
might be Cantonese vegetable bean pot or
chicken livers in peperonata sauce. Sweets
are simple but tempting. *No dogs.*

BAKEWELL   *Green Apple*

Diamond Court, Water Street
MAP 4 D4 *Derbyshire*
Bakewell (062 981) 4404
P Granby Road car park

Open 11–2, also 7–10 Wed–Sat
Closed Sun (except summer), 25 & 26
Dec & 2 wks Jan

Derbyshire cheese pudding £2.50
Banoffi pie £1.20 🫖

In a side street off the town square, this
attractive stone-walled restaurant offers
healthy, innovative cuisine. Owner-chef
Roger Green continues to please with his
menu – aubergine pâté or mackerel and
cider mousse; spinach and mushroom
wholewheat lasagne, salami ratatouille, or
lamb and leek pie, as main course. Puddings include pavlova, banoffi pie or an
imaginative plum cake. Slightly wider
choice in evenings. *No smoking.*

Credit Access, Diners, Visa

BARDEN   *Howgill Lodge*

Nr Skipton
MAP 4 D3 *North Yorkshire*
Burnsall (075 672) 655
P own car park

Open 10–6
Closed Mon, Bank Hols (except Good
Fri), weekdays Oct–Easter & 1 wk Xmas

Roast ham £3.80   Cream tea £1.80
🫖

Enjoying a lovely setting high up in the
Yorkshire Dales National Park, this
homely little restaurant offers peace, quiet
and some satisfying home-cooked fare.
Grilled ham and eggs, sirloin steak and
Scottish smoked trout with salad are
popular main meals, while lighter bites
include sandwiches and salads. Afternoon
tea brings scones and moist chocolate
cake, and there are simple sweets like
seasonal fruit pies and sherry trifle, too.
No dogs.

BARNARD CASTLE   *Market Place Teashop*

29 Market Place
MAP 4 D2 *Co. Durham*
Teesdale (0833) 690110
P Market Place

Open 10–5.30 (Sun from 3)
Closed Sun in Jan–Feb & 10 days Xmas

Leek au gratin £1.95   Steak & kidney
pudding £2.40 🫖

Dating back to 1702, this characterful tea
room with flagstone floor and antique
furniture offers an all-day menu. The
dishes of the day might be spinach, cheese
and brown rice savoury, a tasty steak and
kidney pudding with a generous serving of
vegetables, and there are also snacks on
toast. The cakes on display are mostly
home-made and the scones are freshly
baked. The good selection of teas come in
attractive mock-antique silver pots.

BARNARD CASTLE   *Priors Restaurant*

7 The Bank
MAP 4 D2 *Co. Durham*
Teesdale (0833) 38141
P street parking

Open 10–5 (Sat till 6), June–Sept 10–6
(Sat till 7)
Closed Sun Nov–Easter & 1 Jan & 25
& 26 Dec

Leek croustade £1.75   Cheesecake 90p
🫖

Festooned with hanging plants this pristine vegetarian restaurant cum art and
craft shop displays an appetising selection
of wholefood fare at a self-service counter.
Mrs Prior masterminds the dishes including spicy bean and vegetable casserole,
quiches with excellent wholewheat pastry,
baked potatoes and sandwiches. Robust
salads accompany and upsidedown cake,
Bakewell tart or chocolate cake follow.
Stone walled courtyard for summer eating.
Non-smoking area. No dogs.

Credit Access, Amex, Diners, Visa

BARNSTAPLE   *Lynwood House*

Bishops Tawton Road
MAP 8 B1 *Devon*
Barnstaple (0271) 43695
P own car park

Open 12–2 & 7–9.30 (till 10 in summer)

Duck liver pâté £2.95   Steak sandwich
£4.25   ⊖

Ask for the bar snack menu at this family-run downstairs restaurant in a converted Victorian house. Local produce is used wherever possible and fish dishes are particularly good – from flavoursome fish soup to grilled sprats with mustard seasoning, Devon smoked salmon and lemon mousse with creamy prawn sauce. Equally tasty alternatives include omelettes, salads and home-cooked gammon, with meringue glâcé among tempting sweets. *No dogs.*

Credit Access, Visa

BASLOW   *Cavendish Hotel*

MAP 4 D4 *Derbyshire*
Baslow (024 688) 2311
P own car park

Open 12.30–2

Fennel & dill soup £2.75
Toad-in-the-hole £8.75
⊖ ♥

Sit in the plush, oak-furnished bar or elegantly comfortable lounge at this handsome hotel and enjoy a beautifully presented lunch chosen from a varied and imaginative list. The simplest dishes work best, including creamy chicken and calf's liver terrine, home-made venison sausages, tender grilled sirloin steak and garden-fresh salads. Finish with a rich, tempting dessert like chocolate and rum roulade with vanilla sauce. Polished, professional service. *No dogs.*

Credit Access, Amex, Diners, Visa

BATH   *Bath Puppet Theatre*

Riverside Walk, Pulteney Bridge
Town plan B3 *Avon*
Bath (0225) 312173
P Walcot Street car park

Open 10–5.30
Closed 25 & 26 Dec

Ploughman's £2.25   Coffee walnut
cake 85p

Good quality cooking and bottomless cups of tea go hand in glove at this delightful little coffee shop cum puppet theatre by the weir beneath Pulteney Bridge. Puppeteer owner Andrew Hume is the man also responsible for wholesome snacks such as hearty vegetable soup, toasted sandwiches, quiche, pizzas and garlic bread stuffed with houmous, tomatoes or cheese. On the sweet side, there are delicious cakes, slices and flapjacks. Terrace. *Unlicensed. No smoking.*

BATH   *Canary*

3 Queen Street
Town plan A3 *Avon*
Bath (0225) 24846
P Charlotte Street car park

Open 9.30–5.30, Sun 11–5.30
Closed 1 Jan & 25 & 26 Dec

Honey spiced chicken £2.85   Tuna
& pasta bake £3.10   ⊖ ♥

Live music on Saturday afternoons and wonderful baking create scrambling for tables in this small split-level tea-room. Proprietor Simon Davis's forte is baking – his Alice's fruit cake is full of moist fruits in a dark Guinness-fortified bread. His high-baked scones achieve a surprising lightness and go well with excellent loose leaf teas. Lunchtime sees open sandwiches, rarebits, omelettes and specials like crab cheesecake and fresh salmon. *Non-smoking area. No dogs.*

LVs

BATH   *Moon & Sixpence*

6a Broad Street
Town plan B3 *Avon*
Bath (0225) 60962
P   Broad Street car park

Open   11.30–2.30 & 5.30–10.30 (Fri & Sat till 11)
Closed   1 Jan & 25 & 26 Dec

Egg mayonnaise £3.45   Whole smoked mackerel £3.65   ☺

The delightful fountained courtyard of this wine bar cum restaurant is the perfect spot for a summer lunch. Choose from a super buffet selection of pâtés, quiches, meats and excellent salads, or go upstairs for waitress-service lunches or more elaborate evening meals. Warm pigeon breast with redcurrant jelly, pork with Dijon mustard and cream sauce and monkfish with green peppercorns are typical of the dishes you might find. *No dogs.*

Credit   Access, Amex, Visa

BATH   *Number Five*

5 Argyle Street
Town plan B3 *Avon*
Bath (0225) 444499
P   Walcot Street car park

Open   10am–10pm, Sun 12–2
Closed   Bank Hols

Pitta sandwich £2.95   Trawlerman's pie £4.25   ❦

You can get all the dishes at any time of the day at this stylish, informal place near Pulteney Bridge. There's now a three course fixed-price menu in the evenings, but you can still pop in for a snack. The all-day English breakfast is a treat, or try the generous sandwiches, the twice-baked soufflé or a salad. There are hot dishes too, like lamb chops with rosemary butter and desserts like meringues with whipped cream. Children's portions. *Non-smoking area.*

BATH   *Rossiter's*

38 Broad Street
Town plan B3 *Avon*
Bath (0225) 62227
P   Walcot Street car park

Open   10–5
Closed   Sun & Bank Hols

Cheese soufflé & cider sauce £3.50
Home-made soup £1.75   ❦

Healthy eating plays an important part at this stylish restaurant above Anne Rossiter's household goods store. At lunchtime, the appetising choice ranges from imaginative starters like parsnip and apple soup or mushroom and watercress pâté to vegetarian specials and hormone-free meat dishes such as noisettes of lamb en croûte. From the counter come light scones, flapjacks, hazelnut meringues, ginger cake and filled baps. *Non-smoking area. No dogs.*

Credit   Access, Visa

BATH   *Tarts Restaurant*

8 Pierrepont Place
Town plan B4 *Avon*
Bath (0225) 330280
P   NCP Manvers Street

Open   12–2.30 & 7–10.30
Closed   Sun, 1 Jan & 25 & 26 Dec

Baked avocado filled with prawns & quails' eggs £2.95   Roast lamb cutlets with rosemary £7.80   ☺

Daily specials supplement the regular menus at this alcoved basement restaurant. Follow Stilton and onion soup or smoked salmon and fennel pâté with, perhaps, chicken, mushroom and watercress pancake, whisky-flamed steak, or brill with cucumber and lime hollandaise. Lovely sweets include lemon cheesecake and raspberry and cream-filled hazelnut meringues. Full meals only served Friday and Saturday evenings. *Non-smoking area. No dogs.*

Credit   Access, Visa

BATH   *Theatre Vaults*

Sawclose
Town plan A3 *Avon*
Bath (0225) 65074
P Kingsmead Square

Open 12.30–2.30 & 6–7.30
Closed Sun (also Mon eve when no
performance) & 25 Dec

Smoked salmon & bacon quiche £3
Vegetarian pasty £3   🅟

Snacks and full meals can both be enjoyed
in the lively, atmospheric setting of the
Theatre Royal's stone vaults. At lunchtime
or before a show, there are light bites such
as soup, mushrooms and Gruyère roulade,
tagliatelle carbonara and smoked haddock
crêpe, as well as more substantial offerings
like roast pork, steak and chicken paprika.
Tempting sweets include hazelnut meringue, and there's a shorter more elaborate dinner menu. *No dogs.*

Credit Access, Diners, Visa

BATH   *The Walrus & the Carpenter*

28 Barton Street
Town plan A3 *Avon*
Bath (0225) 314864
P Charlotte Street car park

Open 12–2 & 6–11
Closed Sun lunchtime & 1 Jan
& 25 Dec

Winter vegetable stew £4.05
Cheese & bacon burger £3.85

Open now at lunchtimes as well as for
candlelit evening meals, this friendly,
informal bistro offers appetising dishes at
reasonable prices. Burgers are the mainstay, served with such tasty toppings as
mustard and apple sauce or sour cream
and chives. There are also steaks and
kebabs, plus vegetarian offerings like
sesame seed and aubergine pâté, spinach
lasagne or cheesy lentil loaf. Home-made
cakes and ices for afters. *Minimum charge
£3.65 on Fridays and Saturdays after
7pm. No dogs.*

BEAMINSTER   *N·E·W*
ENTRY   *Tea Shoppe*

6 Church Street
MAP 5 A4 *Dorset*
Beaminster (0308) 862513
P street parking

Open 10–5.30
Closed Wed, also Mon & Tues Xmas–
Easter & 1 Jan & 25 & 26 Dec

Filled omelette £2.75   Chicken & ham
pie £2.95   🅟   🍷

This wonderfully cottage tea shop fits the
bill perfectly. There's a good choice of
loose-leaf teas and a sideboard full of high
quality home baking. There are scones,
buns and cakes (like the light, moist lemon
sponge with a zesty lemon icing) with
coffee and lunchtime sees soup, salads,
jacket potatoes and pretty Danish open
sandwiches. The cream tea has warmed
scones with excellent clotted cream, cakes
and a choice of teas. *No smoking.*

BERKHAMSTED   *Cook's Delight*

360 High Street
MAP 6 D2 *Hertfordshire*
Berkhamsted (044 27) 3584
P street parking

Open 10–9 (Sat 10–3 & 8 till late, Sun
12–5)
Closed Mon–Wed, Bank Hols, 1 wk
Easter & 2 wks Aug

Carrot and seaweed quiche £1.75
Claypot £4.50   🍷

Khaieng Tyler brings an oriental touch to
the vegetarian, macrobiotic and meat
dishes in the tea room and garden behind
an organic health food shop. There is an
exceptional range of teas, a choice variety
of sweet things – like a rich carrot cake –
and savoury dishes that include green lentil
and onion salad, spicy turkey or carrot and
seaweed quiche, and bean casserole. More
elaborate evening dishes, when booking is
essential. Children's portions. *No smoking. No dogs.*

Credit Access, Visa

BERWICK-UPON-TWEED   *Funnywayt'Mekalivin*

53 West Street
MAP 2 D5 *Northumberland*
Berwick-upon-Tweed (0289) 308827
P   Bridge Street car park

Open   12–3
Closed   Thurs, Sun & Bank Hols

Lentil roast £2.75   Venison casserole
£2.85   🍵

Once a craft shop, this quaint little place packed with objets d'art is now a popular restaurant. Owner Elizabeth Middlemiss does all the cooking, from interesting starters like smooth mushroom and sherry soup to tasty entrées – perhaps broccoli and cauliflower crumble or venison casserole – and delicious caramel tart or cheese and oatcakes for afters. Book for fixed-price dinners served Friday and Saturday. *Unlicensed. Non-smoking area. No children under eight. No dogs.*

BERWICK-UPON-TWEED   *Kings Arms Hotel, Hideaway*

Hide Hill
MAP 2 D5 *Northumberland*
Berwick-upon-Tweed (0289) 307454
P   street parking

Open   12–2.30 & 6–10
Closed   25 Dec

Taramasalata £1.25   Rump steak £5.50
€

Simple, satisfying home-cooked fare from a sensibly short menu is available both lunchtimes and evenings at this smart little restaurant. Well-seasoned flavoursome leek and potato soup, freshly prepared chicken liver or fish pâté or seafood salad could precede a generous mixed grill (liver, lamb chop and sausage), fried fish, chicken cordon bleu or a juicy steak. Finish with an ice cream-based dessert or cinnamon-spiced apple pie. *No dogs.*

Credit   Access, Amex, Diners, Visa

BERWICK-UPON-TWEED   *Scotsgate Wine Bar*

1 Sidey Court, off Marygate
MAP 2 D5 *Northumberland*
Berwick-upon-Tweed (0289) 302621
P   Castlegate car park

Open   10–3 & 6.30–10.30 (Fri & Sat
till 11)
Closed   Mon eve, all Sun, 1 Jan & 25
& 26 Dec

Courgette & mushroom bake £2.65
Beef bourguignon £2.95   €

Fresh produce is used to excellent effect for a variety of tasty snacks at this attractive little wine bar. Local smoked trout, Scotch eggs, ploughman's and salads are all popular light bites, while daily-changing hot dishes might include watercress and chicken soup followed by vegetarian mushroom stroganoff or beef and potato pie. To finish, try a hot peach pancake or gin and lime sorbet, or sample the excellent cheeses. Children's menu. *No dogs.*

BEXHILL   *Trawlers*

60 Sackville Road
MAP 6 E4 *East Sussex*
Bexhill (0424) 210227
P   De la Warr Pavilion car park

Open   11.30–2 & 5–9 (Mon till 8)
Closed   Sun & 2–3 days Xmas

Cod & chips £2   Apple pie £1   🍵

Just a short walk from the seafront is this simple, spotlessly clean fish and chip restaurant. The fish is always fresh and is served in generous portions. There's ever-popular cod, plaice, and locally caught huss or skate cooked in a light, crisp batter and served with freshly-made chips. Meat pies and sausages are available for meat-eaters. Locally baked apple pie or pineapple fritters with ice cream round off your meal. Children's menu. *Minimum charge £1. No dogs.*

LVs

BIDDENDEN   *Claris's Tea Shop*

3 High Street
MAP 6 E3 *Kent*
Biddenden (0580) 291025
P village car park adjacent   &

Open 10.30–5.30
Closed Mon & 1 wk Xmas

Poached egg on toast 90p   Coffee
& walnut cake 70p

White china, white tablecloths and water-colours provide the cheerful background for tempting snacks and savoury dishes at this village tea shop. A large variety of cakes and pastries vie with fresh cream meringues and bread pudding. Hot beef and tomato soup or creamed mushrooms on toast make an appetising lunch. There is a good choice of speciality teas. Meals can be enjoyed in the pretty garden in summer. *Unlicensed. No smoking. No dogs.*

BILLERICAY   *Webber's Wine Bar*

2 Western Road
MAP 6 E3 *Essex*
Billericay (0277) 656581
P High Street car park

Open 11–2.30 & 6–10.30 (Mon from 7, Fri & Sat till 11)
Closed Sun, Bank Hols, 2 wks Aug & 1 wk Xmas

Mussels in parsley & white wine £5.95
Hot crab quiche £2.75

Imaginative food and outstanding wines make this lively wine bar a great favourite. Tuck into pâtés, cold meats and impressive salads from the display counter, or choose a blackboard special – perhaps smoked salmon and courgette quiche or rabbit casseroled in a bitter orange sauce. Chilli, garlic mushrooms and jacket potatoes are regular stalwarts, and irresistible sweets include hot sticky toffee pudding. *Minimum charge Friday and Saturday evenings £5. No dogs.*

Credit Access, Amex, Diners, Visa   **LVs**

BILLINGSHURST   *Burdocks*

59 High Street
MAP 6 D3 *West Sussex*
Billingshurst (040 381) 2750
P car park opposite

Open 9.30–5

Closed Mon (except Bank Hols) & 1 wk Xmas

Chicken & broccoli lasagne £2.95
Toasted sandwiches £1.50
Dundee cake 65p   Cherry
Bakewell 65p

★ New owners but the same high standards prevail, and a delightful array of home-baked treats can be enjoyed here or taken home. The cosy, beamed eating area has floral print cloths, antique furniture, and a black-leaded stove laden with, for example, a liberally almond-topped Dundee cake, chocolate fudge cake, Bakewell tart and a masterly light passion cake with butter icing and walnuts. The freshly made sandwiches include granary bread well filled with tender roast beef. A blackboard lists the weekly-changing lunchtime menu with, perhaps, Vichyssoise, country beef casserole and chicken and broccoli lasagne, for the heartier appetite. The loose leaf tea is outstanding in flavour, strength and quality. *Minimum lunchtime charge £2. No dogs.* ★

BIRDLIP

Kingshead House

Nr Gloucester
MAP 5 B2 *Gloucestershire*
Gloucester (0452) 862299
P own car park &

Open 12.15–2.15
Closed Sat & Sun lunch, all Mon

Tomato & mint soup £2.20   Filo pastry
pancake filled with spinach & Gruyère
cheese £3.75   ⊖

Judy Knock's cooking is unfailingly enjoyable at this mellow, welcoming bar. You
can lunch lightly on a plateful of
charcuterie or some first-rate soup, served
with home-baked wholemeal bread, or add
the daily special (perhaps piquant turkey
breasts with ginger) if you're really hungry.
Appetising alternatives include fresh pasta
with garlic mushrooms and a smoked fish
salad, while dessert might be a
mouthwatering walnut tart. *No dogs.*

Credit Access, Amex, Diners, Visa

BIRMINGHAM

Bobby Browns in Town

Burlington Passage, New Street
Town plan C2 *West Midlands*
021-643 4464
P The Pallasades car park

Open 12–2.30 & 6–10.45
Closed Sun lunch & 25 Dec

Fillet of sole with a grape, dry martini &
cream sauce £2.95   Noisettes of lamb in
redcurrant sauce £5.95   ⊖

Vibrant with life and colour, this popular
basement restaurant offers a wide variety
of capably prepared dishes – some simple,
others more exotic. Traditionalists might
opt for soup or pâté followed by steak,
mushroom and Guinness pie or roast
pheasant, while for the more adventurous
there are crudités, chicken in honey and
passion fruit sauce and veal Roquefort.
Toothsome desserts include light and fluffy
lemon crunch. *No dogs.*

Credit Access, Amex, Diners, Visa

BIRMINGHAM

Chung Ying

16 Wrottesley Street
Town plan C3 *West Midlands*
021-622 5669
P NCP in Ladywell Walk

Open 12–11.30 (Sun till 11)
Closed 25 Dec

Sizzling steak Cantonese-style £7
Crispy chicken £6.50

Cantonese dishes are carefully prepared
and full of flavour at this smart, friendly
Chinese restaurant close to the wholesale
market. Excellent dim sum are available
throughout the day, from favourite wafer-
wrapped king prawns to spare ribs in black
bean sauce, yam croquettes with diced
chicken and beef ball dumplings. Note,
too, the delicious hot and sour soup and
main courses such as fried king prawn and
scallop in bird's nest or sliced beef with
mushrooms and bamboo shoots. *No dogs.*

Credit Access, Amex, Diners, Visa

BIRMINGHAM

Forbidden City

36 Hurst Street
Town plan C3 *West Midlands*
021-622 2454
P street parking

Open dim sum 12–6 (full menu till
midnight)

Bean curd roll with diced chicken £1.10
Water chestnut cake £1   ♥

A stone's throw across Queensway from
New Street Station, this Chinese restaurant has many rooms sectioned off with
elaborate screens, and a casino upstairs.
Some forty dim sum dishes are offered
from deep-fried squid, prawn dumplings,
rice-flour pancakes and steamed pork balls
to the quite exceptional bean curd roll,
with diced chicken in a paper-thin deep-
fried pancake. Sweets might be egg waffles
or a water chestnut cake. More elaborate
meals in the evening. *No dogs.*

Credit Access, Visa **LVs**

BIRMINGHAM   *La Galleria*

New Library Complex, Paradise Place
Town plan B2 *West Midlands*
021-236 1006
P NCP in Cambridge Street &

Open 12–2.30 & 5.30–10.30 (Fri &
Sat till 11)
Closed Sun & Bank Hols

Kidneys in red wine £4.75   Ravioli
napoletana £3.55

The cooking has a strong Italian slant at
this popular city-centre wine bar. Fresh
fish is always available, with choices such
as whitebait, sardines, trout and halibut,
and there's a good choice of pasta dishes
and pizzas. Daily specials cater for the
carnivore (perhaps chicken chasseur, kebabs with savoury rice and chilli con carne),
while pleasant sweets like strawberry fool
or chocolate mousse round off one's meal.
No dogs.

Credit Access, Amex, Diners, Visa   **LVs**

BIRMINGHAM   *New Happy Gathering*

43 Station Street
Town plan C3 *West Midlands*
021-643 5247
P Pallasades car park

Open 12–11.45
Closed 4 days Xmas

Toasted prawns with sesame seeds £2
King prawn dumpling £1.40

Light and delicious dim sum suggests an
expert hand in the kitchen at this spacious
first-floor Chinese restaurant in the city
centre. The tempting selection includes
pork and king prawn dumplings, steamed
meat balls with Chinese mushrooms and
deep-fried wun tun. From the main menu
comes excellent hot and sour soup, plus
such enterprising main courses as baked
squid in salt and chilli or steamed chicken
wrapped in lotus leaves. Swift, friendly
service. *No dogs.*

Credit Access, Amex, Diners, Visa

BIRMINGHAM   *La Santé*

182 High Street, Harborne
Town plan A3 *West Midlands*
021-426 4133
P street parking

Open 7pm–10pm (Fri & Sat till 10.30)
Closed Sun, Mon & Bank Hols

Cheese fondue £3.20   Spinach crêpe
£2.60

Francophiles will enjoy the real countryside atmosphere at this quietly elegant
French vegetarian restaurant on the High
Street of a Birmingham suburb. The menu,
which changes fortnightly, is enterprising
with starters like spicy lentil soup and
garlicky breadcrumbed mushrooms preceding leek pie, raclette or courgettes
stuffed with hazelnuts and cheese. Pear
and ginger crumble and mango mousse are
typical sweets. *Unlicensed but bring your
own. No dogs.*

Credit Access, Visa

BISHOP'S CASTLE   *No 7*

7 High Street
MAP 5 A2 *Shropshire*
Bishop's Castle (0588) 638152
P street parking

Open 10–3 (Mon & Sat till 2.30)
Closed Sun & 1 wk Xmas

Bean & mushroom stroganoff £2
Lemon meringue pie 70p 🥄

People sit elbow to elbow at refectory
tables to enjoy the offerings in this tiny
restaurant where the food is simple but
well prepared and full of flavour. There are
vegetarian dishes like layered vegetables
in a light cheesy sauce with salad, and also
roast meats and steak and kidney pie. For
sweet things you'll find the home-made
cakes and sponges, scones, Welsh cakes
and the Bakewell tart very tempting. *Non-
smoking area. No dogs.*

BLANCHLAND   *White Monk Tea Room*

5 The Square, Nr Consett
MAP 3 C2 *Northumberland*
Blanchland (043 475) 276
P village car park

Open 2–5
Closed end Oct–Easter, also Mon–Fri
Easter–Spring Bank Hol

Set afternoon tea £1.65   Tea & cakes
£1.05 🍵

Nancy Morpeth has run this charming
village tea room, just a stone's throw from
the river Derwent, for over 15 years, and
her formula – good home baking and value
for money – is hard to beat. The full-blown
afternoon tea comprises freshly-made
sandwiches of salmon or egg mayonnaise
and buttered brown bread with home-made
jam. Fruity scones or moist walnut cake
are a hearty accompaniment to the good
strong tea. Daintier appetites can settle for
tea with scones or sandwiches. *Unlicensed.*

BLEWBURY   *Lantern Cottage*

South Street
MAP 5 C3 *Oxfordshire*
Blewbury (0235) 850378
P street parking &

Open 3–6
Closed Mon–Fri Jan & Feb &
all Xmas

Set afternoon tea £1.10

Beside the village green, Miss Glover's tiny
timber-framed cottage is the perfect setting
for a thoroughly traditional afternoon tea.
Sit at one of the five tables (each is provided
with a little brass handbell to summon
service) and tuck into hot buttered scones
with delicious home-made jam, featherlight Victoria sponge, miniature meringues, chocolate cake, iced fairy cakes
and a huge pot of tea. *Unlicensed. No
dogs.*

BODIAM   N·E·W   *Knollys*
                               ENTRY

Main Street
MAP 6 E3 *East Sussex*
Staple Cross (058 086) 323
P own car park &

Open 10.30–5.30
Closed mid Oct–Easter

Steak & kidney pie £2.95   Pavlova 95p
🍵

Within sight of Bodiam Castle, this lively,
well-run tea shop takes pride in its large
flower-filled garden – the perfect spot for
a snack on a summer's day. Baking is
Gloria Barratt's forte and her mouthwatering display of teatime treats ranges from
deliciously light scones to a superb cream-
filled Victoria sponge. At lunchtime,
there's home-made soup, sandwiches and
salads, as well as more substantial offerings
like lasagne and macaroni cheese. *No
dogs.*

BOLTON ABBEY   *Bolton Abbey Tea Cottage*

Nr Skipton
MAP 4 D3 *North Yorkshire*
Bolton Abbey (075 671) 495
P Bolton Abbey car park &

Open 9.30–6
Closed weekdays Nov–end Mar

Steak & kidney pie £3   Afternoon tea
£2.75 🍵

Stone-flagged floors, whitewashed walls
and pine furniture add to the appeal of
these two converted cottages next to the
post office. A magnificent display of cakes
near the front door attracts admiring
comments (and plenty of orders) while
savoury snacks include soup, sandwiches,
omelettes and lunchtime dishes such as
gammon and egg. Home-made fruit pie or
sticky toffee pudding for afters. Traditional
Sunday lunch. Eat outside in the sunny
garden if you wish. *No dogs.*

BOOT

Brook House Restaurant

Holmrook, Eskdale
MAP 3 B3 *Cumbria*
Eskdale (094 03) 288
P own parking &

Open 8.30am–8.30pm
Closed 2 days Xmas

Australian crunchy 55p   Spiced lentil
cakes £2.85

Charming new owners continue to maintain high standards at this cosy little restaurant, where hungry fell walkers can now stoke up throughout the year on tasty home-cooked fare. Hearty breakfasts start the day, while from around noon the choice embraces everything from soup and sandwiches to savoury nut loaf, Cumberland sausages and oven-baked trout. A set tea could be a fry-up or traditional scones, and sweet treats include trifle, meringues and tempting cakes. Terrace. *No dogs.*

Credit Access, Visa

BOURNEMOUTH

Carlton Hotel Lounge

East Overcliff
MAP 5 B4 *Dorset*
Bournemouth (0202) 22011
P own car park

Open 12–2.30 & 3.30–5.30

Afternoon tea £5.50   Steak sandwich
with French fries & salad £10.50   🍷

The lounge of this hotel has been splendidly remodelled. You can enjoy your snack overlooking the patio and the seafront beyond, or in leather armchairs by the fire. The afternoon tea is a real feast featuring dainty smoked salmon sandwiches, crumbly scones – with as much strawberry jam and clotted cream as you can manage – and pastries and fresh cakes. A good range of teas accompany these treats. Sandwiches and salads are served from noon to 2.30. *No dogs.*

Credit Access, Amex, Diners, Visa

BOURNEMOUTH

N·E·W
ENTRY

Henry's

6 Lansdowne Road
MAP 5 B4 *Dorset*
Bournemouth (0202) 297887
P street parking &

Open 11.30–2 & 6–10.30
Closed Sun & Mon eves & most Bank
Hols

Vegan burger salad £2   Tipsy
mushroom pie £3.50

'Mention if you are a vegan', one of the boards hung with greenery proclaims in this deservedly popular vegetarian restaurant. The young owners use quality ingredients and plenty of enthusiasm to imaginative effect. Starters include courgette croquettes and lentil pâté followed by vegetarian cottage pie or cheesy mushroom layer. Book in the evening when the menu extends to brazil nut roast and gravy or spinach lasagne. Vegan ice cream and plum crumble complete the occasion. *No dogs.*

LVs

BOURNEMOUTH

Salad Centre

22 Post Office Road
MAP 5 B4 *Dorset*
Bournemouth (0202) 21720
P Bourne Avenue car park

Open 9–5 (July–Sept till 8)
Closed Sun, Good Fri & 25 & 26 Dec

Vegetarian wholemeal pie £2.95   Nut
rissoles & salad £2   🍷   ⊝

Swift, friendly counter service keeps the queues moving at this popular, spotless restaurant decorated with abundant greenery. Hot soup and baked potatoes with tasty vegetarian fillings are supplemented by wholemeal pizzas and quiches, plus a good selection of fresh, healthy salads. Good home baking includes fruit pies, carrot and ginger cake, muesli flapjacks and scones, which can be enjoyed with various teas and herbal infusions. *No smoking. No dogs.*

LVs

BOURNEMOUTH

Superfish

186 Seabourne Road, Southbourne
MAP 5 B4 *Dorset*
Bournemouth (0202) 426158
P Woodside Road car park

Open 11.30–2 & 5.30–11 (Fri & Sat 5–11.30)
Closed Sun & 25 & 26 Dec

Fresh haddock & chips £3.40   Cod & chips £3.25

The newest in this chain of simple restaurants offers the same standard of cooking and service. Pine furniture and red and white tablecloths are spotlessly clean, and the short menu features cod fillet, scampi, huss and, if available, haddock, halibut or lemon sole, all served with tasty chips, hot French bread and a selection of pickles and sauces from a trolley. Ice creams for dessert are served with French wafer biscuits. Children's platter. *No dogs.*

LVs

BOURTON-ON-THE-WATER

Small Talk Tea Room

1 High Street
MAP 5 B2 *Gloucestershire*
Bourton-on-the-Water (0451) 21596
P Station Road car park &

Open 9–5.30 (Fri & Sat in summer till 10)
Closed 25 Dec

Afternoon cream tea £1.85   Homity pie £2.35 🫖

A real delight, this tiny beamed tea room crammed with Cotswold souvenirs offers delicious cakes and pastries throughout the day. At lunchtime, soup, sandwiches, ploughman's, Cotswold pâté and savoury croissants are supplemented by daily specials such as Stilton and walnut flan or sugar-baked ham served with a jacket potato and salad. Full marks too, for the smashing afternoon teas featuring the lightest scones imaginable. *Non-smoking area. No dogs.*

BOWNESS-ON-WINDERMERE

Hedgerow

Greenbank, Lake Road
MAP 3 C3 *Cumbria*
Windermere (096 62) 5002
P street parking

Open 10–9.30 (Nov–Mar till 8)
Closed Mon Nov–Mar & 25 & 26 Dec

Cashew nut & cream cheese pâté £1.50
Bowness bake £4.20

Enjoyable and imaginative vegetarian dishes are offered at this friendly, pine-furnished restaurant. Daily specials support the short regular menu, with choices such as black-eyed bean and fresh mint pâté or creamy garlic mushrooms followed by, say, cheese and lentil rissoles with tomato and red wine sauce or tasty chick pea bake. For the sweet-toothed, there's moist Guinness cake (delicious with cheese), Cumberland date slice or West-morland dream cake. *Non-smoking area.*

Credit Access, Diners, Visa

BRADFORD

Pizza Margherita

Argus Chambers, Hall Ings
MAP 4 D3 *West Yorkshire*
Bradford (0274) 724333
P NCP Hall Ings

Open 11am–11.30pm
Closed 1 Jan & 25 & 26 Dec

Pizza funghi £2.70   Lasagne £2.95

A bright summery restaurant where delicious pizzas are prepared right before your eyes. Lovely crispy bases come topped with everything from simple cheese and tomato to gourmet-style smoked salmon and prawns. To start, try tuna and bean salad or garlicky baked mushrooms, which non-pizza eaters can follow with lasagne or chilli. Rich chocolate fudge cake or Brazilian bombe to finish. *Non-smoking area. No dogs.*

Credit Access, Visa   LVs

BRADFORD-ON-AVON   *Corner Stones*

32 Silver Street
MAP 5 B3 *Wiltshire*
Bradford-on-Avon (022 16) 5673
P   Bridge Street car park

Open 9–5.30
Closed Sun (in winter) & most Bank
Hols

Broccoli, ham & leek bake £2   Pineapple
pavlova 90p   🍵

Sharing premises with their own bread and
cake shop, Jane Harrow and her team are
moving further into the wholefood and
vegetarian end of the market. Open early
with coffee, tea and cakes, which are
substituted at lunchtime by soups, salads
and daily specials like chicken and vegetable crumble and smoked bacon and broccoli
quiche. The afternoon sees tea, sandwiches
and cakes to be enjoyed with a good cup
of tea. French or English wines – non-
alcoholic if you prefer. *No dogs.*

Credit Visa

BRAMPTON   *N·E·W ENTRY*   *Tarn End*

Talkin Tarn
MAP 3 C2 *Cumbria*
Brampton (069 77) 2340
P   own car park   &

Open 12–2
Closed all Feb

Swordfish steak & salad £4.95   Bessie's
slice £1.20   🍵

Jointly owned and run by the Tusching-
hams with their daughter and her chef
husband Domenico Tellatin, this friendly
restaurant offers carefully prepared lunches
six days a week (buffet only available on
Sundays). Tasty moules or creamy broccoli
soup might precede grilled scallops with
bacon, pork loin stuffed with prunes or
braised venison. Lighter dishes include
Welsh rarebit and smoked chicken salad with
pineapple, and there are enjoyable sweets
like lemon meringue pie for afters. *No dogs.*

Credit Access, Amex, Diners, Visa

BRENDON   *N·E·W ENTRY*   *Rockford Cottage Tea Room*

Nr Lynton
MAP 8 B1 *Devon*
Brendon (059 87) 257
P   own car park

Open 10–5
Closed Nov–Easter

Smoked mackerel with gooseberry sauce
£1.75   Treacle tart 50p   🍵

A tea room with a terraced garden overlooking Doone Valley is a delightful setting
in which to enjoy Sylvia and Tony Jeffer-
son's home cooking. Besides a tempting
range of teatime bakes, they offer wholesome savouries such as tasty lentil soup,
cheese and onion pasties and smoked
mackerel with gooseberry sauce. Daily
specials might include cashew nut roast
and desserts like marmalade bread pudding
and lemon curd crunchies. Small portions
for children. *Unlicensed.*

BRIDGEMERE   *Bridgemere Garden World Coffee Shop*

Nr Nantwich
MAP 3 C4 *Cheshire*
Bridgemere (093 65) 381
P   own car park   &

Open 9–5 (till 8.30 in summer)
Closed 25 & 26 Dec

Chicken & mushroom pie £2.80
Beef bourguignon £2.80

Gardeners from all over the North come to
this large, well organised garden centre
and enjoy the pleasant outdoor feel of the
coffee shop during their visit. Savoury
snacks include meaty pork pies, a wide
selection of sandwiches, salads, chilli and
lasagne. Among the home-made cakes and
pastries are custard pies, cream-filled croissants and orange, coffee, date and walnut
and coffee cakes. *Unlicensed. No smoking. No dogs.*

BRIDGNORTH   *Sophie's Tea Rooms*

Bank Street
MAP 5 A2 *Shropshire*
Bridgnorth (074 62) 4085
P town centre car park

Open 10–5.30, Sun 2–6
Closed Sun (except April–Nov),
1 Jan & 25 & 26 Dec

Cashew paella £2.25   Quiche & salad
£1.80

The friendly, hardworking Bennetts offer
an excellent range of home-baked goodies
at their cosy tea room. Typical choices
might include flavoursome scones, almond
slice, caramel shortcake and lemon
meringue pie, all attractively displayed on
a pine dresser. Light savoury snacks
(toasties, salads, hot filled baps) are also
popular, while lunchtime brings more
substantial alternatives – perhaps a traditional roast, or vegetarian chestnut ragout.
Unlicensed. Non-smoking area. No dogs.

BRIDGWATER   *Nutmeg*

8 Clare Street
MAP 8 C1 *Somerset*
Bridgwater (0278) 457823
P Mount Street car park

Open 8–5.30
Closed Sun & May Bank Hols

Roast beef £2.60   Apple cake 35p

Joyce Forbe's simple but well-cooked food
draws crowds to her attractive little café-
restaurant. You can start the day with a
hearty breakfast, or drop in for morning
coffee or afternoon tea to be tempted by
the mouthwatering cakes and pastries.
Lunchtime brings hot savoury dishes like
vegetarian quiche, a roast of the day, pies,
some calorie-counted dishes and a pleasing
selection of salads. Bakewell tart or cream
gâteau for afters. *Non-smoking area. No
dogs.*

LVs

BRIDPORT   *N·E·W ENTRY*   *Morgan's*

6 West Street
MAP 8 C2 *Dorset*
Bridport (0308) 25877
P Gateway supermarket car park

Open 10–2.30 & 7–11
Closed Sun

Grilled sardines £2.95   Leek & celery au
gratin £1.95   🐸

Nick and Nina Morgan are the new
proprietors of this high-street wine bar
(formerly Monique's). Watch the blackboard for daily-changing lunchtime dishes
such as grilled sardines or home-made
celery soup, various salads, plus hot
specials like lamb ragoût, fish pie and
vegetarian pancakes. More adventurous
evening offerings range from steak to veal
escalopes and trout in wine and butter
sauce, with perhaps Austrian coffee cake
for afters. *Non-smoking area. No dogs.*

BRIGHTON   *Al Duomo*

7 Pavilion Buildings
Town plan C3 *East Sussex*
Brighton (0273) 26741
P NCP in Church Street

Open 12–2.30 & 6.30–11.30
Closed Sun & Bank Hols

Pizza marcolino £3.30   Cannelloni
£2.80

Find this little piece of Italy near Brighton's
Royal Pavilion. Pizzas in some 20 different
varieties (including a rolled one) are the
mainstay of the menu, aided by pasta in
tasty if not strictly authentic sauces, crisp
salads and a self-service antipasto table.
Blackboard specials ring the changes –
perhaps halibut with white wine sauce or
veal in various guises. Italian sweets and
strong espresso round off the meal. *No
dogs.*

Credit Access, Amex, Visa

BRIGHTON   *Allanjohn's*

8 Church Street
Town plan C3 *East Sussex*
Brighton (0273) 683087
P NCP Church Street

Open 10–5.30, Fri 9.30–6, Sat 9–6 &
Sun 10.30–3
Closed Most Bank Hols, 25 & 26 Dec

Jacket potato filled with prawns & cheese
£1.75   Seafood platters from £2.80

Check John Haslem's window display for
the day's prizes that he collects fresh from
Billingsgate at this simple little seafood
bar. Eaters-in have a choice of four check-
clothed tables at the back, where they can
tuck into cockles, mussels, prawns and
crab, enjoyed in bowls, on platters, or as
fillings for jacket potatoes and brown
bread sandwiches. Some hot dishes, too,
like plaice and stuffed oysters. *Unlicensed.
No dogs.*

BRIGHTON   N·E·W ENTRY   *Black Chapati*

12 Circus Parade
Town plan C1 *East Sussex*
Brighton (0273) 699011
P street parking &

Open 6–10.30

Closed Mon, Bank Hols & 1st 2
wks Jan

Masala dosa £3.75   Gujerati thali
£4.95   Prawn curry £5.75
Shrikhand £1.25

★ Extrovert owner Steve Funnell took the hippy trail
to India back in the seventies and fell in love with the
food. Today, local Indian chefs are among the regular
clients at his ultra-relaxed restaurant decorated in
minimalist black and white. Wonderfully fresh herbs
and spices enhance every dish on the short menu,
from refreshing bhelpoori to Gujerati thali – a feast
that includes crisply cooked curried vegetables,
superb dhal and wonderful pilau rice – an excellent
introduction to Steve's cooking. Note, too,
imaginative daily specials like fish molee (haddock
chunks in a mild coconut sauce) and, to finish,
deliciously rich, saffron-tinted spiced yoghurt. *No
dogs.* ★

Credit Visa

BRIGHTON   N·E·W ENTRY   *China Garden Restaurant*

88 Preston Street
Town plan B3 *East Sussex*
Brighton (0273) 25124
P street or Regency car park

Open 12–11 (Dim sum 12–4)

Singapore noodles £3.75   Prawn
dumplings £1

The full menu of this stylish, bustling
restaurant is available throughout the day,
but the skilfully prepared dim sum is
offered until 4pm. An excellent choice of
dim sum includes pork dumplings, beef
balls with vegetables, spring rolls and more
exotic items like shark's fin dumpling,
duck's web and mixed meat, and chicken
feet in black bean sauce. Efficient but
friendly staff will be glad to advise on the
more exotic dishes. *No dogs.*

Credit Access, Amex, Diners, Visa

BRIGHTON   *Cripes!*

7 Victoria Road
Town plan B2 *East Sussex*
Brighton (0273) 27878
P street parking

Open 12–2.30 & 6–11.30
Closed 25 & 26 Dec

Spinach, cheese & egg galette £3.65
Mixed nuts & honey crêpe £1.05

Those who like something a bit different should head for this delightfully atmospheric crêperie. Wholemeal buckwheat galettes are freshly made to order with a great range of fillings – from simple cheese and tomato to the more exotic prawns with ratatouille, or chicken livers, spinach and sour cream. For dessert, try a wafer-thin variety with bananas and rum, or even oranges in Grand Marnier. A choice of French or English ciders is the traditional accompaniment. *No dogs.*

BRIGHTON   *Food for Friends*

17a Prince Albert Street
Town plan C3 *East Sussex*
Brighton (0273) 202310
P Town Hall car park

Open 9am–10pm (Sat till 11)

Closed 25 Dec

Savoury crêpe £1.35   Tijuana tortillas £2.65   Black-eyed bean & mushroom stroganoff £1.60 Bonde Napoleon 80p

★ Simon Hope (also author of a book of recipes) is the driving force behind this popular self-service vegetarian restaurant with its simple decor of pine and potted greenery. Imaginative savouries range from exemplary wholemeal quiches, super-fresh salads and splendid soups (try the cheese and lentil, served with lovely granary bread) to a magnificent mushroom and lentil roast or broccoli and black-eyed bean bake. In the morning, breakfast on muesli, muffins and wholemeal croissants, or come for afternoon tea and a mouthwatering selection of cakes and pastries from their own pâtisserie around the corner. *Non-smoking area. No dogs.* ★

Credit Visa **LVs**

Our inspectors never book in the name of Egon Ronay's Guides.

They disclose their identity only if they are considering an establishment for inclusion in the next edition of the Guide.

BRIGHTON   *The Mock Turtle*

4 Pool Valley
Town plan C3 *East Sussex*
Brighton (0273) 27380
P street parking

Open 10–6

Closed Sun, Mon & Bank Hols, 2
wks Autumn & 4 days Xmas

Herb omelette £1.80   Cod &
chips £2.45   Meringue glâcé
£1.25   Cream tea £1.75 🍵

★   A truly scrumptious window display of home-baked
cakes, breads and biscuits draws the customers in to
fill every table at the Chaters' quaint and cottagy tea
shop – now in its fifteenth year. Join them in a
selection that ranges from flavoursome walnut and   ★
currant loaf, fluffy wholemeal scones and shortbread
to buttery French almond cake and fresh cream
gâteau. At lunchtime, traditional light snacks such
as Welsh rarebit and anchovy toast are supplemented
by fresh plaice fillets with chips, omelettes and
breakfast grills. There is a good range of speciality
teas, and you can take home jams and preserves –
and even Christmas puddings. *Unlicensed. No
smoking area. No dogs.*

BRIGHTON   *Pie in the Sky*

87 St James's Street
Town plan D3 *East Sussex*
Brighton (0273) 692087
P meter parking

Open 12–2.30 & 6.30–11.30, Sat & Sun
12–11.30
Closed 1 Jan & 25 & 26 Dec

Deep-pan pizza from £2.25   Choice of
pasta with sauce from £2.60

You're allowed to eat as much as you can
of the home-made pasta dishes at this
simple pasta and pizza restaurant. The
pizzas are deep pan variety and come in
various sizes with a goodly selection of
twenty possible toppings – tuna fish and
banana if you wish! There are a few starters
like vegetable crudités with a dip and some
salads too. The dessert menu offers ice
creams and cheesecakes. Children's portions. *No dogs.*

BRIGHTON   *N·E·W ENTRY*   *Ramada Renaissance Hotel, Barts Bar*

Kings Road
Town plan C3 *East Sussex*
Brighton (0273) 206700
P own car park   ♿

Open 12–11.30pm

Gratinated mussels with garlic £2
Casserole of shellfish £6.50

Coolly sophisticated, with its marble-
topped tables, bentwood chairs and tiled
floor, this brasserie-style bar has a distinctly Continental feel. A mouthwatering
display of seafood on ice indicates the
scope of the menu, which ranges from
simple prawns with mayonnaise dip or
deliciously smooth smoked salmon
mousse, to clam chowder, oysters gratinated with leeks and garlicky shellfish
casserole. Smartly uniformed staff provide
friendly and efficient service.

Credit Access, Amex, Diners, Visa

BRIGHTON   *Samsons*

25 St George's Road, Kemptown
Town plan E3 *East Sussex*
Brighton (0273) 689073
P street parking

Open 6pm–11.30pm (Sun till 11)
Closed 4 days Xmas

French onion soup 95p   ¼lb chilliburger
£3.65

Char-grilled hamburgers served in toasted
poppy seed buns, together with a mixed
salad and baked potato or French fries, are
the speciality of this laid-back restaurant
decorated with sepia photographs of
Brighton in years gone by. Sirloin steak or
tuna fish and vegetarian salads are popular
alternatives, and there's also a quiche and
soup of the day. Finish with banana and
toffee flan or brownies with a hot chocolate
sauce.

BRIGHTON   *Saxons*

48 George Street
Town plan D3 *East Sussex*
Brighton (0273) 680733
P street parking

Open 12–3, also Wed–Sat 7.15–10.15
Closed Sun, Bank Hols & 1 wk Xmas

Chick pea & vegetable curry with brown
rice £1.50   Aubergine stroganoff with
sauté potatoes & vegetables 🍵

Saxon Howard is the force behind this
popular vegetarian restaurant with pine
tables, painted chairs and poster-covered
walls. At lunchtime there is a display of
half a dozen interesting and original salads,
Indian-style snacks and hot dishes of the
day such as a chick pea and vegetable
curry with brown rice and a casserole. In
the evenings meals are slightly more
elaborate. *Unlicensed, but bring your
own wine. No smoking at lunchtime. No
dogs.*

BRIGHTON (HOVE)   *Twizzles*

40 Western Road
Town plan B2 *East Sussex*
Brighton (0273) 774341
P street parking

Open 12–2 & 7–11
Closed Sun, Bank Hols, 4 days Xmas

Enchiladas £1.90   Pinchos (marinated
pork) £2.50

Locals are regular customers at this highly
popular little restaurant specialising in
tapas. Choose from classic enchiladas,
pinchos (succulent, spicy pork on a
skewer), or perhaps quisquilla, a dish of
prawns and tomatoes topped with cheese.
Other options include home-made borsch
and garlic snails, with fresh local fish and
steaks among more conventional entrées.
Grand Marnier glâcé or chocolate mousse
to finish. Arrive early to be sure of getting
a table.

BRISTOL   *Arnolfini Café Bar*

Narrow Quay, Prince Street
Town plan C3 *Avon*
Bristol (0272) 299191
P Unicorn NCP ♿

Open 10am–10pm (Fri & Sat till 10.30),
Sun 12–10
Closed Mon, Bank Hols & 25 Dec–2 Jan

Ham & Gruyère croissant £1.50   Spicy
lamb & spinach £2.75 🍵

Part of an attractive arts complex created
out of dockside warehouses, this popular
café-bar (now open right through the day),
is run with flair and enthusiasm. As well as
home-made cakes and cookies to accompany tea and coffee, there's a short,
imaginative selection of savouries ranging
from soup (the red pepper and tomato is
delicious) and salads to beef and oyster pie,
wonderfully cheesy aubergine parmigiana
or a daily special like marinated pork
kebabs. *Non-smoking area. No dogs.*

BRISTOL

Cherries

St Michaels Hill, High Kings Down
Town plan B1 *Avon*
Bristol (0272) 293675
P   street parking

Open 12–2.30 & 7–11.30
Closed Sun & Bank Hols

Garlic mushrooms £1.60   Lasagne
provençale £4.70

Nothing is too much trouble for the staff
of this informal vegetarian bistro. At
lunchtime, blackboards advertise a short
menu of simple but tasty fare – hearty
soups, ploughman's, quiches and colourful
salads – while at night the choice widens
to include mixed nut pâté and houmous
among starters, perhaps followed by
vegetable and coconut curry or ratatouille-
filled pancakes. Try baked bananas or
vegan gâteau for afters. *No dogs.*

Credit Access, Visa

BRISTOL

Guild Café-Restaurant

68 Park Street
Town plan B2 *Avon*
Bristol (0272) 291874
P   NCP Park Row

Open 9.30–5 (Sat till 4.30)
Closed Sun & Bank Hols (except
Good Fri)

Spinach & feta cheese quiche £3
Tarragon chicken £3.40   ✆

Throughout the day, delicious home-made
cakes and biscuits can be enjoyed with tea
or coffee on the leafy terrace of this
attractive restaurant in a smart little
department store. Lunchtime brings a
short selection of savouries such as tuna
and dill quiche, beef stroganoff with
caraway seed dumplings, or tomato and
aubergine casserole. Lovely fresh salads
too, and enjoyable sweets like moist apple
cake to finish. *Non-smoking area. No
dogs.*

BRISTOL

Rainbow Café

10 Waterloo Street, Clifton
Town plan A1 *Avon*
Bristol (0272) 738937
P   street parking

Open 10–5.30
Closed Sun, Bank Hols & 1 wk Xmas

Bacon & courgette quiche £2.85
Beef goulash with baked potato £3.60
✆   🍵

Enjoy a break at this friendly little café in
Clifton's chic shopping alleys. Excellent
tea and sweet things like crumbly, light
scones and moist tea breads are available
all day. From noon, the choice widens with
a vegetarian soup, quiche and healthy,
interesting salads. Traditional sweets and
home-made ice creams to follow. Tables
outside in summer. Children's portions.
Non-smoking area. No dogs.

LVs

BRISTOL

Wild Oats II

85 Whiteladies Road, Clifton
Town plan A1 *Avon*
Bristol (0272) 734482
P   NCP Clifton Down Shopping Centre

Open 10am–10pm (Mon & Tues till
6pm, Fri & Sat till 10.30pm)
Closed 25 & 26 Dec

Seitan stroganoff £7   Seafood tempura
£8.50   🍵   ✆

Only top-quality natural ingredients, organically grown where possible and free
from chemicals, additives and preservat-
ives, are found at this friendly wholefood
restaurant. Carefully balanced meals could
start with miso soup, move on to vegetable
tempura, wholemeal pizza or quiche served
with salad, or one of the tempting tofu
specials, and end with delicious carob and
cherry gâteau. Excellent choice of teas.
More elaborate evening meals. *Non-smoking area.*

Credit Access, Visa   LVs

BROAD CHALKE   *Cottage House*

South Street
MAP 5 B3 *Wiltshire*
Salisbury (0722) 780266
P street parking

Open 10.30–12.30 & 2.30–5.30
Closed Sat pm (except May–Sept), Sun am, all Mon, 10 days Xmas & restricted opening Feb & Oct

Cream tea with lardy cake £1.90
Wiltshire tea bread 45p 🍵

Fresh trout pâté with hot buttered toast is a delicious new treat on the menu at the tiny tea room attached to the village shop and Post Office belonging to Enid and Ian White. Lovely cream teas are also popular, and there's a fine choice of home-baked goodies, including shortbread, fruit cake, gâteau, chocolate macaroons, almond slice and cream-filled éclairs. Eat in the garden or out on the patio when it's fine. *Unlicensed. No dogs.*

BROADWAY   *Coffee Pot*

76 High Street
MAP 5 B2 *Hereford & Worcester*
Broadway (0386) 858323
P street parking

Open 10.30–5.30
Closed Wed, also Mon–Thurs Nov–Dec, 25 Dec, & all Jan & Feb

Cream tea £1.60   Pork & apricot casserole £3.25 🍵

Just beyond the turn for Stratford, at the top end of town, the Taylors' spick-and-span tea room has many charming features, including a fine display of Staffordshire pottery figures for sale. On the eating side, a blackboard announces dishes of the day such as pizza, bacon and lentil soup or haddock and prawn casserole. There are always plain and toasted sandwiches, plus a tempting array of cakes. Super afternoon teas are a popular option.

BROADWAY   *Collin House Hotel*

Collin Lane
MAP 5 B2 *Hereford & Worcester*
Broadway (0386) 858354
P own car park ♿

Open 12–1.30

Closed 3 days Xmas

Herb cheese pâté £2.50   Duck terrine £1.75   Seafood gratin £4.25   Treacle tart £1.50 🅮

★ Settle in front of an open fire, or admire the view from the garden at John and Judith Mills' ivy-clad Cotswold-stone house. Dinner is quite an elaborate affair, but the lunch menu is suitable for either a light snack or a full meal. You might wish to try their celery soup, served with fresh wholemeal bread, followed by a simple but delicious gratin of poached haddock with mushrooms and prawns, or alternatively plump for herb cheese pâté and wild rabbit cooked with bacon and tarragon. Sweets, too, are most appealing – try the lovely trifle, or bread and butter pudding laced with brandy. Sunday lunch brings a traditional roast. *No dogs.* ★

Credit Access, Visa

BROADWAY   *Goblets*

High Street
MAP 5 B2 *Hereford & Worcester*
Broadway (0386) 852255
P   Lygon Arms car park

Open 12–2.30, 3–5.30 & 6–9.30 (Fri &
Sat till 10)
Closed 2 wks Xmas

Baked avocado & Stilton £2.50
Chicken & leek pie £3.75   🕭

Beams, leaded mullion windows and an
ancient inglenook provide the atmospheric
background for some enjoyable eating at
this cosy little wine bar. Check the blackboard for the day's offerings – perhaps
soup, pâté or garlic mushrooms, followed
by stuffed chicken breast, grilled halibut,
a simple omelette or cauliflower cheese.
For afters, there is a memorable Queen of
Puddings strictly not for the faint-hearted.
Polished, friendly service. *No children. No
dogs.*

BROMLEY   *Hollywood Bowl*

4 Market Parade
MAP 6 D3 *Kent*
01-460 2346
P   meter parking

Open 12–2.45 & 6–11.15 (Fri & Sat till
11.45)
Closed Bank Hols (except Good Fri)

¼lb hamburger de luxe £2.90   Steak on a
stick £4.25

Old-fashioned advertisements adorn the
walls of this informal and well-run American-style restaurant. Cheerful young staff
are kept busy serving predictable but
honestly cooked dishes such as chicken
satay, chilli con carne and succulent,
perfectly cooked meaty hamburgers. Crisp
salads come with a choice of dressing and
American-style desserts include hot
toasted waffles with maple-flavoured
syrup. *No dogs.*

LVs

BURNHAM MARKET   *N·E·W ENTRY*   *Soul Kitchen*

Market Place
MAP 6 E1 *Norfolk*
Fakenham (0328) 738967
P   street parking

Open 10–5
Closed Sun, Mon & Bank Hols

Trawlerman's pie £2.50   Cookie cake
50p   🕭

Pine banquettes, fresh white walls, a
stairway that boasts a twenties-style mural
and red plastic cloths give a country feel to
this stylish establishment arranged on two
floors. Light savoury bites range from
tasty wholemeal sandwiches and farmhouse terrine to blue cheese and celery
quiche. A blackboard advertises daily
specials such as traditional raised pies, and
there are tempting ice creams, cakes and
pastries to finish. *Unlicensed. Non-smoking area. No dogs.*

BURNLEY   *Butterfingers*

10 Halstead House, St James Row
MAP 3 C3 *Lancashire*
Burnley (0282) 58788
P   market car park

Open 8.30–4 (Tues till 2)
Closed Sun, Bank Hols & 3 days Xmas

Chicken hotpot £2.10   Sticky toffee
pudding £1   🍮

Old friends Karen Evans and Jane Connolly
make a fine team at this popular self-
service café. Freshly-made sandwiches and
toasties, filled jacket potatoes and Wensleydale cheese ploughman's are all favourite
light bites, while heartier appetites will
appreciate blackboard specials such as beef
and vegetable soup, steak and mushroom
pie, or a slice of quiche. Simple, enjoyable
puds and cakes for the sweet-toothed.
Unlicensed. No dogs.

LVs

BURY ST EDMUNDS   *Beaumonts*

6 Brentgovel Street
MAP 6 E2 *Suffolk*
Bury St Edmunds (0284) 706677
P Cattlemarket

Open 11.30–2.30
Closed Mon, Sun & Bank Hols

Vegetable crumble with herb sauce £2.20
Mixed pepper and sweetcorn flan 80p

Behind a thriving health food store is a restaurant and homely, upstairs coffee shop. There's a wide variety of salads, and you can choose from vegetarian dishes such as fresh asparagus quiche, cashew nut and bean pâté, freshly baked quiche, or orange and carrot soup with a wholemeal roll. Sweet things include fresh fruit salad, goats milk ice cream and a traditional currant cheesecake. They also serve plain and fruit yoghurts. Eat outdoors in summer. *No dogs.*

Credit Access, Visa

CALDBECK   *Priests Mill*

Wigton
MAP 3 B2 *Cumbria*
Caldbeck (069 98) 369
P own car park &

Open 10–5.30
Closed Mon, weekdays Nov & Dec
& all Jan & Feb

Nutty cheese bake £2.25   Date & walnut slice 45p 🍵

Housed in a restored water mill (together with craft workshops, a gift shop and bookshop), this simple restaurant offers honest, wholesome fare prepared from fresh local produce under the careful supervision of Beryl Hibbs. Help yourself from the tempting display of home-baked goodies – orange gingerbread, carrot cake, scones and lemon slices – or choose a savoury dish like hearty lentil soup, nutty cheese bake or beef and vegetable casserole. *Unlicensed. Non-smoking area. No dogs.*

CALVER BRIDGE   *Derbyshire Craft Centre Eating House*

Nr Baslow
MAP 4 D4 *Derbyshire*
Hope Valley (0433) 31231
P own car park

Open 10–5.30
Closed 25 & 26 Dec, weekdays Jan
& Feb

Game pâté £1.70   Lemon meringue 80p
🏵 🍵

A popular place inside the craft centre where the owner, Janette Beauchamp, presides affably and offers excellent baking to her customers. There are good quiches, tasty home-made soup served with fresh baps, an interesting choice of salads (al dente pasta or raw chopped mushrooms) and filled rolls for a quick bite. Then there is a super array of sweet things, including lightly-glazed, crisp apple tart, scones, cakes and pastries. *Unlicensed. Non-smoking area. No dogs.*

CAMBRIDGE   N·E·W   *Kings Pantry*
ENTRY

9 Kings Parade
MAP 6 D2 *Cambridgeshire*
Cambridge (0223) 321551
P Lion Yard car park

Open 10–5.30
Closed 25, 26 Dec & 1 Jan

Spinach lasagne £2.25   Carrot cake
with cream cheese topping 95p

Frances Sampson conscientiously uses only natural, wholesome ingredients, including rennet-free cheeses, at her basement vegetarian restaurant. Bright and bustling, the friendly staff are keen to explain the daily specials. Start with a split pea and lentil soup followed by a vegetarian chilli, packed with fresh vegetables, or a bulghar wheat and courgette bake. Crisp salads accompany, and moist carrot cake or date slice draw a filling conclusion. *No smoking. No dogs.*

LVs

CAMBRIDGE   *Nettles*

6 St Edwards Passage, Kings Parade
MAP 6 D2 *Cambridgeshire*
P NCP in Lion Yard

Open 9–8
Closed Sun, Bank Hols & 1 wk Xmas

Pasta in mushroom & wine sauce £1.40
Fruit crumble 75p

Take-away is the main trade at this bright, fresh little establishment, although there's limited space for those wishing to enjoy the imaginative wholefood vegetarian fare on the premises. Pasta in mushroom and wine sauce, richly flavoursome vegetable chilli, hearty soups and salads typify the tempting savouries on offer, while puddings include a memorable apple crumble packed with nuts, seeds and dried fruit. *Unlicensed. No smoking. No dogs.*

LVs

CAMBRIDGE   *Upstairs*

71 Castle Street
Map 6 D2 *Cambridgeshire*
Cambridge (0223) 312569
P Shire Hall car park

Open 6.30pm–10pm (Fri & Sat till 10.30 & Sun till 9.30)
Closed Mon & Bank Hols

Lamb couscous £6.10   Lemon chicken £5.25

Middle Eastern dishes collected from owner Virginia La Charité's travels form the basis of the menu offered at this informal little first-floor restaurant decorated with brass lanterns and incorporating Moorish arches. Helpful staff will guide you in your choice – perhaps Chorba (beef soup with lentils and chick peas) followed by stuffed vegetables, chicken in yoghurt sauce or lamb couscous. Fruit pancakes or floating Turkish delight to finish.   *No dogs.*

Credit Access, Visa

CANTERBURY   *Cogan House English Brasserie*

53 St Peter's Street
Town plan C2 *Kent*
Canterbury (0227) 472986
P Marlow car park

Open 10.30am–10.30pm (Sun from 12)
Closed Mon & Bank Hols

Guinea fowl in cider sauce £5   English goat's cheese £2.75   ⊜   ♥

A marvellous 12th-century building houses this lofty restaurant above a shoe shop. Everything on the menu is available throughout opening hours, whether you choose a snack (including open sandwiches, fine English cheeses, crab pâté and soup) or opt for an appetising main dish such as vegetable hotpot, sirloin steak with garlic and parsley butter or lamb and apricot pie. Enjoyable sweets, cakes, scones and teacakes also offered. *Non-smoking area. No dogs.*

Credit Access, Visa

CANTERBURY   *Crotchets*

59 Northgate
Town plan D1 *Kent*
Canterbury (0227) 458857
P St Radigund's car park   &

Open 12–3 & 6.30–12, Sun 12–2 & 7–10.30
Closed 25 & 26 Dec

Beef bourguignon £3.50   Farmhouse pâté £1.40

There's live jazz every night at this informal city centre wine bar where the blackboard announces a constantly changing choice of simple, well cooked snacks. There might be avocado with tuna, stuffed peppers provençal, pizzas, salads, ploughman's and a soup of the day. These can all be accompanied by wonderful garlic bread. For desserts there could be apple pie, a sorbet, or delectable hot chocolate fudge cake. The garden is open in summer.

Credit Access, Amex, Diners, Visa   **LVs**

CANTERBURY — *Pizza Place*

87 Northgate
Town plan D1 *Kent*
Canterbury (0227) 451556
P Northgate car park &

Open 10.30am–11.30pm
Closed 25 & 26 Dec

Pizza toscana £2.55   Chocolate fudge
cake £1.25

Traditional pizzas, American deep dish pizzas or flip-over style crêpe pizzas (all made with wholemeal bases if you perfer), are here at this bright, cheerful restaurant. Over a dozen varieties are on offer (many of which are vegetarian), from a hot Americana to a simple Margherita, supplemented by garlic dough bread, chilli bean dip, salads and pasta dishes too. On the blackboard, specials of the week and sweets of the day are announced. Children's portions. *No dogs.*

LVs

CANTERBURY — *Sweet Heart Pâtisserie*

Old Weavers House, St Peters Street
Town plan C2 *Kent*
Canterbury (0227) 458626
P Westgate car park

Open 9–5.30
Closed 3 wks Jan

Chicken crêpe £3.50   Sachertorte £1.45
🍵

This 15th-century weavers house is at the heart of historic Canterbury. Its ancient timbers now adorn a commendable pâtisserie and tea room. Continental cakes are the forte: mocca torte, bacardi crunchnut, diplomat torte and apple strudel all vie temptingly. Before 2.30pm try the savoury crêpes such as ratatouille or a vege-strudel. Farmer's lunch and quiche lorraine are available all day. In summer sample the excellent teas on the riverside terrace. *Non-smoking area. No dogs.*

CANTERBURY — *Il Vaticano Pasta Parlour*

35 St Margarets Street
Town plan C2 *Kent*
Canterbury (0227) 65333
P Rose Lane car park

Open 11am–11pm, Sun 12–10
Closed 25 & 26 Dec

Gazpacho 95p   Pasta carbonara £3.50
☕

Freshly made pasta is the speciality of this bright, modern little restaurant in the city centre. Choose from five different varieties served with an appetising range of sauces, from bolognese to prawns and mushrooms in a garlicky cheese sauce. Ravioli, cannelloni and lasagne are popular, and to start there's classic minestrone or tuna with haricot beans. Italian desserts, ice creams and sorbets and cheeses also available. *No dogs.*

Credit Access, Amex, Diners, Visa   LVs

CARLISLE — *Hudson's Coffee Shop*

Treasury Court, Fisher Street
MAP 3 C2 *Cumbria*
Carlisle (0228) 47733
P Scotch Street car park &

Open 9.30–5 (Thurs till 4)
Closed Sun, Bank Hols (except Good Fri
& Aug)

Cumberland ham & eggs £2.60
Treasurer's lunch £1.85   ☕ 🍵

With its William Morris wallpaper, bentwood and wicker chairs, and views across an attractive courtyard and mini garden centre, the coffee shop is a pleasant place to enjoy the goodies displayed. Owner Steve Hudson does all the baking. Snacks include good lentil soup, a range of sandwiches, ploughman's, pizzas, and vegetarian quiche. For sweet things there are scones, cakes and gâteaux to enjoy with the fresh looseleaf teas. Children's menu. *No smoking. No dogs.*

LVs

CARTMEL
N·E·W ENTRY

Prior's Refectory Coffee Shop

The Square, Nr Grange-over-Sands
MAP 3 C3 *Cumbria*
Cartmel (053 95) 36267
P own car park

Open 10.30–5
Closed End Oct–1 wk before Easter

Crock of mushrooms £2.25
Fisherman's lunch £2.65 ☺

Part of the Priory Hotel, this friendly little café offers sandwiches and cakes throughout the day, plus appetising home-cooked dishes between 12 and 2pm. Soups are hearty and full of flavour, while tempting local fare ranges from Cumberland sausages with apple relish to smoked fillet of Lakeland trout with horseradish and dill sauce. Other choices include quiche and chicken tikka. Traditional Sunday lunch. *Non-smoking area. No dogs.*

Credit Access

CARTMEL

St Mary's Lodge

Nr Grange-over-Sands
MAP 3 C3 *Cumbria*
Cartmel (053 95) 36379
P own car park

Open 2.30–5
Closed mid Nov–end Mar

Pavlova 80p   Cream tea £1.65

In this delightful little tea room in a quiet, historic village, Mrs Gaskins offers a warm welcome and some quite excellent baking. The full afternoon tea includes brown and white finger sandwiches and super-light scones served with outstanding home-made plum jam. A selection of breads – date and walnut, pineapple or banana – and cakes like chocolate, fruit or a Victoria sponge accompany. Children's portions. *Unlicensed. No smoking. No dogs.*

CASTLE CARY

Old Bakehouse

High Street
MAP 8 D1 *Somerset*
Castle Cary (0963) 50067
P town car parks

Open 9–5 (Mon till 1.30)
Closed Sun & Bank Hols

Spinach & tomato lasagne £1.85
Vegetable crumble £1.85 🍵

Carol Sealey's attractive little wholefood restaurant specialises in freshly prepared, organically grown produce. Her daily-changing lunchtime menus might offer spicy mulligatawny soup followed by fisherman's pie, pizza, quiche or her appetising vegetable and rice bake. Imaginative salads accompany main courses, and sweets include toffee date pudding and lemon mousse. At other times of day enjoy home-baked cakes and scones. *No smoking. No dogs.*

CASTLE CARY

Tramps

Woodcock Street
MAP 8 D1 *Somerset*
Castle Cary (0963) 51129
P museum car park

Open 11.30–3.30
Closed Sun, Mon, 1 Jan & 25 & 26 Dec

Grilled sardines £2.95   Moussaka £2.95

Situated above a well-stocked delicatessen, this village wine bar provides a wide ranging menu using good quality local produce. Platters of salami and other charcuterie, excellent salads or the popular king prawns with garlic mayonnaise vie for attention with the blackboard choice of fresh fish – poached haddock or scallops perhaps. Vegetarian specialities and delicious home-made pastries are also available. More elaborate evening meals.

Credit Access, Visa

CASTLE COMBE   *The Manor House*

Nr Chippenham
MAP 5 B3 *Wiltshire*
Castle Combe (0249) 782206
P own car park

Open 3.30–5.30

Toasted afternoon tea £3.50
Cream tea £3.75 🍵

Enjoying a magnificient rural setting beside the river Bybrook, this creeper-clad 17th-century manor provides a quintessentially English setting for tea. Eat in the panelled lounge or out on the lawn, choosing from three set teas that include such delights as light scones, chocolate eclairs and apple tartlets, toasted honey and walnut bread, hot buttered crumpets and dainty finger sandwiches. Fine tea served from a silver pot. *No dogs.*

Credit Access, Amex, Diners, Visa

CASTLE HEDINGHAM   *Colne Valley Railway Restaurant*

Yeldham Road, Nr Halstead
MAP 6 E2 *Essex*
Hedingham (0787) 61174
P own car park

Open 10–5 (till dusk in winter)
Closed Jan & Feb

Ham & leek roly-poly £3.50   Steamed syrup & ginger pudding £1.25 ☕ 🍵

Mrs Hymas' excellent cooking makes this former British Rail restaurant car well worth branching out for. Delicious home-baked goodies like coffee and walnut cake, featherlight scones and cream-filled gâteaux go down a treat with tea or coffee. At lunchtime, the tempting choice ranges from vegetable soup or smoked mackerel pâté to salmon and asparagus-filled pancakes, courgette quiche and sugar-roast ham, with steamed sponge pudding or strawberry meringue sundae for afters. *Unlicensed. No dogs.*

CASTLETON   *Rose Cottage Café*

MAP 4 D4 *Derbyshire*
Hope Valley (0433) 20472
P village car park

Open 10–6
Closed Fri, 25 Dec & all Jan & Feb

Mince beef pie £1.95   Chicken & mushroom toasted sandwiches £1.55
🍵

Hungry Hope Valley walkers often drop in to Alma Woodgett's welcoming cottage, so hearty soups, meat pies and mixed grills feature prominently on her menu, as well as lighter savouries including toasted sandwiches and baked potatoes. Also on offer all day is a selection of fine traditional home baking: lovely light scones, butter-drenched teacakes, moist chocolate cake, apple pie and almond slice. Garden. *Unlicensed.*

CAULDON LOWE   *Lindy's Kitchen*

Staffordshire Peak Arts Centre,
Nr Waterhouses
MAP 5 B1 *Staffordshire*
Waterhouses (053 86) 431
P own car park

Open 10.30–5.30 (in summer Sat till 7.30)
Closed Mon–Thurs in winter

Staffordshire oatcakes with mushrooms £2.60   Apricot & sultana flapjack 50p

Set high in the Staffordshire Peak District, this former school building offers simple yet interesting vegetarian food. In the mornings there are cakes like lemon curd gâteaux and apple cake. Lunchtime brings hot dishes: satisfying soups, aubergine-filled Staffordshire oatcakes, healthy salads, filled jacket potatoes and very enjoyable mushroom burgers. In the afternoon there is a set cream tea with wholewheat scones, filling savoury sandwiches and cakes. *No smoking. No dogs.*

Credit Access, Amex, Visa

CERNE ABBAS

N·E·W ENTRY

Singing Kettle

7 Long Street
MAP 8 D2 *Dorset*
Cerne Abbas (030 03) 349
P street parking

Open 10.30–5.30
Closed Mon (except Bank Hols),
25 & 26 Dec & weekdays in winter

Dorset cream tea £1.50   Ham platter
£1.50

Visitors to the Celtic Long Man at Cerne
Abbas should also take time to drop in at
Maureen Ranson's cosy tea shop tucked
away in a Georgian terrace and crammed
with old-fashioned bric-a-brac. She bakes
all her own cakes, which you can enjoy
with a refreshing cuppa or as part of a set
afternoon tea featuring lovely scones, local
clotted cream and excellent jam. Light
lunches range from home-made quiche or
pâté with salad to filled jacket potatoes.
Unlicensed. No dogs.

CHATHAM

N·E·W ENTRY

Food for Living Eats

116 High Street
MAP 6 E3 *Kent*
Medway (0634) 409291
P Pentagon car park

Open 9–4.30
Closed Sun & Bank hols

Vegetable bake £1.85   Carrot
soup 75p

At the back of a health food shop in the
high street, this neatly kept self-service
restaurant offers notably flavoursome and
carefully prepared vegetarian fare. Tasty
soups packed with goodies can precede
crunch-topped vegetable bake, lasagne,
various quiches and pizzas, or just a simple
sandwich. Apple crumble or moist, sultana-
studded carrot cake make a pleasant finish.
Friendly service. *Unlicensed. No smoking. No dogs.*

LVs

CHATHAM

Simson's

58 High Street
MAP 6 E3 *Kent*
Medway (0634) 42372
P Brook car park

Open 11.30–2.30 & 7–11
Closed Sun, Mon & 2 wks Jan

Beef & Guinness pie £4.75   Lasagne and
salad £2.85

Decorated with photographs of old
Chatham, this modest little high street
wine bar is of definite interest to local
historians. The staff are friendly and the
cooking is serious fare for healthy appetites. The blackboard menu could offer a
varied range, like pork in sherry, vegetable
samosas, omelettes and simple puddings,
all full of flavour and definitely home-
made. Open-air eating on the patio. *No
dogs.*

Credit Access, Visa LVs

CHATHAM

Where the Dickens

272 High Street
MAP 6 E3 *Kent*
Medway (0634) 813163
P public car parks

Open 12–3, Sat 10.30–4 & Sun
12.30–2.30
Closed Mon & most Bank Hols

Vegetable lasagne £3.95   Wendy's
cheesecake £1.50

Above a health-orientated enterprise off
the High Street is this pleasant restaurant
with bare wooden floors, half-panelled
walls and pine furniture. The menu offers
a simple selection of cakes, wholemeal
sandwiches and vegetable pâté. More substantial dishes include vegetable cheesebake galette, assorted pasta dishes and
organically-grown jacket potatoes. You
are encouraged to help yourself from the
colourful salad cart. More elaborate
evening meals. *No smoking. No dogs.*

Credit Access, Visa

CHEAM
Superfish

64 The Broadway
MAP 6 D3 *Surrey*
01-643 6906
P Park Road car park

Open 11.30–2 (Sat till 2.30) & 5.30–11,
Fri & Sat 5–11.30
Closed Sun & some Bank Hols, 1 wk
Xmas

Cod & chips £2.60   Scampi & chips
£3.95 🍵

A small selection of good fish is on offer at
this spotlessly clean, light and cheerful
place, one of a chain of similar restaurants.
Choose from fillet of plaice, haddock, huss,
sole, whole plaice on the bone and halibut
steaks, all served with well-cooked chips,
nice, crusty French bread and a pickle and
sauce trolley. For sweet there are various
ice creams. Children's platter. *Unlicensed
(but bring your own). No dogs.*

LVs

CHEDDAR
Wishing Well Tea Rooms

The Cliffs
MAP 8 C1 *Somerset*
Cheddar (0934) 742142
P cheese factory car park

Open 10–6
Closed mid Oct–April (except Sun in
Feb, Mar, Oct & Nov)

Jacket potato with scrambled egg £1.95
Fresh salmon salad £3.25 🍵

Mrs. Lewis's fine home baking has delighted visitors to Cheddar Gorge for some
21 years now, and standards remain
consistently high. Light, fluffy scones and
tasty cakes (coffee and walnut, cherry,
orange) accompany afternoon tea, while
savoury snacks available throughout the
day include freshly made sandwiches,
toasties and salads. Lunchtime brings
home-made soup, filled jacket potatoes
and sweets like sherry trifle. Book for
traditional Sunday roast. *Unlicensed.*

CHELTENHAM
Choirs Tea Rooms

5 Well Walk, Clarence Street
MAP 5 B2 *Gloucestershire*
Cheltenham (0242) 510996
P St James' Square NCP

Open 10–6
Closed Sun, 1 Jan & 25 & 26 Dec

Nut loaf & salad £2.95   Hot apricot
crunch £1.10 🕑 🍵

Splendidly restored, these beamed and
bow-windowed tea rooms make a delightfully cosy setting for some excellent home
cooking. Sixteen varieties of cake, from
spicy carrot to hazelnut with Tia Maria,
make teatime special, while savouries
available all day range from winter soups
to wholemeal harvest pie, baked potatoes,
freshly-made sandwiches, quiche and lots
of healthy salads. Three-course evening
meals served on Fridays and Saturdays.
No dogs.

Credit Access

CHELTENHAM
Langtry Pâtisserie & Tea Rooms

56 High Street
MAP 5 B2 *Gloucestershire*
Cheltenham (0242) 575679
P St James Street car park

Open 9–5.30 (Sat till 6)
Closed Sun & Bank Hols

Welsh rarebit £2.35   Gâteau tea £1.50
🕑

Mr Plank's own bakehouse is the source
of all the delicious goodies on offer at this
pretty, spacious tea shop. Choose from a
tempting display of fresh cream cakes,
doughnuts, Danish pastries and flapjacks,
or enjoy his lovely home-baked bread in
sandwiches, or toasted and topped with,
say, mushrooms or scrambled eggs. Tasty
alternatives include soup, salads and a
Cotswold cheese lunch. Ice cream specialities to finish. *Unlicensed. No dogs.*

LVs

CHELTENHAM — *Promenade Pâtisserie*

112 The Promenade
MAP 5 B2 *Gloucestershire*
Cheltenham (0242) 575144
P NCP in Regent Arcade

Open 8–6 (Sun from 10)
Closed 1 Jan & 25 & 26 Dec

Pasty with salad 70p   Pittville tea £1.50
🕭 ☕

In this tea shop, sister to the Langtry, the decor is more modern and modest, but the baking is of the same high standard. Choose from Mr Plank's Danish pastries, éclairs and scones with jam or lemon curd, and whipped cream, or try the sandwiches on a choice of home-made breads. Hot savoury snacks include steak and kidney pies, pasties, and rarebits. Ice cream specialities to follow. *Unlicensed. No dogs.*

LVs

CHELTENHAM — *The Retreat*

10 Suffolk Parade
MAP 5 B2 *Gloucestershire*
Cheltenham (0242) 235436
P street parking

Open 12–2.15 & 6–9
Closed Sun & Bank Hols

Chilli with yoghurt & cucumber dressing £2.55   Chocolate brandy cake £1.10
🕭

Eat in the picturesque courtyard of this popular wine bar near the Ladies' College. Lunchtime (when it's quieter) brings the greatest choice of food, with cold meats and colourful salads being supplemented by appetising daily specials like deep-fried whitebait, lasagne, and cauliflower cheese served with super granary bread. There's soup, pâté and quiche to start, and tasty sweets include bread and butter pudding. *No dogs.*

Credit Access, Amex, Diners, Visa   LVs

CHESTER — *Chester Grosvenor Library*

Eastgate Street
MAP 3 C4 *Cheshire*
Chester (0244) 324024
P NCP in Eastgate Street   ⅏

Open 9.30–5
Closed 25 & 26 Dec

Grosvenor tea £7.50   Terrine of duck with home-made breads £7.50   🕭 ☕

Refurbishment has seen the creation of this new and stylish booklined library lounge, with deep sofas and armchairs. Morning coffee with home-made biscuits and shortbread is followed at lunchtime by smoked salmon, slices of cold beef Wellington or Scottish lobster. Strawberries in season with cream or the splendid Grosvenor cheeseboard round things off. Afternoon tea is also a delight, with finger sandwiches, well-risen scones and home-baked French pastries. *No dogs.*

Credit Access, Amex, Diners, Visa

CHICHESTER — *Chats Brasserie*

Unit 5, Sharp Garland House, Eastgate
MAP 5 C4 *West Sussex*
Chichester (0243) 783223
P Priory car park

Open 9.30–4.30 (Mon from 11, Sat till 5.30)
Closed Sun, also Mon Jan–end Mar, Bank Hols & 3 days Xmas

Avocado & cottage cheese quiche £1.10
Smoked trout & horseradish £2

The bustling, brightly decorated brasserie has a loyal following, which can mean that it gets quite chaotic at times. On offer throughout the day is a good array of snacks such as sandwiches (both open and closed), salads and blackboard specials like liver and onion casserole and chicken provençale. There are tempting puddings too – crème caramel or toffee crunch ice cream, perhaps, and cakes such as apricot slices, date fingers and sponges. *Non-smoking area. No dogs.*

CHICHESTER   *Clinchs Salad House*

14 Southgate
MAP 5 C4 *West Sussex*
Chichester (0243) 788822
P Avenue de Chartres car park

Open 8–5.30

Closed Sun & Bank Hols

Vegetable & cheese layer bake
£1.80   Aubergine & tomato
gratinée £1.80   Egg custard tart
60p   Fresh fruit pavlova 80p   🍵

From early morning the self-service counter offers myriad mouthwatering choices: the range including fruit or cheese scones, Belgian chocolate fudge slice, amazing-looking meringue iced walnut cake with ★ 'hedgehog'-style icing, and fresh fruit pies. At ★ lunchtime these are augmented by vegetarian daily specials like parsnip and tomato bake, leek and egg mornay and an assortment of salads from simple grated carrot to brown rice, bean sprout, red cabbage and beetroot and other composites. Beverages include a range of teas including herbal ones. The decor is plain and unfussy so the many satisfied customers can concentrate on enjoying their excellent food. Children's portions.

LVs

CHICHESTER   *St Martin's Tea Rooms*

St Martin's Street
MAP 5 C4 *West Sussex*
Chichester (0243) 786715
P St Martin's car park

Open 10–6
Closed Sun, Mon, Bank Hols & 1 wk Xmas

Iced carrot cake 95p   Aduki bean pie £2
🍵

Keith Nelson's good old-fashioned tea rooms and quiet secluded garden offer quality and charm, nestling behind a simple façade. All day there are baked items like wholemeal scones, a masterful rich, spicy iced carrot cake and crispy oatmeal flap-jacks. At lunchtime there's a daily chang-ing salad, soup and a hot dish, like aduki bean pie, usually geared to vegetarians. Salads and sandwiches, including a toasted banana variety, are also available. The loose leaf tea makes an exceedingly good cup. *No smoking. No dogs.*

CHIPPING CAMPDEN   *Greenstocks*

Cotswold House Hotel, The Square
MAP 5 B2 *Gloucestershire*
Evesham (0386) 840330
P street parking

Open 9.30am–10.30pm

Brie puffs with spicy tomato sauce £2.65
Almond & apple pie with Cotswold cream
£1.65   🍵   🍵

Part of the Cotswold House Hotel, this smart, terracotta-floored establishment is open for tempting snacks throughout the day. Hearty breakfasts and coffee-time pastries are followed at lunchtime by, perhaps, a hearty soup, a light quiche and delicious puddings like apple and almond pie. Afternoon tea brings savoury dishes as well as cakes and scones, and the evening menu includes extras such as T-bone steaks. *No dogs.*

Credit Access, Amex, Diners, Visa

CHIPPING CAMPDEN — *Kings Arms Hotel, Saddle Room*

The Square
MAP 5 B2 *Gloucestershire*
Evesham (0386) 840256
P The Square &

Open 12–2

Steak & kidney pie £3.95   Seafood bake
£3.25   🍴

The panelled bar or the walled garden are the best spots to choose for enjoying a first-rate lunch at this 16th century Cotswold stone hotel in the market square. Start with soup, chicken liver pâté or fresh grilled sardines, and go on to chicken tikka, pasta provençale or mussels in a distinctive sauce of white wine, tomato, garlic and herbs. For afters try the interestingly named chocolate lovers' delight, banoffi pie or chocolate and mint mousse. *No dogs.*

Credit Access, Visa

CHIPPING NORTON — *Nutters*

10 New Street
MAP 5 B2 *Oxfordshire*
Chipping Norton (0608) 41995
P tourist office car park

Open 9.30–6 (till 5.30 in winter)
Closed Sun, Mon (except Bank Hols)
& 1 wk Xmas

Tuna & mushroom lasagne £1.95   Hot
potato scones with cheese 75p   🍵

The emphasis is on healthy and enjoyable eating at Elizabeth Arnold's pin-bright restaurant with a pretty walled garden. Wholemeal scones and a delicious sugar and fat-free fruit cake are typical of her home-baked offerings, while appetising lunchtime savouries range from flavourful soups, salads and filled jacket potatoes to vegetarian lasagne and savoury flans. To finish, try the apple charlotte or fresh fruit salad. *Non-smoking area. No dogs.*

CHISLEHURST — *Mrs Bridges' Kitchen*

49 Chislehurst Road
MAP 6 D3 *Kent*
01-467 2150
P street parking

Open 8–1.30
Closed Sun, Bank Hols, 2–3 wks
summer & 1 wk Xmas

Gardener's chicken £2.20   Home-made
treacle tart 70p   🍵

A smashing farmhouse breakfast featuring egg, bacon, sausage and tomato served with a hunk of crusty bread and a warming cup of tea kicks the day off to a great start at this popular café opposite the station. Lunchtime brings soup, omelettes, ploughman's, pizzas and bumper toasted sandwiches, as well as more hearty main dishes like chicken casserole, grilled steak or gammon with pineapple. *No dogs.*

Credit Access, Visa   LVs

CHRISTCHURCH — *Salads*

8 High Street
MAP 5 B4 *Dorset*
Christchurch (0202) 476273
P Saxon Square car park

Open 10–3
Closed Sat, Sun & Bank Hols

Artichoke & cheese flan 80p   Mixed
bean & potato pie 90p   🍵

Healthy and enjoyable eating is the order of the day at this friendly establishment. Food is served at a counter from where you might choose corn and carrot bake or artichoke and cheese flan accompanied by freshly prepared salads including spicy bean or broccoli. A range of unusual breads such as turmeric or walnut is also available. Spoil yourself with a delicious sweet like chocolate and vanilla sponge, soft fruit gâteau or strudel. *Unlicensed. No smoking. No dogs.*

LVs

CIRENCESTER   *Brewery Coffee House*

Brewery Court
MAP 5 B3 *Gloucestershire*
Cirencester (0285) 4791
P Brewery car park

Open 10–5.30
Closed Sun, 1 Jan & 25 & 26 Dec

Vegetable terrine £1.95   Apple muffins
£1

Cirencester Workshops for the Arts provide the setting for this airy coffee house,
which offers delicious home baking from
light wholemeal scones to passion cake.
More substantial choices are available at
lunchtime – spinach roulade, stir fry
vegetables, quiches, salads and nut roast
for vegetarians, and chicken Veronique,
spicy Cotswold sausage or fisherman's
bake for meat-eaters. Grapefruit mousse
or pineapple and peach cream pie to end.
No smoking lunchtimes. No dogs.

Credit Access, Amex, Diners, Visa

CIRENCESTER   *N·E·W ENTRY*   *No. 1*

1 Brewery Court
MAP 5 B3 *Gloucestershire*
Cirencester (0285) 69290
P Brewery car park

Open 10–5
Closed Sun, 25 & 26 Dec

Vegetable layer £2.75   Beef carbonnade
£2.95   🐾

In a courtyard near the town's craft
workshops, this smart eaterie provides
flapjacks, brownies, apple and cinnamon
cake, apricot slices and banana and walnut
cake among others all day, together with
savoury items such as ham and pineapple
quiche, pâté, baked potatoes and salads.
Hot dishes appear at midday, and always
include one vegetarian (try ratatouille au
gratin) and one meat dish like liver and
bacon or spicy rice and pork. Pleasant
sweets. *Minimum charge £1.50 12–2. No
smoking lunchtime. No dogs.*

CIRENCESTER   *Shepherds Wine Bar*

Fleece Hotel, Market Place
MAP 5 B3 *Gloucestershire*
Cirencester (0285) 68507
P own car park

Open 10.30am–10.30pm (till 6 in
winter)

Artichoke soup £1.35   Pork, apple &
sage pie £3.50   🥧

Linked by a cobbled courtyard to the
Fleece Hotel, this pleasant wine bar is open
for morning coffee and afternoon tea as
well as for light meals. Herby blue cheese
tart, smoked chicken and avocado salad,
braised spicy sausages and pork, sage and
apple pie typify the imaginative, freshly
prepared dishes on offer. Finish with richly
indulgent raspberry cheesecake or a platter
of English cheeses. Fine wine selection.
No dogs.

Credit Access, Amex, Diners, Visa

CLARE   *Peppermill Restaurant*

Market Square
MAP 6 E2 *Suffolk*
Clare (0787) 278148
P street parking

Open 11–4.30, Oct–May 12–2
Closed Sun & Mon

Fisherman's pie £2.70   Fruit cake 75p
🥧   🐾

Roger Steele cooks everything to order at
this cottagy beamed restaurant, and the
results are well worth the short wait.
Besides tasty light snacks (scones, sausage
rolls, omelettes, sandwiches and jacket
potatoes), they offer full lunches that
might start with a hearty vegetable soup,
followed by chicken in red wine, sirloin
steak or deliciously sauced nut roast, and
end with moist bread and butter pudding.
Evening meals by arrangement only. *No
dogs.*

Credit Access, Amex, Diners, Visa

CLARE   *Ship Stores*

22 Callis Street
MAP 6 E2 *Suffolk*
Clare (0787) 277834
P street parking

Open 7.30–6.30
Closed 25 Dec

Set tea 80p   Mushrooms on toast 65p

Joyce Kies' sound home baking is at the heart of the simple choice of food available at this charming little tea room in the village stores. Throughout the day (it starts here at 7.30) you can tuck into well-risen scones, rich, moist teabreads (try the rich fruit variety) and lovely light chocolate gâteau. On the savoury side, there are popular snacks like bacon sandwiches, baked beans on toast, ploughman's and cheesy jacket potatoes. Eat on the patio in summer. *Unlicensed.*

CLAWTON   N·E·W ENTRY   *Court Barn Country House Hotel*

Nr Holsworthy
MAP 8 B2 *Devon*
North Tamerton (040 927) 219
P own car park

Open 3–5.30
Closed 1st wk Jan

Meringue & clotted cream £1.60   Court Barn Special tea £3.25 🍵

A few minutes from the A38 Launceston–Bideford road, Robert and Susan Woods' peaceful hotel is just the place for a traditional Devon cream tea. Sit in the comfortable lounge, or out on the patio when it's fine, and enjoy Susan's superbly light scones served with tasty jam and thick, yellow cream, delicious cakes and featherlight meringues. Cucumber sandwiches and toasted teacakes are also available, together with an impressive selection of quality teas. *No dogs.*

Credit Access, Amex, Diners, Visa

CLEVEDON   N·E·W ENTRY   *Murrays*

91 Hill Road
MAP 5 A3 *Avon*
Clevedon (0272) 874058
P street parking

Open 10–5
Closed Sun, Mon & Bank Hols

Macaroni with vegetables & cheese £1.75
Chicken curry £1.85 🅑 🍵

Packed tables at all times of the day testify to the popularity of Gail Murray's cooking at this friendly little tea shop. Her home-baked goodies make a fine display – try the lovely oven-warm scones served with good strawberry jam and thick clotted cream or the rich fruit cake with a refreshing brew. From noon, consult the blackboard for the day's specials – perhaps crusty tuna bake, chicken curry or lasagne – or just settle for a freshly made salad or sandwich.

CLEVELEYS   N·E·W ENTRY   *Wholefood & Vegetarian Restaurant*

44 Victoria Road, West, Nr Blackpool
MAP 3 B3 *Lancashire*
Blackpool (0253) 865604
P street parking

Open 10–5 Mon–Sat (Sun from 12)
6.30–10 Fri only
Closed 5 days Xmas

Fresh pineapple & kiwi pavlova £1.10
Homity pie £2.75 🍵

Situated above a wholefood shop, this smart, bentwood-furnished restaurant offers carefully prepared, healthy snacks throughout the day. Sandwiches, omelettes, jacket potatoes and some good home baking fill morning and afternoon gaps, while lunchtime brings flavourful soups, salads, a daily quiche and appetising specials like tangy mushroom stroganoff. Hot fruit crumble to finish. *Minimum charge £3 Friday evening. No smoking. No dogs.*

G. K. Chesterton
1874–1936

Tea, though an oriental
Is a gentleman at least;
Cocoa is a cad and coward,
Cocoa is a vulgar beast.
The Song of Right and Wrong

R. H. Barham
1788–1845

'Tis not her coldness, father,
That chills my labouring breast;
It's that confounded cucumber
I've ate and can't digest.
'The Confession'

Oscar Mendelsohn

Breathes there a man with nose so dead
Who never to himself has said:
'One pickled onion, one shallot,
Would raise this dish to what it's not'?
'Pickled Onions', in *A Salute to Onions* (1966)

Anonymous

I eat my peas with honey,
I've done it all my life.
It makes the peas taste funny
But it keeps them on the knife!
Manners

CLIFTON DYKES   *Wetheriggs*

Nr Penrith
MAP 3 C2 *Cumbria*
Penrith (0768) 62946
P own car park &

Open 10–5.30
Closed weekdays Nov–Feb

Mushroom flan £2.50
Bran muffins 35p 🍵

American Sunday brunch is hugely popular at this friendly restaurant – part of a complex that includes weaving and pottery workshops, a museum and a sculpture garden. At other times enjoy tasty bran muffins, fruity scones and delicious banana and walnut cake, or opt for more substantial savouries like soups, jacket potatoes and excellent deep quiches. Try their quality ice creams and specialist teas. Set meals in the evening. *No smoking.*

Credit Access, Visa

CLIFTONVILLE   *Batchelor's Pâtisserie*

246 Northdown Road, Nr Margate
MAP 6 F3 *Kent*
Thanet (0843) 221227
P street parking

Open 8.30–6
Closed Sun, Mon, Bank Hols & 2 wks Xmas

Quiche & coleslaw £1.05   Swiss truffle torte £1.20 🍵

Lucerne-born Franz Ottiger offers a small taste of Switzerland in his spotlessly clean pâtisserie in the bustling town centre. Drop in for the lightest imaginable croissants, a sausage roll or quiche with coleslaw. Satisfy a sweet tooth with one of many delicious cakes and pastries like macaroons, chocolate truffle torte or Black Forest gâteau. Strong, foamy espresso coffee provides the final touch. *Unlicensed. No dogs.*

COCKERMOUTH   *Quince & Medlar*

13 Castlegate
MAP 3 B2 *Cumbria*
Cockermouth (0900) 823579
P Market Street car park

Open 7pm–9.30pm (Fri & Sat till 10), Sun 12.30–8

Closed Sun (winter), Mon (except Bank Hols), & 3 wks winter

Mixed vegetable curry £4.75
Brazil nut crown £4.95   Caponata £1.65   Normandy apple tart £1.80

★ Susan and Jonathan Whitehead-Whiting make a splendid team at this cosy vegetarian restaurant in a listed Georgian building near the castle. Both Mediterranean and Eastern influences can be seen throughout Susan's imaginative, monthly-changing menus, with choices like flavoursome aubergines in sweet and sour sauce, flageolet bean dip and ginger cheese pâté among starters, plus such appetising main courses as black-eyed bean, vegetable and pasta casserole, ratatouille pancakes or crunchy nut and seed bake to follow. End memorably with lovely lemon cheesecake, sticky toffee pudding or hazelnut and carrot cake. *No smoking. No dogs.* ★

Credit Access, Visa

COLCHESTER   *Bistro Nine*

9 North Hill
MAP 6 E2 *Essex*
Colchester (0206) 576466
P NCP Stockwell St

Open 12–1.45 & 7–10.45
Closed Sun, Mon, Bank Hols & 1 wk
Xmas

Stilton & onion soup 95p   Chicken stir
fry £3.95   ⊜

Here's a lively informal place offering
simple snacks to one side and more
substantial meals to the other. The ingredients, including the herbs and spices, are
fresh and well cooked and the vegetables
crisp. From the snack menu try the spinach
and cheese samosas, the crab and watercress mousse or the beef daube if you're
extra hungry. Keep room for the bread and
butter pudding unusually sweetened with
marzipan. *No dogs.*

Credit Access, Visa

COLCHESTER   *Poppy's Tea Room*

17 Trinity Street
MAP 6 E2 *Essex*
Colchester (0206) 65805
P Osbourne Street car park

Open 9.30–4 (Fri & Sat till 5.30)
Closed Sun & Bank Hols

Spinach & ham quiche £2.95   Chocolate
roulade £1.30

Poppies ramble over the tablecloths and
curtains at this very pretty little tea room
near a large shopping precinct. Call in for
a reviving cuppa and a delicious sweet
something, such as gooey hazelnut and
chocolate meringue, coffee and walnut
cake or an almond slice. Lunchtime brings
generously served savouries like chicken
and tarragon pancakes, smoked mackerel
and cheese platter, jacket potatoes and
sandwiches. *No dogs.*

Credit Visa

COLLIER STREET   *Butcher's Mere*

Nr Marden
MAP 6 E3 *Kent*
Collier Street (089 273) 495
P own car park

Open 10–7 (Thurs from 2)

Cream tea £1.95   Fruit cake 75p   🫖

Louise Holmes' popular tea room is idyllic
with a picture postcard garden beside an
old-fashioned duck pond complete with
little wicket bridge. The baking on offer is
a treat: light scones, delicious fruit jams,
good fat-free sponges with real butter
cream and golden brown meringues. Dia-
betic cream teas are available. Among the
cakes are orange and lemon, moist fruit,
marble cake and chocolate or hazelnut log.
Service is relaxed and chatty. *Unlicensed.*
No smoking. No dogs.

COMPTON   *Old Congregational Tea Shop*

Nr Guildford
MAP 6 D3 *Surrey*
Guildford (0483) 810682
P street parking

Open 10.30–5.30
Closed Mon (except Bank Hols),
Tues & 1 wk Xmas

Welsh rarebit £1   Bakewell tart 60p
🫖

Sally Porter lives in a converted Congregational church on the B3000, where she
also serves excellent afternoon teas to an
appreciative clientele. Delicious scones are
complemented by thick cream and Sally's
lovely home-made jam, while coffee and
walnut cake is another speciality. Savoury
snacks range from soup and toasted
sandwiches to ham and leek quiche made
with tasty, home-cooked ham and rich,
buttery pastry. *Unlicensed. Non-smoking
area.*

CONGLETON   *Odd Fellows Wine Bar & Bistro*

20 Rood Hill
MAP 3 C4 *Cheshire*
Congleton (0260) 270243
P street parking

Open 12–2 & 6.45–11 (Sun till 10.30)
Closed Sun lunch, Bank Hol Mons
& 25–27 Dec

Savoury cheese pâté £1.95   Drunken
bullock £5.25   ♉

The Kirkham brothers' popular and atmospheric restaurant consists of a first-floor
bistro, a ground-floor wine bar and a
courtyard for open-air eating. Starters and
main courses are not as good as they once
were, although the menu is imaginative
and varied, including herrings in Madeira
sauce, rare roast beef, lamb kebabs and
Greek salad. Puddings are the best part of
the meal, from delicious lemon meringue
pie to rich chocolate and ginger trifle.
Outstanding wines.

Credit Amex, Visa

CONISTON   *N·E·W ENTRY*   *Jumping Jenny at Brantwood*

Brantwood
MAP 3 B3 *Cumbria*
Coniston (0966) 41715
P Brantwood House car park

Open 10.30–5 (till 4 mid Nov–mid Mar)
Closed Mon & Tues (mid Nov–mid Mar)

Grasmere gingerbread 45p   Potted trout
£2.35

The stables at John Ruskin's former
Lakeland home are now attractively converted into this atmospheric café with a
distinctly Victorian feel. A huge kitchen
table groans under a wealth of wholesome
home baking – rich fruit cake, tea breads
and scones – while a blackboard displays
the day's lunchtime savouries. These range
from simple starters like mushroom and
nut pâté to hearty casseroles like navarin
of lamb and beef in Guinness. *No dogs.*

CORSE LAWN   *Corse Lawn House*

Nr Gloucester
MAP 5 B2 *Gloucestershire*
Tirley (045 278) 479
P own car park &

Open 12–2 & 7–10

Baked crab in filo pastry £4.50
Feuilleté of wild mushrooms £5.50
Leek & watercress soup £2.25
Strawberry shortcake £2.75   ♉

★ Relax in the bar lounge of this old coaching inn and
savour Barbara Hine's exquisite cuisine. Using only
the freshest ingredients she combines textures,
flavours and sauces to produce an enticing array of
dishes. Light meals or starters encompass Mediterranean fish soup, venison sausages, pâté au Cognac
or terrine of vegetables. Heartier main courses range
from vol-au-vent of quail's eggs and feuilleté of calf's
sweetbreads to scallops with noodles. The mousse of
three chocolates – light, dark and white – is a
delightful decadence, or round off refreshingly with
fresh figs and an Armagnac sorbet. Traditional
Sunday lunch. Children's portions. Garden. ★

Credit Access, Amex, Diners, Visa **LVs**

COVENTRY   *Herbs*

28 Lower Holyhead Road
MAP 5 B2 *West Midlands*
Coventry (0203) 555654
P street parking

Open 6.30pm–9.30pm
Closed Sun & Bank Hols

Pancake with asparagus & pine kernels
£1.65   Red cabbage & mushroom
hotpot £4.25

The food at this prettily decorated restaurant is mainly vegetarian, but there is always a fish and a meat dish as well. Try the Caponata, consisting of chilled aubergines, celery, onions and olives with garlic bread, or spaghetti with green vegetable and cheese sauce. Desserts include carrot pudding and pashka (glâcé fruit in curd cheese and sour cream). As much fresh cona or decaffeinated coffee as you like is served with sugared almonds. *No smoking. No dogs.*

Credit Access, Visa

We publish annually
so make sure you use the current edition.

CRANBROOK   N·E·W ENTRY   *Cranes*

2 Waterloo Road
MAP 6 E3 *Kent*
Cranbrook (0580) 712396
P street parking

Open 12–2
Closed Sun

Ratatouille flan & salad £2.85   Roast
beef & Yorkshire pudding £3.50   ☺

After visiting the renowned Cranbrook windmill, this cosy little restaurant makes an attractive spot for a delicious, bistro-style lunch prepared with flair by Jeremy & Wendy Pook. Eat as little or as much as you fancy – from home-made soup or pâté, garlic mushrooms and prawn salad, to roast beef with Yorkshire pudding, fresh fish and chicken casserole. Enjoyable gâteaux and fresh fruit flans to finish. More elaborate evening meals. *No dogs.*

Credit Access, Visa

CROYDON   *Hockneys*

98 High Street
MAP 6 D3 *Surrey*
01-688 2899
P NCP at rear

Open 12–10.30
Closed Sun, Mon, Bank Hols, 1 wk
Easter, 2 wks Aug & 2 wks Xmas

Spicy mushroom soup £1.10   Lasagne
£3.30   ☺

Melon with coconut and ginger sauce, spicy mushroom soup or houmus are some of the starters which might appear on the menu in this friendly wholefood vegetarian restaurant. Main dishes of spinach lasagne or shish kebabs can be followed by a choice of cakes and sweets, including rum and raisin parfait. Counter service till 5.30pm, then table service and slightly higher prices. Book for dinner. *Unlicensed, so bring your own wine. No smoking. No dogs.*

Credit Access, Amex, Diners, Visa   **LVs**

DARTINGTON   *Cranks Health Food Restaurant*

Shinners Bridge, Nr Totnes
MAP 8 C2 *Devon*
Totnes (0803) 862388
P own car park

Open 10–5

Closed Sun (except in summer),
1 Jan & 25 & 26 Dec

Mushroom stroganoff £2.75
Chilli bean casserole £2.90
Vegetable crumble £2.75   Apricot
slice 70p 🫖 🐾

★ A rural branch of a leader in vegetarian and wholefood
catering – and all you might expect from them. The
pleasant rustic decor, within a large complex with
cider press and shops, provides pleasing surroundings in which to enjoy the food. Hot dishes include a
daily soup, splendid pizzas, ever-changing quiches,
mushroom stroganoff or well seasoned vegetable pie,
all served with a good selection of salads from large
earthenware dishes. There are wholesome sweet
things too: flapjacks, fruit slices or apple and pear
crumble, and excellent cheeses. Eat outside on the
terrace in summer. *Non-smoking area. No dogs.* ★

LVs

DARTMOUTH   *Spinning Wheel Café*

Hauley Road
MAP 8 C3 *Devon*
Dartmouth (080 43) 2645
P Mayor's Avenue car park ♿

Open 10.30–5
Closed Mon end Nov–end Mar, 1 Jan
& 25 & 26 Dec

Cream tea £1.70   Welsh rarebit £1.10
🐾

Enjoy the Merediths' sound home cooking
out on the sunny courtyard (a blaze of
colour in summer), or in the cosy beamed
tea shop itself, in the company of their
resident ghosts. The menu is kept simple
– local crab and salmon feature in salads
and sandwiches and there are warming
soups, omelettes and things on toast, too.
On the sweet side, tuck into lovely fresh
scones with clotted cream and jam, moist,
light coffee or vanilla sponge, flapjacks
and meringues. *Unlicensed.*

DENT   *Dent Crafts Centre*

Helmside, Nr Sedbergh
MAP 3 C3 *Cumbria*
Dent (058 75) 400
P own car park

Open 10–5.30
Closed 3 Jan–10 Mar

Smoked trout pâté £1.95   Carob crunch
60p 🐾

This is a fascinating little craft centre set
up in a group of stone and slate outhouses.
On sale are wooden goods and the work of
local painters and etchers. Inside, there is
a flagstone-floored café selling salads,
ploughmans, baked potatoes and filled
baps. Cakes include orange, date and
walnut, coffee and chocolate biscuit cake.
You can sit on the terrace while you eat
and watch the carpenters at work. Children's portions. *No smoking. No dogs.*

Credit Access, Visa

DERBY   *N·E·W ENTRY*   *Cutlers Bistro*

22 Irongate
MAP 5 B1 *Derbyshire*
Derby (0332) 368732
P Assembly Rooms car park

Open 10–2.30 & 7–9.45
Closed Sun, Mon eve & Bank Hols

Butter bean & cider casserole £2.20
Brie & bacon jacket potato £1.60

Above a shop just outside the city centre, this simple little bistro serves appetising home-cooked meals in a friendly atmosphere. Soup, pâté and taramasalata with hot pitta makes tasty snacks or starters, while main courses range from French onion tart, pizza and quiches to vegetarian lasagne and fish moussaka. There are toasted sandwiches and filled jacket potatoes, too, plus popular sweets like chocolate fudge cake to finish. *Non-smoking area. No dogs.*

Credit Access, Visa

DERBY   *Lettuce Leaf*

21 Friar Gate
MAP 5 B1 *Derbyshire*
Derby (0332) 40307
P Friar Gate car park &

Open 9.30–7.30
Closed Sun & Bank Hols

Nut roast £3.25   Broccoli & mushroom pie £2.95

Cathie Shepherd continues to maintain her high standards in her popular vegetarian restaurant. A blackboard lists such daily specials as marrow provençale, quiches, tomato and courgette bake with fresh vegetables and a cheesy topping and perhaps a vegetable hotpot. Snacks include 'things' on toast, omelettes, flans and open sandwiches. There is a good selection of home-baked cakes and biscuits. *Non-smoking area. No dogs.*

LVs

DEVIZES   *Wiltshire Kitchen*

11 St John's Street
MAP 5 B3 *Wiltshire*
Devizes (0380) 4840
P market square car park &

Open 9.30–5.30

Closed Sun, Bank Hols & 1 wk Xmas

Spiced chicken with coriander £3.50   Spinach & mushroom lasagne £3.20   Almond & lemon tart £1.30   Ginger & apple cake £1.50 🍵

★   Just the sort of place that every country town should have – and doesn't. Ann Blunden's enthusiasm for cooking is a real delight. Her lovely salads and gorgeous looking quiches are staples, but the ever-changing hot dishes at lunchtime are the real treats. Delicately delicious vegetable and mushroom soup, served with granary bread, can be followed by sweetbreads perfectly cooked in a subtle yet positive sauce, and there's a delectable ginger and apple pudding to round off a memorable meal. Other choices might be fish roulade, spinach and mushroom lasagne or roast beef. Good speciality teas, lovely cakes and an outstanding elderflower wine by the glass complete the picture. Outdoor eating. *No smoking. No dogs.*   ★

DISS
Weavers

Market Hill
MAP 6 E2 *Norfolk*
Diss (0379) 2411
P Market Place car park

Open 12–2 & 7–9.30 (Fri & Sat till 10)
Closed Sat & Bank Hol Mon lunches, all
Sun & 1 Jan, 25 & 26 Dec

Hungarian pork goulash £2.75
Summer pudding 95p 🫖

Informality is the keynote of this charming restaurant-cum-wine bar in the town centre. At lunchtime, consult the blackboard for simple, wholesome fare like creamy cauliflower and almond soup, lasagne, smoked Suffolk ham salad and delicious seasonal desserts. The evening menu is more elaborate, but friendly young owners the Bavins will happily serve a glass of wine and a snack at the bar counter. *No dogs.*

Credit Access, Visa

DODD WOOD
Old Sawmill

Underskiddaw, Nr Keswick
MAP 3 B2 *Cumbria*
Keswick (0596) 74317
P own car park &

Open 10.30–5.30
Closed end Oct–2 wks before Easter

Cumberland ham salad £2.90   Apple pie
80p 🫖

A few miles north of Keswick on the A591 and surrounded by woodland is this simple place in what was once a sawmill. Here Mrs Hotton both cooks and serves behind the counter. The menu is the same all day: woodman's lunch (like ploughman's), various salads and sandwiches (home-cooked succulent gammon, perhaps) and home-made soup. There are fruit pies and various cakes like gingerbread and a fruit cake that is moist and full of fruit. Children's portions. *Unlicensed. No smoking. No dogs.*

DORCHESTER
Potter In

19 Durngate Street
MAP 5 B4 *Dorset*
Dorchester (0305) 68649
P Waitrose car park

Open 10–5
Closed Sun & Bank Hols

Lentil bake £2.95   Dorset cream tea
£1.65 🫖 🍵

Mrs Armstrong's home baking is a strong attraction at this popular little self-service restaurant sharing space with the Dorset Craft Guild Shop. Delicious scones, chocolate cake, fruit slices and zesty lemon meringue pie go down well with a good cuppa, while light lunchtime dishes like lentil soup, pizzas, quiches, omelettes and generous salads are supplemented by a daily special such as pork casserole. Garden. *Non-smoking area. No dogs.*

LVs

DORRINGTON
Country Friends

Nr Shrewsbury
MAP 5 A1 *Shropshire*
Dorrington (074 373) 707
P own car park

Open 12–2
Closed Sun, Mon & 2 wks Oct

Baked stuffed peach £3.60   Chicken &
sorrel quennelles £4.20 🫖

Six miles south of Shrewsbury, this restaurant serves bar snacks at lunchtime only. The seating is comfortable and the large collection of pictures, figurines and objets d'art provides plenty to admire. The cooking is simple but imaginative with dishes such as blue cheese doughnuts and salad. Desserts are excellent, or you could sample the wide variety of English cheeses. Real coffee and a range of teas are served. Eat in the garden in summer. Children's portions. *No dogs.*

Credit Amex, Diners, Visa

DUNSTER   *Tea Shoppe*

3 High Street
MAP 8 C1 *Somerset*
Dunster (0643) 821304
P street parking

Open 9–6

Closed weekdays Nov–mid Dec
& all Jan & Feb

Vegetable casserole £3   West
Country treacle tart £1   Cheese
& pâté board £1.60   Toasted tea
cake 75p

Yorkshire couple Pam and Norman Goldsack fell in
love at first sight with this delightful tea shop in a
15th-century cottage on Dunster's lovely High
Street. Now the new owners, their enthusiasm is
★ reflected in friendly, caring service plus top-quality ★
baking and produce. Lunchtime brings superb soups
(try carrot and coriander or leek and potato),
imaginative pâtés and such delicious main dishes as
herby local sausages with home-made mustard,
fisherman's casserole and an excellent quiche salad.
Round it all off with sensational lemon cheesecake,
fresh strawberry meringue or something from the
lavishly laden cake counter. Cheese and pâté boards
provide savoury alternatives. Children's menu. *Non-
smoking area.*

EARDISLAND   N·E·W   *Elms*
                          ENTRY

Leominster
MAP 5 A2 *Hereford & Worcester*
Pembridge (054 47) 405
P own car park

Open 2.30–5.30 (summer till 6)
Closed Sun (in June) & Sept–Spring
Bank Hol (except Easter)

Cream tea £1.50   Farmhouse tea £2

Mary Johnson not only runs the farm and
the guest house, but also finds time to turn
her hand to some good, old-fashioned
home baking for this spotless little tea
room. The formula is simple – a cream tea
with plain scones, home-made jam and
whipped cream, or the farmhouse version
with bread and butter, wholemeal fruit
scones, moist, dark fruit cake and nice
light Victorian sandwich. *Unlicensed. No
smoking. No dogs.*

EAST BUDLEIGH   *Grasshoppers*

16 High Street
MAP 8 C2 *Devon*
Budleigh Salterton (039 54) 2774
P car park opposite

Open 10–5.30
Closed Mon (except Bank Hols), 25 Dec,
1st wk May & 2 wks mid Oct

Beef cobbler £3.15   Devon cream tea
£1.60

Peggy Cooke's home-baked goodies are
available throughout the day at this tiny
gift and tea shop. Look out for her sponges,
lardy cake, Viennese shortbread and coconut chocolate crunch, or choose a savoury
like smoked mackerel pâté, a ploughman's
or a generous salad. Lunchtime brings
such tasty offerings as herby lamb casserole, Devonshire chicken, fish pie and
devilled kidneys, with homely puddings –
apricot sponge, treacle tart – for afters.
Unlicensed. No smoking.

EAST MOLESEY   *Hampton Court Brasserie*

3 Palace Gate Parade, Hampton Court
MAP 6 D3 *Surrey*
01-979 7891
P   Palace Gate Parade

Open   12–3 & 7–11
Closed   1 Jan & 25 & 26 Dec

Spinach roulade £2.45   Poached
chicken with crab mousse £7.25   ℰ

New owners have changed the name but
not the quality at this chic brasserie near
the Thames. Choose a single course or a
full meal from the imaginative, frequently
changed menus: perhaps herby pancakes
with cheese and ham followed by calf's
liver with mustard grain sauce, lamb hot
pot or baked sea bass with Pernod.
Enjoyable sweets, good wines and delightful service complete the picture. *No dogs.*

Credit   Access, Amex, Diners, Visa

EAST MOLESEY   *Superfish*

90 Walton Road
MAP 6 D3 *Surrey*
01-979 2432
P   public car park to rear   &

Open   11.30–2 (Sat till 2.30) & 5.30–11,
(Fri & Sat from 5)
Closed   Sun & some Bank Hols

Cod & chips £2.60   Scampi & chips
£3.95   🍴

A small selection of good fish is on offer at
this spotlessly clean, light and cheerful
place, one of a chain of similar restaurants.
Choose from fillet of plaice, haddock, huss,
sole, whole plaice on the bone and halibut
steaks, all of which are served with well-
cooked chips, nice, crusty French bread
and a pickle and sauce trolley. For sweet
there are various ice creams. Children's
platter. *No dogs.*

LVs

EASTBOURNE   *Byrons*

6 Crown Street, Old Town
MAP 6 E4 *East Sussex*
Eastbourne (0323) 20171
P   street parking

Open   12.30–1.30 (strictly by
arrangement only)

Closed   Sat lunch, all Sun, Bank
Hols & 1 wk Xmas

Spinach mousse £2.45   Braised
oxtail with port £5.25   Beef olives
£5.20   Cognac & white wine
sorbet £1.95   ℰ

★   It is essential to book in advance if you wish to lunch
at this charming little restaurant. There are only half
a dozen pink linen-clad tables, but the cooking is of
star quality and served with skill and sophistication
by the professional and dedicated hosts, Simon and
Marion Scrutton. Simon is the chef, while Marion
presides with great presence over the front of house
activities. Only first-rate ingredients are used to
create dishes of imagination and style, full of delicate
flavour, such as Toulouse sausage with onion
marmalade, or prune ice cream. Fresh local fish is
served as available. There is a selection of excellent
British farmhouse cheeses. Children's portions on
request. *No children under 5. No dogs.*   ★

Credit   Amex, Diners, Visa

EASTBOURNE
Qualisea

9 Pevensey Road
MAP 6 E4 *East Sussex*
Eastbourne (0323) 25203
P Arndale car park

Open 11.30–8
Closed Sun & 2 days Xmas

Plaice & chips £1.50   Egg, sausage &
chips £1.40 🍲

Michael Cosma has been preparing fish
and chips in his very popular and exceedingly efficient restaurant for over twenty
years now. Besides his good, moist fresh
fish (cod, haddock, plaice and cod's roe) all
in good crisp batter, there are other snacks
with chips such as fried eggs, hamburgers,
chicken or sausages. There's a very simple
dessert choice. House wine is available by
the glass. *No dogs.*

LVs

EASTLEIGH
Piccolo Mondo

1 High Street
MAP 5 C4 *Hampshire*
Eastleigh (0703) 613180
P Southampton Road car park

Open 12–2.30 & 6.30–11 (Thurs–Sat
till 11.30)
Closed Sun & Bank Hols

Antipasto misto £3.50   Tortellini
parmigiana £3.50

Favourite Italian dishes are carefully prepared and enjoyable at this delightfully
informal, pine-furnished restaurant. There
are plenty of pizzas, pasta, veal and chicken
dishes to choose from, as well as interesting
ways with fish (try red mullet in a white
wine and tomato sauce) and delicious daily
specials like herby home-made sausages.
A range of imaginative ice creams and
excellent espresso to finish. *No dogs.*

Credit Access, Amex, Diners, Visa   **LVs**

ELLAND
Berties Bistro

7 Town Hall Buildings
MAP 4 D4 *West Yorkshire*
Halifax (0422) 71724
P Town Hall car park &

Open 7pm–11pm, Sun 5pm–
9.30pm

Closed Mon, 1 Jan & 25 & 26 Dec

Curried prawns £2.45   Crab
mousse £2.35   Lemon sole in
batter with mango sauce £5.85
Chicken en croûte with prawns
& herb cheese £5.90 🥂

★ For imaginative, creative flair and skill in cooking it
is difficult to beat the weekly-changing menus of
Michael Swallow at this Victorian-style bistro with
open bookshelves and old prints enhancing the
image. Open your account with mushroom and ★
walnut soup, French leaf salad, chicken and spinach
terrine or curried mushroom and bacon tartlet.
Poached salmon in watercress and scampi sauce,
moussaka, chicken in Pernod sauce, beef goulash,
lemon sole or vegetarian lasagne are just some of the
delicious main dishes. For afters you are spoilt for
choice: Berties bombe, Bailey's Irish Cream cheesecake, damson and whisky ice cream or white wine
syllabub. Children's menu. *No dogs.*

ELY
N·E·W
ENTRY
Old Fire Engine House

St Mary's Street
MAP 6 E2 *Cambridgeshire*
Ely (0353) 2582
P street parking

Open 10.30–5.30
Closed 10 days Xmas

Apple & hazelnut pie with cinnamon
£1.20   Rabbit & pork in mustard
& parsley £6.95

Near the cathedral, this homely restaurant
also houses a gallery featuring the work of
local artists. Eat in the tile-floored dining
room, or out in the lovely garden on sunny
days – a particularly idyllic spot for
morning coffee or traditional teas featuring
cucumber sandwiches, scones and lovely
cakes like ginger or lemon. Lunchtime
brings such treats as rich lamb and
vegetable soup, seasonal salmon (with
excellent hollandaise), and delicious
brandy and wild apricot ice cream. *No
dogs.*

EMBLETON
Wythop Mill

Nr Cockermouth
MAP 3 B2 *Cumbria*
Bassenthwaite Lake (059 681) 394
P own car park

Open 10.30–4 (Sun till 6 in summer)
Closed Mon, Tues, most Bank Hols & all
Jan–Feb

Ham & French bean flan £3.90   Apricot
& nut flapjack 60p

Part of a millhouse and museum beside a
mountain river, this is a real family
enterprise, that offers a friendly welcome
and imaginative, wholesome food. There is
a delightful coarse-textured sardine and
lentil pâté, spinach and cottage cheese
pancake or savoury flan. Sweets include
enormous portions of excellent creamy
home-made ice cream. Morning coffee and
afternoon tea also come with lovely home-
made goodies. More elaborate evening
meals in summer on Thursday and Friday
evenings. *No smoking. No dogs.*

ETON
Eton Wine Bar

82 High Street
MAP 6 D3 *Berkshire*
Windsor (0753) 854921
P High Street car park

Open 12–2.30 & 6–11, Sun 12–2 &
7–10
Closed Easter Sun & 3–4 days Xmas

Seafood cocotte £3.95   Chocolate,
apricot & almond florentine £2.35   ℰ

The food is full of interest at this stylish
wine bar where the blackboard advertises
the constantly changing bill of fare. Start
with a warming soup like Cheddar, celery,
cauliflower and leek, or perhaps a light
curried prawn and cucumber mousse.
Tasty dishes to follow might include
chicken and tarragon bake or seafood and
almond pancake. Elegant sweets such as
brandy snap basket with raspberries and
cassis cream. *No dogs.*

Credit Access, Visa

EWELL
Superfish

9 Castle Parade, By-pass Road
MAP 6 D3 *Surrey*
01-393 3674
P street parking &

Open 11.30–2 (Sat till 2.30) & 5.30–11,
Fri & Sat 5–11.30
Closed Sun & some Bank Hols

Cod & chips £2.60   Scampi & chips
£3.95

A small selection of good fish is on offer at
this spotlessly clean, light and cheerful
place, one of a chain of similar restaurants.
Choose from fillet of plaice, haddock, huss,
sole, whole plaice on the bone and halibut
steaks, all of which are served with well-
cooked chips, nice, crusty French bread
and a pickle and sauce trolley. For sweet
there are various ice creams. Children's
platter. *No dogs.*

LVs

FALMOUTH — *Pandora Inn*

Restrongnet Passage, Nr Mylor Bridge
MAP 8 A3 *Cornwall*
Falmouth (0326) 72678
P own car park

Open 12–5 & 7–10
Closed 25 Dec

Grilled mackerel with walnut butter
£3.25 Pandora club sandwich with
French fries £2.50 🍵

Seek out this delightful white-washed
thatched pub on the creek about four miles
north of Falmouth off the A39. Upstairs in
the restaurant or in the garden there is a
traditional Cornish tea with home-made
scones, clotted cream and a nice pot of tea.
There's also bar food at lunchtimes and in
the evening: salads, smoked fish, moules
marinière and sandwiches. Desserts include lemon meringue pie and chocolate
fudge cake.

Credit Access, Visa

FALMOUTH — *Secrets*

6 Arwenack Street
MAP 8 A3 *Cornwall*
Falmouth (0326) 318585
P Quay car park

Open 10–5 & 7–10
Closed Sun, also Mon & Tues Oct–
Easter, most Bank Hols & 2 wks Feb

Steak & kidney pie £2.95 Austrian
coffee cake 95p 🍵

Enjoy the harbour views from the terrace
of this attractive restaurant run by enthusiastic new owners. Cakes, pastries and
generously filled sandwiches available
throughout the day are supplemented at
lunchtime by hearty soups (try spicy beef),
filled jacket potatoes, salads, savoury
pancakes and blackboard specials like
pizza or tuna quiche. Bread and butter
pudding or treacle tart for afters. More
elaborate evening menu. *Non-smoking
area. No dogs.*

Credit Access, Visa

FELIXSTOWE — *N·E·W ENTRY* — *Hamiltons Tea Rooms*

134 Hamilton Road
MAP 6F2 *Suffolk*
Felixstowe (0394) 282956
P street parking

Open 10–5 (till 2 Wed)
Closed Sun & Bank Hols

Quiche & salad £1.85 Apple & sultana
cake 45p 🍵

Fresh flowers decorate each table at these
pleasant tea rooms above a row of shops
opposite the post office. Drop in for
elevenses or afternoon tea and let friendly
uniformed waitresses serve you scones and
cakes from the attractive sideboard display.
Summer lunchtimes bring quiche and
salads based on, say, ham off the bone,
while in the winter there are warming
casseroles and Cornish pasties. Toasted
sandwiches also available. *Unlicensed.
Non-smoking area. No dogs.*

FROGHALL — *The Wharf Eating House*

Foxt Road, Nr Cheadle
MAP 5 B1 *Staffordshire*
Ipstones (053 871) 486
P own car park

Open 11–5.45 (mid Mar–Spring Bank
Hol & Oct till 5)
Closed Mon & Nov–mid Mar

Afternoon tea £2.25 Turkey & egg pie
£2.25 🍵

Whether you eat in the lovingly restored
Old Mill Eating House or while you are
gliding along the Caldon Canal in a horse-
drawn narrow boat, the setting is delightful. Everything, including the bread, is
home-baked and the lunchtime buffet
choice includes pâté, pizzas, savoury pies,
and jacket potatoes. In the afternoon, teas
are served with scones, cream and home-
made preserves, as well as cakes, pastries
and biscuits. Good pot of tea. Children's
menu. *No dogs.*

Credit Access, Visa

FROME   *Old Bath Arms*

1 Palmer Street
MAP 5 B3 *Somerset*
Frome (0373) 65045
P own car park

Open 12–1.45
Closed Sun, Bank Hols & 25 Dec–3 Jan

Steak & kidney pudding £2.50   Lamb
casserole & parsley dumplings £2.50
🍵

Tony Thorp's melt-in-the-mouth pastry
transforms homely sweets like raspberry
and apple pie or treacle tart into something
special at this pleasant two-room establishment in an old stone building. His wife
Jane prepares the savoury dishes for their
popular buffet-style lunches, with choices
like sliced roast beef, meat pie, generously-
topped pizzas, quiches and cold cuts, plus
a few simple salads. Full evening meal. *No
dogs.*

Credit Access, Visa

FROME   *Settle*

15 Cheap Street
MAP 5 B3 *Somerset*
Frome (0373) 65975
P market place

Open 9–5.30 (Thurs till 2, 6 in
summer) Sun 2.30–6

Closed Sun Oct–April, 1 Jan,
Good Fri, & 25 & 26 Dec

Wild rabbit pie £4.75   Old-
fashioned cheese pudding £3
Fresh cream layer cake £1.10
Cinnamon toast 35p 🍵 🍵

★ A tiny stream runs through Cheap Street, a picturesque walkway with many historic buildings, including this cosily rustic tea shop. Enthusiastic owner
Margaret Vaughan offers an extensive menu of home-
made dishes, using local produce and traditional
recipes wherever possible. Cakes and breads baked
in the adjoining bakery include cheese muffins,
treacle cake ('shepherd's purse') and nutty poppyseed
cake, while on the savoury side there are delights
like cider-enriched chicken casserole and priddy
oggies – cheese pastries filled with pork, bacon and
Cheddar. Homely sweets and English cheeses to
finish. *Non-smoking area. No dogs.* ★

Credit Access, Visa

GATESHEAD   *Marks & Spencer Garden Restaurant*

Unit 46, Metro Centre
MAP 4 D2 *Tyne & Wear*
Tyneside (091) 493 2222
P Metro Centre car park ♿

Open 10–7.30 (Thurs till 8.30), Sat
9–5.30
Closed Sun & 25 & 26 Dec

Beef steak pie £1.90   Lemon torte 90p

Using the food we know and enjoy from
their food halls, this bright, smart and
spotless in-store restaurant is understand-
ably very popular. It offers snacks like
quiches, salads, ploughman's and pastries
– like cheesecake with a nice crisp biscuit
base – all day, and supplements these with
hot dishes at lunchtime. These might be
steak pie with chunks of tender beef,
chicken tikka and fish with real chips.
Children's menu. *No smoking. No dogs.*

GLASTONBURY

Ploughshares Café

4a High Street
MAP 5 A3 *Somerset*
Glastonbury (0458) 31004
P Abbey car park

Open 9am–9.30pm
Closed Tues

Tandoori tofu burger £1.50
Black cherry tofu cheesecake 75p
🍵

Latter-day hippies find a haven at this informal café, part of a cluster of shops known collectively as the Glastonbury Experience. Uncompromisingly vegan and using only organic produce, the short menu offers imaginative delights like tofu kebabs on rice with spicy peanut sauce and deep-fried vegetables with tomato chutney. Throughout the day, excellent cakes and pastries such as apple and ginger slice are served with a wide range of teas. Patio. *Unlicensed. Non-smoking area.*

GLASTONBURY

Rainbow's End Café

17a High Street
MAP 5 A3 *Somerset*
Glastonbury (0458) 33896
P St Johns Square

Open 10–4.30 (Tues from 9.30)
Closed Wed Sept–June, Sun, Bank Hols
& 2 wks Xmas

Greek cheese pie £1.40   Vegetable
lasagne £1.40   ☺   🍵

Wholefood and vegetarian snacks are the speciality of this informal little café, where cakes and biscuits, muesli and simple sweets (lemon meringue pie, Bakewell tart), can be enjoyed in the small garden throughout the day. At lunchtime, the choice expands to include soup, delicious wholemeal quiches (cheese and asparagus), pizzas and jacket potatoes, as well as more substantial offerings like vegetable crumble bake or popular Greek cheese pie. *Non-smoking area. No dogs.*

GOSFORTH

Girl on a Swing

1 Lansdowne Place
MAP 4 D2 *Tyne & Wear*
091-285 9672
P street parking   &

Open 6.30pm–11.30pm
Closed Sun & Bank Hols

Papas arequipena £2.90   Boreks £3.60

A frequently changing range of international wholefood vegetarian dishes is on offer at this pleasant restaurant. French onion soup, Ukranian bortsch, Greek salad or stuffed vine leaves for starters, main dishes like spicy stewed okra, boreks (Filo pastry around spinach and feta cheese) and a Peruvian potato, cheese and chilli dish. Sweets include apricot and chocolate roll or gooseberry fool. Booking is advisable. *No dogs.*

GRANGE-IN-BORROWDALE

Grange Bridge Cottage

Nr Keswick
MAP 3 B2 *Cumbria*
Keswick (0596) 84201
P village car park

Open 10–5.30
Closed Mon (except Bank Hols & July–
Sept), also Nov–Easter (except occasional
weekends)

Lasagne with side salad £1.90   Filled
jacket potatoes £1.50   🍵

Old timbers, a flagstoned floor and pew seating create a delightful setting for a snack at Ron and Joan Norey's stone cottage next to a narrow bridge across the Derwent. Joan's fine home baking, which you can enjoy at any time of the day, includes wholemeal scones, fruit shortbread and delicious cakes like orange seed or carrot, while savoury alternatives range from soup and jacket potatoes to cottage pie and excellent home-cooked gammon. *Unlicensed. No smoking. No dogs.*

GRANGE-OVER-SANDS   *At Home*

Danum House, Main Street
MAP 3 C3 *Cumbria*
Grange-over-Sands (044 84) 4400
P   car park behind post office

Open 10–2
Closed Mon, 1 wk Xmas, all Feb & Nov

Chicken liver pâté £1.95   Spinach &
mushroom quiche £2.95

The Johns have added a smart bar to the
lower area, giving it a wine bar atmosphere,
while the upper area is reminiscent of a
French café. The restricted menu offers
minestrone, various sandwiches and
quiches and an excellent chicken liver pâté.
There are tempting traditional sweets:
apple and blackberry pie, sticky toffee
pudding and Queen of puddings with a hot
jammy filling and light meringue. More
elaborate meals are served in the evenings.
No dogs.

Credit Access

GRANTHAM   *Knightingales*

Guildhall Court, Guildhall Street
MAP 4 E4 *Lincolnshire*
Grantham (0476) 79243
P   Morrisons car park

Open 9.30–4.30
Closed Sun & Bank Hols (except Good
Fri)

Mushroom & cashew nut lasagne £2.35
Chocolate, chestnut & brandy gâteau 95p

Fresh flowers and classical music create a
pleasant atmosphere at this attractively
modern wholefood and vegetarian restaurant where you will find tasty food at low
prices. Consult the blackboard for the
day's tempting dishes: perhaps parsnip
and apple soup or herby cheese pâté
followed by lasagne, a filled jacket potato
or cheese and walnut burgers. There's
always a choice of salads, and sweets
include homemade cakes, brown sugar
meringues and deliciously moist Bakewell
tart. *No dogs.*

GRASMERE   *Baldry's*

Red Lion Square
MAP 3 B2 *Cumbria*
Grasmere (09665) 301
P   Garden Centre car park

Open 9.30–5.30 (till 7.30 in summer)
Closed Thurs in winter & weekdays
Nov–mid Mar (except Xmas)

Vegetable cassoulet £2.95   Hot sticky
gingerbread with rum butter 95p   🐾

Paul and Elaine Nelson's efforts to provide
good wholesome food certainly pay off.
Superb open sandwiches can be enjoyed
with houmous, sugar roast ham or wholemeal quiches, while daily specials might
include vegetarian curry or beef cobbler.
Try Paul's lovely ice cream for afters, or
sample his mother's excellent lemon cake.
Sunday roasts for both vegetarians (chestnut and mushroom loaf) and carnivores
(prime beef). *Minimum lunchtime charge
£2.50. No smoking. No dogs.*

GRAYS   *R. Mumford & Son*

8 Cromwell Road
MAP 6 E3 *Essex*
Grays Thurrock (0375) 374153
P   car park opposite

Open 11.45–2.15 & 5.30–10.30 (Sat till
11)
Closed Sun, Bank Hols (except Good
Fri) & 10 days Xmas

Iced melon £1.20   Cod & chips £3.10

Daily trips to Billingsgate mean that the
fish is super-fresh and in abundant variety
at this bright, modern restaurant. Typical
choices include lemon sole, plaice, skate
wing and rock eel, all lightly battered, full
of flavour and served with good, crisp
chips. Watch out, too, for seasonal specialities such as halibut, crab, lobster and
salmon. Chicken and steak are also available, and there's ice cream to finish.
Minimum charge £2.75. No dogs.

LVs

GREAT BARTON   *Craft at the Suffolk Barn*

Fornham Road
MAP 6 E2 *Suffolk*
Great Barton (028 487) 317
P own car park

Open 10–6 (Sun from 12)
Closed Mon, Tues & Xmas–mid Mar

Fudge cake 40p   Walnut tea bread 25p

Follow signs to the Wild Flower Garden to reach this converted barn in the midst of the Suffolk countryside, where Margaret Ellis runs this tea shop and a small garden centre specialising in unusual herbs. Her home baking repertoire embraces ginger shortbread, flapjacks, chocolate fingers, coffee sponge, dream cake and Canadian fruit cake with the added flavours of coconut and pineapple. Sandwiches and ploughman's at lunchtime. *Unlicensed. No dogs.*

GREAT TORRINGTON   *Rebecca's*

8 Potacre Street
MAP 8 B1 *Devon*
Torrington (0805) 22113
P School Lane car park

Open 9am–10pm
Closed Sun & 3 days Xmas

Welsh pancakes £1.75   Rebecca's tart
£1.75 🍴

Drop in throughout the day at the Lillys' bright little restaurant for a quick snack or full meal. Toasted teacakes and hot croissants with cherry jam start the day, followed by such tempting lunchtime offerings as Welsh mushroom pancakes or creamy cucumber salad, local trout, liver and bacon or traditional homity pie. Lovely puddings and various set teas (including Pooh's, with a honey-smothered muffin). Children's menu. *No dogs.*

Credit Access, Amex, Diners, Visa   **LVs**

GREAT TORRINGTON   *Top of the Town*

37 South Street
MAP 8 B1 *Devon*
Torrington (0805) 22900
P South Street car park

Open 10–5 (till 3 in winter), Sun 12–3
Closed 26 Dec

Braised pork cutlets £3   Mixed grill £4
🥗 🍴

Walk a short way from the town square to this simple little restaurant. In the morning there are home-made scones, gâteaux or fruit pies. The lunchtime fare is home-made: soups, pâtés, well flavoured beef casserole with fresh vegetables, omelettes or lamb chops. To finish there are traditional puddings like mince tart or rice pudding. Afternoon tea is served in the garden in summer. Traditional roast on Sunday. Children's menu. *No dogs.*

Credit Access, Visa

GREAT YARMOUTH   *Friends Bistro*

55 Deneside
MAP 6 F1 *Norfolk*
Great Yarmouth (0493) 852538
P King Street car park

Open 10–4
Closed Sun & Bank Hols

Nut roast £3.25   Lancashire hot pot
£2.95

Recently moved from the ground floor to the first, this friendly restaurant decorated in twenties style offers an appetising daytime selection of snacks. Cheese or fruit scones, sausage rolls and cakes start the day, followed at noon by hot dishes like cheese and onion quiche, baked mushrooms, lasagne and chicken in pastry. Don't miss their light, moist tipsy cake for afters. *Minimum lunchtime charge £3. No dogs.*

Credit Access, Visa   **LVs**

GRIMSBY
The Granary

Haven Mill, Garth Lane
MAP 4 F4 *Humberside*
Grimsby (0472) 46338
P Baxter Gate car park

Open 10.30-2 & 7.30-10
Closed Mon eves & all Sun, Bank Hols
& 1 wk Xmas

Fisherman's pot £3.85   Banoffi pie
£1.25

Top-quality produce is prepared with gusto at this informal restaurant in a stylishly converted granary. Lunchtime fare is slightly simpler than the evening menu, which might include gazpacho followed by perfectly grilled whole plaice with cheese and garlic prawns, duckling with fresh blackcurrants or a prime juicy steak. To finish, choose a delicious sweet like summer pudding or rich raisin, nut and fudge flan. *No dogs.*

Credit Access, Visa

GRIMSBY
Leon's

Riverside, 1 Alexandra Road
MAP 4 F4 *Humberside*
Grimsby (0472) 56282
P Baxter Gate car park &

Open 11.30-2 & 5.30-10,
Sat 11.30-10
Closed Sun, Mon & 2 wks Xmas

Haddock & chips £2.90   Plaice & chips
£3.40 🍵

A fish merchant for nearly 40 years, there's little Leon Marklew doesn't know about the trade, and his enthusiasm and professionalism are hallmarks of this deservedly popular restaurant. Haddock, skate and plaice emerge crisp and succulent from fryers filled with pure vegetable fat that's filtered twice daily. Chicken and sausages, too, plus classic accompaniments like mushy peas and a good strong cup of tea. Children's menu. *Non-smoking area. No dogs.*

HADLEIGH
Earlsburys, Janet's Coffee Shop

30 High Street
MAP 6 E2 *Suffolk*
Hadleigh (0473) 827092
P street parking

Open 9-4.30 (Wed till 1)
Closed Sun & Bank Hols

Chicken & asparagus pie £1.85
Banana split 75p 🍴 🍵

Entrance to Janet Ruffell's delightful coffee shop is via Earlsburys food store. You can sit at gingham-covered tables or in the little walled garden to enjoy tasty vegetable soup with lovely wholemeal bread, followed by ham salad or ploughman's, or a hot lunchtime dish like chicken and asparagus pie. Sandwiches, cakes and scones, to be enjoyed with a refreshing cup of tea, are available all day, and homely sweets include blackcurrant and apple pie. *Unlicensed. No dogs.*

HARROGATE
Bettys

1 Parliament Street
Town plan B3 *North Yorkshire*
Harrogate (0423) 64659
P Union Street car park

Open 9am-9pm (from 9.30 Sun)
Closed 1 Jan & 25 & 26 Dec

Yorkshire rarebit with ham £3.65   Deep-fried granary mushrooms £3.20 🍴
🍵

Select one of the rare coffees or an unusual tea and enjoy the morning café concert at this genteel tea room, the first of the Betty chain (established 1919). Their own baked cakes include hazelnut meringue, Viennese Sachertorte, florentines or try a warm Yorkshire fat rascal with butter. More substantially there are rarebits made with Yorkshire ale, haddock and prawns au gratin or light omelettes served by uniformed waitresses. Children's menu. *Non-smoking area. No dogs.*

Credit Access, Visa **LVs**

HARROGATE   *William & Victoria Downstairs*

6 Cold Bath Road
Town plan B3 *North Yorkshire*
Harrogate (0423) 506883
P street parking

Open 12–2 & 6.30–10
Closed Sat lunch, all Sun & Bank Hols

Poached salmon with cucumber sauce
£4.95   Pork spare rib chop with apple
£4.95   ⊖

An attractive basement wine bar offering a blackboard menu of capably prepared favourite dishes served in friendly, informal style. Stilton and garlic pâté, soup and rough country terrine are typical starters, while main courses might include flavoursome beef goulash, seafood mornay, lasagne or vegetarian aubergine and tomato bake. Popular sweets like raspberry and apple crumble, treacle tart and banoffi pie for an enjoyable finish. *No dogs.*

Credit Access

HARROGATE   *William & Victoria Restaurant*

6 Cold Bath Road
Town plan B3 *North Yorkshire*
Harrogate (0423) 521510
P street parking

Open 6.30pm–10pm
Closed Sun, 26 Dec, 1st wk Jan and last wk Aug

Hot creamed prawns with lobster sauce
£2.25   Beef casserole £4.95   ⊖

Robin Straker is a convivial host in this smart but informal restaurant set above the wine bar of the same name. Here you can choose a satisfying snack or a larger meal from a varied blackboard menu. Main dishes, such as tarragon poached salmon, or chicken breast with rosemary cream, make use of good quality produce at a price that does not stagger the customers. Varied sweets including banana and caramel pie. *No children under 11. No dogs.*

Credit Access

HARWICH   N·E·W ENTRY   *Ha'Penny Pier*

The Pier at Harwich, The Quay
MAP 6 F2 *Essex*
Harwich (0255) 241212
P own car park

Open 12–2 & 6–9.30
Closed 25 Dec

Cod & chips £3.75   Ha'penny pie £3.25

Locally caught seafood is the big attraction at this bright, friendly ground-floor restaurant overlooking the harbour. Follow a plate of cockles, or smoked haddock and mushrooms in creamy cheese sauce with a huge portion of crisply fried cod or plaice served with smashing chips and homemade tartare sauce. Lasagne and rump steak for confirmed carnivores, and gooey, ice cream-based desserts for a sweet finale. *No dogs.*

Credit Access, Amex, Diners, Visa

HATTON   N·E·W ENTRY   *Hatton Craft Centre*

Nr Warwick
MAP 5 B2 *Warwickshire*
Claverdon (092 684) 3350
P own car park   &

Open 9–5
Closed Mon (except Bank Hols), 1 Jan, 25, 26 Dec & 1st 2 wks Jan

Beef stew & dumplings £2   Selection of cakes 40p   ⊖

The farm shop and café of this award-winning craft centre are housed in a converted barn where a stone counter displays a mouthwatering array of home baking – try perhaps the light, moist yoghurt cake or delicious almond-iced vanilla sponge. At lunchtime, there's an appetising choice of hot dishes, which might include beef stew and dumplings, turkey curry or a traditional roast, as well as cold meats and salads. *Unlicensed. No smoking. No dogs.*

HAWES   *Cockett's Hotel*

Market Place
MAP 3 C3 *North Yorkshire*
Hawes (096 97) 312
P   Market Place

Open 10.30–12 & 3–5
Closed mid Nov–mid Mar

Cream tea £1.90   Date & walnut loaf
60p   🍵

Sound baking skills produce the range of
delicious cakes on offer in this pleasant
market-place hotel, including memorable
lemon and chocolate sponges, good meringues and lovely light scones served with
tasty jams such as home-made gooseberry.
Biscuits, crisp shortbread, date and walnut
loaf and flapjacks are also popular choices.
For morning coffee or afternoon tea sit in
the pleasantly traditional restaurant or, if
weather is fine, relax in the courtyard. *No
dogs.*

Credit Access, Visa

HAWKSHEAD   *Minstrels Gallery*

The Square
MAP 3 B3 *Cumbria*
Hawkshead (096 66) 423
P   street parking

Open 10.30–5.30
Closed Fri & all mid Dec–mid Feb

Chicken omelette £2.95   Lemon &
ginger slice 70p   🄴   🍵

There's a cosy, friendly atmosphere at the
Russell's gift shop in a 15th-century
building, where visitors can enjoy some
tasty home cooking with a good cup of
tea. Sit on old settles around refectory
tables and nibble at scones, gingerbread,
slices, various cakes (after 2pm) and
sandwiches. From noon, omelettes, salads
and daily specials like chicken and mushroom pie join the menu, together with
homely sweets such as wholewheat fruit
crumble. *Unlicensed. No smoking.*

HAWORTH   *N·E·W ENTRY*   *Weavers*

15 West Lane
MAP 4 D3 *West Yorkshire*
Haworth (0535) 43822
P   Museum car park

Open 7pm–9.30pm, Sun 12–2.30
Closed Sun (Easter–Oct), Mon, 1st
2 wks July and 1 wk Xmas

Yorkshire pudding £1.50   Breast of
chicken with tarragon sauce £6.25
🄴

You can order just one course or enjoy a
full meal at this delightfully informal
restaurant. Jane Rushworth's repertoire
embraces the thoroughly traditional –
Yorkshire pudding with onion gravy,
pinkly roasted lamb and steamed pudding
with custard – as well as the more exotic –
spicy vegetable parcels accompanied by
excellent vegetable chutney, or monkfish
medallions with tomato sauce. Whatever
you choose, don't miss the splendid home-
baked bread. *No dogs.*

Credit Access, Amex, Diners, Visa

HEACHAM   *N·E·W ENTRY*   *Miller's Cottage Tea Room*

Caley Mill
MAP 6 E1 *Norfolk*
Heacham (0485) 70384
P   own car park   ♿

Open 10.30–5.30 (Easter–Whitsun from
12)
Closed weekdays Easter–Whitsun & all
Oct–Easter

Quiche & salad £2.20   Scones with jam
& cream 50p   🄴   🍵

England's only lavender farm makes a
delightfully fragrant setting for afternoon
tea or a light lunch. Enjoy the rustic charm
of the old miller's cottage or sit outside on
the flower-filled patio or in the beautifully
tended riverside garden. As well as delicious cakes and pastries (note especially
the coconut tartlets and Bakewell tart),
there are sandwiches and salads, ploughman's, quiches and sausage rolls available
right through the day. *Unlicensed. No
dogs.*

HEMEL HEMPSTEAD   *N·E·W ENTRY*   *Gallery Coffee Shop*

Old Town Hall Arts Centre, High Street
MAP 6 D2 *Hertfordshire*
Hemel Hempstead (0442) 42827
P street parking

Open 10.30–4.30
Closed Sun, Bank Hols, 2 wks late
summer, & 1 wk Xmas

Buckwheat pancake with mushroom &
watercress filling £3.45   Hazelnut
meringue cake £1.30   🍴

Part of a bustling arts centre, this bright,
lofty brasserie hums with life at lunchtime.
Hardworking   Alyson   Blackmore   is
responsible for the tempting choice of
food, which ranges from simple sandwiches, soup and pâté to delicious daily
specials – neatly scripted on a blackboard
– such as broccoli and cream cheese
roulade, roast pork Dijonnaise and spaghetti with aubergine and tomato. Lovely
sweets, too, like hot chocolate pudding,
plus some excellent home baking. *No
dogs.*

HENLEY-ON-THAMES   *Barnaby's Brasserie*

2 New Street
MAP 5 C3 *Oxfordshire*
Henley-on-Thames (0491) 572421
P King's Road car park

Open 12–2 & 7–10.30
Closed Sun lunch & all 1 Jan
& 25 & 26 Dec

Barbecued ribs £5.85   Sole stuffed with
smoked salmon £5.85   ⊖

Enjoy a light bite or a full meal at this
relaxed, brasserie-style restaurant in a
smartly modernised 14th-century building.
The main menu ranges from home-made
soup and snails to pizzas, burgers, steaks
and kebabs, while a daily-changing supplement offers specials like venison ragout or
red mullet niçoise. Pancakes layered with
brandy butter, orange sauce and cream are
a popular way to finish. *No dogs.*

Credit Access, Visa   **LVs**

---

*Changes in data sometimes occur in
establishments after the Guide goes to press.*

*Prices should be taken as indications
rather than firm quotes.*

HENLEY-ON-THAMES   *Copper Kettle*

18 Thameside
MAP 5 C3 *Oxfordshire*
Henley-on-Thames (0491) 575262
P station car park

Open 10–6 (Nov–Mar till 5)

Cauliflower cheese £2.25   Toasted
tea cake 50p   🍴

Start the day with a hearty breakfast at
this charmingly chintzy tea room, where
pictures and ornaments decorate the walls
and in the conservatory an old hansom cab
is to be found. In the morning plump for
sandwiches and freshly-baked cakes, to be
followed at lunchtime by perhaps soup,
chicken and mushroom pie or delicious
home-cooked ham. A fine choice of set
teas round off the day. *Minimum lunchtime charge £1.75. Non-smoking area.
No dogs.*

HEREFORD

N·E·W ENTRY

Fat Tulip

**The Old Wye Bridge,
2 St Martin's St
MAP 5 A2 *Hereford & Worcester*
Hereford (0432) 275808
P** street parking

Open 12–2 & 7–10

Closed Sun, Bank Hols & 10 days Xmas

Grilled sardines £3.75   Mussels in almond & garlic butter £2.95
Fresh mango parfait £2.95
Strawberry tart £2.95   ☕

★ This delightfully named bistro is found next to the Old Wye Bridge in the town centre. The atmosphere is informal and charming, with paper covers and fresh flowers on each table, and white-painted walls hung with stylish photographs. Presentation is simple and only the freshest and best produce is used to create the very tasty dishes served here. Sample the delights of fresh river prawns with garlic, ginger and spring onions, or the more substantial roast duck with orange and green peppercorn sauce. Puddings are elegant and there is a small, but most interesting, cheese board. The espresso coffee is outstanding. Children's portions. *No dogs.* ★

Credit Access, Amex, Visa

HEREFORD

Marches

**Union Street
MAP 5 A2 *Hereford & Worcester*
Hereford (0432) 355712
P** Gaol Street car park ♿

Open 8.30–5.30
Closed Sun & Bank Hols

Spinach flan 75p   Vegetarian lasagne £1.30   ☕ 🍵

One complex houses this wholefood restaurant along with a gift gallery and a health food shop. At least twelve different fresh and varied salads are offered, and other dishes include a choice of soups, wholemeal flans, a daily hot special and main courses like nut roast or cashew nut risotto. Fresh fruit salad, fruit pies and lemon meringue pie to follow, or try the flapjacks or gâteau. Speciality teas are available. *Non-smoking area. No dogs.*

Credit Access, Visa   **LVs**

HEREFORD

Nutters

**2 Capucin Yard, Church Street
MAP 5 A2 *Hereford & Worcester*
Hereford (0432) 277447
P** NCP Widemarsh Street ♿

Open 9.30–5
Closed Sun & most Bank Hols

Vegetable lasagne £2.30   Vegetarian pizza 85p   🍵

'Fodder' has changed its name to 'Nutters' but the healthy outlook remains the same at this popular vegetarian restaurant tucked away in a courtyard. The menu varies according to who's cooking that day, but there's always a flavour-packed soup – like nicely spiced carrot and onion – filled rolls, jacket potatoes, quiches and a selection of crunchy fresh salads, as well as filling specials like wholemeal pasta with eggs. Finish with chocolate cheesecake or ginger shortbread. *No smoking. No dogs.*

HERSTMONCEUX   *Praise the Lord*

Gardner Street
MAP 6 E4 *East Sussex*
Herstmonceux (0323) 833219
P street parking

Open 9–5.30
Closed Mon, also 3wks Dec–Jan

Sussex cream tea £2.50   Mushroom
pasty £2.50   🍵

A steady stream of locals buy cakes,
biscuits and French sticks, baked while
they watch. In the cosy eating area are
pretty flower-patterned cloths and a big,
plate-adorned dresser. Savoury snacks
include excellent mini-quiches with good
crisp wholemeal pastry and sausage rolls.
Cakes range from rock cakes to a light
fresh sponge topped with chocolate and a
walnut. Tea is a good, fresh brew of nice
colour and flavour. Garden. *Unlicensed.*
Non-smoking area. No dogs.

Credit Access, Visa

HIGH LORTON   *White Ash Barn*

Nr Cockermouth
MAP 3 B2 *Cumbria*
Lorton (090 085) 236
P own car park

Open 12.30–5.30
Closed end Oct–1 wk before Easter

Chicken liver pâté £1.85   Lemon
cheesecake £1   🍵

A raftered, early 18th-century barn houses
this delightful tea room and gift shop,
where the Georges offer a warm welcome
and some enjoyable home cooking. Light
lunches feature salads with quiches and
cold meats (including delicious home-
baked gammon), while at teatime Mrs
George produces super scones, sandwiches
and a trolley laden with goodies like
chocolate sponge, lemon fridge cake and
date and walnut slice. Garden. *Unlicensed.*
No smoking. No dogs.

HONITON   N·E·W ENTRY   *Dominoes*

178 High Street
MAP 8 C2 *Devon*
Honiton (0404) 3510
P Dowle Street Car Park

Open 12–2.15 & 7–10.15
Closed Sun, Bank Hols & 4 days Xmas

Steak & oyster pie £4.90   Lamb satay
£4.95   🍷

A smart yet informal wine bar with rustic
furnishings and a lively atmosphere. The
imaginative menu ranges far and wide in
its dishes – from taramasalata, tacos and
falafel among snacks or starters to main
dishes such as crispy Szechuan duck, lamb
satay or steak and oyster pie. Grills and
burgers are also available, as are jacket
potatoes, salads and savoury filled croissants at lunchtime. Simple sweets. *No
dogs.*

Credit Access, Visa

HOPE   *Hopechest*

8 Castleton Road, Nr Sheffield
MAP 4 D4 *Derbyshire*
Hope Valley (0433) 20072
P village car park

Open 9.15–5
Closed Sun, Mon, 1 Jan & 25 & 26 Dec

Home-baked ham with salad £1.75
Fruit cake 70p   🍵

In the heart of the Hope Valley, this
friendly little tea room is run by three
retired schoolteachers. High marks go to
such excellent snacks as home-baked ham
and salad, ham and leek quiche, good
flavoured shortbread, a scrumptious
Bakewell tart and whatever else takes the
cook's fancy that day. The tea is good and
the coffee always fresh. Eat outside in
summer. *Unlicensed. No smoking. No
dogs.*

Credit Access, Visa

HORSFORTH   *Stuarts Wine Bar*

166 Town Street
MAP 4 D3 *West Yorkshire*
Leeds (0532) 582661
P   street parking

Open   12–2 & 7.15–10
Closed   Mon eve, all Sun, Bank Hols
& last 2 wks Aug

Mixed meat salad £4.95   Garlic prawns
£2.25   ℰ

A very popular establishment at the top
end of Town Street in which old photographs grace the walls. Most in demand is
the cold buffet selection consisting of cuts
of beef, pork, ham and chicken with a large
variety of serve-yourself salads, prefaced
by soup, garlic prawns, pâté or avocado.
Hot choices include grilled trout, steak au
poivre, Oriental-style vegetables or chicken
stuffed with Stilton and almonds. Chocolate and brandy mousse or fruit crumble
to follow. *No children. No dogs.*

HUNGERFORD   *Bear, Kennet Room*

41 Charnham Street
MAP 5 C3 *Berkshire*
Hungerford (0488) 82512
P   own car park   ♿

Open   12.15–2 & 7.30–9.30 (Fri & Sat
till 10)
Closed   25 Dec

Mussels in white wine & cream £4
Trout stuffed with herbs £7.30   ℰ

Off the comfortable bar of the welcoming
Bear is a small dining room looking over a
street of old and very attractive terraced
cottages. It serves both snacks and full
meals from a seasonally changing menu.
The selection of English farmhouse
cheeses with the baked onion soup makes
a good meal, or you might choose layered
nut slice with an optional poached egg or
the smoked salmon and winter fruit salad.
Eat out on the terrace in summer. *No
dogs.*

Credit   Access, Amex, Diners, Visa

HUNGERFORD   *N·E·W ENTRY*   *Behind the Green Door*

50 Church Street
MAP 5 C3 *Berkshire*
Hungerford (0488) 82189
P   Church Street car park

Open   12–2.30 & 6 30–10.30 (Sun
from 7)
Closed   1 Jan, 25 & 26 Dec

Cumberland sausage £2.45   Pasta
bake £4.15   ℰ

Eat at the bar or at dark polished tables at
this comfortable restaurant converted from
a pub by owner Jenny Wratten's husband.
Crudités with a blue cheese dip, Welsh
rarebit and garlic mushrooms all make
simple snacks or starters, while main
courses include grilled lamb chops, a daily
fresh fish dish and chicken in a creamy
white wine sauce. Desserts like rich chocolate and brandy mousse or traditional rice
pudding round things off. *No dogs.*

Credit   Access, Visa

HUNTINGDON   *Old Bridge Hotel Lounge*

1 High Street
MAP 6 D2 *Cambridgeshire*
Huntingdon (0480) 52681
P   own car park

Open   10am–midnight

Pigeon & steak pie £6.95   Stir-fried
salami, bacon & mushrooms £6.45
ℰ   🍵

A tempting cold buffet is laid out in the
leafy glass-fronted terrace lounge of this
attractive hotel. Take your pick from cold
meats, fresh salmon, crisp salads, and a
selection of salamis with parmesan and
olives, or choose an appetising hot dish
such as Gruyère cheese fritters, jugged
venison or chilli bean pancakes with
mushroom sauce. Afternoon tea is served
in the elegant main lounge or out in the
garden on sunny days. *No dogs.*

Credit   Access, Amex, Diners, Visa

HYTHE   *Natural Break*

115 High Street
MAP 6 F3 *Kent*
Hythe (0303) 67573
P car park opposite police station

Open 9–5
Closed Sun, Good Friday & 25, 26 Dec

Jacket potato & cheese 95p   Courgette
& onion quiche 95p

Pine furniture, bare floorboards and a
relaxed atmosphere combine to make this
tiny vegetarian snack bar (part of a health
food shop), a pleasant place to enjoy a
quick bite. Early in the day cakes like
poppy seed and almond or deliciously moist
carrot cake are displayed on the counter.
Savoury choices such as home-made
soups, celery and walnut quiche, salads
and pizzas are available for lunch. *Unlicensed (bring your own). No smoking.
No dogs.*

ILKLEY   *Bettys*

32 The Grove
MAP 4 D3 *West Yorkshire*
Ilkley (0943) 608029
P town-centre car park

Open 9–5.30, Sat & Sun 9–7
Closed 25 Dec

Full English breakfast £5.25   Haddock
& prawns au gratin £3.35   🅱 🐾

Rarebits made with Yorkshire ale, pork
sausages and bacon, a Yorkshire cheese
lunch of blue and white Wensleydale with
fruit chutney, celery and granary bread are
some of the traditional favourites at this
graciously styled tea shop. Uniformed
waitresses will guide you through the cake
trolley featuring delectable vanilla hearts,
curd tarts, almond macaroons and rich
fruit cake. Excellent tea and rare coffee
selection. *Non-smoking area. No dogs.*

Credit Access, Visa   **LVs**

IPSWICH   *Marno's*

14 St Nicholas Street
MAP 6 F2 *Suffolk*
Ipswich (0473) 53106
P St Nicholas Street car park   &

Open 10–3 (Thurs–Sat till 10)
Closed Sun & Bank Hols

Pasta with mushrooms, cheese & white
wine cream sauce £2.10   Nut roast
£2.10   🐾

Pine furniture, wall posters and a corner
selling second-hand clothes are the setting
for some hearty vegetarian food. Choose
from the counter display a crisp salad or a
filling and tasty bean and vegetable soup
served with a wedge of decent wholemeal
bread. Hot daily specials could include
mushroom and lentil bake, Spanish pudding with peppers, or cheese and potato
casserole. Fruit salad, meringues and
banana and walnut cake to finish. *Non-
smoking area. No dogs.*

LVs

IPSWICH   *Mortimers Oyster Bar*

Wherry Quay
MAP 6 F2 *Suffolk*
Ipswich (0473) 230225
P on the quay

Open 12–2 & 7–9 (Mon till 8.30)
Closed Sat lunch, all Sun & Mon, Bank
Hols, 2 days Easter & 2 wks Xmas

Seafood gratin £3.50   Grilled oysters
mornay £4.25

Above the more sophisticated Mortimer's
restaurant is this simpler branch of the
operation which offers inexpensive meals
of good quality. Decor is simple, with white
walls, arty tablecloths and napkins, and
the windows look out over Ipswich docks.
Oysters, fresh or grilled mornay, fish
lasagne or smoked haddock kedgeree
emphasise the fishy slant to the menu, and
plain puddings include crème caramel,
fruit salad and Greek yogurt with honey.
Children's portions. *No dogs.*

Credit Access, Amex, Diners, Visa

IPSWICH   *Orwell House*

4a Orwell Place
MAP 6 F2 *Suffolk*
Ipswich (0473) 230254
P Cox Lane car park

Open 12–2, also Wed–Sat
7pm–10pm

Spinach & beanshoot pancake
£1.95   Tagliatelle with mussels
£2.25   Escalope of pork £4.95
Chicken marengo £4.85 🍵

★ John Gear's cooking is as consistently excellent
whether you're dining in his formal upstairs restaurant or staying, just-a-bite fashion, at ground-floor
level and ordering from the short bistro menu. The
monthly-changing selection is nicely varied and ★
might typically include herby game pâté, avocado
and mushroom hot pot and tagliatelle carbonara
among starters, followed perhaps by wonderfully
light and fluffy omelette Arnold Bennett, sirloin steak
bordelaise or ham and Stilton-stuffed pork served
with sage and coriander sauce. Irresistible desserts
like hot apricot Charlotte portugaise and coffee
gâteau St. Honore make a perfect finale. *No dogs.*

Credit Access, Amex, Visa

KENDAL   *Corner Spot Eating House*

2 Stramongate
MAP 3 C3 *Cumbria*
Kendal (0539) 20115
P Blackhall Road car park

Open 8.30–4.45
Closed Sun, Thurs & Bank Hols

Quiche, baked potato & salad £1.70
Lemon meringue pie 40p

Cakes and sweets galore are to be found at
this sunny first-floor tea room, including
wholemeal scones, French apple tart,
maids of honour and raspberry shortbread,
as well as seasonal fruit pies and baked
egg custard. Savoury alternatives like
home-made soup and fresh brown bread
sandwiches, a variety of hot quiches and
filled jacket potatoes are especially popular
with lunchtime shoppers, which means
that seats can be hard to find on market
days!

Credit Access, Amex, Diners, Visa   **LVs**

Any person using our name
to obtain free hospitality is a fraud.

Proprietors, please inform
Egon Ronay's Guides and the police.

KENDAL   *The Moon*

129 Highgate
MAP 3 C3 *Cumbria*
Kendal (0539) 29254
P Brewery car park opposite

Open 6pm–10pm (till 9.30 in winter), Fri & Sat till 11 (till 10 in winter)

Closed 1 Jan & 25 & 26 Dec

Beef stroganoff £4.65   Spinach, cheese & mushroom pancake £3.99   Vegetable ragout £4.50   Tropical fruit meringue £1.75

★ This is wholefood cooking at its very best. Striking decor, a mix of prints and paintings and enjoyably bizarre musk lends character and mood to Val Macconnell's delightful restaurant. Sit at gingham-clothed tables and watch the menu change as you eat – a sign of how freshly cooked the food really is. There are no pretentions here, but the food is innovative and exciting; start with mackerel pâté or watercress and avocado mousse, to be followed by haddock and spinach pilaff or well seasoned chilli vegetable and ricotta tortellini bake. A wedge of real cheesecake or a strawberry and hazelnut meringue rounds off a wonderful meal. ★

Credit Access, Visa

KENDAL   *Nutters*

Yard 11, Stramongate
MAP 3 C3 *Cumbria*
Kendal (0539) 25135
P New Road car park

Open 9.30–6.30
Closed Sun & Bank Hols

Vegetable lasagne £2.75   Blackberry & apple meringue 80p 🍵

Once the servants' quarters and stables of a 17th-century house, this friendly, relaxed restaurant offers an appetising choice of carefully prepared fare. Consult the blackboard for the day's selection – perhaps nourishing minestrone followed by Cumberland sausages, beef and vegetable pie or a baked potato filled with pork goulash or cheese and leeks. Lemon meringue pie, sticky toffee pudding and fruit cake for the sweeter tooth. *Non-smoking area. No dogs.*

LVs

KENDAL   *Waterside Wholefoods*

Kent View
MAP 3 C3 *Cumbria*
Kendal (0539) 29743
P riverside car park

Open 9–4
Closed Sun, 1 Jan & 25 & 26 Dec

Turkish pilaff with yoghurt & banana £2.25   Leek & mushroom roulade £2.25

Sharing its premises with a wholefood shop, this solid and reliable restaurant is set out in two rooms with pine tables. There are watercolours for sale, and you can sit out by the River Kent on sunny days. The day's specials appear on a blackboard and a large array of salads is also offered. Dishes incorporate herbs, spices and fresh fruits and are both tasty and satisfying. Plain cakes, ice creams and fruit flan follow. Children's portions. *Unlicensed. No smoking. No dogs.*

KENILWORTH

N·E·W ENTRY

Ana's Bistro

121 Warwick Road
MAP 5 B2 *Warwickshire*
Kenilworth (0926) 53763
P own car park

Open 7–10.30
Closed Sun, Mon, Bank Hols, 1 wk
Easter & 3 wks Aug

Chicken in courgette & sweetcorn sauce
£3.95   Smoked mackerel mousse £1.65
⊖

Robust, capable cooking based on prime produce makes for enjoyable eating at this friendly basement bistro. Choose a full meal or just the main course from a menu that mixes regular favourites like soup, pâté, steak and grilled plaice with constantly changing specials such as sliced melon with oranges and port, or mushrooms and prawns with herby garlic butter. Alternatives might include sautéed lamb in green peppercorn and sherry sauce or tandoori pork with rice. *No dogs*.

Credit Access, Amex, Diners, Visa

---

*We welcome bona fide recommendations or complaints
on the tear-out pages at the back of the book
for readers' comments.*

*They are followed up by our professional team,
but do complain to the management on the spot.*

KENILWORTH

George Rafters

42 Castle Hill
MAP 5 B2 *Warwickshire*
Kenilworth (0926) 52074
P street parking

Open 12–2 & 7–10.30
Closed 26 Dec

Suprême Louis £4.95   Beef &
mushrooms in Guinness pie £3.95

A friendly, informal restaurant near the castle where the food is well prepared and full of interest. Follow light, subtly flavoured prawn mousse or deep-fried goat's cheese with possibly pigeon en croûte served with a rich game sauce, Mediterranean seafood casserole or individual beef, mushroom and Guinness pie. There's always a daily fish and vegetarian special, and tempting sweets include fruit meringue and banoffi pie. *No dogs*.

Credit Access, Amex, Diners, Visa

KESWICK

Bryson's Tea Room

42 Main Street
MAP 3 B2 *Cumbria*
Keswick (0596) 72257
P car park at rear

Open 9–5.30
Closed Sun & end Oct–Easter

Quiche & salad £2.60   Cumberland
farmhouse tea £1.60

Above the Bryson's bakery shop, with its tempting display, is their immensely popular tea room. Everything here is unpretentious, wholesome and good – reflecting the output of the bakery below. Hot snacks include Cumbrian ham and eggs, Borrowdale trout with almonds and Cumberland sausages. The set afternoon tea has scones, moist, fruity malt loaf, tea bread and cakes from the trolley. Children's menu. *Unlicensed. No dogs*.

KEW   *Original Maids of Honour*

288 Kew Road
MAP 6 D3 *Surrey*
01-940 2752
P street parking &

Open 10–5.30

Closed Sun, Mon & Bank Hols

Maid of honour 75p   Home-made
soup 95p   Set lunch £4   Cream
cakes from 65p

★ The Newens family have forged a reputation based
on a century of exemplary baking at this olde-worlde
tea shop opposite Kew Gardens. Everything is baked
in their own kitchen including the lightest imaginable
mille-feuilles, airy sponges, cream horns, fruit tarts,
éclairs, brandy snaps and Henry VIII's reputed ★
favourite, puff pastry maids of honour. The charmingly old-fashioned shop adjoins the tea room with
wheelbacked chairs and old wooden tables bedecked
with fresh flowers. Mouthwatering sausage rolls,
steak pies, Cornish pasties and chicken and ham pies
satisfy a savoury palate. Substantial hot lunches and
set afternoon teas are available. Children's portions.
No dogs.

KEW   *Pissarro's*

1 Kew Green
MAP 6 D3 *Surrey*
01-940 3987
P street parking

Open 11.30–3 & 5.30–11, Sun 12–2
& 7–10.30
Closed Good Fri, Easter Sun & 3 days
Xmas

Fish pie £3.25   Lasagne £3 🍽

Near the main entrance to Kew Gardens is
this pleasant rustic wine bar where the
friendly staff create a relaxing atmosphere.
Smoked mackerel mousse, escalope of veal
in marsala sauce, fillet steak chasseur and
breast of chicken with asparagus in tomato, mushroom and white wine sauce
feature on the blackboard menu, and an
excellent traditional roast is available on
Sundays. The cold buffet is an alternative,
and desserts include mousses, cheesecake
and coffee cream. *No children.*

Credit Access, Visa

KEW   *Wine & Mousaka*

12 Kew Green
MAP 6 D3 *Surrey*
01-940 5696
P street parking

Open 12–2.30 & 6–11.30
Closed Sun, Bank Hols & 3 days Xmas

Moussaka £3.85   Tava £4.95

A smart, bustling Greek restaurant overlooking Kew Green where the tables are
closely packed, the atmosphere informal
and the food delicious. Oregano-scented
meats fresh from the charcoal grill are a
favourite choice – try juicy pork kebabs,
poussin or cumin-flavoured lamb sausages.
Herby meatballs and dolmades, and classic
starters such as houmus and taramasalata,
are notably well executed. Simple sweets.
No dogs.

Credit Access, Amex, Diners, Visa   **LVs**

KIDDERMINSTER   *Natural Break*

6 Blackwell Street
MAP 5 B2 *Hereford & Worcester*
Kidderminster (0562) 743275
P   Swan Centre car park

Open 9.30–4.30 (Sat till 5)
Closed Sun & Bank Hols (except
Good Fri)

Bacon & mushroom pasty 85p   Salad
portion 46p

At the sister branch of the two Worcester
establishments there is the same sort of
choice of healthy food to eat in or take
away. Wholemeal flans with tasty fillings
like mushroom and celery can be enjoyed
with a choice of imaginative salads (try
cheese and carrot or pasta and fruit).
Alternatives include bacon and mushroom
pasties and there is a short list of tempting
sweets. *Unlicensed. Non-smoking area.
No dogs.*

LVs

KING'S LYNN   *Antonio's Wine Bar*

Baxter's Plain
MAP 6 E1 *Norfolk*
King's Lynn (0553) 772324
P   Blackfriars Street car park at rear

Open 12–2 & 7–11.30
Closed Sun, Mon, Bank Hols & 2 wks
Aug

Italian bean soup £1.30   Tagliatelle
£3.10   ℰ

A lovely wine bar, close to the town
shopping centre, dominated by the ebulli-
ent Antonio. A full range of Italian favourites – antipasto, pasta and amply filled
pizzas – is available, plus fresh crab salad
or smoked prawns. Pasta dishes include
spaghetti or tagliatelle bolognese and
macaroni paesana. Home-made minestrone
and lasagne are particularly popular and
there is a delicious Italian trifle or crème
caramel and cheeses to follow. *No dogs.*

KINGSTON   *La La Pizza*

138 London Road
MAP 6 D3 *Surrey*
01-546 4888
P   street parking

Open 5.30–midnight
Closed 1 Jan & 25 & 26 Dec

Baked dough sticks £1   American hot
pizza £3.20

The atmosphere is relaxed and welcoming
at this cheerful Italian restaurant offering
over 25 different varieties of freshly prepared pizzas. Traditional dough bases
come generously topped with everything
from simple tomato, herbs and mozzarella
to red salmon, tuna, prawns and anchovies.
Lasagne and cannelloni are popular alternatives, and starters include minestrone,
garlic mushrooms and salads. Finish with
an excellent ice or splendidly rich chocolate
mousse. *No dogs.*

LVs

KINVER   *Berkeley's Bistro*

High Street, Nr Stourbridge
MAP 5 B2 *Staffordshire*
Kinver (0384) 873679
P   car park opposite

Open 12–2 & 7–10
Closed Sun, 26–31 Dec

Veal kidneys with tomato & pasta £2.75
Turkey escalopes £5.50

A well-established bistro, popular both for
snacks and more leisurely meals. A blackboard announces the day's lunchtime
dishes, and there is also a more extensive
menu available. Choose from such light
dishes as chicken liver with fresh apple in
a cream and sage sauce, minute steak
Lyonnaise and baked egg with tomato and
pepper, or more substantial dishes like
noisette of pork with a well-flavoured port
wine sauce or fillet steak Diane. Simple
sweets. *No dogs.*

Credit Access, Amex, Diners, Visa

KIRKBYMOORSIDE

Hatters Castle Coffee Shop

Market Place
MAP 4 E3 *North Yorkshire*
Kirkbymoorside (0751) 32471
P street parking

Open 9.30–6 (till 9.30pm in summer)
Closed 24 Dec–early Feb

Steak pie £2.80   Hatters special
breakfast £2.95   🅔 🍵

Enjoy some capable cooking and the friendly ambience at this attractively decorated coffee shop. Whilst you look out over the market square you can enjoy quiches, Welsh rarebit, a selection of salads, or open sandwiches on excellent fresh bread with crab, ham, beef or prawns. Main dishes include steak, pork chops and various omelettes. For the sweet-toothed there is the strong flavour of Yorkshire curd tart, or light, tasty scones and fruit pies. *Unlicensed (bring your own). Non-smoking area.*

LAMBERHURST

The Down

Lamberhurst Down
MAP 6 E3 *Kent*
Lamberhurst (0892) 890237
P own car park

Open 10–5.30
Closed Mon (except Bank Hols), Tues
& all Nov–Mar

Kentish cream tea £1.75   Early spring
tea £1.30

Julia Latter, the new owner, has made some changes to this old favourite: the shop is now a craft shop, the tea room is lighter, brighter and more cottagy, and the garden has been converted into a car park. Good, moist cakes, teabreads and a selection of scones are served throughout the day. There are lardy cakes, crumbly butter shortbread, honey and oatmeal slices and a range of cream teas: a children's tea, 'Grandma's favourite' tea and a farmhouse tea. *Unlicensed. No smoking. No dogs.*

LANCASTER

Libra

19 Brock Street
MAP 3 C3 *Lancashire*
Lancaster (0524) 61551
P street parking

Open 9–9 (Mon till 6, Tues & Wed till 8)
Closed Sun, Bank Hols & 1 wk Xmas

Tagliatelle bake £2.35   Harvest pie £2

The atmosphere is relaxed and informal at this friendly vegetarian restaurant where the snacks are all healthy and delicious. Muesli biscuits, fruity wholemeal scones and poppyseed cake go down well with a choice of speciality herb teas, while on the savoury side there are attractive salads, excellent houmus and hot dishes like creamy soup, leek and mushroom pie or stuffed aubergines. More elaborate evening meals. *Non-smoking area. No dogs.*

LAUNCESTON

The Greenhouse

Madford Lane
MAP 8 B2 *Cornwall*
Launceston (0566) 3670
P market car park

Open 10–4; in summer 9–5 & Fri 7–10
Closed Sun & Bank Hols (except 25 Dec)

Blackeye bean & vegetable stew £1.75
Green bean & mushroom bake £2.60
🍵

This bright self-service vegetarian restaurant near the town square is run by Julie and Peter Strong. An excellent range of speciality teas goes well with Julie's tempting home-made cakes, including banana and nut, carrot, apple and lemon. For lunch, there's soup or houmus followed by crisp salads, quiche, courgette and tomato bake or a daily special like aduki bean pie. Friendly and informal service compliments the leisurely atmosphere. Waitress service on Friday evenings in summer. *No smoking. No dogs.*

LAVENHAM
N·E·W
ENTRY
The Great House

Market Place
MAP 6 E2 *Suffolk*
Lavenham (0787) 247431
P   Market place

Open 9.30–2.30 & 3–5
Closed Mon in winter & 3 wks Jan

Cream tea £1.90   Summer buffet £3.95
🍵

Built in the 14th and 15th centuries, and much renovated since, this house was once lived in by the poet Stephen Spender. The dining room has a large red brick fireplace, a central oak beam and white dado panelling. From 9.30 breakfast is available, followed by morning coffee with scones, cakes and delicious sweets. Noon to 2.30 brings lunch – smoked calf's liver with shallots, smoked fish pancakes or an outdoor buffet. From 3 to 5 tea can be taken in the garden.

Credit Access, Amex, Visa

LEAMINGTON SPA
Alastairs

40 Warwick Street
MAP 5 B2 *Warwickshire*
Leamington Spa (0926) 22550
P   street parking

Open 12–2.30 & 7–11
Closed Sun & Bank Hol lunches & all 1
Jan & 25 & 26 Dec

Beef bourguignon £3.75   Lamb
Kashmir £3.75

A lively and informal cellar wine bar with a terrace and garden for al fresco eating and drinking. Cold meats and salads are attractively displayed, and there's an appetising choice of daily hot dishes chalked up on a large blackboard. Starters like calamari, pâté, smoked salmon and taramasalata can be followed by such enjoyably prepared stalwarts as curry, lasagne, duck with green pepper or pork in a creamy tarragon sauce. *No dogs.*

Credit Access, Visa

LEAMINGTON SPA
Mallory Court

Harbury Lane, Tachbrook Mallory
MAP 5 B2 *Warwickshire*
Leamington Spa (0926) 30214
P   own car park

Open 3.30–5

Full afternoon tea £7.50   Chicken
sandwich £3.50 🍵

Enjoy a splendid afternoon tea in the elegant drawing room, pretty lounge or out on the terrace of this superb country house. The set tea is quite a feast, including dainty, freshly made sandwiches (lovely smoked salmon), light, crumbly scones served with good jam and thick cream, featherlight sponges and a gorgeously moist, marzipan-topped fruit cake. Excellent speciality teas provide the perfect accompaniment. *No children under 12. No dogs.*

Credit Access, Amex, Diners, Visa

LEAMINGTON SPA
Piccolino's

9 Spencer Street
MAP 5 B2 *Warwickshire*
Leamington Spa (0926) 22988
P   Chapel Street car park

Open 12–2.30 & 5.30–11 (Sun till
10.30 & Fri till 11.30), Sat 12–11.30
Closed 3 days Xmas

Pizza siciliana £3.45   Lasagne £3.35

A cheerful, brightly decorated Italian restaurant where customers can watch their pizzas being baked to order. Choose from 18 different toppings, including Speedy Gonzales (mozzarella, gorgonzola and tomato), and Red Hot Mama (chilli beef and cheese), on a solid base. Pasta appears in all its popular varieties, and there are also steaks and spit-roast chicken, crisp salads and simple sweets. *Non-smoking area. No dogs.*

Credit Access, Visa

LEAMINGTON SPA   *Regency Fare*

72 Regent Street
MAP 5 B2 *Warwickshire*
Leamington (0926) 25570
P Park Street car park

Open 9–6
Closed Sun & Bank Hols (except May Day)

Steak & kidney pie £4.50   Roast beef & Yorkshire pudding £5.25   ☻

This simple town-centre restaurant doubles as a tea room when not serving lunches, with the set afternoon tea including sandwiches and other savouries, cakes and scones. Coffee is also served all day with cakes. Main meals at midday range from sole in white wine, salmon pie, steak and kidney pie and beef bourguignon to omelettes and a choice of salads. Steamed jam sponge, bread and butter pudding or apricot crumble to follow. *Non-smoking area.*

Credit Access, Visa   **LVs**

LEAMINGTON SPA   *Ropers*

1a Clarendon Avenue
MAP 5 B2 *Warwickshire*
Leamington Spa (0926) 316719
P Russell Street car park

Open 8am–10.30pm (Sun from 10)
Closed 25 & 26 Dec

Savoury pancakes £4.80   Stuffed peppers £3.95   🍶

Early breakfasts start the day at this leafy, conservatory-style brasserie, which also offers super snacks and main meals. Generously-filled granary sandwiches, excellent houmus and pitta, filled jacket potatoes and delicious salads are typical light bites, while the hungry can tackle anything from smoked haddock and spinach lasagne to beef and Guinness pie or pork in a creamy Calvados sauce. Pecan pie or pastries to finish. *No dogs.*

Credit Access, Amex, Visa

LEDBURY   *Feathers Hotel*

High Street
MAP 5 A2 *Hereford & Worcester*
Ledbury (0531) 5266
P town car park

Open 12–2 & 7–9.30

Home-made hamburger with salad £3.95
Beef & venison pie £3.50   ☻

This listed Elizabethan hotel with its beautiful half-timbered façade is a major landmark of Ledbury High Street. The cold table is the lunchtime centrepiece with a selection of cold meats, salads, and a low-calorie slimmer's special, plus an array of home-made sweets. Hot dishes are also available, including a sustaining home-made soup or pâté as starters, and beef and venison pie or home-made hamburger with salad.

Credit Access, Amex, Diners

LEEDS   *Salvo's*

115 Otley Road, Headingley
Town plan B1 *West Yorkshire*
Leeds (0532) 755017
P street parking

Open 12–2 & 6–11.30
Closed Sun, 1 Jan & 25 & 26 Dec

Pizza gallo d'oro £3.75   Tortellini con piselli £3.50

Pizzas are the popular choice at this lively restaurant on the A660 about three miles from the city centre. Massive pizzas with a variety of tasty toppings, including seafood and smoked salmon with capers, are made to order by a cheerful chef who sings his way through their preparation. A large blackboard menu offers a number of fresh fish, pasta and meat dishes. Daily specials widen the choice further and sweets include apple and honey strudel, chocolate whisky cake or fresh pineapple. *No dogs.*

LEEDS   *Strawberryfields Bistro*

159 Woodhouse Lane
Town plan B1 *West Yorkshire*
Leeds (0532) 431515
P NCP in Woodhouse Lane

Open 11.45–2.30 & 6–11
Closed Sat & Bank Hol lunches, all Sun
& 25 & 26 Dec

Red bean moussaka £3.85   Cumin
chicken £5.75

Popular with hungry students, this bright,
friendly bistro has something for everyone
on its wide-ranging menu. Pizzas and
burgers are favourite light bites, and there
are also salads, vetegarian specials and
main dishes ranging from goulash to
sauced sirloin steak. Lunchtime-only extras include ploughman's, savoury flans
and filled jacket potatoes, and apple muesli
crumble and Mississippi mud pie feature
among desserts. *No dogs.*

Credit Access, Visa   **LVs**

LEINTWARDINE   *Selda Coffee & Crafts*

Bridge Street, Nr Craven Arms
MAP 5 A2 *Hereford & Worcester*
Leintwardine (054 73) 604
P street parking

Open Nov–Mar 11–3.30, April–June
9.30–6, July–Aug 9–6.30, Sept–Oct 10–
5.30
Closed Sun & Mon Nov–end Feb

Home-made soup 80p   Toffee slice 45p
🍵

In a lovely tranquil setting, opposite the
village green, cheery Mrs Kidd presides
over her tea rooms where she exhibits local
artists' work. In addition she offers good
cooking and a well brewed pot of tea. Her
menu includes excellent gooey toffee slice
and moist date and walnut loaf, cream teas
in summer and snacks like well flavoured
leek and potato soup, Hereford rarebit with
cheese and apple, omelettes and vegetarian
lasagne. *Unlicensed. No smoking. No
dogs.*

LEOMINSTER   *Granary Coffee House*

6 South Street
MAP 5 A2 *Hereford & Worcester*
P Saveright car park

Open 7–2
Closed Sun & Bank Hols

Lasagne £1.60   Lemon meringue pie
45p

This popular, cheerful coffee house offers
excellent fare in its maze of rooms. On the
heavily laden counters are freshly made
scones, well flavoured banana cake, and
generous portions of tangy lemon meringue pie. At lunchtime, when you may
need to share a table, choose from jacket
potatoes, quiches with good pastry and
tasty fillings, ham-off-the-bone, large well
seasoned Scotch eggs and a dozen or so
salads. *No dogs.*

LEWES   *Old Candlemaker's Café*

The Old Needlemakers, West Street
MAP 6 D4 *East Sussex*
Lewes (0273) 480268
P West Street car park ᬓ

Open 9.30–5
Closed Sun, some Bank Hols & 2 days
Xmas

Home-made quiche & mixed salads £1.95
Carrot cake 75p 🍵

A sympathetically restored 19th century
candle and needle factory now houses a
series of craft shops and a delightful café.
Loyal and enthusiastic customers are
prepared to queue for some time. The
cakes, some home-baked, include chocolate brownies, date slice, sticky iced buns
and caramel slice. Lunch leads with a
home-made soup – parsnip and curry or
Jerusalem artichoke – with pasta, leaf and
bean salads, wholemeal based pizzas and
jacket potatoes. Children's portions. Terrace. *Unlicensed.*

LEWES   *Pattisson's Restaurant*

199 High Street
MAP 6 D4 *East Sussex*
Lewes (0273) 473364
P North Street car park

Open 9.30–2.30 & 7.30–9.15
Closed Mon eve, all Sun, Bank Hols
& 10 days Xmas

Cheese scone 32p   Braised pork with
beer & apples £4.50   🍵

A quiet retreat in the busy High Street for
morning coffee with pleasing home-bak-
ing, and enjoyable lunches. At lunchtime
there is a help-yourself cold table with a
dozen or so salads, ham-off-the-bone,
quiches and pâtés. The hot dishes include
tasty wholesome split pea soup, a daily
special like a generous portion of boiled
ham and parsley sauce, and strawberry and
rhubarb fool – a harmonious marriage of
natural flavours. More elaborate evening
meals. *No smoking mornings.*

Credit Visa

LINCOLN   *Troffs*

Top of Steep Hill
MAP 4 E4 *Lincolnshire*
Lincoln (0522) 510333
P Castle Hill car park

Open 11am–11pm
Closed 25 & 26 Dec

Bacon, lettuce & tomato sandwich £2.50
Vegetable casserole £4.50   🍵

Part of Harveys Restaurant, this bright,
informal restaurant is to be found near the
cathedral entrance. Enjoyable snacks are
freshly cooked and full of flavour, from
cheese and ale fondue to juicy steak or
vegetarian burgers, seafood lasagne and
chicken strips in creamy mushroom sauce
served with rösti potatoes. Finish with
chocolate cake or a lavish ice cream.
Double-decker sandwiches, toasted teacakes and shortbread are served until 6.
No dogs.

Credit Access, Visa

LINCOLN   *N·E·W ENTRY*   *Whites*

The Jews House, 15 The Strait
MAP 4 E4 *Lincolnshire*
Lincoln (0522) 24851
P Danesgate car park

Open 11.30–5
Closed 26 Dec & 2 wks Jan

Lincolnshire bacon cakes £2.70
Continental shortbread cheesecake £1.60

A huge charlotte royale replete with
sponge swirls dominates a window full of
indulgently tempting home-made chocolate gâteaux, continental orange cheesecake, peach roulade and rock cakes. Fresh
flowers dress antique tables in the oldest
lived-in house in Europe. By night a
restaurant, light lunches include shrimp
and haddock gratin, kidneys in batter and
cheesy stuffed aubergine. *No children
under six. Non-smoking area. No dogs.*

Credit Access, Visa

LINCOLN   *Wig & Mitre*

29 Steep Hill
MAP 4 E4 *Lincolnshire*
Lincoln (0522) 35190
P Castle Square car park

Open 8am–midnight
Closed 25 Dec

Stilton, port & celery pâté £2.65   Coffee
& walnut pavlova £1.65

Combining the best elements of pub and
wine bar this 'eating, meeting, drinking,
reading place', as the advertising suggests,
succeeds on all counts. Newspapers and
fresh flowers bedeck the homely beamed
and brickwork interior. Home-made food
is available all day. Broccoli and mushroom
soup can precede pork and Stilton casserole or avocado cheesy bake with rich
passion fruit ice cream or chocolate mille-
feuille to finish. It's well worth the steep
walk. Traditional Sunday lunch. Garden.

Credit Access, Amex, Diners, Visa

LIVERPOOL   *Everyman Bistro*

Hope Street
Town plan F4 *Merseyside*
051-708 9545
P street parking

Open noon–11.30
Closed Sun & Bank Hols & 3 days Xmas

Leek almond pancake £1.50   Pork
coriander & rice £2.80   ⊟

Patrick Byrne and David Scott have built
up an enthusiastic following for their
imaginative, delicious food offered at this
popular bistro beneath the Everyman
Theatre. Super salads (Chinese leaf, orange
and poppyseed, pasta with broad beans
and pesto dressing) accompany flavoursome quiches, savoury pancakes and
pizzas. Meaty main dishes such as coriander pork with rice are enjoyable alternatives and sweets and cheeses are good.
Non-smoking area. No dogs.

LVs

LIVERPOOL   *Streets*

4 Baltimore Street
Town plan F5 *Merseyside*
051-709 2121
P street parking

Open 12–11.30 (Sat, Sun & Bank Hols
from 7pm)
Closed 25 Dec

Chicken cacciatore £3.40   Fillet steak
with mushroom & cream sauce £7.50
⊟

Relax in this comfortable wine bar where
friendly staff will serve you with simple but
tasty dishes. The printed menu is supplemented by blackboard specials offering
generous portions of such dishes as
chicken with almond sauce, beef celestine,
and char-broiled swordfish all served with
seasonal vegetables. Soups, salads and
pâtés are available for those with a lighter
appetite. The list of sweets include chocolate fudge cake and fresh fruit pie and
cream.

LOW LAITHE   *N·E·W ENTRY*   *Carters, Knox Manor*

Summerbridge, Nr Harrogate
MAP 4 D3 *North Yorkshire*
Harrogate (0423) 780607
P own car park

Open 10.30am–10.30pm

Nidderdale smoked Scottish salmon
£3.95   Creamed Italian pasta £2.65

A large blackboard lists a wide selection of
fresh seafood dishes in this smart brasserie
open right throughout the day. Customers
might choose a starter of baked crab with
cheese and asparagus sauce or large
butterfly prawns with garlic; a knox trio of
fresh salmon, lemon sole and lobsters with
white wine sauce to follow, and for a
refreshing finish – lemon chiffon torte. In
addition there is a simple light-lunch and
dinner menu (soups, pies and pasta), and
afternoon tea. *No dogs.*

Credit Access, Visa

LUCCOMBE CHINE   *Dunnose Cottage*

Nr Shanklin
MAP 5 C4 *Isle of Wight*
Isle of Wight (0983) 862585
P own car park

Open 10.30–5.30 (summer till 6.30)
Closed weekdays in winter

Chocolate cake 60p   Fried plaice with
chips £3.10   🍵

A delightful, old thatched cottage pleasantly situated on a cliff-top walk between
Shanklin and Ventnor. Sit in the pretty
garden or inside to enjoy a sandwich, snack
or salad from the day-long menu. Additional choices at lunch and suppertime
include fried fish, lamb chops and steak
pie. Cream teas and ice creams are the
highlight of the day with home-made
scones, cakes and a fresh pot of tea. Book
for the traditional Sunday lunch.

LUDLOW

Aragon's

5 Church Street
MAP 5 A2 *Shropshire*
Ludlow (0584) 3282
P Castle Square

Open 11–10
Closed 25 & 26 Dec

Crab au gratin £2.95   Stuffed
chicken £7.50

The friendly atmosphere here is enhanced
by a smart setting of polished wooden
tables, cloth napkins and comfortable
seats. The dishes are simple, but are
carefully cooked and served. A good variety
of starters and snacks are offered, such as
a delicious tomato soup, or baked potatoes.
There is a good selection of traditional and
deep-pan pizzas, with small-sized pizzas
for children. Snacks are served all day, as
well as cakes, gâteaux and cream teas. *No
dogs.*

Credit Access, Amex, Diners, Visa

LUDLOW

Hardwicks

2 Quality Square
MAP 5 A2 *Shropshire*
Ludlow (0584) 6470
P castle car park &

Open 10–5 (Nov–April till 4, except
Tues till 2.30)
Closed Sun, Good Fri & 3 days Xmas

Norwegian liver bake £3.20   Leek &
mushroom bake £2.80 🍵

In their immensely popular little restaurant
the Peters' counter displays delicious
cakes. From lunchtime onwards there are
well prepared hot dishes: soup of the day
(carrot or lentil, perhaps), mushroom
strogonoff or macaroni and gammon bake
with a thick creamy sauce and well made
salads. On that display are pineapple and
ginger or chocolate biscuit cake or a rich
moist fruit cake. Eat on the terrace in
summer. *Non-smoking area. No dogs.*

---

*Prices given are as at the time of our research
and thus may change.*

LUDLOW

Olive Branch

2 Old Street
MAP 5 A2 *Shropshire*
Ludlow (0584) 4314
P Upper Galdeford car park

Open 10–5 (Oct–Apr till 3 weekdays),
Sat 10–5, Sun 12.15–5
Closed 2 wks Xmas

Spinach lasagne £1.95   Ratatouille
£1.95

In a busy spot in the town centre stands
this friendly little vegetarian restaurant.
Sit at pine tables to enjoy the daily
changing specials featured on a central
blackboard. Lunchtime offers may include
aubergine bake or pasta verdi while regu-
larly available dishes are pizza, oven-fresh
quiche and filled baked potatoes all served
with crunchy-fresh salads. Cakes and
biscuits like chocolate cake and flapjacks
are also available all day long. *Non-
smoking area.*

LUSTLEIGH   *Primrose Cottage*

Nr Newton Abbot
MAP 8 C2 *Devon*
Lustleigh (064 77) 365
P street parking

Open 10–5.30 (till 5 in winter)

Closed weekdays end Nov–beg.
Mar & 4 wks Xmas

Cream tea £2.20   Summer salad
£3   Pork & bramley bake £4.90
Cakes from £1 ☕ 🐾

★ The setting – a yellow thatched cottage in a delightful Dartmoor village, is idyllic. The hosts, Roger and Miranda Oliver, epitomise geniality, but the star attraction here is their exquisite home baking. Irresistible chocolate cake, hazelnut meringues, eclairs, treacle tart, fruit sponge and apple strudel beckon you from a lace hung table. The lightest scones, brown or white, are served with two jams and local clotted cream. At lunchtime try the carrot soup, chicken and mushroom bake with wine and tarragon sauce or pizzas. After sampling the edible delights browse through the antiques for sale upstairs. Children's portions. Garden. *Unlicensed.* ★

LYMPSTONE   *River House*

The Strand
MAP 8 C2 *Devon*
Exmouth (0395) 265147
P village car park

Open 12–1.30

Closed Sun, Mon & Bank Hols

Spinach & mushroom pancake
£5.75   Tagliatelle salad £5.75
Fresh salmon kedgeree £5.75
Moussaka £5.75 ☕

★ Marvellous views from the Wilkes' first-floor restaurant across the river Exe to Powderham Castle are matched by Sheila's super cooking throughout a fixed-price light lunch menu. Fish plays an important part, with beautifully light seafood tartlets, or fillets of sole wrapped around giant prawns and monkfish, among typical treats. Other options might include herby baked eggs with tomatoes, fillet steak in brandy and pepper sauce or wild duck sauced with orange and Grand Marnier. Lovely sweets, too, include chocolate mousse, raspberry trifle, lemon soufflé and sorbet-filled strawberry ice cream. All dishes are priced at £5.75. *No children under five. No dogs.* ★

Credit Access, Amex, Visa

LYNTON   *Lee Cottage*

Lee Abbey
MAP 8 B1 *Devon*
Lynton (059 85) 2621
P own car park

Open 11–12 & 1–5

Closed Sun & early Sept–end
May

Ploughman's £1.80   Cream tea
£1.40   Filled rolls with salad
garnish 80p   Chocolate sponge
60p   ☕ 🍵

★ Run by Lee Abbey Christian Community, this
attractive little tea room reached by a winding cliff-
top road has a beautiful countryside setting. The
cottage nestles in the valley below the main abbey
complex, and from its garden and veranda the
tranquillity of the scene can be enjoyed. The cream
teas are not to be missed with warm, freshly baked
scones, generous portions of jam and clotted cream.
Lovely light Victorian sponges with coffee, chocolate
or jam fillings are a treat to taste. At lunchtime
(served between 1 and 2.30) there are rolls with
adventurous fillings and a choice of either Stilton or
double Gloucester ploughman's. Only open during
summer months. *Unlicensed.* ★

LYONSHALL   *Church House*

Kington
MAP 5 A2 *Hereford & Worcester*
Lyonshall (054 48) 350
P own car park ♿

Open 10–12 & 3–5.30

Closed 25 & 26 Dec

Set afternoon tea £2.15   Lemon
spicy cake 46p   Wholemeal
scones with jam & cream 45p
Coffee cake 40p   🍵

A well run guest house is the site of this quality
Edwardian-style tea room with tables outside looking
across a gentle pastoral scene. The adjoining craft
shop specialises in Edwardian books and bric-a-brac.
★ Each table is set with a different bone china tea
service. Even the cakes are home-made from Edwardian recipes – lemon spicy sponge, chocolate
'naughty' cake (forget the calories), almond and
raisin bake and a rich, dark, slightly tipsy fruit cake.
The full Edwardian tea (order in advance) has dainty
finger sandwiches; the simpler tea offers excellent
fruit or wholemeal scones and a tray of delectable
cakes. The freshly brewed loose-leaf tea is a real
treat. *Unlicensed. No smoking (except outdoor
tables). No dogs.* ★

LYTCHETT MINSTER

Slepe Cottage Tea Rooms

Dorchester Road, Poole
MAP 5 B4 *Dorset*
Morden (092 945) 281
P own car park

Open 10.15–5.45 (Sun from 2)
Closed Mon (except Bank Hols) & end
Oct–1 Mar

Cheese on toast with poached egg £1.40
Mushroom omelette £2   🍵 ❤

On sunny days, tea in the garden is a favourite treat at the Middles' white-painted, thatched cottage standing on the A35 Dorchester road, two miles outside the village. Lovely Dorset clotted cream accompanies home-baked scones, or you can opt for delicious cucumber sandwiches and a choice of cakes like zesty orange, lemon, coffee or chocolate sponge. Light lunches from 12 to 2 include simple snacks like omelettes, salads and cheese on toast. *Unlicensed. No smoking. No dogs.*

LYTHAM

N·E·W ENTRY

Bennett's Bistro

15 Park Street
MAP 3 C3 *Lancashire*
Lytham (0235) 739265
P Pleasant Street car park

Open 12–2.30
Closed Sun, Mon, Bank Hols (except
Good Fri) & 31 Dec

Double decker sandwich £2.90   Savoury
pancake £3.25

The atmosphere is wonderfully relaxed and informal at this cosy bistro run by a talented young team. There's a wide choice of imaginative snacks at lunchtime (jokey titles abound), including an excellent braised onion stuffed with savoury sausage, crispy tacos, slices of black pudding served with rice and a cider and apple sauce, and spicy spare ribs. To finish, try light and fluffy lemon mousse on a biscuit base or hot fruit pie. More elaborate meals in the evening.

LYTHAM

Lytham Kitchen

9 Market Square
MAP 3 C3 *Lancashire*
Lytham (0253) 736492
P street parking

Open 10–5
Closed Sun, Mon, Bank Hols & 25 & 26
Dec

Fresh cod crumble £2.85   Florentines
65p

New owners are continuing the high standards set at this popular self-service restaurant with its booth-style seating. Traditional cooked breakfasts start the day, while freshly made sandwiches and a huge array of cakes and pastries are favourite snacks throughout opening hours. At lunchtime the choice expands to include omelettes, home-made flans and tasty main dishes like liver and onions, beef bourguignon or pork in barbecue sauce. *No dogs.*

LVs

MANCHESTER

N·E·W ENTRY

Brasserie St Pièrre

57 Princess Street
MAP 3 C4 *Greater Manchester*
061-228 0231
P Meter parking

Open 12–2 & 6.30–11, also Bank Hols
7–11
Closed Sat lunch, all Sun & 2–3 days
Xmas

Creamed smoked haddock pancake £2
Fillet of veal with lemon & chives £7.50

A young team runs this smart city-centre brasserie in friendly, efficient style. Tempting French menus change frequently and include substantial starters such as veal and pistachio nut terrine served with crisp salad and fresh redcurrant sauce that are mini meals in themselves. Equally appealing main courses range from goujons of lemon sole with tomatoes and potatoes to chicken bonne femme, and there are delicious sweets to finish. *No dogs.*

Credit Access, Amex, Diners, Visa

MANCHESTER   *Greens*

43 Lapwing Lane, Didsbury
MAP 3 C4 *Greater Manchester*
061-434 4259
P street parking

Open 10–9.30 (till 5 Tues)
Closed Sun, Mon, Bank Hols
& 10 days Xmas

Nut & mushroom burger 95p   Black
Forest trifle £1.25

Friendly owners Michael Fawcett and Mick
Burton offer an imaginative vegetarian
selection at their popular, pine-furnished
restaurant. The regular menu, which
ranges from soup and houmus with pitta,
to sandwiches, nut roasts and tofu burgers,
is supplemented by daily specials such as
the outstanding peanut, almond and pepper loaf. Super salads too, and delicious
sweets like plum and apple crumble or
Black Forest trifle. Bring your own wine
(no corkage). *No dogs.*

MANCHESTER   *N·E·W ENTRY*   *Siam Orchid*

54 Portland Street
MAP 3 C4 *Greater Manchester*
061-236 1388
P NCP Chorlton Street

Open 11.30–2.30 & 6.30–11
Closed Sun lunch & 25 & 26 Dec

Red beef curry £4.50   Thai chicken
salad £3.20

Friendly staff at this bustling, popular little
restaurant near the city centre are always
ready to help newcomers to the Thai
cuisine. Rice forms the centrepiece of every
meal and is eaten with a number of side
dishes such as pork with sweet basil,
excellently-flavoured squid salad, creamy
chicken curry and stir-fried beef with oyster
sauce. Sweets are light, fruity and refreshing. Advisable to book in the evening.
Non-smoking area. No dogs.

Credit Access, Diners, Visa

MANCHESTER   *Woo Sang*

19 George Street
MAP 3 C4 *Greater Manchester*
061-236 3697
P NCP Faulkner Street

Open 12–11.45
Closed 25 & 26 Dec

Dim sum from £1   King prawns in black
bean sauce £7.80

Right in the heart of Manchester's China-
town, this popular first-floor restaurant
offers an extensive à la carte selection of
competently prepared dishes, including
over two dozen dim sum. Follow spicy
spare ribs or wun tun soup with, say,
glutenous rice dumpling with assorted
meat, pork satay kebabs, beef with bamboo
shoots and mushrooms or chicken with
sweet ginger and pineapple. Simple sweets
to finish. *No dogs.*

Credit Access, Amex, Diners, Visa   **LVs**

MANCHESTER   *Yang Sing*

34 Princess Street
Map 3 C4 *Greater Manchester*
061-236 2200
P NCP in Portland Street

Open 12–11
Closed 25 Dec

Dim sum £1   Cantonese-style fillet
steak £6

Booking is advisable at this bustling
basement Cantonese restaurant, where the
food is carefully prepared and authentic.
The dim sum range includes masterful
char sui bao and a magnificent sticky rice,
and on the extensive main menu you will
find everything from noodle soups to crab
dumplings, squid in black bean sauce, stir-
fried clam and vegetables and steamed
chicken and sausage. Glass walls enable
you to watch the fascinating kitchen
activity. *No dogs.*

Credit Access, Amex   **LVs**

MARKET HARBOROUGH   *Taylors Fish Restaurant*

Adam & Eve Street
MAP 5 C2 *Leicestershire*
Market Harborough (0858) 63043
P St Mary's Road car park &

Open 10.30–2 & 7–10
Closed Mon & Tues eves in winter, all
Sun & 1 Jan & 25 & 26 Dec

Halibut steak & chips £3.20   Smoked
mackerel salad £1.85

Whether you enjoy waitress service upstairs, or serve-yourself downstairs, the
quality and range of fresh fish is the same
at this popular and long-established restaurant. Cod, haddock, plaice, halibut,
dogfish and skate are all crisply battered
and served with tasty home-made chips.
Alternatives include chicken, pies and cold
meat salads, together with a coffee shop
menu offering filled rolls, toasted sandwiches and scones. *Non-smoking area.
No dogs.*

LVs

MARLBOROUGH   *Polly*

26 High Street
MAP 5 B3 *Wiltshire*
Marlborough (0672) 52146
P street parking

Open 8.30–6, Sat 8–7, Sun 9–7

Closed 1 Jan, 1st two Fri & Sat in
Oct & 3 days Xmas

Set afternoon tea £2.05   Fish
mousse & salad £2.65   Home-
baked gammon £3.65   Salmon &
spinach roulade £3.95 ✿

★ Epitomising the traditional tea room, our 1985 'Tea
Place of the Year', remains, through years of staff
dedication, one of Britain's best. A feast of home-
made meringues, chocolates and gâteaux grace pine
dressers and lace-hung tables. Lunch stars pâtés, fish
mousse, natural soups and quiches served with
imaginative salads supplemented by veritable treats
of daily specials such as fresh smoked trout.
Afternoons see sumptuous set teas – try the light
lemon and kiwi fruit gâteau – with a menu of ice-
cream creations for children. Queuing likely at
weekends. *Minimum charge of £2.05 after 3pm.
Non-smoking area. No dogs.* ★

Credit Access, Amex, Diners, Visa

MARLOW   *Burgers*

The Causeway
MAP 5 C3 *Buckinghamshire*
Marlow (062 84) 3389
P Pound Lane car park

Open 8.30–5.30
Closed Sun, Bank Hols

Steak & kidney pie £2.70   Black Forest
gâteau 95p ✿

Enjoying a prime corner location near
Marlow bridge, this spotlessly-kept tea
shop offers a superb selection of cakes,
pastries and chocolates – all made on the
premises by long-established Swiss owners
the Burger family. Black Forest gâteau is
their speciality, but close competition
comes from the lovely florentines, choux
buns, fresh cream cakes and torten.
Savoury options include spinach quiche.
Unlicensed. No dogs.

LVs

Samuel Butler
1835–1902

The hen is only an egg's way of making another egg.
Life and Habit

––––––––––

Jonathan Swift
1667–1745

Fish should swim thrice: first it should swim in the sea . . .
then it should swim in butter, and at last, sirrah, it
should swim in good claret.
Polite Conversation

––––––––––

William Shakespeare
1564–1616

. . . who can . . . cloy the hungry edge of appetite
By bare imagination of a feast?
Or wallow naked in December snow
By thinking on fantastic summer's heat?
Richard II

––––––––––

Alexander Pope
1688–1744

Fame is at best an unperforming cheat;
But 'tis substantial happiness to eat.
Mr D'Urfey's Last Play

MATLOCK   *Strand Restaurant*

43 Dale Road
MAP 4 D4 *Derbyshire*
Matlock (0629) 4444
P   Matlock Bridge car park

Open 10–2 & 7–10
Closed Sun & 1 wk Xmas

Beef & mushroom carbonnade £2.95
Mexican beef tacos £4.25   ✍

Judith Mason used to sell home-made cakes through Harrods. Now she and her husband run a restaurant in this converted Victorian draper's shop. The atmosphere is informal and interesting, with some seating on a gallery and attractive cast iron pillars and balustrades. Cakes and scones are served in the morning and lunch begins at noon, offering cheerful snacks like chilli, quiche or salad. The menu is more elaborate in the evening. Wednesday night go Italian with pizza and pasta dishes. *No dogs.*

MATLOCK   *Tall Trees*

Oddford Lane, Two Dales, Darley Dale
MAP 4 D4 *Derbyshire*
Matlock (0629) 732932
P   own car park   ⅊

Open 9–5.30
Closed 1 wk Xmas

Smoked seafood & avocado flan £3
Treacle & walnut tart £1.20

In the grounds of a small garden centre, this pine-furnished tea room offers an interesting line in lunchtime specials. Typical choices might include mushrooms in garlic mayonnaise, lamb, orange and Rosemary pie, vegetable biryani, Stilton and walnut flan, or cider-baked gammon. To finish, perhaps hazelnut and coffee meringue or fruit and yoghurt syllabub. Jovial staff serve cakes and biscuits throughout the day. *Non-smoking area. No dogs.*

MAWGAN   *Yard Bistro*

Trelowarren Estate, Nr Helston
MAP 8 A3 *Cornwall*
Mawgan (032 622) 595
P   own parking   ⅊

Open 11–2
Closed Mon (Oct–end Nov) & all Dec–end Mar

Pâté £2   Crab ploughman's £2.50
✍   🫖

Forming one side of the courtyard of a country mansion is this attractive bistro in the old coach house, where the atmosphere is informal and the offerings tasty. Coffee only until noon, and then the menu covers soup, garlic bread, ploughman's, smoked mackerel, quiche, beef or crab salad, egg mayonnaise, baked potatoes and a dish of the day such as courgette and cauliflower gratinee. For dessert, sample the chocolate brownies, Mississippi mud pie or fruit crumble. More elaborate evening meals. *No dogs.*

Our inspectors never book in the name of Egon Ronay's Guides.

They disclose their identity only if they are considering an establishment for inclusion in the next edition of the Guide.

MELMERBY   *Village Bakery*

Penrith
MAP 3 C2 *Cumbria*
Langwathby (076 881) 515
P own car park

Open 8.30–5 (Sun from 9.30)

Closed Mon (except Bank Hols) &
25 Dec–wk before Easter

Set tea £4   Cumberland sausage
£4.25   Spiced vegetables with
brown rice £3.95   Date & treacle
slice 30p

★ The Whitleys and their team use only the best quality
ingredients for their delicious food. Organic English
wheat is locally stoneground and vegetables are
home grown organically. The building is a converted
barn with a lovely conservatory, and there is old pine
furniture with pretty Laura Ashley cloths in the
upstairs restaurant. To start the day excellent
breakfast with endless cups of good coffee, quality
teas and light, crisp wholemeal croissants is served.
At other times there are fresh salads, good flavoured
cheesebreads, a delightful set afternoon tea, home-
made fresh fruit ice cream. Tempting lunchtime
snacks might include creamy vegetable pie or beef
and garlic casserole. *No smoking. No dogs.* ★

Credit Access, Visa

MENTMORE   *Stable Yard Craft Gallery & Tea Room*

Nr Leighton Buzzard
MAP 5 C2 *Bedfordshire*
Cheddington (0296) 668660
P own car park   &

Open 10–6
Closed Mon (except Bank Hols), Tues &
1 wk Xmas

Quiche & salad £2.15   Apple pie £1.25

A converted stable block houses this little
tea room and delightful craft shop. Admire
the traditional country surroundings as
you tuck into a simple savoury snack like
pizza, sausage rolls or wholemeal quiche,
or indulge yourself with a selection from
the sweet items on offer – including
chocolate brownies, eccles cakes, bread
pudding and caramel squares. Tables are
put out on the cobbled courtyard in
summer. *Non-smoking area. No dogs.*

MIDDLEWICH   *Tempters*

11 Wheelock Street
MAP 3 C4 *Cheshire*
Middlewich (060 684) 5175
P street parking

Open 12–2 & 5.30–10
Closed Sun eve, all Mon & Bank Hols

Chilli pancake with garlic bread £2.15
Chicken & Stilton roulade £6.30

There is a relaxed and happy atmosphere
in this pleasant split-level wine bar furnished with natural wood tables. The menu
offers traditional items, like celery soup,
Lancashire hotpot, steaks, chicken Kiev,
jacket potatoes and cheesecake – but all
home-made. No short cuts are taken in
this kitchen! All ingredients are fresh and of
good quality, nicely seasoned and cooked
with care. Good wines and coffee. Sweets
include chocolate biscuit crunch and Gaelic
coffee trifle. *No children. No dogs.*

Credit Visa

MIDSOMER NORTON   *Mrs Pickwick*

70 High Street
MAP 5 A3 *Avon*
Midsomer Norton (0761) 414589
P   street parking

Open 9–6
Closed Sun & Bank Hols

Cauliflower cheese £1.50   Bath bun 40p
🍴

Friendly little tea rooms behind and above a high-street cake shop. All through the day there's a good selection of pastries and confectionery, including custard slices, Bath buns, scones and cheesecakes. Sandwiches, rolls and toasted snacks provide tasty savoury bites, and lunchtime brings soup, hot pasties and omelettes. Daily specials like macaroni cheese or cottage pie are marked up on a blackboard menu. *Unlicensed. No dogs.*

LVs

MILTON ERNEST   N·E·W ENTRY   *The Strawberry Tree*

Radwell Road
MAP 6 D2 *Bedfordshire*
Oakley (023 02) 3633
P   own car park   &

Open 11.30–5.30
Closed Mon & Tues & all Jan

Fisherman's muffin £2.95   Almond cheesecake with fresh strawberry sauce £1.80   🍴

John and Wendy Bona make you feel really welcome at their impeccably kept little thatched cottage. John bakes all the mouthwatering cakes and pastries (the multi-layered strawberry and cream gâteau is perfectly light and moist), and there are some excellent savouries, too. Try, perhaps, toasted muffins topped with hot tuna or cheese, generously filled wholemeal sandwiches and superb home-smoked gammon salad. *Unlicensed (bring your own wine). No dogs.*

MINSTEAD   *Honey Pot*

Nr Lyndhurst
MAP 5 B4 *Hampshire*
Southampton (0703) 813122
P   own car park

Open 10.30–5.30
Closed Nov–spring

Toasted teacake 90p   Beehive tea £1.90
🍵

You can take your tea either in the pretty garden bordering on a buttercup meadow or in the extension of the thatched cottage. Friendly ladies will serve you with a range of set teas such as the Queen Bee Tea, with good home-made scones, quality jams and super thick, yellow cream, and well-made cakes, pastries and biscuits. There are savoury items too: home-cooked boiled bacon, sandwiches and filled rolls and a hot dish of the day. Home-made desserts and a range of ices to follow. *No dogs.*

MONTACUTE   *Montacute House Restaurant*

Montacute House
MAP 8 C1 *Somerset*
Martock (0935) 824575
P   own cark park   &

Open 11.30–5
Closed Good Fri & end Oct–Easter

Ploughman's £1.95   Ham salad £2.95
🍴 🍵

After enjoying the splendours of the 16th-century National Trust house and its fine gardens you can retire to the old laundry to enjoy a snack or tea. At lunchtime there are soups, ploughman's, flans with potato and salad, sandwiches and an occasional hot special such as chicken in tarragon. In the afternoon a good range of excellent baking appears: plain or wholemeal scones, moist, tangy lemon cake, flapjacks and a delicious fruit cake made with cold tea. *Non-smoking area. No dogs.*

Credit Access, Amex, Diners, Visa

MORDEN   *Superfish*

20 London Road
MAP 6 D3 *Surrey*
01-648 6908
P Safeway supermarket car park &

Open 11.30–2 (Fri & Sat till 2.30)
& 5.30–11 (Fri & Sat from 5)
Closed Sun & Bank Hol lunches

Cod & chips £2.60   Skate & chips
£3.95

A small selection of good fish is on offer at this spotlessly clean, light and cheerful place, one of a chain of similar restaurants. Choose from fillet of plaice, haddock, huss, sole, whole plaice on the bone and halibut steaks, all of which are served with well-cooked chips, nice, crusty French bread and a pickle and sauce trolley. For sweet there are various ice creams. Children's platter. *No dogs.*

LVs

MOUSEHOLE   *N·E·W ENTRY*   *Annie's*

2 Fore Street
MAP 8 A3 *Cornwall*
Penzance (0736) 731635
P Harbour car park

Open 10–6
Closed late Oct–Easter (except 3 wks Xmas)

Lasagne £2.50   Date & walnut slice 40p

Near the harbour, this bright, friendly tea shop offers a simple but appealing selection of home cooking. Bakewell tart, rich chocolate fudge cake and lemon slice are typical teatime fare, while savoury items range from filled jacket potatoes, sandwiches and rolls, huge bowls of delicious soup and freshly made salads to cheese ratatouille and daily specials such as liver and bacon. Homely sweets like apple crumble to finish. Small portions for children. *Unlicensed.*

NEW ROMNEY   *Country Kitchen*

18 High Street
MAP 6 E3 *Kent*
New Romney (0679) 64642
P street parking &

Open 7.30–5 (Wed till 4 & Sat till 3)
Closed Mon pm, all Sun, Bank Hols, 2–3 days Xmas & New Year

Chicken breast with tarragon sauce
£3.45   Walnut sundae £1.15

Owners Mr Spee and Mr Brown will bake from as early as 2am if need be to meet the demand for their cooking at this popular oak-beamed restaurant. The tempting selection of sweet treats includes fresh cream cakes, Danish pastries, scones and fruit pies, while for a savoury snack there are sausage rolls, pasties, quiches and filled rolls. Lunchtime adds soup, omelettes, fried fish and a hot daily special like a filling steak and vegetable pie. *No dogs.*

Credit Access, Visa

NEWARK   *Gannets*

35 Castlegate
MAP 5 C1 *Nottinghamshire*
Newark (0636) 702066
P street parking

Open 10–4.30
Closed Sun, Bank Hols & 1 wk Xmas

Rissoles with yoghurt sauce £2.75
Boboutie £2.95

Hilary Bower offers wholesome fresh dishes at her very popular little self-service restaurant. The display of hot and cold food and crisp, imaginative salads is supplemented by specials chalked up on the blackboard. There are soups (carrot and fennel, cream of cauliflower and spicy lentil) and hot dishes such as courgette and tomato savoury and fish pie. Sweets include a delicious carrot cake and ginger, orange and caramel pie. *No smoking lunchtimes. No dogs.*

NEWCASTLE UPON TYNE   *Mather's*

4 Old Eldon Square
MAP 4 D2 *Tyne & Wear*
091-232 4020
P NCP in Newgate Street

Open 9.30am–10.30pm
Closed Sun, Bank Hols & 2 wks Aug

Pâté & garlic bread £1.85   Chilli con
carne £2.85   ☕

Robust and dependable cooking is offered
in this simply furnished, informal basement
bistro, where you can have a snack or a
full meal at any time of the day. There are
always vegetarian choices – Spanish omelette, ratatouille salad or baked potatoes,
and always three soups like tomato and
basil or vegetable. Hamburger, salad, chips
or spaghetti bolognese are offered as main
courses or you might just want a sandwich.
Blackberry Romanoff, cheesecake or banana boat if you fancy something sweet.

LVs

---

*Any person using our name
to obtain free hospitality is a fraud.*

*Proprietors, please inform
Egon Ronay's Guides and the police.*

NEWMARKET   *Jane's Wine Bar*

29 High Street
MAP 6 E2 *Suffolk*
Newmarket (0638) 668031
P town-centre car parks

Open 9–4.30
Closed Sun & Bank Hols

Portuguese eggs & salad £2.80   Apple
& blackberry meringue £1   ☕ ☕

A spiral staircase leads down from a dress
shop to this pretty basement restaurant,
where at lunchtimes you can snack on
open sandwiches and filled rolls or choose
something more substantial like a warming
soup, honey-baked ham or a savoury crêpe.
Mornings and afternoons bring a small but
moreish selection of cakes and sweets to
enjoy with tea and coffee, including fruit
choux log, scones and chocolate eclairs.
No dogs.

Credit Access, Amex, Diners, Visa   LVs

NEWPORT   *N·E·W ENTRY*   *Full of Beans*

69 Pyle Street
MAP 5 C4 *Isle of Wight*
Isle of Wight (0983) 522218
P Pyle Street car park

Open 9–6 (Thurs till 3)
Closed Sun, Bank Hols & 1 wk Xmas

Chilli bean casserole £1.95   Carrot &
apple soup £1.25

Rough-hewn plank walls adorned with
mirrors and pictures combine with pine
furniture to give a rustic appearance to
this tiny café situated behind a wholefood
shop. Hot dishes of the day might be
ratatouille, flagelot bean stew, nut roast or
risotto served with a selection of delicious
salads. Soup, baked potatoes or one of the
several types of quiche are alternatives,
and sweets include apple crumble or date
slices. Range of teas, including herbal.
Unlicensed. No smoking.

LVs

NEWPORT   *God's Providence House*

12 St Thomas Square
MAP 5 C4 *Isle of Wight*
Isle of Wight (0983) 522085
P   Pyle Street car park

Open 10–5
Closed Sun & Bank Hols

Carrot, onion & cumin pie £1.70
Lemon meringue pie 90p 🐾 ⊖

Dating from 1701, this fine town house boasts Georgian bow windows and a shell canopy over the main entrance. Sandwiches, cakes, scones and light bites accompany tea and coffee in the restaurant, where tasty lunches featuring choices like steak pie and the day's roast are also served. Climb the carved oak staircase to the Upstairs Parlour for a mainly vegetarian selection – wholemeal quiches, jacket potatoes and hot specials such as broccoli cheese bake. *Non-smoking area. No dogs.*

NORTHALLERTON   *Bettys*

188 High Street
MAP 4 D3 *North Yorkshire*
Northallerton (0609) 5154
P   town centre car park

Open 9–5.30 (Sun from 10)
Closed 1 Jan, Easter Sun & 25 & 26 Dec

Yorkshire rarebit with ham £3.30
Cream tea £2.20 ⊖ 🐾

Every town deserves a traditional tea shop like Bettys. Select one of the special rare coffees – Peruvian Chanchamayo – or an unusual tea – special Tippy Assam – to accompany a richly spiced Yorkshire fat rascal or one of the alluring array of tea breads and cakes. The lightest omelettes, Yorkshire cheese lunch with apple chutney or mushrooms on toast are freshly cooked and served all day by delightful, uniformed waitresses. Expect to queue for a short while. *No dogs.*

LVs

NORWICH   *Britons Arms Coffee House*

9 Elm Hill
MAP 6 F1 *Norfolk*
Norwich (0603) 623367
P   street parking

Open 9.30–5
Closed Sun & Bank Hols

Hot choux puff with seafood filling £2.50
Chicken & chive tart £2.35 🐾

Enjoyable light snacks are available throughout the day at this ancient half-timbered cottage with a garden terrace for alfresco eating. A fine brew accompanies open sandwiches and freshly baked scones, flapjacks and cakes, while lunchtime brings delicious dishes like Swedish herring, chicken and chive tart and baked potatoes with a tasty bolognese filling. Finish with chocolate roulade or banana and hazelnut meringue. *Minimum lunchtime charge £1.50. Non-smoking area. No dogs.*

NORWICH   *Café La Tienda*

10 St Gregory's Alley
MAP 6 F1 *Norfolk*
Norwich (0603) 629122
P   Pottergate car park

Open 10–5
Closed Sun & Bank Hols

Carrot & thyme soup £1.50   Aubergine & parmesan bake £2.80

Sit at simple pine tables and benches and tuck into some deliciously wholesome fare at this unfussy little restaurant. Blackboard specials such as delicate green pea soup and richly sauced aubergine and vegetable bake back up the short regular menu of hot pitta with tasty fillings, taramasalata, crab pâté and fresh, colourful salads. To finish, try the apple crumble with home-made yoghurt or rich, moist carrot cake. *Non-smoking area.*

NORWICH   *Swelter's*

Woburn Court, 8 Guildhall Hill
MAP 6 F1 *Norfolk*
Norwich (0603) 612874
P Theatre Royal car park

Open 11.30–2.30 & 5.30–10.30
Closed Mon & Tues eves, all Sun, Bank
Hols & 25–30 Dec

Moussaka £2.50   Garden salad £1.95
℗

A fetching central display of crisp salads,
raised pies, meats, terrines and cheeses
catches the eye at this smartly rustic city
wine bar. Help yourself, or go for something hot like home-made vegetable soup
followed by a hearty daily special such as
chicken and almond gratin and finish with
deliciously moist banana bread. Good
choice of wines by the glass from the
Cruover machine. More elaborate evening
meals with waitress service. *Non-smoking
area. No dogs.*

LVs

NORWICH   *Waffle House*

39 St Giles Street
MAP 6 F1 *Norfolk*
Norwich (0603) 612790
P St Giles car park

Open 11–10 (Fri & Sat till 11)
Closed Sun, Bank Hols & 3 days Xmas

Ham, cheese & mushroom waffle £2.60
Bananas & cinnamon waffle £1.20

Hanging plants, bamboo chairs and pine
tables contribute to the homely atmosphere at this popular restaurant specialising in waffles. Generous toppings range
from relatively simple ham with cheese
sauce and mushrooms, or tuna mayonnaise, to a delicious daily special like
garlicky courgettes provençale followed
by, say, a traditional sweet waffle served
with chocolate mousse, nuts and cream.
*Bring your own wine (no corkage). Non-
smoking area. No dogs.*

LVs

NOTTINGHAM   *Pagoda*

31 Greyfriar Gate
MAP 5 C1 *Nottinghamshire*
Nottingham (0602) 501105
P Greyfriar Gate NCP

Open 12–4.30 & 6.30–12, Sun
noon–midnight
Closed 25 Dec

King prawns with black bean sauce £6.30
Steamed dry beef balls £1.15

Cantonese cooking is the speciality of this
modest Chinese restaurant near the city
centre. Dim sum snacks like paper-
wrapped prawns and crispy pancake rolls
are a popular option between noon and
4.30, while more substantial dishes range
from familiar favourites (roast Peking
duck, sweet and sour pork) to such exotic
offerings as baked silver pomfret or
steamed eel with black beans and chilli.
Fruit fritters for dessert. *No dogs.*

Credit Access, Amex, Diners, Visa   **LVs**

NOTTINGHAM   *The Q in the Corner at Ziggi's*

3 Victoria Street
MAP 5 C1 *Nottinghamshire*
Nottingham (0602) 506956
P Fletcher Gate

Open 9.30–5
Closed Sun & Bank Hols (except
Good Fri)

Vegetarian moussaka £2   Carrot
cake 55p

Tired shoppers can seek refuge and a
refreshing cup of tea at this pleasant
restaurant in the corner of a fashion shop.
Toffee shortbread, flapjacks, date shortcake, florentines and cheese or fruit scones
are the staple fare along with salads and
quiches. Hot dishes are well presented and
include lasagne, filled jacket potatoes and
a vegetarian option. Congenial service
overseen by the Stevensons. Set afternoon
teas in summer. *Unlicensed. No dogs.*

Credit Access, Visa

NOTTINGHAM
N·E·W ENTRY
Shôgun

95 Talbot Street
MAP 5 C1 *Nottinghamshire*
Nottingham (0602) 475611
P NCP in Wollaton Street

Open 12–2
Closed Sun, Mon, 25 & 26 Dec & 1 Jan

Beef teriyaki lunch £4.95   Tempura
lunch £4.95

The only Japanese restaurant in Nottingham offers a good introduction to Japanese food. The staff offer helpful advice on what to choose and how to eat it. The basic set lunch gives a choice of several main dishes, from yakiniku to chicken katsu, all served with salad, rice, soup and a dessert. The domburi lunch includes tempura and beef strips and vegetables in a spicy sauce. A more elaborate and expensive à la carte menu is available for lunch and dinner. *No dogs.*

Credit Access, Amex, Diners, Visa

NOTTINGHAM
Ten

10 Commerce Square, off High
Pavement
MAP 5 C1 *Nottinghamshire*
Nottingham (0602) 585211
P Commerce Square

Open 5.30–11 (Sat 12–11.30)
Closed Sun, Mon & Bank Hols (except
Good Fri & 25 Dec eve)

Cauliflower & mushroom pie £3.50
Tofu & sweet pepper pâté £1.20

Go downstairs into a converted warehouse, through a door and come out, almost miraculously, into a spacious room overlooking rooftops. Malcolm Tandy's vegetarian menu includes such carefully prepared dishes as cashew nut, avocado and mushroom noisettes in vine leaves, or couscous and sweet peppers filled with broccoli in a cassis sauce. On Saturdays a snack menu, featuring soups, burgers, and home-made baked beans, is available all day. *No dogs.*

Credit Access, Visa

OFFHAM
Old Post House

Nr Lewes
MAP 6 D4 *East Sussex*
Lewes (0273) 477358
P own car park

Open 2–5.30, Sat & Sun 10–12.30
& 2–6
Closed Tues, Wed, Thurs & all
weekdays (Oct–Apr)

Sussex cream tea £1.95   Old Post
House tea £2.45 ☙

Caring owners Joyce and Peter Standley continue to provide visitors with a warm welcome and top quality home baking at their immaculately-kept tea room. Cakes range from a tempting fruit cake to a tangy lemon cake or a popular coffee and walnut gâteau. Wonderful shortbread – and the wholemeal scones must not be missed. Set teas only at the weekends. There's a fine garden with good views for outdoor eating. *Minimum charge at weekends and peak times £1. Unlicensed. No smoking. No dogs.*

OMBERSLEY
Ombersley Gallery Tea Room

Church Terrace, Nr Worcester
MAP 5 B2 *Hereford & Worcester*
Worcester (0905) 620655
P street parking

Open 10–5
Closed Sun & Mon & 24 Dec–1 Feb

Ploughman's lunch £1.50   Boozy
chocolate mousse 95p ☙

Opposite the church, this convivial little tea room shares a half-timbered house with an antique and picture gallery. Delicious home baking includes orange and apricot teabread, chocolate fudge cake and marzipan slices, while for a light savoury snack try a warm croissant filled with tasty egg mayonnaise. Lunchtime brings soup, jacket potatoes, salads and pâté, plus more substantial dishes like devilled pork chops. *Unlicensed. No smoking. No dogs.*

OSWESTRY   *Good Companion*

10 Beatrice Street
MAP 5 A1 *Shropshire*
Oswestry (0691) 655768
P street parking

Open 11.45–2 & 6.30–10.15
Closed Sun & Mon lunch, all 1 Jan
& 25 & 26 Dec

Shropshire pie £3.85   Walnut fudge &
honey tart £1.50   🍵 🍷

New owners are raising standards even
higher at this welcoming town-centre wine
bar. Gordon Tipton looks after customers
while wife Marjorie produces delicious
light dishes for a short, constantly
changing menu. Typical delights might
include creamy parsnip soup with wonderful garlic bread, smoked haddock and
cheese quiche, jacket potato with ham and
celery mayonnaise and roast gammon
salad. To finish, try the superb walnut
fudge and honey tart. *No dogs.*

Credit Amex, Diners

OXFORD   *Browns*

7 Woodstock Road
Town plan C1 *Oxfordshire*
Oxford (0865) 511995
P meter parking

Open 11am–11.30pm (Sun & Bank Hols
from noon)
Closed 5 days Xmas

Roast ribs £5.15   Chocolate pie £1.35
🍷

Bright, spacious and festooned with greenery, this bustling restaurant provides an
attractive setting for some enjoyable eating. The American-influenced menu
includes stylish snacks like spaghetti with
meat sauce, hot pastrami on rye and crab
and avocado salad, as well as more tradi-
tionally British offerings – fisherman's pie,
chargrilled lamb or a daily special of, say,
oxtail in tomato soup. Croissants and
coffee until noon and scones for afternoon
tea. *Non-smoking area.*

OXFORD   N·E·W ENTRY   *Café M.O.M.A.*

Museum of Modern Art,
30 Pembroke Street
Town plan C4 *Oxfordshire*
Oxford (0865) 722733
P Westgate car park   ⅊

Open 10–5 (Sun from 2)
Closed Mon, 1 Jan & 25 & 26 Dec

Stuffed aubergine £2.20   Apricot upside
down cake 65p   🍵

Owned and run by the Museum of Modern
Art and housed in its basement, this
friendly café offers cakes and pastries, tea
and coffee, all day long. Lunchtime
savouries could include a delicious herby
tomato soup and a tasty cheese and onion
quiche served with crisp, fresh salad. More
robust options might be beef carbonnade,
stuffed aubergines with noodles, or braised
pork chops. Desserts like pavlova and
baked apples to follow. Afternoon tea only
on Sunday. *Non-smoking area.*

OXFORD   *Heroes*

8 Ship Street
Town plan D3 *Oxfordshire*
Oxford (0865) 723459
P Broad Street car park

Open 9–7.30 (Sat & university hols
till 5)
Closed Sun, 5 days Easter & 10 days
Xmas

Crispy bacon sandwich £1   Bread &
butter pudding 45p   🍷

New owners are continuing the successful
formula of this popular city-centre
sandwich bar, where granary, white,
French and pitta bread come crammed
with super fillings. Choices range from
roast chicken and egg mayonnaise to hot
specials like sweet and sour ham in pitta.
Try tasty mushroom soup to start and the
favourite bread and butter pudding for
afters. Toasted snacks, cooked breakfasts
and croissants served until 11am. *Unlicensed. Non-smoking area. No dogs.*

OXFORD   *Munchy Munchy*

6 Park End Street
Town plan B3 *Oxfordshire*
Oxford (0865) 245710
P Worcester Street car park

Open 12–2.10 & 5.30–10

Closed Sun, Mon, Bank Hols, 3
wks Aug–Sept & 3 wks Dec–Jan

Beef with laos & cardamom £3.95
Lamb with celery seeds & sour
cream £4.85 Asparagus in crab
meat sauce £4.95

★ By stark contrast the unpretentious decor, pine
tables and tiled floor highlight Ethel Ow's sumptuous
interpretation of Indonesian and Malaysian cuisine.
She selects the best at the market and with an exotic
mix of herbs and spices produces about six anony-
mous dishes. There are no starters so order a range
of dishes from possibly lamb with nutmeg, clove,
cinnamon and aubergine; grey mullet in hot and sour
sauce with turmeric, lime leaves and lemon grass or
chicken with cardamom and cumin. Paw-paws,
mangos and ice-cream make a refreshing end to a
meal. Book at weekends. Children welcome except
Friday and Saturday evenings. *Unlicensed (bring
your own). Non-smoking area. No dogs.* ★

OXFORD   *Randolph Hotel Lounge*

Beaumont Street
Town plan C3 *Oxfordshire*
Oxford (0865) 247481
P own car park &

Open 3–6

Set afternoon tea £4.50

Traditional afternoon tea can be enjoyed
in the lofty, elegant lounge of this fine
Victorian hotel. Sit at crisply-clothed tables
and tuck into neat finger sandwiches,
scones spread with super thick clotted
cream, and a selection of pastries including
chocolate eclairs, fruit tartlets, meringues
and moist Madeira cake. At other times,
tea and coffee with biscuits, sandwiches
and Danish pastries are available. *No dogs.*

Credit Access, Amex, Diners, Visa

OXFORD   *St Aldate's Church Coffee House*

94 St Aldate's
Town plan D4 *Oxfordshire*
Oxford (0865) 245952
P Westgate car park

Open 10–5
Closed Sun, Bank Hols & 4 days Xmas

Peach curry £1.75 Chocolate caramel
shortbread 50p

All the profits from this enterprising self-
service coffee house, next door to St
Aldate's, go to church funds. Throughout
the day home-baked goodies like bread
pudding, chocolate caramel shortbread,
scones and moist lemon banana cake are
served, along with filled jacket potatoes.
Lunchtime brings tasty main dishes such
as lamb in orange or chicken with walnuts
and there is always a vegetarian option.
Unlicensed. No smoking. No dogs.

LVs

PAINSWICK   *Cup House*

Bisley Street
MAP 5 B2 *Gloucestershire*
Painswick (0452) 812322
P   street parking

Open 10–1.45 & 2.45–5
Closed Sun am, all Wed, 25 & 26 Dec &
3rd wk Jan

Toasted sandwich £1.40   Cream tea
£1.50

When the sun shines, you can sit out on
the sheltered patio of this cottagy little tea
room to enjoy a simple snack. Scones,
flapjacks, cakes and slices accompany cups
of tea and coffee, while lunchtime brings
soup, fish and chips, quiche and ham or
cheese and egg salad. Freshly-cut sandwiches and poached egg or beans on toast
provide popular light bites. In winter,
choose from a few hot specials like steak
and kidney pie. *Unlicensed. No dogs.*

PAINSWICK   *Painswick Hotel*

Kemps Lane
MAP 5 B2 *Gloucestershire*
Painswick (0452) 812160
P   own car park

Open 12.30–2
Closed Sun

Buffet lunch £3.75   French apple flan
95p   ℰ

The summer buffet at this elegant and
civilised hotel has long been popular. Along
with a choice of ten salads there are cold
meats, jacket potatoes and also a daily hot
dish, perhaps blanquette of lamb, steak
and kidney pudding or beef bourguignon.
To follow there are gâteaux and fresh fruit
salads among the sweets. Log fires in
winter when choice is restricted to a hearty
soup, filled rolls, sandwiches, pâté and
ploughman's. *Non-smoking area.*

Credit Access, Amex, Diners, Visa

PARKGATE   *Chompers*

The Parade
MAP 3 B4 *Cheshire*
051-336 1567
P   car park at rear

Open 5.30–11 (Sat till 11.30), Sun 12–
11

Seafood kebab £6.95   Chicken tikka
£5.95   ℰ

Overlooking the Dee estuary (binoculars
and crayons for capturing the scene are
provided), this smartly informal restaurant
offers a most imaginative range of dishes.
Look for choices like deep-fried mushrooms stuffed with Brie and almonds,
vegetable chilli served with potato skins
and sour cream and fresh sardines in a
garlicky tomato sauce. Pizzas and hamburgers are simpler alternatives. Sunday
brunch is very popular. *No dogs.*

Credit Access, Amex, Diners, Visa   **LVs**

PATELEY BRIDGE   *Willow*

Park Road
MAP 4 D3 *North Yorkshire*
Pateley Bridge (0423) 711689
P   Park Road car park

Open 12–2 & 6.30–9.30
Closed Sun eve, all Mon, Tues, Bank
Hols (except Good Fri & 25 Dec) & 2 wks
Feb

Grouse in red wine & herb sauce £7.50
Smoked oyster & bacon kebabs
£2.40   ☙

At this pleasant beamed restaurant the
imaginative menu is described on a blackboard: perhaps ramekin of chicken with
spinach or savoury éclairs to start; duck
and orange pie or pork fillet with savoury
apple stuffing for the main course. Tempting sweets include chocolate and brandy
fudge cake and Dutch apple flan. After
dinner relax in one of the big comfy lounge
chairs for coffee. There is a simple menu
at lunchtime. *No dogs.*

Credit Access, Amex, Visa

PENSHURST

Fir Tree House Tea Rooms

Nr Tonbridge
MAP 6 E3 *Kent*
Penshurst (0892) 870382
P street parking ও

Open 3-6
Closed Mon in season (except Bank Hols when closed Tues) also Nov–Dec

Set afternoon tea £2.10   Tea & home-made cakes £1.70 🍵

Caroline Fuller-Rowell looks after visitors to her delightful tea room and pretty rear garden with charm and efficiency. Sit on Victorian pews at bare oak tables decorated with fresh flowers to enjoy her set afternoon teas featuring light, warm scones with cherry jam and cream, wholemeal bread sandwiches and delicious cakes – perhaps tangy lemon sponge, coffee and walnut or moist fruit. There's a good choice of quality teas. *Unlicensed. No smoking.*

PLUMTREE

Perkins Bar Bistro

Station Road
MAP 5 C1 *Nottinghamshire*
Plumtree (060 77) 3695
P own car park

Open 12-2 & 7-10

Closed Sun, Mon, Bank Hols & 1st wk Sept

Blanquette d'agneau à l'ancienne £4.65   Poached salmon with prawns dugléré £5.95   Braised woodpigeon with fresh oranges £5.25   Hazelnut meringue gâteau £1.75 🥧

★ The quality of Tony Perkins' cooking and the friendly atmosphere created by Wendy Perkins and their staff ensure that this stylish bistro in a converted railway station is always busy. A blackboard lists dishes made of top quality fresh produce expertly handled in traditional styles. Begin with game soup, chicken liver and pork terrine, jellied eels or cheese, nut and brandy pâté. Follow with poulet bonne femme, pot-roasted quail with grapes and almonds, filet de porc Mexicaine, delice de sauman dugléré, or a daily special like entrecôte marchand de vin. Don't miss the tempting sweets: chocolate pot, crème caramel, poached pear, or fluffy lemon soufflé. It is advisable to book. *No dogs.* ★

Credit Access, Amex

POLPERRO

Captains Cabin

Lansallos Street
MAP 8 B3 *Cornwall*
Polperro (0503) 72292
P village car park

Open 12-2.30 & 7-10.30
Closed Sun, Mon & Tues (Nov–Mar), & all Jan

Monkfish mornay £6.25   Veal Marsala £6.95 🥧 🍵

The seafood couldn't be fresher at this low-beamed restaurant by the harbour. Whiting, sole, pollock, plaice and codling are all lightly fried and served with 'proper' chips, while for a treat there's dressed crab, lobster or a daily special like delicious seafood paella. Meat and chicken dishes ring the changes while soup, sandwiches and ploughman's provide lighter snacks. Homely sweets (many ice cream-based) to finish, and more elaborate evening meals. Children's menu.

Credit Access, Amex, Diners, Visa

POOLE   *Inn à Nutshell*

27 Arndale Centre
MAP 5 B4 *Dorset*
Poole (0202) 673888
P Kingland car park

Open 9.30–5
Closed Sun & Bank Hols

French onion soup £1.90   Cheese
& oatmeal roast £1.75   🅔   🍲

A popular formula of wholefoods and healthy eating keeps this self-service café bustling. Vegetable soups top the daily specials followed possibly by cheese and oatmeal roast and filling apple and walnut slice or carob cake. Regular features include morning coffee and hot rolls through to crunchy wholemeal quiches, nutty salads and generously topped jacket potatoes complemented by English fruit wines or flavoured milk. Children's portions. *No smoking. No dogs.*

Credit Access, Amex, Diners, Visa   **LVs**

PORTSMOUTH (SOUTHSEA)   *Country Kitchen*

59 Marmion Road
MAP 5 C4 *Hampshire*
Portsmouth (0705) 811425
P car park opposite

Open 9–5
Closed Sun & Bank Hols

Fruit & coconut chunk 50p   Home-made
potato cakes & mixed salad £2.40   🍲

Eat healthily and well at this popular little self-service vegetarian restaurant. The hot savoury choice embraces substantial soups like butter bean and vegetable as well as melt-in-the-mouth quiches (try deliciously creamy sweetcorn and onion) and appetising daily specials such as cauliflower bake or potato pancakes. Excellent salads too, and fresh fruit crumble for afters. There's a wide choice of teas to enjoy with delicious home-baked cakes and slices. *Unlicensed. No smoking. No dogs.*

LVs

PORTSMOUTH (SOUTHSEA)   *Rosie's Vineyard*

87 Elm Grove
MAP 5 C4 *Hampshire*
Portsmouth (0705) 755944
P street parking

Open 7pm–10.30pm (till 11 in summer),
also Sun 12–2
Closed 1 Jan & 22–27 Dec

Seafood pancakes £4.25   Spinach &
ham cannelloni £3.60   🅔

Enjoy the buzzing atmosphere both inside this Continental-style wine bar and, on fine summer evenings, outside in the pergola-covered garden. A variety of unpretentious but well-cooked dishes is listed on blackboards in the window and behind the bar. Starters include devilled mushrooms and taramasalata; then choose a main course like moussaka, smoked haddock bake or ratatouille wholemeal pancake, followed by cherry and almond pie, hot waffles, ice cream or cheese. *No dogs.*

Credit Access, Visa

POULTON-LE-FYLDE   *Anna's Bistro*

15 Breck Road
MAP 3 B3 *Lancashire*
Poulton-le-Fylde (0253) 882336
P town centre car parks

Open 8.30–3.30
Closed Wed, Bank Hols & 2 wks Xmas

Mushroom omelette £1.20   Toasted
teacake 35p

You can watch Anna Pawson and her team busily preparing the dishes as you order your choices from the menu at the counter. You might try the freshly cooked ham or the soup made from the ham stock. There are omelettes, pizzas and wholemeal sandwiches – regular, open and toasted. A small selection of tempting home-made cakes and pies is on offer. Breakfasts include bacon and egg barmcakes, and there are more elaborate meals in the evenings. Children's portions are available. *Unlicensed.*

RAMSGATE   *Sands*

12 Cliff Street
MAP 6 F3 *Kent*
Thanet (0843) 586911
P street parking

Open 12–2.30 & 7–11
Closed Sun & Bank Hols

Chicken crêpe £3.95   Deep-fried
Camembert with cranberry sauce £1.60

Imaginative, highly enjoyable food served
in a friendly, informal atmosphere makes
for satisfaction all round at this pleasant
wine bar. Choices embrace favourites like
home-made soup, lasagne and steak and
kidney pie, as well as spicy, herby pasta,
mushrooms with blue cheese dip, savoury
crêpes and chicken Elizabeth. Simple
sweets (profiteroles, fruit crumble) to
finish. Good selection of wines by the
glass. *No dogs.*

Credit Access, Amex, Diners, Visa

READING   *Mama Mia*

11 St Mary's Butts
MAP 5 C3 *Berkshire*
Reading (0734) 581357
P shopping centre car park

Open 12–2 & 6–10.30, Sat 12–10.30
Closed Sun & 25 & 26 Dec

Spaghetti carbonara £4.25   Avocado
vinaigrette £1.50   ☺

Friendly and efficient service generates a
sense of well-being at this popular Italian
and French restaurant near the Broad
Street Mall. Authentic dishes in impressive
variety – plenty of pastas, pizzas, and
sauced steaks and escalopes – are decently
cooked, largely to order. Try garlicky
Steak Mama Mia with tomatoes and mushrooms or veal with parmesan and herbs.
To follow there are gâteaux and Italian-
style trifle. *No dogs.*

Credit Access, Amex, Diners, Visa

RICHMOND   *Refectory*

6 Church Walk
MAP 6 D3 *Surrey*
01-940 6264
P NCP at station   &

Open 10–2 (Sun from 12)
Closed Mon & Bank Hols

Chicken & mushroom pie £3.20
Flapjacks 55p   ☕

Harriet and Martin Steel bring a love of
traditional and regional British cooking to
this delightful eating place opposite the
church. At lunchtime choose granary
bread with potted meat, a savoury flan, or
something more substantial like chicken
and mushroom pie or beef and orange
casserole. Scones, slices and gingerbread
accompany morning coffee. Delightful
puddings like walnut butterscotch tart,
and more elaborate evening meals. *Minimum lunchtime charge £2.25.*

Credit Access

RICHMOND   *Richmond Harvest*

5 Dome Buildings, The Quadrant
MAP 6 D3 *Surrey*
01-940 1138
P Lichfield Terrace

Open 11.30–11 (Sun till 10.30)
Closed 1 Jan & 25 & 26 Dec

Guacamole £1.75   Red bean chilli £2.85

Local office workers and shoppers know a
good thing when they see one. They flock
here to satisfy their appetites with freshly-
prepared items from both blackboard and
printed menus. Choose tasty split pea
soup, haricot beans with fresh vegetables
and tomato dressing, or quiche with
wholemeal pastry. There are also salads,
vegan dishes, and desserts like chocolate
cake, walnut date slice, carrot cake and
hot fruit crumble. Herbal teas also feature.
No dogs.

LVs

RICHMOND   *Wildefoods*

96 Kew Road
MAP 6 D3 *Surrey*
01-940 0733
P street parking

Open 9–7, Sun 12–5
Closed Sun in winter & 3 days Xmas

Vegetarian crêpe 55p   Wholemeal pizza
65p 🍵 🐾

Everything is freshly prepared and enjoyable at this attractive wholefood shop that has a few tables around the display cabinet. The simple but appetising selection, available right through the day, includes Greek yoghurt with honey, filled rolls and sandwiches, crunchy salads, wholemeal quiches and mixed vegetable pizzas. For a virtuous finale, try the surprisingly rich but fat-free fruit cake – excellent with a fragrant speciality tea. *Unlicensed. No smoking. No dogs.*

RINGMER   *Coffee House*

72 Springett Avenue
MAP 6 D4 *East Sussex*
Ringmer (0273) 812855
P street parking ﾠ♿

Open 9.30–2 (Sun from 12)
Closed Mon, Good Friday, 1 wk April &
1 wk Oct

Two-course lunch £3.50   Scone &
butter 40p 🐾

Pristine is the only word to describe the inside of this licensed coffee house restaurant with its immaculate pine tables and pleasant simple decor. Equally impressive are the professional-looking home-made gâteaux and pastries in the small glass counter. The day starts with egg and bacon and later a set lunch is available – liver and bacon perhaps, pork and mushroom casserole, or roast chicken. On Wednesday to Saturday evenings there is a set dinner at £7. *No smoking. No dogs.*

RIPON   *N·E·W ENTRY*   *The Upper Loft*

Ripon Small Shops, Duck Hill
MAP 4 D3 *North Yorkshire*
Ripon (0765) 5283
P street parking

Open 10.30–5.30 (Sat & Sun till 7, Mon
& Tues in winter till 4.30)
Closed Wed (in winter) & 25 Dec

Steak & kidney pie £2.45
Cherry pie £1

Found on the first floor of a small shopping arcade, this timbered tea room is an attractive setting for capable cooking and friendly service. Plain or toasted sandwiches and salads are on the simple menu alongside creamed smoked haddock with poached egg, Welsh rarebit and cottage pie. Daily specials might include minute steak or curry filled vol-au-vents. The pear and strawberry flan is a tasty choice from the selection of cakes and flans on offer. *Non-smoking area. No dogs.*

ROCHESTER   *Casa Lina*

146 High Street
MAP 6 E3 *Kent*
Medway (0634) 44993
P Blue Boar Lane car park

Open 9.30am–10pm
Closed Sun & Mon, Bank Hols, 1st 2
wks Oct & 1 wk Xmas

Spaghetti bolognese £3.50   Pizza casa
nostra £5 🐾

Delicious, authentic-tasting pizzas are the main attraction at this friendly little high-street pizzeria. Watch Italian-born Mrs Syer and her husband at work in the open kitchen piling high the crisp bases with everything from simple mozzarella and tomato to the lavish casa nostra featuring a dozen ingredients. Tasty alternatives include pasta and fish dishes, grills and omelettes, as well as salads and sandwiches. *No dogs.*

Credit Access, Visa

ROMSEY

Cobweb Tea Rooms

49 The Hundred
MAP 5 C4 *Hampshire*
Romsey (0794) 516434
P Love Lane car park

Open 10–5.30 (Bank Hol Sun from 2.30)
Closed Sun, Mon (except Bank Hols), last wk Sept, first wk Oct & 1 wk Xmas

Steak & ale pie £2.50 Chocolate hazelnut torte 90p 🍵

Angela Webley's excellent home baking attracts locals and tourists alike to this homely little tea room. Typical temptations might include buttery shortbread, moist coconut-coated madeleines, iced sponges and chocolate cream gâteau. Those with a savoury tooth can choose from toasted sandwiches and cheese or pâté platters, plus lunchtime specials such as pork casserole or meat pie. Set teas also served. Patio for fine weather. *Non-smoking area. No dogs.*

ROMSEY

Latimer Coffee House

11 Latimer Street
MAP 5 C4 *Hampshire*
Romsey (0794) 513832
P own car park

Open 9–5.30, Oct–Easter 9.15–5
Closed Sun, 1 Jan & 25 & 26 Dec

Savoury flan £1.35 Toasted teacake 35p 🍵

Delightfully cottagy inside, this popular town-centre tea room also has a small rear garden where snacks can be enjoyed in summer. Choose from home-made scones and cakes in such tempting combinations as carrot and cinnamon or coconut and cherry. Lunchtime brings a daily vegetable soup, filled jacket potatoes, appetising quiches (maybe tuna or ratatouille), a selection of imaginative salads and traditional or vegetarian pasties. *No dogs.*

ROSS-ON-WYE

Meader's

1 Copse Cross Street
MAP 5 A2 *Hereford & Worcester*
Ross-on-Wye (0989) 62803
P Bowling Green car park ♿

Open 10–3

Hungarian layered cabbage £2.40
Lasagne & salad £2.50

Hungarian-born Andras Weinhardt offers hearty lunchtime dishes from his native land like bean soup, layered cabbage and pork or beef goulash (delicious with paprika potatoes) at this welcoming town-centre restaurant. Other tasty choices include grills, roasts, and vegetarian specials (nut roast, vegetable curry), plus such tempting sweets as chocolate brandy fudge cake or fresh fruit salad. Set price evening meals. Children's menu. *Non-smoking area. No dogs.*

ROTTINGDEAN

Rottingdean Pâtisserie

32 High Street
MAP 6 D4 *East Sussex*
Brighton (0273) 32180
P West Street car park

Open 10–4.30 (Sat & Sun till 5)
Closed Mon (except Bank Hols), 1 Jan & 25 & 26 Dec

Welsh rarebit £1.75 Quiche & salad £1.75

A splendid array of home baking attracts both locals and tourists to this Victorian tea shop just a few yards from the seafront. Typical delights include chocolate éclairs and coffee choux buns, floury scones, fresh cream gâteau and iced sponges, while light lunches, served from noon, offer soup and salads, filled jacket potatoes and toasted sandwiches, quiche and a ploughman's platter. Patio. *Unlicensed.*

ROWLANDS CASTLE   *Coffee Pot*

14 The Green
MAP 5 C4 *Hampshire*
Rowlands Castle (0705) 412538
P street parking

Open 9–5 (Sun & Bank Hols
from 2.30)
Closed 1 Jan & 25 & 26 Dec

Millionaire's shortbread 40p   Passion
gâteau 75p 🍵

Mrs Lomer runs this delightfully higgledy-
piggledy little tea room on the village
green with great panâche. She's a dab
hand in the kitchen and her delicious
sausage rolls, pasties and savoury pies
(sausage, egg and bacon) are just right for
hollow tummies. Soups and sandwiches
are available too, along with light scones
and expertly baked cakes like marmalade
or cherry. Sit in the garden on sunny days.
Unlicensed. No smoking. No dogs.

RYE   *Swiss Pâtisserie*

50 Cinque Ports Street
MAP 6 E3 *East Sussex*
Rye (0797) 222830
P car park opposite

Open 8–4.30 (Tues till 12.30)
Closed Sun, Bank Hols & all Jan

Sausage & French bread £1   Mille-
feuille 42p

Claude Auberson is the man responsible
for the delicious home-baked goodies on
offer at this busy and popular tea room.
An excellent jumbo sausage makes a lovely
lunchtime snack, while other tempting
choices include savoury pies, soups and
open sandwiches. On the sweet counter a
wonderfully light sachertorte laced with
apricot jam and chocolate, scrumptious
cream slices, liberally filled chocolate
éclairs or, more simply, an apple slice or
Bakewell tart. *Unlicensed. No smoking.
No dogs.*

RYTON-ON-DUNSMORE   *Ryton Gardens Café*

National Centre for Organic Gardening,
Wolston Lane
MAP 5 C2 *Warwickshire*
Coventry (0203) 303517
P own car park ♿

Open 9–5
Closed 25 & 26 Dec

Mushroom roast £3.20   Vegetable
risotto £2.85 🍵

Part of the National Centre for Organic
Gardening, this friendly, unpretentious
café not surprisingly uses only organically
grown, freshly prepared produce. The
daily-changing hot selection might include
flavourful tomato and carrot soup followed
by vegetable crumble, spinach quiche or
onion tart – all delicious with either crisp
vegetables or salad. Finish with moist
prune cake or cream-filled wholemeal
sponge topped with fresh peaches. *No
smoking. No dogs.*

Credit Access, Visa

ST ALBANS   *Kingsbury Mill Waffle House*

St Michael's Street
MAP 6 D2 *Hertfordshire*
St Albans (0727) 53502
P own car park

Open 11–6 (till 5 in winter), Sun 12–6
Closed Mon (except Bank Hols), Tues &
10 days Xmas

Ratatouille & cheese waffle £2.50
Spiced fruit waffle £1.20 🍵

An ancient mill on the river Ver is the
atmospheric setting for John and Doreen
Gazes' excellent range of waffles. Sweet or
savoury toppings, both hot and cold, on
plain or wholewheat bases, are full of
surprises: try cheese sauce and mushrooms
or a blackboard special like curried mince
with coconut and banana. Chocolate
mousse with nuts and cream is a typically
exotic ending. Eat on the patio in summer.
Unlicensed. No smoking. No dogs.

ST MARGARET'S AT CLIFFE   *Roses*

High Street
MAP 6 F3 *Kent*
Dover (0304) 852126
P car park at rear

Open 10.30–1 & 2.30–5
Closed Sun & Mon (except Bank Hols),
2 days Xmas & 2 wks Feb

Scone with jam & cream 80p   Chocolate
fudge cake 50p   🍵

Joyce Grimer's excellent home baking
makes this pretty little craft and tea shop
something special. Sit at one of the four
cane tables decorated with floral-patterned
china cups and silk flower arrangements,
or out in the garden on sunny days. Tuck
into her lovely light scones, gooey, cream-
filled meringues and wonderful cakes like
iced lemon sponge or rich chocolate fudge
cake – all delicious with a fine pot of
excellent loose leaf tea. *Unlicensed. Non-
smoking area. No dogs.*

ST MARY'S   *Tregarthens Hotel*

Isles of Scilly
MAP 8 A2 *Cornwall*
Scillonia (0720) 22540
P street parking

Open 12.30–1.45
Closed 1 Nov–mid Mar

Hot smoked mackerel with horseradish
£2.50   Cream cheese & pineapple open
sandwich £1.50

Picture windows look out onto the terrace
where you can eat on fine days. Lunchtime
snacks available at the bar give sufficient
choice for either a quick bite or a main
meal. Among the offerings are local crab,
hot smoked mackerel with horseradish
butter, jacket potatoes with various fillings, ploughman's, sandwiches and there
is always a hot dish of the day. Simple
puddings include fruit pie and ice creams.
No dogs.

Credit Access, Amex, Diners, Visa

ST MICHAEL'S MOUNT   *Sail Loft*

The Harbour, Nr Marazion
MAP 8 A3 *Cornwall*
Penzance (0736) 10748
P in Marazion

Open 10.30–5.30 (weather & tide
permitting)
Closed beg Nov–end Mar

Seafood pie £3.60   Cream tea
£1.75   🍵

Take the ferry at high tide or walk across
a cobbled causeway for a meal adventure
at this cleverly converted boathouse. An
enticing menu, with local fish a feature,
abounds in home-made soups, seafood pie,
pâté, salads and flans, plus a daily special
(perhaps tarragon chicken) and a three-
course roast lunch on Sundays. Drink a
fine pot of tea and enjoy the home-made
baking: oatcakes, Victoria sponge, fruit
pies and syllabubs. *No smoking. No dogs.*

Credit Access, Amex, Diners, Visa

SALISBURY   *Just Brahms*

68 Castle Street
MAP 5 B3 *Wiltshire*
Salisbury (0722) 28402
P town centre car park

Open 12–2 & 7–10 (Fri & Sat till 10.30)
Closed Sun & Bank Hols

Spinach soup £1.25   Ginger roulade
£2.50   🍵

A trendy wine bar stylishly run by young
proprietor Stephen Hamson. A single
course section on the main bistro menu
offers competently cooked Stilton and leek
quiche, vegetarian or fishy crêpes, sauté of
mushrooms with home-made soups to
start. Daily specials, possibly venison and
chestnut pie, complement with a blackboard announcing sweets including ginger
roulade and crème brûlée. Candelit lace
tables with fresh flowers. *No children. No
dogs.*

Credit Access, Amex, Visa

SALISBURY   *Mainly Salads*

18 Fisherton Street
MAP 5 B3 *Wiltshire*
Salisbury (0722) 22134
P central car park

Open 10–5
Closed Sun, Bank Hols & 1 wk Sept

Cossack pie £1.15   Dutch apple
pie 58p 🍵

Ron and June Ceresa offer good, imaginative food in their self-service vegetarian
restaurant. There are attractive composite
salads and lunchtime hot dishes like cheese
and onion pie and a nicely flavoured curried
nut loaf. In addition there are pizzas,
quiches, pasta dishes and various tempting
sweet things. With morning coffee and
afternoon tea, a selection of home-made
cakes. *Minimum lunchtime charge
£1.75. Unlicensed. No smoking. No
dogs.*

LVs

SALISBURY   *Michael Snell*

8 St Thomas's Square
MAP 5 B3 *Wiltshire*
Salisbury (0722) 336037
P town centre car park

Open 9–5.30 (Sat from 8.30)
Closed Sun, Bank Hols and 3 days Xmas

Moonraker vegetable pie £2.80   Coffee
meringue 89p 🍵

Tucked between a church and a rushing
weir, this bustling tea room – which spills
onto the pavement in summer – twins as a
shop selling home-made chocolates, teas
and pâtisserie. More substantially, at
lunchtime choose from the daily billed hot
dish, voluminous salads or piping hot
asparagus and cheese flan, with home-
made ice creams and gâteaux to finish.
Children's menu for under 10s. Cream
teas. *Minimum charge £3 at lunchtime.
Unlicensed. Non-smoking area. No dogs.*

SANDWICH   *N·E·W ENTRY*   *Pinkies*

7 King Street
MAP 6 F3 *Kent*
Sandwich (0304) 612019
P street parking

Open 9–5
Closed Wed, 25, 26 Dec & 2 wks
Jan–Feb

Stilton & walnut open sandwich £1.75
Passion cake 75p 🍵

Dating back to 1390, this quaint cottage
boasts a stylishly modern decor. Here the
Ickes produce a vast selection of tempting
snacks throughout the day, from imaginative open sandwiches (perhaps salt beef
or Stilton and walnuts) to vol-au-vents,
mumbled eggs (scrambled with cheese and
mushrooms) and quiches. Set teas offer a
range of home-made cakes and an excellent
choice of specialist brews. *Unlicensed.
Non-smoking area.*

Credit Amex

SELWORTHY   *Periwinkle Cottage Tea Rooms*

Selworthy Green, Nr Porlock
MAP 8 C1 *Somerset*
Porlock (0643) 862769
P church car park

Open 10–5
Closed 1 Nov–14 Mar

Chicken & leek pie with cream sauce
£2.95   Turkey pie £2.95 🅔 🍵

At the heart of a picture postcard village,
this thatched cottage stands on a flower-
bordered green. Inside, the sideboard
displays fresh meringues, treacle tart, a
light sponge with a lemon filling, coffee
and walnut gâteau, Dutch apple flan and
other excellent examples of home baking.
At lunch time choose from glazed roast
ham, pies, pâtés and ploughman's. Crumbly scones, home-made jams and fresh
clotted cream complete a tea-time treat.
Unlicensed. No dogs.

SETTLE   *Car & Kitchen*

Market Place
MAP 3 C3 *North Yorkshire*
Settle (072 92) 3638
P Market Place

Open 9.30–5 (Sun from 11)
Closed Wed (Jan–mid Mar) & 1 Jan
& 25 & 26 Dec

Pasta with mushrooms, bacon & garlic
cheese £2.40   Curried chicken
mayonnaise £2.20

Above a gift store in the market place is
this convivial little coffee shop where home
baking is available in the mornings and
afternoons and lunchtime sees more substantial choices. Shortbread, flapjacks,
teacakes, scones and date and walnut loaf
are stalwarts, and the set tea includes a
range of tempting cakes. Snacks in the
savoury line include quiche, meatloaf,
baked potatoes and interesting dishes like
aubergine parmesan. *Unlicensed. No
dogs.*

Credit Access, Visa

SHEFFIELD   *Just Cooking*

16 Carver Street
MAP 4 D4 *South Yorkshire*
Sheffield (0742) 27869
P NCP in Carver Street

Open 11–3.30 (Sat from 10)

Closed Sun, Mon, Bank Hols
(except Good Fri), 3 wks Aug–Sept
& 1 wk Xmas

Chicken simla £3.95   Spinach &
lentil roulade £2.60   Bacon &
Emmenthal pie £2.95   Fruit
brûlée £1.20

★ Owners John Craig and Brian Rosen and their staff
alike, are justly proud of this airy self-service
restaurant with its really friendly atmosphere and
first-class food. The constantly changing range of
dishes, all prepared with imagination and flair from
the finest ingredients, might include Stilton and
apple strudel, vegetable lasagne, lamb and apricot
casserole or a deliciously mild and creamy simla
served with brown rice and a crisp, colourful salad.
For dessert, feast on moist coffee gâteau, raspberry
roulade or perhaps a wickedly rich sherry trifle. Full
meals are served on Friday evenings. *Minimum
lunchtime charge £2. Non-smoking area. No dogs.*   ★

SHEFFIELD   *Toff's Restaurant & Coffee House*

23 Matilda Street, The Moor
MAP 4 D4 *South Yorkshire*
Sheffield (0742) 20783
P Matilda Way car park &

Open 10–4.30
Closed Sun & Bank Hols

Savoury tartlets £1.65   Beef stroganoff
£3.25

Garden-style furniture and an abundance
of greenery lend a summery air to this
friendly restaurant. Drop by, morning or
afternoon, for tea, coffee and cakes, or
make it a lunchtime visit when the choice
includes quiche and salad, interesting
terrines (perhaps chicken, cheese and herb)
and warming casseroles. To finish, try a
dessert like apple frangipane or the rich,
moist chocolate fudge cake delicately
flavoured with orange. *No dogs.*

LVs

SHERBORNE
N·E·W ENTRY
Church House Gallery

Half Moon Street
MAP 8 D1 *Dorset*
Sherborne (0935) 816429
P Long Street car park

Open 9.30–5 (till 2 Wed)
Closed Sun & Bank Hols

Sherborne tea £1.95 Cheese platter
£2.50 ☕ 🍵

Nestling in the shadow of Sherborne Abbey, this ancient almshouse is today a thriving coffee shop and art gallery. Good home cooking is the big attraction here and only the very best ingredients are used – try, for example, the superb orange sponge, made with fresh juice and butter, or the lovely light wholemeal scones. On the savoury side there are pizzas, crisp salads and jacket potatoes. *Unlicensed. Non-smoking area.*

Credit Access, Visa

SHIPTON
Beningbrough Hall Restaurant

Nr York
MAP 4 E3 *North Yorkshire*
York (0904) 470666
P own car park &

Open 12–5.30
Closed Mon, Fri & Oct–Easter (except weekends in Nov & Dec)

Chicken & mushroom pie £2.75 Home-made strawberry gâteau 70p ☕ 🍵

In the grounds of a National Trust Georgian country house is this pleasant self-service restaurant (entry fee of £1.50 is returnable if you stay less than an hour). The weather dictates the choices: on cooler days there is home-made soup and hot pies, and there are always salads with pâté, quiche, coronation chicken or cold meats. Everything is home-made and there are lots of scones, biscuits, gâteaux and hot tarts in winter. *Non-smoking area. No dogs.*

SHOREHAM-BY-SEA
Cuckoo Clock

74 High Street
MAP 6 D4 *West Sussex*
Shoreham-by-Sea (0273) 453853
P Ship Street car park

Open 10.30–5.30
Closed Sun, Bank Hols & 2 wks Sept

Lemon layer cake 40p Steak & kidney pudding £2.80 🍵

Mr Sheppard has welcomed visitors to his little tea room right in the centre of Shoreham for a quarter of a century. He's renowned for his all-day fry-ups and lunchtime daily specials: a roast of the day, classic toad-in-the-hole, liver and bacon and shepherd's pie. Round off your meal with lemon pancakes, fruit pie or good steamed pudding. There are fresh cut sandwiches, home-made scones and various set teas with a good choice of blends. *Unlicensed. Non-smoking area. No dogs.*

LVs

SHREWSBURY
Cornhouse Restaurant & Wine Bar

59 Wyle Cop
MAP 5 A1 *Shropshire*
Shrewsbury (0743) 231991
P NCP Wyle Cop &

Open 12–2.30 & 6.30–10.30
Closed some Bank Hols

Moussaka £3.75 Herrings in sour cream £1.50 ☕

Enjoyable, home-cooked fare is the order of the day here. Amongst lots of greenery and oak furniture, warm yourself in front of the open fire before selecting from the short, daily-changing menu. Try, perhaps, a delightful carrot and orange soup, followed by moussaka, tender minced lamb in béchamel sauce, or opt for a chargrilled steak. Round things off with a delicately spiced apple pie. Friendly service. *No dogs.*

Credit Access, Visa

SHREWSBURY — Delanys Vegetarian Restaurant

St Julian's Craft Centre, St Alkmunds Square
MAP 5 A1 *Shropshire*
Shrewsbury (0743) 60602
P NCP Wyle Cop

Open 11–2.30
Closed Sun & Bank Hols

Spicy butter bean casserole £1.65
Devon apple cake 75p 🍵

Jazz music accompanies the healthy snacks served in the converted vestry of St Julian's church. Order at the counter from a simple selection that ranges from morning coffee and cakes to tasty lunchtime offerings like courgette and tomato quiche, cheese-topped vegetable bake, spicy butter bean casserole and lovely fresh, imaginative salads. Try banana and pineapple crumble to finish – unusual and highly successful. *No smoking.*

LVs

SHREWSBURY — Delanys Vegetarian Restaurant

Wyle Cop
MAP 5 A1 *Shropshire*
Shrewsbury (0743) 66890
P NCP Wyle Cop &

Open 9.30–5.30, also Thurs–Sat 7–10
Closed Sun & Bank Hols

Hungarian mushroom soup £1.30
Aubergine & potato curry £3 🍵

Watercolours of old Shrewsbury and a collection of theatrical masks adorn the walls of this stylish branch of the original Delanys. Daily blackboard specials supplement the regular menu and a typically appetising selection could include Chinese parsnip soup, wholemeal quiche, an excellent chick pea and mushroom loaf or cheesy nut and vegetable bake. Finish on a luxurious note with smooth, light chocolate and hazelnut mousse.

LVs

SHREWSBURY — The Good Life

N·E·W ENTRY

Barracks Passage, Wyle Cop
MAP 5 A1 *Shropshire*
Shrewsbury (0743) 50455
P NCP Wyle Cop

Open 9.30–3.30 (till 4.30 Sat)
Closed Sun, Bank Hols

Spinach moussaka £1.30   Chocolate rum & raisin flan 75p

Friendly owner Mrs Weston and her staff are responsible for the truly tempting array of goodies offered at this bright, wholefood restaurant. Imaginative quiches, savoury nut loaves and filled jacket potatoes go beautifully with crunchy-fresh salads, and there's always soup and a daily hot special like five-bean cheesepot. Finish with scones, date slice or a magnificent chocolate, rum and raisin flan. *Non-smoking area. No dogs.*

LVs

SIDBURY — Old Bakery

Nr Sidmouth
MAP 8 C2 *Devon*
Sidbury (039 57) 319
P village car park

Open 9.30–1 & 2–6
Closed Sun, Good Fri & mid Oct–Easter

Clotted cream meringue 95p   Cottage tea £1.60 🍵

Antique bedstead panels decorate the walls of this immaculately kept village tea room, run with care and pride by Jeanne Selly. Super home baking is her speciality, and afternoon teas are a positive feast of lovely light scones, wonderful clotted cream meringues and a tempting choice of cakes such as date and walnut, lemon sponge, almond slices and buttery shortbread. The pretty little garden makes a delightful spot for summer snacking. *Unlicensed. No smoking.*

SKELWITH BRIDGE   *Chesters*

Nr Ambleside
MAP 3 B3 *Cumbria*
Ambleside (0966) 32553
P own car park

Open 10.30–5.30
Closed 25 & 26 Dec & 4 days Jan

Cheesy bean bake £2.75   Rich seed cake
90p ❤

Enjoying a pretty riverside setting next to
Skelwith Bridge, this appealing café shares
space with the showroom and shop of a
restored slate works. A splendid array of
home baking includes coffee and chocolate
gâteaux, seed and fruit cakes and fruity
scones. At lunchtime there's home-made
soup, pork and Stilton pâté, houmous, plus
lots of salads and appetising hot choices
like cheesy bean bake or beef and Guinness
pie. Terrace. *Non-smoking area. No dogs.*

SKIPTON   *Herbs*

Healthy Life Natural Food Centre,
10 High Street
MAP 4 D3 *North Yorkshire*
Skipton (0756) 60619
P car park at rear of Town Hall

Open 9.30–5
Closed Sun, Tues, 1 Jan & 25 & 26 Dec

Nut cutlets with plum sauce £2.65   Leek
& mushroom bake £2.65

This bright, clean café above a wholefood
shop is especially popular on market days.
Specials of the day can include vegetable
lasagne or broccoli quiche. The menu
offers home-made soup, pâté and various
salads and sandwiches. Among the sweet
dishes are chef's specialities of the day
such as pineapple fruit cake or almond and
raisin tart. Several blends of tea are
available, including a selection of herbal
brews. Children's portions. *No smoking
after 11.30 am. No dogs.*

SOLIHULL   *Bobby Browns*

165 High Street
MAP 5 B2 *West Midlands*
021-704 9136
P Civic Centre car park

Open 12–2 (Sun till 3) & 7–10.30
(Fri & Sat till 11)
Closed most Bank Hols

Lasagne £3.85   Lamb St Clementine
£5.95 ⊟

In a handsome stone house on the High
Street, this cosy restaurant offers light bar
snacks at ground level and appetising main
meals above. Tasty onion soup or smoked
chicken might precede lasagne, tender
lamb noisettes or filling beef and Guinness
pie and there is always a vegetarian main
dish available. Lemon crunch remains the
pick of the home-made desserts. Helpful
and engaging service. *No dogs.*

Credit Access, Amex, Diners, Visa

SOUTH MOLTON   *N·E·W ENTRY*   *Corn Dolly*

115a East Street
MAP 8 B1 *Devon*
P street parking &

Open 9.30–6 (Sat 10–6)
Closed Sun, Mon & Bank Hols

Kings Ransom tea £2.50   Chocolate
cake 70p ⊟ ❤

A delicious ham sandwich made with
quality local ham and fresh wholemeal
bread exemplifies the good standards at
this tea shop. Try one of seven set teas:
apple pie tea with real Bramley filling,
seafarer's tea with smoked mackerel and
gooseberry sauce, or a children's Little
Jack Horner tea. Home-made rhubarb
cake, lemon curd sponge and coconut slice
are among a delectable selection. Sally
Cooper and Dorothy Tomkins have lauda-
bly chosen quality over quantity. *Unlicensed. No dogs.*

SOUTH MOLTON   *Stumbles Wine Bar*

131 East Street
MAP 8 B1 *Devon*
South Molton (07695) 4145
P own car park

Open 10.30–2.30 & 7–11 (from 6.30 in summer)
Closed Sun, 1 Jan & 25 & 26 Dec

Peperoni pizza £2.50   Tagliatelle carbonara £3.50 🍵

Capably cooked, interesting dishes feature in this smart wine bar with a garden. Starters at lunchtime include prawns with aïoli, stir-fry chicken livers and baked eggs with asparagus cream. There are more substantial dishes too, like chicken baked with Gruyère and served with fresh crisp vegetables. Pizzas and pastas with various sauces and garnishes are also on offer. To finish try the light raspberry soufflé, meringues or chocolate roulade. Children's portions are available. *No dogs.*

Credit Access, Amex, Diners, Visa

SOUTHAMPTON   *La Margherita*

4 Commercial Road
MAP 5 C4 *Hampshire*
Southampton (0703) 333390
P car park at rear

Open 12–2.15 & 6.30–11.30
Closed Sun & Bank Hols

Pizza Margherita £2.80   Pasta with a choice of sauces £3.25

The interior of this Italian restaurant matches the boldly painted exterior, with loud music, colourful decor and a lively atmosphere. Familiar choices on the menu range from steak, veal and chicken dishes to pasta and fish. Pizzas with names like Superman and Sophia Loren have numerous toppings – ham and cheese with pineapple, and peppers with ham and mushrooms. Tuna fish and butter bean salad is a possible starter, with cheesecake or gâteau for a sweet finish. *No dogs.*

Credit Access, Amex, Diners, Visa   **LVs**

SPETISBURY   *Marigold Cottage*

High Street, Blandford Forum
MAP 8 D2 *Dorset*
Blandford (0258) 52468
P own car park

Open 10–5.30
Closed Mon

Baked gammon & pineapple £3.40
Baked potato with tuna & pasta £1.65
🍷

The McCracken family have taken over this pretty sixteenth century cottage tea room. They offer various lunchtime specials like roast beef, fish pie and salads, but you can also choose from a range of sandwiches and filled jacket potatoes too. The set Dorset cream tea has warm scones with clotted cream and a selection of tempting home-made cakes. A set price menu (£8.50) is available in the evening. Children's menu. Garden. *No dogs.*

Credit Access, Visa

SPILSBY   *Buttercross Restaurant*

18 Lower Market
MAP 4 F4 *Lincolnshire*
Spilsby (0790) 53147
P market square car park

Open 10–4.30
Closed Sun, Tues, Bank Hols (except May Day), 1 wk July & 1 wk Dec

Deep-fried vegetable pancakes with sweet & sour sauce £2.20   Normandy chicken £2.65 🍷

The Bosketts' delightfully informal restaurant overlooks the Buttercross in the town centre. They serve coffee, lunches and teas. Lunch might include cock-a-leekie soup or chicken liver pâté, roast of the day, seafood mornay, omelettes, steaks and vegetarian dishes. Sweets such as raspberry cheesecake and home-made ice creams. Afternoon tea offers scones, sandwiches and moist chocolate cake. Full meals Friday and Saturday evenings. *Minimum lunchtime charge £1.75. No dogs.*

STADDLE BRIDGE   *Cellar Bar at the Tontine*

Nr Northallerton
MAP 4 D3 *North Yorkshire*
East Harlsey (060 982) 671
P own car park

Open 11.30–3 & 7–11

Closed 1 Jan & 25 & 26 Dec

Steak au poivre £8.80   Chicken
Jo Jo £6.95   Moules marinière
£2.95   Osso buco £6.95   ☕

★ Excellent service and a lively, relaxed atmosphere can be enjoyed in this attractive cellar bar. From the imaginative menu chalked up on a blackboard, snackers can plump for fettuccine pasta with cream and bacon, fried black pudding and garlic mushrooms with provençale sauce. A more substantial choice might include roast rack of lamb with rosemary and garlic – served tender and pink and with perfectly cooked fresh vegetables – salmon Wellington, calf's liver with Madeira sauce or duck breast au Cassis. The sweets too are a treat: baked Alaska, sticky toffee pudding, rich creamy chocolate mousse or chocolate nut cake. ★

Credit Access, Amex, Diners, Visa

STAMFORD   *George of Stamford*

St Martin's High Street
MAP 6 D1 *Lincolnshire*
Stamford (0780) 55171
P own car park

Open 9am–11pm

Warm salad of monkfish £4.90   Fresh
fruit pavlova £2.55   ☕ 🍷

One can eat in the bar or on the pretty cobbled patio, but the bright and airy garden lounge of this old coaching inn has the best choice of snacks for just-a-biters. A cold buffet offers roast meats, salmon and fresh salads, while hot options might include fritto misto, grilled lamb-burgers with yoghurt dressing and fried pork with rigatoni in tomato sauce. Soup, open sandwiches and delicious sweets and pastries complete the picture. *Non-smoking area. No dogs.*

Credit Access, Amex, Diners, Visa

STAMFORD   *Mr Pips Coffee Shop & Restaurant*

11 St Mary Street
MAP 6 D1 *Lincolnshire*
Stamford (0780) 65795
P Wharf Road car park

Open 9.30–4.30
Closed Sun & Bank Hols

Vegetable soup 90p   Smoked haddock in
cider sauce £2.25   🍷

Part of a 16th-century listed building, this warmly inviting coffee shop offers enjoyable snacks throughout the day. A fine old sideboard displays tempting goodies such as oven-warm scones, apricot cream sponge and delicious lemon and brandy syllabub. At lunchtime, appetising daily specials such as pork and mushroom pie supplement the regular choice of home-made soup and various pâtés, vegetarian quiche and imaginative filled jacket potatoes. *No dogs.*

Credit Access, Visa

Ogden Nash
1902–71

By undraped nymphs
I am not wooed;
I'd rather painters painted food . . .
'The Clean Platter' in *The Face is Familiar* (1954)

C. Herman Senn

Oh, I am a festive chafing dish,
I foam, and froth, and bubble,
I sing the song of meat and fish,
And save a deal of trouble.
Chafing Dish and Casserole Cookery (1908)

Jonathan Swift
1667–1745

Promises and pie-crust are made to be broken.
Polite Conversation

'Saki' (H. H. Munro)
1870–1916

I believe that I once considerably scandalised her
by declaring that clear soup was a more important
factor in life than a clear conscience.
The Blind Spot

STEVENAGE

De Friese Coffee Shop

71 High Street, Old Town
MAP 6 D2 *Hertfordshire*
Stevenage (0438) 720519
P street parking

Open 9.30–5.30 (Wed till 2), Sat 8.30–5, Sun 11–5
Closed 25 & 26 Dec

Ham sandwich & salad 90p   Home-made
ice cream cone 50p   🍵

A simple, friendly little high street shop with pine tables at the back where customers can sample a wide range of cheeses (over 80 different varieties) and ice creams, all washed down by delicious fresh ground coffee. Enjoy your cheese in a salad, sandwich or ploughman's adding home-made soup to start and perhaps chocolate fudge cake, apple pie or a super praline or raspberry ice for afters. *Unlicensed. No smoking.*

Credit Visa   LVs

STONHAM ASPAL

Stonham Barns

Pettaugh Road, Nr Stowmarket
MAP 6 E2 *Suffolk*
Stowmarket (0449) 711755
P own car park   &

Open 10–5.30 (Nov–Easter till 4.30)
Closed Mon & 1 wk Xmas

Ploughman's £2   Treacle tart & cream
£1.20   🍵 🍴

A group of attractively converted barns house this informal restaurant with adjoining garden centre and farm shop. In summer a cold buffet (12–2pm) offers salads, cold cuts and ploughman's, while in winter there's a lunchtime choice of three or four hot dishes such as beef and prune casserole. Day-long home-baked treats could include a moist and delicious sultana whisky cake. Small portions for children. Outdoor eating. *No dogs.*

Credit Access, Visa

STRATFORD-UPON-AVON

N·E·W ENTRY   ### Café Natural

Unit 1, Greenhill Street
MAP 5 B2 *Warwickshire*
Stratford-upon-Avon (0789) 415741
P NCP Market Square   &

Open 9–5.30
Closed Sun, 1 Jan, 25 & 26 Dec

Mushroom & tomato lasagne £1.90
Apple & hazelnut crumble £1.50
🍵 🍴

Helpful, smiling staff add to the convivial atmosphere at this bright little vegetarian café. Try one of the day's specials, like popular cheese-topped potato and aubergine pie, or opt for a regular favourite such as spinach roulade, cashew nut croquettes or spicy peanut balls. There are colourful, imaginative salads and tempting sweets like apricot crunch. Cakes and pastries available all day. *Unlicensed. No smoking. No dogs.*

Credit Access, Visa   LVs

STRATFORD-UPON-AVON

Pinocchio

6 Union Street
MAP 5 B2 *Warwickshire*
Stratford-upon-Avon (0789) 69106
P street parking

Open 12–2 & 6–11
Closed Sun, 1 Jan & 25 Dec

Pizza Pinocchio £4.25   Rigatoni with
onions, bacon, chilli, tomato & cream
£4.25

An agreeable and informal restaurant specialising in Sicilian-style cuisine with notably good home-made pastas and pizzas. Starters include traditional minestrone and large mushrooms stuffed with ricotta cheese and spinach. Pasta dishes will be traditional favourites; the crisp, well-baked pizzas may be topped with various choices including a generous portion of herby vegetables. Veal and chicken dishes are offered as alternatives. *No dogs.*

STRATFORD-UPON-AVON   *Slug & Lettuce*

38 Guild Street
Map 5 B2 *Warwickshire*
Stratford-upon-Avon (0789) 299700
P NCP in Market Place

Open 12–2 & 6–10, Sun 12–1.30 &
7–9.30
Closed 1 Jan, 25 & 26 Dec

Smoked chicken & avocado salad £3
Burgundy mushrooms & bacon £2.50
🍵

You can watch the chef cooking in the
open kitchen area, and even listen to him
singing if you're lucky, in this stylish
bistro-style pub. Fresh local produce is the
basis for such enjoyably prepared offerings
as celery and almond soup or black pudding
with apple sauce followed by, say, calf's
liver and onions, pork chop with mushroom and Stilton sauce, or fillet steak au
poivre. The wine list is interesting and
varied, and booking is advisable.

Credit Access, Visa **LVs**

STROUD   *Mother Nature*

2 Bedford Street
MAP 5 B3 *Gloucestershire*
Stroud (045 36) 78202
P John Street car park

Open 9–4.30
Closed Sun & Bank Hols

Vegetable lasagne £3.10   Breton pie
£3.10 🍵 🍷

Quality wholefood ingredients are carefully
prepared to provide consistently enjoyable
eating at this smart vegetarian restaurant
behind a health food shop. Throughout
the day cakes, biscuits, samosas and bhajis
are available, while at lunchtime the choice
widens to include soup, quiches, colourful
salads and specials such as vegetable curry
or pasta milanaise. Fruit-based desserts or
cheeses to finish. *No dogs.*

LVs

STROUD   *N·E·W ENTRY*   *The Old Lady Tea Shop*

1 Threadneedle Street
MAP 5 B3 *Gloucestershire*
Stroud (045 36) 2441
P John Street Car Park

Open 9.30–4.30 (till 2 Mon & Thurs)
Closed Sun & all Bank Hols

Toasted sandwich £1.00   Home-made
cakes from 25p 🍷

Named in remembrance of London's famous Old Lady of Threadneedle Street, Mrs
Walker's pleasant first-floor tea shop offers
a short selection of home-baked goodies
from her husband's bakery below. Light,
fresh scones, Chelsea buns, doughnuts
and gooey caramel shortbread are all
popular with a choice of teas, espresso or
cappuccino. Hot snacks are limited to
toasted sandwiches, pizzas and filled jacket
potatoes. *Unlicensed. No dogs.*

STUDLEY   *Interesting Things*

8 Marble Alley, Nr Alcester
MAP 5 B2 *Warwickshire*
Studley (052 785) 3964
P car park opposite

Open 10–5
Closed Sun, Mon, Bank Hols (except
Good Fri) & 1 wk Xmas

Cheese flan £1.15   Griddle cake £1.05

After browsing round Dawn and Rob
McKees' gift shop, go upstairs to their
friendly coffee shop for an enjoyable light
snack. Throughout the day there's a fine
selection of home baking, including crumbly scones, fresh cream gâteau, chocolate
cake and sticky treacle tart. Lunchtime
brings a short menu of sausage rolls,
salads, jacket potatoes, a daily hot special,
like steak and kidney pie or lasagne, and
choice of savoury flans. *Unlicensed. Non-
smoking area. No dogs.*

SWAFFHAM   *Red Door*

Market Place, 7 London Street
MAP 6 E1 *Norfolk*
Swaffham (0760) 21059
P street parking

Open 9.30–5 (Sun from 11 & till 3 in winter), also Fri & Sat 7pm–9pm
Closed Mon, some Bank Hols & 2 wks Jan

Cheese & vegetable pie £2.80
Afternoon tea £2.40   ☙

A splendid array of home-baked goodies accompany tea or coffee taken at the Spencers' town-centre restaurant. Look out for a delicious Norwegian apple cake, chocolate caramel shortbread, light, fruity scones and iced honey and nut cake. Lunch here on a ploughman's, omelette or salad, or tuck into something more substantial like pork and plum pie, burgundy beef or fried haddock. On Friday and Saturday evenings additional blackboard specials are available. *No dogs.*

Credit Access, Visa

SWINDON   *Acorn Wholefoods*

40 Havelock Street
MAP 5 B3 *Wiltshire*
Swindon (0793) 39396
P Market Street car park

Open 10–6
Closed Sun & Bank Hols

Cream of leek & celery soup £1
Mushroom & almond risotto £2.65

The Hardings' self-service wholefood restaurant above their health food shop is a popular place for enjoyable vegetarian, vegan and a few seafood dishes. Smartly uniformed girls help you choose from the colourful counter display of crunchy-fresh salads and hot snacks like flavoursome cashew nut lasagne, pizzas, quiches and filled jacket potatoes. Nice cakes (carob, date and walnut slice) are served all day. *Unlicensed (bring your own – £1 corkage). Non-smoking area. No dogs.*

Credit Access, Visa   **LVs**

TANGMERE   *N·E·W ENTRY*   *River Kwai*

Arundel Road, Chichester
MAP 6 D4 *West Sussex*
Chichester (0243) 773294
P own car park

Open 12–2.30 & 6–11.30
Closed Sun & 3 days Xmas

Kao pud £4.50   Sen mee rad nay £3.50

A section of the menu at the Panichs' pretty Thai restaurant, with its gentle oriental music, is devoted to quick lunch or supper rice and noodle dishes. Kao pud has fried rice with chicken, pork and crab meat or prawns. There are Thai hot and sour soups, various egg dishes and satay with delicious peanut sauce. The sarong-clad waitresses and cheerful staff are very welcoming. *No children. No dogs.*

Credit Access, Diners, Visa

TARR STEPS   *Tarr Farm*

Dulverton
MAP 8 C1 *Somerset*
Winsford (064 385) 383
P Exmoor National Parks car park

Open 11–5.30
Closed end Oct–end Mar

Cottage pie £2.50   Prawn salad £2.80
☙

If you are taking a drive to see the renowned Tarr Bridge, thought by some to date from the Bronze Age and by others from Medieval times, you should take time out to visit Deborah Connell's farmhouse tea room. Enjoy scones and clotted cream, biscuits or cakes, or a light lunch of soup, pasties, quiche or salad (from 12.30 to 2.30) in the cool, plain interior or outside on rustic furniture in the summer. Sweets include apricot crumble, lemon mousse and cheesecakes.

TAUNTON   *Bow Bar*

Castle Hotel, North Street
MAP 8 C1 *Somerset*
Taunton (0823) 272671
P Castle Green car park

Open 12–2 & 3–6
Closed Sun & Bank Hols

Asparagus flan £1.95   Herb pancakes
provençale £2.25

Enjoyable light lunches are served in this
spacious, lofty bar, part of the Castle Hotel.
Poached egg florentine and leek and
mushroom tartlet are typical starters, while
main courses range from cream cheese
roulade and cucumber vinaigrette to
noodles with flaked cod and delicious
cottage pie. Salads, sandwiches and jacket
potatoes also available, plus homely sweets
like bread and butter pudding. Also open
for afternoon tea. *Non-smoking area. No
dogs.*

TAUNTON   N·E·W
                    ENTRY   *Porters*

49 East Reach
MAP 8 C1 *Somerset*
Taunton (0823) 256688
P Victoria Gate car park

Open 12–2 & 7.30–10.30
Closed Sat lunch, all Sun, Good Fri,
25 & 26 Dec

Spinach & walnut lasagne £4.50   Deep
fried Camembert £1.60   🍵

Leafy plants decorate the Porters' cheerful
wine bar with its own tiny courtyard for
summer snacking. Check the blackboard
for the day's enterprising specials – perhaps pea and mint soup or smoked haddock
pâté followed by trout with celery sauce or
tender chicken in cream and thyme. Open
sandwiches make lighter lunchtime alternatives, and there's a delicious lemony
treacle tart for afters. *Non-smoking area.
No dogs.*

Credit Access, Visa

TICEHURST   N·E·W
                   ENTRY   *Plantation Tea Company*

1 High Street
MAP 6 E3 *East Sussex*
Ticehurst (0580) 200015
P street parking

Open 9–5
Closed Mon

Quiche & salad £2.15   Sussex apple
cake 80p   ⊖

In an area rich in National Trust properties
to visit, this neat little café – run by friendly
owners Michelle and Melvyn Vinall – makes
a pleasant place to stop for refreshment.
Early birds can start the day with a
breakfast-style egg and bacon muffin,
while lunchers might settle for home-made
soup and a sandwich – or something more
substantial like steak and mushroom pie.
Teatime treats, temptingly displayed in the
window, could include a feathery lemon
sponge. *Unlicensed.*

TIDESWELL   *Poppies*

Bank Square, Tideswell, Nr Buxton
MAP 4 D4 *Derbyshire*
Tideswell (0298) 871083
P street parking

Open 12–2 & 6–11
Closed Sun lunch, all Mon, Feb & 2 wks
May

Country vegetable soup £1.45   Salmon
steak £6.45

A friendly, homely atmosphere pervades
this informal little restaurant with its
colourful display of poppies. The simple
menu of well-prepared and generous dishes
includes some vegetarian choices. There is
vegetable soup with home-baked wholemeal bread, mushroom and herb pâté
houmus with garlic bread, meat loaf, trout
and a chilli bean and vegetable casserole.
Sweets could be apple, sultana and cinnamon pie or ice cream and seasonal fruits.
No dogs.

Credit Access, Visa

TISSINGTON   *Old School Tea Rooms*

Nr Ashbourne
MAP 4 D4 *Derbyshire*
Parwich (033 525) 467
P own car park

Open 2.30–5.15 (Bank Hols & school
hols from 11)
Closed Oct–Easter

Cream tea £1.50   Chocolate cake 55p
🍵

Faithful customers can't keep away from
this delightful tea room (formerly the
village school), set in a wonderfully peaceful corner of the English countryside.
Excellent afternoon teas are the big attraction here, with crumbly oven-warm scones
served with fruity jam and thick local
cream, dainty sandwiches (usually cucumber and egg mayonnaise), and a small
choice of cakes – perhaps tangy lemon, or
rich chocolate sponge. Eat outside in the
garden if the sun shines. *Unlicensed. No
smoking. No dogs.*

TIVERTON   *Angel Foods*

1 Angel Terrace
MAP 8 C1 *Devon*
Tiverton (0884) 254778
P Phoenix Lane car park

Open 8.30–5.30 (Thurs till 2.30)
Closed Sun, Bank Hols & 4 days Xmas

Angel burger £1.70   Greek salad £1.05
🅔 🍵

Shelves lined with beans and pulses
surround customers eating at this tiny café
at the back of a wholefood shop.
Refreshing herbal teas go well with sweet
treats like lemon Madeira cake and orange
carob flapjack, as well as savouries such
as curried vegetable pasty and jacket
potatoes. Lunchtime brings imaginative
soups (cauliflower and coriander),
delicious homity pie, pizzas, healthy salads
and vegetable bakes. Yoghurt or fruit
crumble to finish. *Unlicensed. No smoking. No dogs.*

TOLWORTH   *Superfish*

59 The Broadway
MAP 6 D3 *Surrey*
01-390 2868
P Tolworth car park to rear

Open 11.30–2 (Sat till 2.30) & 5.30–
10.30 (Fri & Sat 5–11)
Closed Sun, Mon & Bank Hols (except
Good Fri)

Cod & chips £2.60   Scampi & chips
£3.95 🍵

A small selection of good fish is on offer at
this spotlessly clean, light and cheerful
place, one of a chain of similar restaurants.
There are fillets of plaice, haddock, huss,
sole, whole plaice on the bone and halibut
steaks all served with well-cooked chips,
nice, crusty French bread and a pickle and
sauce trolley. For sweet there are various
ice creams. Children's platter. *No dogs.*

LVs

TORQUAY   *The Mulberry Room*

1 Scarborough Road
MAP 8 C2 *Devon*
Torquay (0803) 213639
P street parking

Open 10–5 (Sat till 3)
Closed Mon, Tues & Bank Hols

Pork chop & apple sauce £2.75   Lemon
meringue pie £1.20 🅔 🍵

Lesley Cooper runs her homely little back
street tea room with charm and friendliness. A table by the door displays freshly
baked cakes (Devon apple, banana, lemon)
available throughout the day, while at
lunchtime the savoury choice includes
soup, sandwiches and ploughman's, salads
with quiche or honey-baked ham, plus
peanut rissoles and a tasty hot special such
as beef casserole or cottage pie. Finish
with chocolate mousse or individual sherry
trifle. Roast Sunday lunch.

TOTNES   *Above Town Wholefood Eating House*

77 High Street
MAP 8 C2 *Devon*
Totnes (0803) 864025
P Rotherfold car park

Open 12–2.30 & 7–10 (Fri & Sat only)
Closed Sun, Mon, Bank Hols & 2 wks
Oct

Salad niçoise £1.75   Chicken curry
£2.95 🍵

Quality ingredients, many organically
grown, are carefully used to produce an
interesting menu in this bright informal
first floor restaurant. June Palk and ex-
physicist Guy Jenkins offer a short but
changing selection including houmus,
Spanish hors d'oeuvre or Italian carrot
salad for starters, followed by croissant
stuffed with feta cheese and spinach,
spaghetti with tuna sauce, spicy bean stew
or lamb cutlets. Tempting sweets feature
gingerbread pudding and greek yoghurt
and honey. *No smoking.*

*We publish annually
so make sure you use the current edition.*

TOTNES   *Willow*

87 High Street
MAP 8 C2 *Devon*
Totnes (0803) 862605
P Leechwell Street car park

Open 9–5 (from 10 in winter) & Tues–
Sat 6.30–10
Closed Tues & Thurs eves in winter, all
Sun & 1 wk Xmas

Couscous with peanut sauce £2.20
Organic mushroom crumble £2.30

The atmosphere is welcomingly informal
at this pleasant vegetarian wholefood
restaurant. Organic vegetables, free range
eggs and rennet-free cheeses are basic to
the dishes. There's an Indian menu on
Wednesdays and live music on Friday
evenings. The rich filling bean soup has a
lovely subtle flavour and the celeriac
cutlets come with excellent brown rice and
a tangy tomato sauce. Sweet things include
fresh cream buckwheat gâteau. *No smoking.*

TREBARWITH STRAND   *House on the Strand*

Nr Tintagel
MAP 8 B2 *Cornwall*
Camelford (0840) 770326
P street parking

Open 10am–10pm
Closed end Oct–early Mar

Beef stout casserole £5.20   Aduki bean
& vegetable pie £4.25 🍵

Close to the beach, this lively, family-run
bistro offers an imaginative selection of
dishes throughout its opening hours.
Subtly spiced curries are a house speciality,
while other tasty offerings range from crab
pâté and cheese rarebit to chicken loaf
with tomato and chilli sauce, steak and
Cheddar pancakes and vegetarian bean
casseroles. Sweet treats include sticky
toffee pudding and chocolate fudge cake.
Terrace. *Non-smoking area. No dogs.*

Credit Access, Visa

TREBARWITH STRAND   *The Old Millfloor*

Tintagel
MAP 8 B2 *Cornwall*
Camelford (0840) 770234
P own car park

Open 2–5.30 (in winter Sat and
Sun from 12)

Closed Mon & also every weekday
between Oct–April

Sandwich with side salad 80p
Farmhouse beef pie £2.25
Omelette £2.25   Cornish cream
tea £2

★ A steep path sweeps down to Janice Waddon-Martyn's
delightful 16th century house set beside a stream
and in the most delightful garden. Her baking is
quite outstanding, and whether you choose her hot
fresh scones, strawberry cream flans, scrumptious
coffee cake or delicious chocolate cake, you are sure
to be satisfied. If you are looking for a savoury snack
you will find excellent ploughman's with tasty cheese
or hot dishes like omelette with garlic, peppers and
onions, real Cornish pasties, chicken pilau or beef
pie. Stop by for a cup of Earl Grey, Assam, Darjeeling
or Ceylon tea in this most English of places. More
elaborate meals are served in the evenings. *Unlicensed.* ★

TRESCO   *Island Hotel Restaurant*

Isles of Scilly
MAP 8 A2 *Cornwall*
Scillonia (0720) 22883

Open 12.30–1.30, Sun 1–1.45
Closed mid Oct–mid Mar

Smoked mackerel with cucumber &
horseradish sauce £1.50   Cold meat
platter £5.50

Enjoy the views of the sea from the picture
windows of this airy restaurant set in
splendid sub-tropical gardens. Local fish
and seafood feature prominently on the
light lunch menu, ideal for just-a-biters.
Salads with fresh crab or melon, cream
cheese, prawns and smoked salmon are
inviting, or go for a daily special such as
lemon sole or John Dory. Alternatives
include various meat, chicken and lobster
dishes and there's an excellent cheeseboard. Set lunch only on Sunday. *No dogs.*

TUNBRIDGE WELLS   *Cheevers*

56 High Street
MAP 6 E3 *Kent*
Tunbridge Wells (0892) 45524
P street parking

Open 12–2.30
Closed Sun, Mon, Bank Hols, 1 wk
spring & 2 wks autumn

Rack of lamb £6.95   Fettucine with
ham, veal & cream £4.35

Tim Cheevers and his proficient staff offer
a daily-changing lunchtime menu at this
small, stylish restaurant. The simply prepared food is fresh and imaginative, including such dishes as delicately flavoured
mousse of crab wrapped in spinach with
excellent muesli-walnut bread, duck
roasted with spring onions and ginger and
fillet of brill with dill and tomatoes. There
are tempting desserts too. The set evening
menu is more expensive. *No dogs.*

Credit Access, Visa

TUNBRIDGE WELLS *Delicious*

14 Mount Pleasant
MAP 6 E3 *Kent*
Tunbridge Wells (0892) 47134
P Calverley Ground car park

Open 9.30–5
Closed Sun & Bank Hols

Cauliflower cheese £1.95   Jacket potato with corn, sultanas & mayonnaise £1.75

This spacious, bright, clean self-service restaurant is popular with mothers and young children in the mornings. Early in the day a wide range of cakes and amply filled sandwiches are offered. Lunch, from 11.30, gives a good choice of savoury dishes such as pasta, cottage pie and cauliflower cheese, all well cooked and very popular. Later in the day cakes, sandwiches and tea are served. *Unlicensed. Non-smoking area.*

LVs

TUNBRIDGE WELLS *Downstairs at Thackeray's*

85 London Road
MAP 6 E3 *Kent*
Tunbridge Wells (0892) 37559
P street parking

Open 12.30–2.30 & 7–11

Closed Sun, Mon, Bank Hols & 1 wk Xmas

Pasta with leeks & parmesan £1.95   Pork rillette with green peppercorns £1.95   Chicken with yoghurt £5.90   Ginger & toffee pudding £1.95   🅰 🍵

★ The former home of the Victorian novelist William Makepeace Thackeray now houses an elegant restaurant and this small intimate bistro-style restaurant and patio with lots of flowers and friendly, professional service. The cooking is very sound and the ingredients of high quality. A blackboard describes set lunches but the menu offers such simple dishes as fresh pasta with leeks or noisettes of pork with an apricot and green peppercorn stuffing. The set lunch might be a perfectly poached egg in a pastry case with well flavoured duxelle and classic hollandaise or breast of chicken cooked in yoghurt and spices with delicious vegetables and a zesty orange burnt cream. *No dogs.* ★

Credit Access, Visa

TUNBRIDGE WELLS *Pilgrims*

37 Mount Ephraim
MAP 6 E3 *Kent*
Tunbridge Wells (0892) 20341
P street parking

Open 9am–8pm (Mon till 5)
Closed Sun & Bank Hols

Spinach lasagne £2.25   Asparagus savoury £2.25   🍵

Delicious vegetarian fare keeps this leafy, pine-furnished restaurant, at the back of a health food shop, busy throughout the day. Crisp, imaginative salads go well with hot lunchtime dishes like wholemeal pizza, moussaka or courgette casserole, and there's fresh fruit trifle for afters. Cakes and pastries include excellent wholemeal scones, cheesecake and moist banana, pineapple and walnut cake. *Minimum lunchtime charge £1.50. Non-smoking area. No dogs.*

TUTBURY   *Cornmill Tea Room*

Cornmill Lane, Nr Burton upon Trent
MAP 5 B1 *Staffordshire*
Burton upon Trent (0283) 813300
P own car park

Open 10–5
Closed Sun, Mon & Bank Hols

Welsh rarebit £1.80   Mushroom
omelette £2.10

The original water wheel – dating back to 1705 – still remains at this charming beamed tea room in a converted corn mill beside the river Fleam. Savoury snacks like Welsh rarebit, ham and mushroom omelette, salads and cucumber sandwiches are popular, and they are matched by super scones, featherlight sponges and toasted teacakes to enjoy as part of an excellent-value set afternoon tea. Eat in the garden on sunny days. *Unlicensed. No smoking. No dogs.*

ULLSWATER   *Rampsbeck Hotel*

Watermillock, Nr Penrith
MAP 3 C2 *Cumbria*
Pooley Bridge (085 36) 442
P own car park

Open 12–2, also Easter–end Oct
3.30–5.30
Closed 3 Jan–mid Feb

Deep-fried Brie £3.25   Lemon
cheesecake £1.75   ᴇ

Admire the view across Ullswater from the French windows of this pleasant hotel bar, where delicious light lunches are served. Deep-fried Brie with a garlicky tomato coulis, wild mushroom quiche and vegetable ravioli with minced lamb sauce are typically imaginative choices, while equally tempting sweets include individual heart-shaped chocolate cakes filled with fudge cream and traditional baked lemon cheese-cake. Summer teas in the comfortable lounge. Garden.

Credit Access, Visa

ULLSWATER   *Sharrow Bay Country House Hotel Lounge*

Pooley Bridge, Nr Penrith
MAP 3 C2 *Cumbria*
Pooley Bridge (085 36) 301
P own car park

Open 4–4.45
Closed Dec–end Feb

Afternoon tea only £6.50

★   Sink into a deep comfortable sofa and relax in a timeless country house bedecked with flowers, object d'art, fine furniture, crystal and chandeliers. The scene is set for the most exquisite afternoon tea – which cascades over several tables. A choice of loose-leaf teas served in elegant china is accompanied by hot buttered white and brown toast, wholemeal and fruit scones with jam and thick cream, bread and butter, rhubarb jam with a hint of ginger, home-made biscuits, cakes and finger sandwiches. Halfway through the feast, freshly made tea is offered. The service is quite delightful. *Unlicensed. No smoking. No children. No dogs.*   ★

ULVERSTON

Renaissance Bistro

17 Fountain Street
MAP 3 B3 *Cumbria*
Ulverston (0229) 52299
P car park opposite

Open 10-5
Closed Sun & Bank Hols

Vegetable cheese pie with jacket potato
£1.85   Lemon meringue pie 75p

This bustling, well-run bistro forms part of a lively arts centre and is a popular new face in the town. Join the throngs calling in for tea or coffee with cakes and pastries or for more substantial meals. The choice includes delicious home-made soups like cream of tomato and carrot, also wholemeal quiches, jacket potatoes, crisp salads and a hot daily special. Portions are generous, and service is helpful and efficient. *No dogs.*

UPPER SLAUGHTER

Lords of the Manor Hotel

Bourton-on-the-Water
MAP 5 B2 *Gloucestershire*
Cotswold (0451) 20243
P own car park

Open 12.30-2
Closed Sun & Bank Hols

Stuffed breast of chicken £4.95   Exotic
fruit gâteau & ice cream £2   ❷

On sunny days enjoy a light lunch in the lovely gardens of this fine old house. The civilised bar and lounges provide elegant alternatives for a short, tempting selection of seasonally-changing dishes. Subtly seasoned watercress soup or a leaf salad with oak-smoked fish might precede tasty chicken breast filled with Shropshire blue, or steak, kidney and mushroom pie. Finish with hot rhubarb crumble, rice pudding or the cheeseboard. *No dogs.*

Credit Access, Amex, Diners, Visa

WALBERSWICK

Potters Wheel

The Green
MAP 6 F2 *Suffolk*
Southwold (0502) 724468
P street parking

Open 10.30-5.30
Closed Tues & Nov-Mar

Avocado baked in cheese, tomato & nut
stuffing £3.25   Cream tea £1.50   🍵

Lesley Scott's unbounded enthusiasm attracts a steady stream of customers to her charming tea room. They come for the mouth-watering scones and cakes (rich fruit, tangy lemon curd), and for the appetising and varied lunches. A typical selection from the blackboard might include soup or pâté followed by chicken curry or mushroom stroganoff, with fruit crumble or syllabub for afters. Table d'hôte dinner Friday and Saturday evenings.

Credit Access

WALLINGFORD

Annie's Tea Rooms

79 High Street
MAP 5 C3 *Oxfordshire*
Wallingford (0491) 36308
P Castle Street car park

Open 10-5 (till 5.30 in summer), Sun
2.30-5.30
Closed Sun (Sept-May), Wed & Bank
Hols

Cream tea £1.60   Egg mayonnaise
sandwich 90p   🍵

Fresh flowers decorate each table at these pin-neat tea rooms near the town centre. Set teas featuring some fine home baking – toasted teacakes served piping hot, scones with lovely plum jam – are a real treat, and there are delicious cakes, like traditional jam sponge, to enjoy with morning coffee too, Lunchtime brings open sandwiches, salads and ploughman's, as well as soup, jacket potatoes and a daily hot dish. *Unlicensed. No smoking.*

WALLINGFORD   *Lamb Coffee Shop*

Lamb Arcade, High Street
MAP 5 C3 *Oxfordshire*
Wallingford (0491) 33581
P   Castle Street car park

Open   10–5, Sat 9.30–5.30
Closed   Sun & 25 & 26 Dec

Fillet of pork in mustard sauce £2.95
Seafood strudel £2.95   🍵

When you reach the top floor of the antique arcade set in a Georgian hotel, you'll find the Taskers' small self-service coffee shop. A blackboard menu offers specials like pâtés, home-made soups, filled jacket potatoes, tuna niçoise, roast chicken, rollmop herrings and freshly made salads. There's a fine array of home-made goodies for sweets such as caramel shortbread or fresh cream meringues. A large selection of speciality teas, along with traditional varieties, is offered. Children's portions.

WALTON-ON-THE-NAZE   *Naze Links Café*

Old Hall Lane
MAP 6 F2 *Essex*
P   Naze car park   &

Open   9–5.30
Closed   Mon (Apr, May & Oct) & all Nov–end Mar

Home-made quiche & salad £1.95
Custard tart 35p   🍵

Right on the cliff top you will find this café with a sunny terrace offering views of the coastline up to Harwich and Felixstowe. It doubles as a souvenir shop, but the home baking is a strong attraction, and ranges from savouries like sausage rolls, toasted sandwiches, made-to-order filled rolls, quiches and ploughman's. Sweet delights on offer include fruit cake, coconut cake, iced coffee and walnut sponge, bread pudding, apple pie and egg custard tart. *Unlicensed.*

WANSFORD-IN-ENGLAND   *Haycock Hotel Lounge*

London Road, Nr Peterborough
MAP 6 D1 *Cambridgeshire*
Stamford (0780) 782223
P   own car park

Open   12–10.30

Mushrooms in garlic £3.25   Lasagne £4.85   🍵

The riverside garden, comfortable bar and lounge provide a choice of settings to suit everyone at this old coaching inn. A tempting cold buffet offers cold cuts and salads, while appetising hot dishes range from soup and herby baked mushrooms to stir-fried vegetables with black beans and seafood pancakes, plus steaks, chops and sausages barbecued in the garden on fine days. Scones, cakes and sandwiches for afternoon tea. *No dogs.*

Credit   Access, Amex, Diners, Visa

WANTAGE   *Vale & Downland Museum Centre*

Old Surgery, Church Street
MAP 5 C3 *Oxfordshire*
Wantage (023 57) 66838
P   Civic Hall car park

Open   10.30–4.30, Sun & Bank Hols 2.30–5
Closed   Mon & 1 wk Xmas

Asparagus quiche & salad £2.50
Lemon sponge 50p   🍵

A 17th century cloth merchant's house now contains Wantage's museum of local life and its coffee shop. A favourite with locals who meet here to enjoy a range of cakes (like lemon sponge, coffee cake and flapjacks baked by volunteers) and the Earl Grey or Darjeeling tea and fresh coffee. You can also have a light lunch of soup, savoury pies, pâté, jacket potatoes and salads, all attractively displayed at the self-service hatch. *Unlicensed. No smoking. No dogs.*

WARE   *Sunflowers*

7 Amwell End
MAP 6 D2 *Hertfordshire*
Ware (0920) 3358
P car park next to Ware Station

Open 10-5 (Thurs till 1.30)
Closed Sun & Bank Hols

Leek croustade £1.50   Mixed pepper
quiche 79p

Above a small wholefood shop is this very
simple vegetarian restaurant which, although rather sparse, offers tasty, wholesome dishes. Making use of mostly organic
produce, they will tempt you with good
soups, leek and mushroom pie (with light
wholemeal pastry and a generous tasty
filling), salads, filled jacket potatoes and
vegeburgers. There's a good selection of
sweet things too, including generous portions of moist passion cake or a winter
tart. *No smoking. No dogs.*

LVs

WAREHAM   *N·E·W ENTRY*   *Priory Hotel*

Church Green
MAP 5 B4 *Dorset*
Wareham (092 95) 51666
P own car park

Open 3-5

Priory 'Ritzy' tea £5.50   Pot of tea
& gâteau £2.30 🍵

Just a short walk from Wareham's riverside
car park and you can take tea with elegance
in the drawing room or riverside garden of
the 16th century Priory. Stephen West's
kitchen provides lovely gâteaux and shortbreads, a generous pot of good tea and at
lunchtime, light snacks and sandwiches.
The Ritzy tea is a feast – cucumber and
fresh salmon sandwiches, warm scones
with Dorset clotted cream and a slice of
gâteau. *Minimum charge £3. No children. No dogs.*

Credit Access, Amex, Diners, Visa

WARMINSTER   *Jenner's*

45 Market Place
MAP 5 B3 *Wiltshire*
Warminster (0985) 213385
P car park at rear

Open 9.30-5.30
Closed Sun Oct-Mar & all 25 Dec-2 Jan

Leeks au gratin & salad £2.95   Red
pepper & nut risotto £2.15 🍵

Stock up at the wholefood counter after
enjoying your snack in the café or in the
courtyard with its small arts and crafts
market. Pleasant waitresses serve you with
salads, flapjacks, carob cakes, cookies,
sandwiches or moist, fruity date and walnut
slice along with your choice of traditional
or herbal teas. There are summer cream
teas and more elaborate meals on Friday
and Saturday evenings and Sundays. *Unlicensed, but bring your own. No smoking. No dogs.*

WARMINSTER   *Vincent's*

60 East Street
MAP 5 B3 *Wiltshire*
Warminster (0985) 215052
P street parking

Open 11.45-2.30
Closed Sun & Mon lunch & 3-4 wks
from 26 Dec

Chicken salad £2.85   Spinach & cream
cheese pancake £2.15 🅔 🍵

Anne Werrell's Belgian origins shine
through in her robust, enjoyable cooking
at this pleasant restaurant which has a
charming patio for alfresco eating. Vegetable soup, savoury pancakes and salad
niçoise are typical light lunchtime dishes
or starters, while more substantial offerings include brill in lemon and parsley
sauce, calf's liver Lyonnaise and fillet
steak. Don't miss the delicious treacle tart
for afters. More elaborate evening meals.
No dogs.

Credit Access, Visa

WARSOP

Goff's

4 Burns Lane
MAP 5 C1 *Nottinghamshire*
Mansfield (0623) 844137
P car park opposite

Open 12–2
Closed Sat, Mon & Bank Hols

Creamed garlic mushroom salad £1.95
Fillet of beef au poivre £5.95

The lunch menu here is good value for money; only fresh ingredients are used and Lynne and Graham Goff give a warm, friendly welcome to their many guests. It is possible to have just a starter, such as bolognese pancake or melon with fresh fruit and ginger, followed by a delicious, fluffy, sticky, hot toffee pudding. Main courses are imaginatively cooked by the bold confident chef, and an à la carte menu is available for lunch and dinner. *No dogs.*

Credit Access, Amex, Diners, Visa

WARWICK

Bar Roussel

62a Market Place
MAP 5 B2 *Warwickshire*
Warwick (0926) 491983
P Market Place car park

Open 11.30–2.15 & 7–9.45
Closed Sun lunch & 25 Dec

Brazil nut rissoles with mushroom sauce £2.95 Prawns in garlic mayonnaise £1.70 ℮

The atmosphere is relaxed and friendly at this comfortable and popular wine bar. A cold counter featuring quiches, pâtés and salads is supplemented by daily hot specials from the blackboard that always include a flavoursome soup (like our fresh tomato and orange), as well as more substantial dishes such as stuffed peppers and lamb with rosemary. Simple home-made sweets include raspberry sorbet and lemon meringue pie. *No children. No dogs.*

LVs

WARWICK

Brethren's Kitchen

Lord Leycester Hospital
MAP 5 B2 *Warwickshire*
Warwick (0926) 492797
P own car park &

Open 10–5
Closed Sun & Nov–Easter

Filled jacket potato £1.40 Leycester loaf 45p

Vivienne Robinson runs this characterful tea room, in the heart of the Lord Leycester Hospital, with immense charm and friendliness. Her short, uncomplicated menu includes a choice of freshly made sandwiches (egg and cress, salmon and cucumber), salads and a delicious cheese and onion quiche, together with some lovely home-baked goodies – perhaps chocolate gâteau, cherry shortbread or tangy lemon sponge. Consistently enjoyable standards; friendly, informal service. *Unlicensed. No dogs.*

WARWICK

Charlotte's Tea Rooms

6 Jury Street
MAP 5 B2 *Warwickshire*
Warwick (0926) 498930
P market place

Open 10–5.30 (Sun from 11)
Closed 25 & 26 Dec & 2 wks Nov

Chicken & mushroom pie £2.95
Scones with cream & jam £1.50

On a handsome street in historic Warwick this quintessentially English tea shop is run with great charm by Mrs Lubrano. Accomplished home baking produces a good selection of cakes (moist banana and coffee sponge) and scones to enjoy with a fragrant brew, while at lunchtime there is soup and a robust daily special such as chuck steak casserole with dumplings. Omelettes are available all day. *Unlicensed. No smoking. No dogs.*

WARWICK   *Piccolino's Pizzeria*

31 Smith Street
MAP 5 B2 *Warwickshire*
Warwick (0926) 491020
P Nibbs car park

Open 12–2.30 & 5.30–11 (Fri & Sat till 11.30 & Sun till 10.30)
Closed 25 & 26 Dec

Piccolino's pizza £3.40   Lasagne £3.50

The pizza dough is kneaded in full view of the customers here, and toppings added before baking in the corner oven in this simple friendly pizzeria just out of the centre of Warwick. All the usual permutations of toppings are available, and a short selection of starters include minestrone and antipasto. Pasta dishes are also on the menu, and desserts are simple – cheesecake, profiteroles and Italian ice creams. *No dogs.*

Credit Access

WATERPERRY   *Waterperry Gardens Tea Shop*

Waterperry Horticultural Centre, Nr Wheatley
MAP 5 C3 *Oxfordshire*
Ickford (084 47) 254
P own car park

Open 10–5.30 (Sat & Sun till 6 & winter till 4.30)
Closed 1 wk Xmas

Chicken pie & salad £3.10   Carrot cake 55p 🍵 ☕

Part of a horticultural centre that includes a plant and garden shop and lovely ornamental gardens, this simple tea room offers a selection of interesting snacks to enjoy with a reviving brew. A long self-service counter displays scones, caramel shortbread, flapjacks and delicious cakes, such as tangy lemon, while at luchtime you can tuck into soup and ploughman's, cheese flan or chicken pie. *Non-smoking area. No dogs.*

Credit Access, Amex, Visa

WELLS   *Cloister Restaurant*

Wells Cathedral
MAP 8 D1 *Somerset*
Wells (0749) 76543
P market place

Open 10–5 (Sun from 2); Nov–Feb 11–4 & Sun 2–5
Closed 2 wks Xmas

Vegetable bake £1.80   Ham & broccoli flan £1.35 🍵

The splendid stone-vaulted cloisters of Wells Cathedral make a splendid setting for appetising snacks available throughout the day. Home baking is much in evidence on the self-service counter, which offers scones, flapjacks and fruit cakes, along with soup and a daily-changing savoury flan at lunchtime. Other midday options might include chicken curry or cauliflower cheese, with delicious hot tropical trifle for afters. *No smoking. No dogs.*

WELLS   *Good Earth*

4 Priory Road
MAP 8 D1 *Somerset*
Wells (0749) 78600
P own car park

Open 9.30–5.30
Closed Sun

Brazil nut roast £1.40   Pineapple upside down pudding £1.15 🍵 ☕

Healthy snacks based on natural, unrefined produce can be enjoyed at this rustic wholefood restaurant with a leafy courtyard. Traditional cakes such as Somerset apple dappy and flapjacks go well with speciality teas and pure fruit juices, while the savoury choice extends from soup, salads, pizzas and flans to daily specials like mushroom and cashew nut pie. Now open for restaurant meals Wednesday to Saturday. *Non-smoking area. No dogs.*

Credit Access

WEST BYFLEET   *Janes Upstairs*

51 Old Woking Road
MAP 6 D3 *Surrey*
Byfleet (093 23) 40366
P car park opposite

Open 12–2 & 6–10
Closed Sun, Mon & some Bank Hols

Lemon sole £4.50   Egg mayonnaise
£1.20   ☻

Jane is from the family which has brought
us the Superfish chain. She runs this pretty
and friendly little fish restaurant above the
local branch. The main courses are the
splendid fresh fish from downstairs, with
their lovely crisp batter and excellent chips.
She offers simple starters like consommé,
prawn cocktail and egg mayonnaise. To
finish, there are a couple of home-made
sweets like crème caramel and delicious
rum and raisin chocolate mousse. *No dogs.*

Credit Visa   LVs

WEST BYFLEET   *Superfish*

51 Old Woking Road
MAP 6 D3 *Surrey*
Byfleet (093 23) 40366
P car park opposite   &

Open 11.30–2 (Sat till 2.30) & 5.30–
10.30 (Fri & Sat till 11)
Closed Sun & some Bank Hols

Cod & chips £2.60   Scampi & chips
£3.95

A small selection of good fish is on offer at
this spotlessly clean, light and cheerful
place, one of a chain of similar restaurants.
There are fillets of plaice, haddock, huss,
sole, whole plaice on the bone and halibut
steaks all served with well-cooked chips,
nice, crusty French bread and a pickle and
sauce trolley. For sweet there are various
ice creams. Children's platter. *No dogs.*

LVs

---

*Changes in data sometimes occur in
establishments after the Guide goes to press.*

*Prices should be taken as indications
rather than firm quotes.*

WESTFIELD   *Casual Cuisine*

Church Lane, Nr Hastings
MAP 6 E4 *East Sussex*
Hastings (0424) 751137
P own car park

Open 12–2 & 7–9.30
Closed Sun–Tues, Bank Hols (except
Good Fri), 2 days Xmas & all Jan

African bobotie & rice £2.95   Turkey in
spicy peanut sauce £4.95   ☻

A cosmopolitan menu sets the tastebuds
tingling at this informal, bistro-style restaurant run with great enthusiasm by Tony
and Heather Symonds. Lunchtime brings
a wide-ranging choice from the blackboard
– perhaps crab pâté or mushrooms à la
grecque, followed by chicken Mexican or
an interesting special like spicy African
bobotie. More elaborate evening meals are
served and simple sweets include home-
made ices. Garden. *Non-smoking area.
No dogs.*

Credit Access, Amex, Diners, Visa

WHITBY *Magpie Café*

14 Pier Road
MAP 4 E2 *North Yorkshire*
Whitby (0947) 602058
P Khyber Pass Street

Open 11.30–6.30

Closed Nov–1 wk before Easter

Lemon sole & chips £3.50   Black Forest trifle £1.10   Sticky sultana loaf £1.10   Crab & prawn salad £4.95

★ Go for the superbly fresh seafood at this lovely café which looks out on to the fishing quay below. It has been run by the Mckenzie family for over 40 years, and they are still full of zest for the job. The set lunches are difficult to resist, with Whitby crab to start, and main courses featuring cod, haddock, plaice, sole, lobster and, for meat-eaters, steak, grilled ham or turkey breast. Chips are excellent, as are the salads which include salmon, crab or de-luxe fish platter. Home-made sweets to finish such as lemon trifle, Yorkshire curd cheesecake, or several gluten-free, wholefood and fat-free choices. Cakes accompany afternoon tea. Children's menu. *Non-smoking area. No dogs.* ★

WILLERBY   N·E·W ENTRY   *Cedars at Grange Park Hotel*

MAP 4 E3 *Humberside*
Hull (0482) 656488
P own car park &

Open 10am–10.30pm

Pizza Napoli £3.60
Chicken Kiev £4.40

Sit in the friendly, informal bar or leafy conservatory of this popular hotel to browse through the vast menu of brasserie-style snacks available. Pizzas and pasta dishes are abundantly well represented, there are ploughman's and smashing French bread sandwiches, plus more substantial offerings such as beef stroganoff or steak tartare. Cakes and scones accompany morning coffee and afternoon tea, and sweets include exotic speciality ices. *No dogs.*

Credit Access, Amex, Diners, Visa

WILLERBY *Raffaele's*

Well Lane
MAP 4 E3 *Humberside*
Hull (0482) 652616
P own car park

Open 12–2 & 7–11
Closed 2 days Xmas

Pizza Margherita £2.90   Spaghetti
Carbonara £3.60

Marble-topped tables and Italian flag colours create the setting for the competently prepared Italian food in the Willerby Manor Hotel. Try the steaming hot minestrone or the avocado with seafood filling as a starter. Main dishes include various pastas and pizzas like pescatore pizza with prawns, mussels and calamari and tagliatelle with ham and mushrooms in béchamel sauce or canelloni with spicy tomato and salami filling. *No dogs.*

Credit Access, Amex, Visa

WILLITON   *Blackmore's Bookshop Tea Room*

6 High Street
MAP 8 C1 *Somerset*
Williton (0984) 32227
P street parking

Open 9–5.30 (Sat till 1pm)
Closed Sun & Bank Hols

Cottage pie £1.95   Lasagne £2.05

At the back of a small bookshop, this simply decorated and cosy tea room offers a tempting selection of home-made fare. Savoury snacks include jacket potatoes with a variety of fillings like bacon, onion and garlic butter, shepherd's pie, vegetable casserole, plus a range of salads. A daily selection of cakes could include flapjacks, fruit slices or coffee cake. In the summer you can eat out on the patio.

WILLITON   *N·E·W ENTRY*   *Orchard Mill*

off Bridge Street
MAP 8 C1 *Somerset*
Williton (0984) 32133
P own car park &

Open 10–6
Closed Tues (in winter), Mon, Jan & Feb

Pork in cider sauce £2.95   Steak & Guinness pie £2.95

Standing beside a working 17th-century waterwheel, the original mill house is now the setting for some robust, wholesome cooking. Lunchtimes are a highlight, when soup can be followed by grilled gammon or wholemeal pasta cheesebake and, finally, delicious blackcurrant crumble. Lighter alternatives include quiches, ploughman's and jacket potatoes, while sandwiches, salads, splendid cakes and scones are available all day. Traditional Sunday lunch. *Unlicensed. No smoking. No dogs.*

WIMBORNE MINSTER   *Quinneys*

26 West Borough
MAP 8 D2 *Dorset*
Wimborne (0202) 883518
P street parking &

Open 9.15–5.15
Closed Sun, Mon, 1 Jan & 25 & 26 Dec & 1 wk Spring Bank Hol

Fried liver & grilled bacon £3.60   Dorset cream tea £1.75 ❤

Quite simply the best tea and coffee house in the area. The Skidmore family have been running their bakery and eating house for almost a quarter of a century now, and they continue to delight customers with such favourites as coffee and walnut cake, macaroons, shortbreads, scones, and their renowned Dorset apple cake. A traditional English breakfast is available along with teacakes and crumpets, and a blackboard lists lunchtime options such as chicken and leek soup and grilled trout. Children's menu. *Non-smoking area. No dogs.*

WINCHELSEA   *Finches of Winchelsea*

12 High Street
MAP 6 E4 *East Sussex*
Rye (0797) 226234
P street parking

Open 10.30–6 & 7.30–9.30 (Fri & Sat)
Closed Wed (Nov–April)

Wiener schnitzel £3.60   Coffee & walnut gâteau 80p

Next to the village Post Office, this cottagy little restaurant makes a delightful place to linger over a good range of home-cooked snacks. New chef-patron Dik Evans offers a particularly appetising lunchtime selection, from excellent vegetable or chilli pasties to fishermen's pie, ploughman's and a speciality veal dish. Splendid home baking too: look out for the delicious lemon gâteau and nutty, chocolate-covered Ischler biscuits. Garden. *Non-smoking area. No dogs.*

Credit Access, Amex, Diners, Visa

Owen Meredith
1831–91

He may live without love – what is passion but pining?
But where is the man who can live without dining?
Lucile

Bennett Cerf

Good manners: The noise you don't make when you're
eating soup.
Laughing Stock (1945)

Marie Dressler

If ants are such busy workers, how come they find time
to go to all the picnics?
Cited by Cowan in *The Wit of Women*

P. B. Shelley
1792–1822

Though we eat little flesh and drink no wine,
Yet let's be merry: we'll have tea and toast;
Custards for supper, and an endless host
of syllabubs and jellies and mince pies,
And other such lady-like luxuries.
Letter to Maria Gisborne

WINCHELSEA   *Winchelsea Tea Room*

Hiham Green
MAP 6 E4 *East Sussex*
Rye (0797) 226679
P   street parking

Open   2.30–6 (Sat & Sun from 12)
Closed   Mon, Fri & Dec–end Feb

Quiche & salad £1.80   Smoked
mackerel fillets £1.65   🍵

A delightfully old-fashioned tea room with
lace curtains at the window and a central
table piled high with Linda Rankin's home-
baked goodies. Look out for her light
scones, tangy lemon gâteau, gooey caramel
slice and rich fruit cake, or opt for a simple
savoury like Welsh rarebit or a toasted
sandwich. Other tasty lunchtime snacks
include baked mackerel fillets, a Cheddar
ploughman's and filled jacket potatoes.
No dogs.

Credit   Access, Visa

WINCHESTER   *Mr Pitkin's*

4 Jewry Street
MAP 5 C3 *Hampshire*
Winchester (0962) 69630
P   library car park in Jewry Street

Open   11.30–2.30 & 6–11
Closed   25 Dec

Chicken & ham pie £4.25   Sole stuffed
with prawns £4.25   🏠

Bare wooden floors, poster-framed wine
labels and an abundance of greenery
combine to produce a very pleasant setting
for sampling the excellent food in this wine
bar underneath a restaurant. Brunch consists of croissants, kedgeree, kippers and
coffee, and other hot dishes on offer are
sole with prawns and vegetable or chicken
and ham pie. The menu is varied and
includes five vegetarian choices, as well as
a selection of salads, cold meats, quiches
and cheeses. Gâteau or cheesecake for
afters. *Non-smoking area (lunchtimes).*

Credit   Access, Amex, Diners, Visa

WINDERMERE   *Miller Howe Hotel*

Rayrigg Road
MAP 3 C3 *Cumbria*
Windermere (096 62) 2536
P   own car park

Open   3–5
Closed   early Dec–mid Mar

Afternoon tea £3   🍵

Enjoy the magical view from the terrace
while you take afternoon tea or retreat to
the peaceful, antique-filled lounges of this
much-loved Lakeland hotel. Friendly staff
will serve you with freshly baked scones
and a lovely moist fruit loaf, together with
a mouthwatering selection of cakes such
as cream-filled brandy snaps and baby
meringues, chocolate éclairs, butterfly
buns and delicious little fresh raspberry
tartlets. *No smoking.*

Credit   Access, Amex, Diners, Visa

WINDERMERE   *Miller Howe Kaff*

Alexandra Buildings
MAP 3 C3 *Cumbria*
Windermere (096 62) 2255
P   own parking

Open   10–4
Closed   Sun & 25 & 26 Dec

Vegetable terrine £1.90   Banana, walnut
& ginger pie with butterscotch sauce
& cream £1.25   🍵

Produce made at John Tovey's celebrated
Miller Howe Hotel is the basis for the
gourmet dishes (at budget prices) offered
at this bright little café sharing space with
a kitchenware shop. Typical delights might
include a colourful vegetable terrine, sole
stuffed with salmon and avocado, super
salads and irresistible sweets like hot
strawberry and apple pie or Grand Marnier-
laced chocolate slice. *No smoking. No
dogs.*

WINDERMERE

Victoria Cottage

21 Victoria Street
MAP 3 C3 *Cumbria*
Windermere (096 62) 5234
P street parking

Open 12–5.30 (Sun from 2.30)
Closed Thurs, all Jan–Feb

Cumbrian rarebit £1.50   Lancashire
muffins 60p   🍵   🍵

Philip and Jane Butcher run their delightful
little tea shop with great professionalism.
Simple snacks like home-made pâté and
filled granary baps are available all day,
while hot lunchtime dishes might include
wine-enriched cottage pie. Exemplary
cream teas could feature a splendidly rich
orange fruit cake served, North Country
style, with Cumbrian farmhouse cheese.
Lovely Lakeland brew, too, specially
blended for Lakes water. More elaborate
evening menu. *No smoking.*

WINDSOR

Angelo's Wine Bar

5 St Leonards Road
MAP 6 D3 *Berkshire*
Windsor (0753) 857600
P William Street car park

Open 12–2.30 & 5.30–11
Closed Sun & Bank Hols

Moules marinière £3   Chicken Kiev
£5.85

In this simple little Italian restaurant with
a small bar area there are some pleasant,
honest dishes to enjoy. For starters, you
might like the home-made minestrone or
the egg mayonnaise with a pleasing garnish
and for a choice of main course perhaps
the escalope Neopolitan with good spaghetti, chicken Kiev or grilled sole. There
are some nice sweets like apple pie, ice
creams and fresh fruit in season. Children's
portions. *No dogs.*

Credit Access, Amex, Diners, Visa

WINDSOR

Dôme

5 Thames Street
MAP 6 D3 *Berkshire*
Windsor (0753) 864405
P King Edward Court car park

Open 9–11 (Sun till 10.30)
Closed 25 & 26 Dec

Continental breakfast £2.20   Croque-
monsieur £1.80   🍵

Go through the lively bar and café to the
restaurant area at the rear, where French
posters adorn the high walls. Croissants
or pain au chocolat are served all day, or
you can opt for one of the house specialities
which range from pâté, Brie Amandine and
filled baguettes to steaks, chilli, omelettes,
charcuterie or an imaginative salad served
in a deep white china bowl. Excellent citron
pressé, and good sweets and coffees. *No
children after 7.30 unless accompanied
by an adult. No dogs.*

Credit Access, Amex, Visa

WIRKSWORTH

Crown Yard Kitchen

Heritage Centre, Market Place
MAP 4 D4 *Derbyshire*
Wirksworth (062 982) 2020
P street parking

Open 9–5
Closed Sun (in winter) & 25 & 26 Dec

Cod mornay £1.95   Apple strudel 85p
🍵

Adjoining the town's Heritage Centre, this
bright, airy restaurant makes a useful stop
for a good hot lunch. Satisfying alternatives might include moussaka, cod mornay
and shepherd's pie. There are lighter
choices too, like jacket potatoes, and
various salads. Cakes, biscuits and specialist teas are available all day, and service is
friendly and helpful. On Friday and Saturday evenings a more sophisticated menu
operates. *No smoking lunchtime. No
dogs.*

WOKINGHAM   *Setters Bistro*

49 Peach Street
MAP 5 C3 *Berkshire*
Wokingham (0734) 788893
P   Easthampstead Street car park

Open 12–2.30
Closed Sun & Bank Hols

Chicken Kiev £5.95   Jugged venison
£7.50   ℗

Overlooking the main street, this pleasant restaurant has a relaxed '60s' feel to it. A blackboard lists the lunchtime specials: leek and potato soup, courgette and prawn au gratin, chicken goulash, beef curry, steak and kidney pie, or cauliflower cheese. Puddings are particularly good; banana cake with rum butter, treacle tart or oranges in caramel. More elaborate meals in the evening. *No dogs.*

Credit Access, Amex, Diners, Visa

WOODBRIDGE   *The Wine Bar*

17 The Thoro'fare
MAP 6 F2 *Suffolk*
Woodbridge (039 43) 2557
P   Oak Lane car park

Open 12–2 & 7.30–9.30
Closed Sun, Mon & 25 & 26 Dec

Pigeon breast with bacon & red wine
sauce £2.50   Cabbage & pickled walnut
timbale with red pepper sauce £4.90

In this pretty upstairs wine bar Sally O'Gorman offers imaginative dishes chalked upon a blackboard. Try the spicy black bean soup or the prawn-filled pancakes with delicious bread for starters. Main courses could be stuffed loin of pork with kumquats, quail on croutons, or an interesting salad with lemony vinaigrette. Don't miss the delicious sweets like home-made brown bread ice cream or Calvados and apple cheesecake. *No children. No dogs.*

WOODSTOCK   *Brothertons Brasserie*

1 High Street
MAP 5 C2 *Oxfordshire*
Woodstock (0993) 811114
P   street parking

Open 10.30am–10.30pm
Closed 1 Jan & 25 & 26 Dec

Brothertons smokies £2.50   Chocolate
mousse £1.75

Pine tables, polished floorboards and genuine gas lighting provide the uncluttered setting at this town-centre brasserie. Morning coffee and croissants and afternoon tea and scones flank the lunchtime offerings of baked smokies, garlic steak, chicken stuffed with hazelnuts and Camembert or one of the week's specials like best end of lamb with mint and red wine sauce. Sweets include rum truffle cake and a quite superb apple crumble.

Credit Access, Amex, Diners, Visa

WOODSTOCK   *Feathers Hotel, Garden Bar*

Market Street
MAP 5 C2 *Oxfordshire*
Woodstock (0993) 812291
P   street parking

Open 12.30–2.15

Feathers salad £4.50   Supreme of
chicken £4.50

The delightful garden makes a lovely setting in which to enjoy some imaginative dishes available from the bar menu of this renowned town-centre hotel. Soup of the day or deep-fried mushrooms with garlic mayonnaise might precede orange-flavoured venison casserole, chicken supreme in a mildly curried sauce or a herby ham and onion quiche. Round things off with chocolate mousse or a satisfying hot sweet. *No dogs.*

Credit Access, Amex, Diners, Visa

WOODSTOCK — *Feathers Hotel Lounge*

Market Street
MAP 5 C2 *Oxfordshire*
Woodstock (0993) 812291
P street parking

Open 3.30–5.30

Afternoon tea £4.50 🥄

The elegant panelled lounge of this town-centre hotel provides the perfect setting for afternoon tea. The set price menu allows you to choose from China or Ceylon tea and includes a selection of fresh sandwiches followed by scones with jam and delicious whipped cream, and finishes with a choice of home-made cakes – brandy snaps, lemon cake or shortbread. Attractive crockery and courteous service add an extra feel of elegance. *No dogs.*

Credit Access, Amex, Diners, Visa

WOOL — *Rose Mullion Tea Room*

3 Station Road, Nr Wareham
MAP 8 D2 *Dorset*
Bindon Abbey (0929) 462542
P own car park &

Open 8.30–5
Closed Mon (except Bank Hols), 2 wks Xmas

Mushroom & nut fettucine £2.50
Dorset cream tea £1.80

New family owners are running this pretty little tea room attached to a 16th-century thatched cottage. Oven-warm scones, rich, moist fruit cake and toasted teacakes remain favourite teatime treats, while lunch could be a three-course special (perhaps egg mayonnaise followed by Dorset hot pot, with peach and apple crumble for afters) or something light like Welsh rarebit, a burger or filled jacket potato. Traditional Sunday roast available. Garden. *Non-smoking area. No dogs.*

WOOLPIT — *The Bakery*

Nr Bury St Edmunds
MAP 6 E2 *Suffolk*
Elmswell (0359) 40255
P street parking

Open 12–2.30
Closed Sun & Mon

Game pie £3.60   Roast Suffolk ham
£4.20 🌣

Mellow red-brick walls, quarry tiles on the floor and refectory-type tables set the scene in this pleasant restaurant. At lunchtime there are simple choices like soup of the day, ploughman's, fish or country pâté, pizza, tasty poacher's pie, good-looking Suffolk ham on the bone and salads. There is always a vegetarian dish of the day. In the evenings there is a fixed price dinner menu. *Non-smoking area. No dogs.*

WOOTTON BASSETT — *N·E·W ENTRY* — *Emms*

147 High Street
MAP 5 B3 *Wiltshire*
Wootton Bassett (0793) 854783
P street parking

Open 9.30–5
Closed Sun, Bank Hols, 1 Jan
& 25 & 26 Dec

Vegetarian bean soup 85p   Chicken
casserole £2.85

Polished cooking, a pristine interior and the personal service of Marilyn O'Hara make this smart café opposite the church eminently visitable. Fresh home-made soup, cakes and savouries can be eaten in or taken away. At lunchtime there is a vegetarian choice – savoury pancakes, soup or quiche – and plenty for the children. Follow chicken and almond tomato crevettes or beef bourguignon with a mouth-watering chocolate roulade. Freshly brewed afternoon tea with delicious scones. *No dogs.*

WOOTTON COMMON   *N.E.W ENTRY*   *Lugleys Tea Gardens*

Staplers Road
MAP 5 C4 *Isle of Wight*
Isle of Wight (0983) 882202
P Own car park

Open 10–5
Closed Bank Hols & Oct–end May

Egg baked with smoked haddock £2.25
Strawberry shortcake £1

Angela Hewitt pays commendable attention to detail at her pretty country restaurant where teas, coffees and light lunches can be enjoyed either in the delightful garden or airy conservatory. Potted shrimps, Welsh rarebit and crusty bread with gourmet sausages, home-baked ham, or fresh salmon, all make delicious midday snacks. For sweet-tooths there's banana cheesecake, gâteau St. Emilion, scones and seasonal strawberry shortcake.

Credit Access, Amex

WORCESTER   *Natural Break*

4 The Hopmarket/17 Mealcheapen
Street
MAP 5 B2 *Hereford & Worcester*
Worcester (0905) 26654/26417
P Cornmarket pay & display   &
(Hopmarket)

Open 10–4, Sat 10–5 (Mealcheapen Street from 9.30)
Closed Sun & Bank Hols (except Good Fri)

Cheese & onion quiche 85p   Fruit pie 75p

There are now three branches (see Kidderminster), in this chain of self-service restaurants, all offering freshly cooked sweet and savoury items throughout the day. Crunchy, imaginative salads – sweetcorn, butter bean and broccoli – go beautifully with tasty flans like cheese and spinach or chicken and celery, and there are pasties, sausage rolls and sandwiches, too. Sweet treats include lemon meringue pie and cherry slice. *Unlicensed. Non-smoking area. No dogs.*

LVs

WORTHING   *Fogarty's*

10 Prospect Place, off Montague
Street
MAP 6 D4 *West Sussex*
Worthing (0903) 212984
P Prospect Street car park

Open 9.30–5

Closed All Sun & Mon, most Bank Hols, 2 wks Feb & last wk Sept–1st wk Oct

Asparagus, celery & mushroom flan £1.80   Strawberry tartlet £1.20   Wholemeal flan & salad £2.80

★ Marjorie Denney and her daughter Jane Ambridge keep the compact counter of their simply furnished and spotlessly maintained, quarry-tiled tea room, laden with the output of their hard working kitchen. There will be honey and brandy walnut loaf, eye-catching, tasty and liberally filled strawberry tartlets and buttery shortbread, topped with caramel and chocolate among the treats. Well brewed coffee comes in individual pots. At lunchtime neat blackboards list daily specials like broccoli and smoked haddock flan or gammon ham Hawaiian. There's a tempting range of salads too. *Non-smoking area upstairs. No dogs.* ★

WORTHING   *Mr Pastry*

8 Warwick Lane
MAP 6 D4 *West Sussex*
Worthing (0903) 212780
P Guildbourne Centre car park

Open 9-5
Closed Sun & most Bank Hols

Cheese salad £1.50   Danish pastry 50p
🫖

Choose your cakes and pastries from the pâtisserie adjoining this neat, pine-furnished café in a little shopping arcade, and they will be brought through to your table. Sweet treats like Danish pastries, rum truffles, mille-feuilles, chocolate cake and flapjacks are all very enjoyable, while on the savoury side there are pasties and quiches, sausage rolls, sandwiches and steak and kidney pie. *Unlicensed. Non-smoking area. No dogs.*

WORTHING   *Nature's Way Coffee Shop*

130 Montague Street
MAP 6 D4 *West Sussex*
Worthing (0903) 209931
P street parking

Open 9.30-5
Closed Sun & Bank Hols

Spinach & Stilton pancakes £1.70
Chick pea casserole £1.70 🫖

Imaginative vegetarian fare is the speciality of this spacious, self-service restaurant above a wholefood shop. A wide range of salads, delicious wholemeal flans (try Stilton and celery), soup and jacket potatoes are backed up by daily hot dishes – perhaps chick pea casserole, broccoli and walnut bake or leek and cauliflower lasagne. Finish with a simple fruit trifle or a superb carrot cake. *Unlicensed. Non-smoking area. No dogs.*

Credit Access **LVs**

WORTHING   *N·E·W ENTRY*   *River Kwai*

16 Ambrose Place
MAP 6 D4 *West Sussex*
Worthing (0903) 211901
P street parking

Open 12-2.30 & 6-11.30
Closed Sun & 3 days Xmas

Pud Thai £4.50   Kao pud £3.50

In a side street off the main shopping street the friendly River Kwai provides good food in stylish surroundings. The menu offers a balanced selection of authentic oriental dishes: interestingly named 'son-in-law's eggs' has a subtle sweet and sour sauce; beef with oyster sauce has a crisp, sharp flavour; carefully prepared prawns with asparagus is another tasty item. The waitresses will offer friendly advice to customers unfamiliar with the oriental dishes. *No children. No dogs.*

Credit Access, Diners, Visa

YARM   *Coffee Shop*

44 High Street
MAP 4 D2 *Cleveland*
Eaglescliffe (0642) 782101
P own car park

Open 9-5
Closed Sun & Bank Hols

Yorkshire curd cake 90p   Quiche
lorraine 95p 🫖

Climb to the top floor of a gift shop in Yarm's main street to reach this delightful coffee shop. There are simple snacks like mulligatawny soup with just the right hint of curry, quiches, a variety of omelettes and filled jacket potatoes, salads or toasted sandwiches. You can choose more substantial dishes like lasagne with salad and cheesy prawns with a provençale sauce. There is a tempting display of sweets and a good selection of cheese too. Eat alfresco in the courtyard in summer. *No dogs.*

YARMOUTH   *Jireh House*

St James's Square
MAP 5 C4 *Isle of Wight*
Isle of Wight (0983) 760513
P in square

Open 8.45–6
Closed Jan & Feb

Shepherd's pie £1.65   Lemon & almond
gâteau £1   🍵

The atmosphere is cosy and relaxing at
this antique-furnished tea room in a 17th
century building on the main square. A
tempting range of home baking – from
scones and shortbread to lemon and
almond gâteau or banana cake – accompanies a good cup of tea, while lunchtime
brings such popular savouries as macaroni
cheese, ploughman's and shepherd's pie.
Toasted sandwiches, filled jacket potatoes
and various salads are also available, plus
homely sweets like rhubarb crumble. *No
dogs.*

YEOVIL   *Trugs*

5 Union Street
MAP 5 A4 *Somerset*
Yeovil (0935) 73722
P Peter Street car park

Open 9–5.30
Closed Sun & Bank Hols

Vegetable moussaka £2.10
Chilli beef crumble £2.30   🥮 🍵

Near the town centre is this spacious pine-
furnished wholefood bistro serving food
all day. The display of crisp salads and
sweets, like toffee date pudding, is inviting.
A blackboard lists the day's specials, which
always include one meat, one chicken, one
fish and three or four vegetarian dishes,
one of which is vegan-based. Examples are
tuna and mushroom tagliatelle and cauliflower cheese. *Non-smoking area. No
dogs.*

LVs

YORK   *Bees Knees*

Millers Yard, Gillygate
Town plan C1 *North Yorkshire*
York (0904) 624045
P NCP in Clarence Street

Open 10–5 (Oct–May till 4)
Closed 1 Jan & 25 & 26 Dec

Quiche & salad £2.15   Mushroom soup
& roll £1   🍵

Enjoy a healthy, well balanced and pains-
takingly prepared meal at this simple
wholefood café with its own bakery.
Typical savoury items might include cheese
and potato pie, tofu burgers, samosas and
fluffy tomato and courgette quiche, all
delicious with crunchy-fresh salads incorporating beans and grains. Apple juice
sweetens the excellent cakes, and tempting
desserts like apricot macaroon make a fine
finish. *Unlicensed. No smoking. No dogs.*

YORK   *Bettys*

6 St Helens Square
Town plan C2 *North Yorkshire*
York (0904) 659142
P St Saviour Gate car park

Open 9am–9pm (Sun from 9.30)
Closed 1 Jan & 25 & 26 Dec

Salmon & prawn salad £3.75   Cheese &
bacon potatoes £2.20   🥮 🍵

Unashamedly old fashioned dishes, made
with quality ingredients, are served by
neatly uniformed waitresses. Ceiling fans
hum leisurely to the refrains of the evening
pianist evoking a bygone era. Rarebits
made with Yorkshire ale and dressed with
delicious chutneys or the fried fillet of
haddock with chips are favourites. Choux
pastries, fruit cakes and Yorkshire curd
tart are irresistible. Try the home-made
soup with a cheese and herb roll. Excellent
tea and coffee selection. *No dogs.*

Credit Access, Visa LVs

YORK   *Mulberry Hall Coffee Shop*

Stonegate
Town plan C1 *North Yorkshire*
York (0904) 620736
P St John Street car park

Open 9.30–4.30
Closed Sun, Bank Hols & 1st wk Jan

Welsh rarebit £3   Yorkshire curd tart
60p 🍵

Tucked away in historic Stonegate, above a china shop, this elegant coffee house makes an ideal spot for lingering over tea or coffee. Ginger and chocolate or moist fruit cake, pear tart, cheesecakes and almond slice make a tempting display on the sweet trolley, while savoury options range from freshly-made sandwiches (perhaps egg and cress), to smoked salmon pâté, Welsh rarebit and prawn or mushroom vol-au-vents. *Unlicensed. No dogs.*

Credit Access, Visa

YORK   *Oat Cuisine*

13a High Ousegate
Town plan C2 *North Yorkshire*
York (0904) 627929
P Piccadilly car park

Open 12–3 & 7–11

Closed Sun, 25 & 26 Dec & 1st
wk Jan

Tostada £2.95   Cottage cheese & fresh fruit platter £2.50   Fresh asparagus flummery wrapped in filo pastry £5.35   Hazelnut & passion fruit roulade £2.25 🥗

★ Simplicity and elegance combine to provide the perfect setting for careful cooking and friendly service at this informal vegetarian restaurant. Lunches, dinners and lighter meals served throughout the day are of a high standard. Courgette and mushroom lasagne or tagliatelle provençale are on the lunchtime menu or opt for superb Oat Cuisine club sandwich of houmus, lettuce, tomato, mayonnaise, cheese, cucumber, egg and avocado. A variety of Mexican specialities like huevos rancheros, tostadas and burritos are also available with delicious sweets to follow, such as hazelnut and passion fruit roulade or apricot and almond strudel. Book at weekends. *Minimum charge £2.50 at busy times. Non-smoking area. No dogs.* ★

Credit Access, Amex, Visa

YORK   *St Williams College Restaurant*

3 College Street
Town plan C1 *North Yorkshire*
York (0904) 34830
P St Johns car park in Lord Mayors Walk

Open 10–5 (Sun from 10.30)
Closed 1 Jan, Good Fri & 25 & 26 Dec

Coq au vin £2.50   Beef bourguignon
£2.50 🥗

The building of St Williams College date back as far as 1461, but the coffee shop and courtyard now sport modern furniture. A tempting array of goodies awaits you: tasty Yorkshire curd tarts in good crisp pastry, fresh light fruit, cheese or plain scones, banana flan and traditional trifle. Hot specials range from macaroni cheese to Lancashire hotpot, and lunchtime savoury snacks include raised pies, pâtés, terrines and cold meats, quiches and a choice of salads. *Non-smoking area. No dogs.*

YORK   *Taylors Tea Rooms*

46 Stonegate
Town plan C2 *North Yorkshire*
York (0904) 622865
P Minster car park

Open 9–5.30
Closed 1 Jan & 25 & 26 Dec

Mushroom & blue Wensleydale omelette
£3.20   Toasted Yorkshire loaf 65p ☕
🍵

A delightfully old-fashioned menu matches
the nostalgic charms of these tea rooms
situated above a shop selling teas and
coffees in a 16th-century building. Begin
the day with teacakes, muffins, omelettes
or rarebits. At lunchtime, salads, sandwiches and things-on-toast are offered,
while afternoon treats include cakes and
pastries and rich fruit cakes served, Yorkshire style, with Wensleydale cheese. *Unlicensed. Non-smoking area. No dogs.*

Credit Access, Visa

YORK   *Wholefood Trading Company*

98 Micklegate
Town plan B2 *North Yorkshire*
York (0904) 656804
P Nunnery Lane car park

Open 11–4
Closed Sun, Bank Hols & 3 days Xmas

Quiche & salad £2.80   Artichoke soup
£1.10

Straightforward, nourishing vegetarian
fare is the hallmark of this friendly little
restaurant above a wholefood shop. Thick
vegetable soups served with lovely wholemeal bread, quiches, crunchy salads, mushroom and aubergine moussaka and jacket
potatoes are all popular choices at lunchtime, and there's always a vegan dish of
the day. Sweets include fruit crumble and
trifle, nice cakes like fresh ginger or halva
at other times. *No smoking. No dogs.*

LVs

SCOTLAND

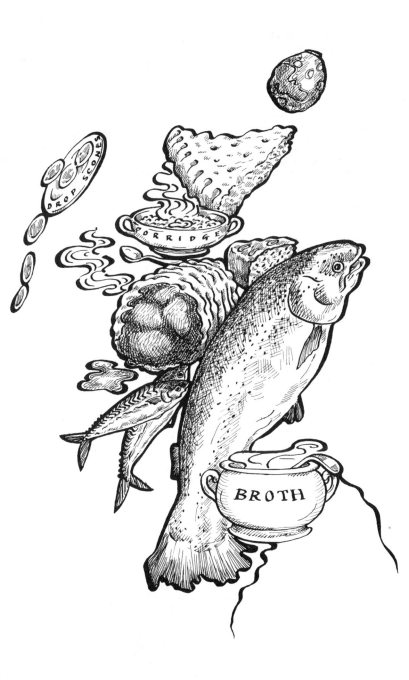

ABOYNE

Ballater Road
MAP 1 C3 *Grampian*
Aboyne (0339) 2249
P street parking

Open 11–6
Closed mid Oct–end Mar

Chicken fillets £3   Sausage, egg
& chips £3.75 🍵

Alford House Restaurant

Part of a stone terrace on the A93, this simple little tea room offers good home baking and hearty unpretentious meals. At lunchtime tuck into Scotch broth followed by local beef sausages, roast brisket (hot or as part of a salad), haddock or crispy chicken. Chips with everything for high tea from 4.30, and Scotch pancakes, scones and shortbread are delicious with home-made jams and a strong brew. *Unlicensed. No smoking. No dogs.*

ALLOWAY

Mount Oliphant Farm
MAP 2 B5 *Strathclyde*
Alloway (0292) 43644
P own car park ♿

Open 12–2
Closed 1 Jan

Game pâté with oatcakes £1.50
Fresh grilled salmon £4.55 🍵

Burns Byre Restaurant

Robert Burns lived at this small working farm for ten years as a boy, and the original cattle byre has now been turned into a delightful restaurant. The farm's own finest produce features in such tempting lunchtime dishes as spring lamb cutlets, prime sirloin steak and baked ham with orange and cider sauce, while the local waters provide wonderfully succulent salmon. More elaborate evening meals. *No dogs.*

Credit Access, Amex, Diners, Visa

ARDENTINNY

Loch Long, Argyll
MAP 2 B4 *Strathclyde*
Ardentinny (036 981) 209
P own car park

Open 12–2.30 & 6.30–9.30
Closed Nov–mid Mar

Musselburgh pie £3.75   Wild duck
breast in honey £6.85 🍵

Ardentinny Hotel Buttery

The beamed Buttery at this friendly old inn beside Loch Long is a pleasant spot in which to enjoy some appetising home cooking. Lunchtime brings tasty snacks like thick soup with granary bread, marinated herrings, toasties and savoury pancakes, as well as more substantial offerings such as venison casserole or fried haddock. Smoked salmon and steaks join the menu at night, and there are tempting sweets to finish. *Non-smoking area.*

Credit Access, Amex, Diners, Visa

ARISAIG

MAP 1 B3 *Highland*
Arisaig (068 75) 651
P village car park

Open 8.30–10 & 12–2
Closed Oct–Easter

Beef bourguignon £3.75   Trout pâté
£2.20 🍵

Old Library Lodge & Restaurant

Run in friendly fashion by the Broadhursts, this charming old restaurant enjoys a waterside setting on the road to the Isles. The day starts early with good hearty breakfasts, then at lunchtime a blackboard menu offers home-made soups served with lovely wholemeal bread, ploughman's, quiches and salads, marinated local herrings and appetising hot dishes such as beef bourguignon. Fruit crumble or ice cream to finish. More elaborate evening meals. *No dogs.*

BALFRON   *Coffee Mill*

151 Buchanan Street
MAP 2 C4 *Central*
Balfron (0360) 40145
P Co-op car park

Open 10–5 (Wed till 1)
Closed Sun, 1 Jan & 25 Dec

Gammon cheese & pineapple open
sandwich £1.30   Home-made soup
45p 🍵

A tiny tea room on the main thoroughfare
of this quiet Stirlingshire village in which
Evelyn Warnock provides a selection of
uncomplicated snacks and teas. Home-
made soups, open sandwiches, baked beans
on toast and baked potatoes form the
savoury choices, and sweet things include
scones with jam, fruit tartlets and sponge
gâteaux layered with fresh whipped cream.
Everything is available all day long and the
cooking is consistently good. *Unlicensed.*
No dogs.

COLBOST   *Three Chimneys*

Nr Dunvegan, Isle of Skye
MAP 1 A2 *Highland*
Glendale (047 081) 258
P own car park

Open 12.30–2

Closed Sun & mid Oct–Easter

Skye prawn salad platter £7.25
Hot marmalade pudding £2.50
Chicken & pasta salad £3.50
Shortbread with ice cream £1.50
🍵 🍵

★ In a stone cottage on the B884, Eddie and Shirley
Spear offer imaginative, skilfully prepared food
featuring the abundant fresh fish and produce of
Skye. A more charming spot it would be hard to find:
stone walls, a beamed ceiling, pretty ornaments and ★
pots and pans around a fireplace and fresh flowers
on every table. You might start with a delicious
carrot and lentil soup with home-made bread and
pale fresh butter. The fresh daily quiche could be a
perfect creamy crab with a choice of salads. Home-
made brown-bread ice cream with a blackcurrant
sauce or outstanding shortbread are among the
desserts. There is a more elaborate evening menu.
No dogs.

Credit Access, Visa

Any person using our name
to obtain free hospitality is a fraud.

Proprietors, please inform
Egon Ronay's Guides and the police.

CRINAN   *Crinan Coffee Shop*

CRINAN
By Lochgilphead
MAP 2 B4 *Strathclyde*
Crinan (054 683) 261
P village car park ♿

Open 9–5 (July–Sept till 7)

Closed Nov–mid Mar

Cheese & onion quiche £1.10
Open sandwiches from £1.25
King size, yachtsmen's sausage
rolls £1.10   Chocolate roulade
85p   Doughnut 40p 🍵

★ The cooking is faultless and the setting – on the quayside of the Crinan canal overlooking the moored fishing boats – is quite charming. Once the stables for the barge horses, the rough stone walled interior with its tiled floor and pine tables now displays today's hub of enterprise – a pine counter burgeoning enticingly with shortbread, fruit slices, coffee gâteaux, coconut fudge and chocolate caramel slices of exquisite quality. Lunchtimes bring a softly filled Stilton and courgette quiche in perfect pastry (a fine example of this much denigrated dish), open sandwiches and giant sausage rolls, rounded off with a moist chocolate roulade studded with fresh strawberries. Children's portions. *No dogs.* ★

CULLIPOOL   *Longhouse Buttery*

Isle of Luing, By Oban
MAP 2 B4 *Strathclyde*
Luing (085 24) 209
P own car park ♿

Open 11–5

Closed Sun & early Oct–mid May

Prawn salad £5   Frozen orange
cream £1.60   Cullipool mixed
platter £7.85   Egg mayonnaise
sandwich £1.90 🍵

★ Make the journey by ferry over to the Isle of Luing in order to sample the spectacular views from the large bay window of this spotless little restaurant. Also breathtaking is the standard of the cooking by Audrey Stone, and her partner Edna Whyte is sure to give you a very warm welcome. Food is available all day, from artichoke soup, venison pâté and open wholemeal sandwiches to home-baked gammon and fresh island seafood – try the Cullipool platter with wild salmon, lobster, prawns, squat lobster tails and pickled salmon. Finish up with fresh fruit salad, triple meringue or frozen Cullipool chocolate pot. Children can choose what they want from the kitchen. *No dogs.* ★

DALBEATTIE   *Coffee & Things*

32 High Street
MAP 2 C6 *Dumfries & Galloway*
Dalbeattie (0556) 611033
P Town Hall car park

Open 10–5
Closed Sun, Mon, Bank Hols (except
Good Fri, Easter Mon & Aug Bank Hol)
& 1 Jan–early Mar

Galloway lamb casserole £3.25   Cottage
pie and vegetables £2.95 🍵

You can buy antiques and gifts as well as
enjoy some fine home baking at Mr
Rangecroft's pretty little coffee shop.
Light, flavoursome scones, shortbread,
treacle fingers and deliciously moist chocolate cake all go well with an excellent
brew. At lunchtime the daily-changing
menu offers such hearty dishes as stuffed
beef olives, sweet and sour pork casserole,
and a steamed syrup sponge for afters.
Friendly service from smartly uniformed
waitresses. *Minimum lunchtime charge
£1.50. No dogs.*

DIRLETON   *Open Arms Hotel*

MAP 2 C4 *Lothian*
Dirleton (062 085) 241
P own car park &

Open 12.30–2
Closed Sun, 25 & 26 Dec & 1 wk Jan

Chicken, leek & potato pie £3.85
Cranachan with blackcurrants £1.50 ⊖

This comfortable lounge, with a coal fire
in winter, provides a relaxed stopping
place. A hearty appetite will be satisfied by
the generous portions of dishes like a
warming broth, mussel and onion stew,
braised beef or baked ham. However, if it's
a snack you're after, try an original salad
or a vegetarian lasagne, which will leave
room for a delicious sweet like creamy
cranachan with nicely tart blackcurrants.
Garden open in summer. *No dogs.*

Credit Access, Amex, Diners, Visa

DRYBRIDGE   *N·E·W ENTRY*   *The Old Monastery*

Nr Buckie
MAP 1 C2 *Grampian*
Buckie (0542) 32660
P own car park

Open 12–2
Closed Sun, Mon, Bank Hols & 3 wks
Jan & 2 wks Nov

Morayfish feast £4.50   Breast of chicken
with mild Dijon mustard sauce £3.95

This charming building was erected by the
Benedictines in the early 1900s. The bar,
where lunches are served, is an extension
to the cloisters and has Gothic-style rattan
chairs with pine tables. Local produce is
cooked with skill and the menu offers
chicken terrine, minute steak with Madeira
and mushroom sauce, or poached salmon
with prawn, cream and wine sauce followed
by grape and port trifle or meringues with
redcurrants. More elaborate evening
meals. *No children under 6. No dogs.*

Credit Access, Amex, Diners, Visa **LVs**

DRYBURGH ABBEY   *Orchard Tearoom*

Nr St Boswells
MAP 2 D5 *Borders*
St Boswells (0835) 22053
P street parking &

Open 10–5.15 (till 5.30 Sat),
Sun 2–5.30
Closed end Oct–end Mar

Scone with butter & jam 55p
Home-made soup 60p 🍵

Run with vivacity by Fiona Lynn, this
attractive tea shop overlooking the river
Tweed nestles right in the heart of Scott
country. Tuck into home-made cakes and
biscuits, light cheese or plain scones,
buttered fruit gingerbread and moist lemon
sponge – all delicious with a flavoursome
brew. Soup, sandwiches and bacon rolls
are the only savouries, but three-course
lunches and high teas can be provided if
ordered in advance. *Unlicensed.*

DULNAIN BRIDGE

Muckrach Lodge Hotel

Nr Grantown-on-Spey
MAP 1 C3 *Highland*
Dulnain Bridge (047 985) 257
P own car park

Open 12–2

Gammon sandwich £1.90   Mille-feuille
£1.30

The bar of the hotel makes a cheerful, popular spot for lunch, offering honest, simple food: freshly cut granary bread sandwiches (well filled with roast pork and Dijon mustard), salads and soups. Chicken liver pâté with Cognac or home-made potted ham are also tempting. The sweets are especially good – mille-feuille plump with cream and topped with melted chocolate is a good choice. There is a good all-Scottish cheeseboard. The coffee is freshly ground. *No dogs.*

Credit Access, Amex, Diners, Visa

DUMFRIES

Opus Salad Bar

95 Queensberry Street
MAP 2 C6 *Dumfries & Galloway*
Dumfries (0387) 55752
P street parking

Open 9–5 (Thurs till 2.30)
Closed Sun & Bank Hols

Vegetable crumble £1.70   Cauliflower
cheese £1.70   🍵 🍮

Standards are consistently high at the Hallidays' bright little first-floor café to be found in a gift shop just off the town's main shopping square. Make your selection from the self-service counter, where lunchtime choices such as delicious shepherd's pie, crunchy cauliflower cheese, quiche and up to ten different salads are backed up throughout the day by filled rolls, scones, cakes, figgy fingers and simple sweets. Children's menu. *Non-smoking area. No dogs.*

Credit Access

DUNDEE

Raffles Restaurant

18 Perth Road
MAP 2 C4 *Tayside*
Dundee (0382) 26433
P street parking

Open 10–9 (Fri & Sat till 10.30)
Closed Sun, Mon, 2 wks July & 2 wks
Jan

Lamb korma £4.50   Beef oriental £4.95
🍮

The key to the successful menu of this busy bistro – a campus favourite – is variety. The fare alters daily, ranging from a hearty cooked breakfast or home-baked cakes and scones, to a midday meal of brains in garlic butter, spinach mornay pancake, pork schnitzel or guinea fowl with lemon sauce. Vegetarian choices too; try pan fried trout with chives or vegetable lasagne. Evening booking advisable, particularly Friday and Saturday. *No dogs.*

DUNKELD

*N·E·W
ENTRY*

Tappit Hen

7 Atholl Street
MAP 2 C4 *Tayside*
Dunkeld (035 02) 472
P street parking

Open 10.30–5
Closed Sun, Mon & Thurs in winter
& 2 wks Xmas

Minestrone soup 85p   Millionaire's
shortbread 60p

A really friendly atmosphere pervades this little restaurant underneath a gift shop. Pine tables and walls covered with pictures enhance the simple choice of well-prepared food. Savoury choices are made up of rolls and sandwiches filled with beef, tuna or egg and cress perhaps. Oatcakes, crumpets and muffins complement the three different types of scone, and excellent home baking includes coffee and chocolate cakes, fruit cake, shortbread and rock cakes. *Non-smoking area. No dogs.*

Credit Visa

DUNOON   *Black's Tea Room*

144 Argyll Street
MAP 2 B5 *Strathclyde*
Dunoon (0369) 2311
P Moir Street car park

Open 8.45–5
Closed Sun, 1 & 2 Jan, 25 & 26 Dec

Bridie with beans 75p   Black cherry
gâteau 85p

In the main street of this waterfront town
a warm welcome awaits you at Mrs Black's
unpretentious little tea room, sharing
premises with her own bakery, which
provides cakes and scones throughout the
day. Gorge yourself on rum-based tipsy
cake, pineapple tart or warm crumpets
with cherry filling, or try savoury items
like soup, jacket potatoes, filled rolls, steak
pie or bridie (a Scottish favourite consisting
of herby sausagemeat in flaky pastry).
Unlicensed. No dogs.

We welcome bona fide recommendations or complaints
on the tear-out pages at the back of the book
for readers' comments.

They are followed up by our professional team,
but do complain to the management on the spot.

EDINBURGH   *Le Café Noir*

Waverley Market, Waverley Bridge
Town plan D3 *Lothian*
031-556 1374
P St James's Centre   &

Open 8am–midnight (Thurs–Sat till
1am)
Closed 1 Jan

Smoked mackerel salad £1.75   Jamaican
rum cake 95p

Strikingly fashionable with its matt black
decor and outdoor tables arranged beside
a fountain and ornamental pool, this stylish
cafe is part of the Waverley Market
shopping precinct. The day starts with
coffee and croissants from 8am, moving
on via cakes and pastries to elegant light
lunches featuring roast beef, ham, seafood
and pâté with a selection of appetising
salads. More substantial meals are available
in the adjoining bistro. *No dogs.*

Credit Access, Amex, Diners, Visa   **LVs**

EDINBURGH   *Café Saint Jacques*

King James Thistle Hotel,
Leith Street
Town plan D2 *Lothian*
031-556 0111
P NCP in St James Centre

Open 12.30–2
Closed 25 & 26 Dec

Hors d'oeuvre £4.95   Stir fried curried
vegetables £3.25   🅑 ♣

Lavish hors d'oeuvre lure you to a central
display at this smart French-style restaurant on the third floor of a modern hotel. If
you choose a light meal, start with hot or
cold soup and proceed to mussels in white
wine, ginger and cream sauce, salad niçoise
or an omelette of your choice. Generous
Danish-style open sandwiches are not for
the faint-hearted. Select a Scottish or
French cheese in preference to the less
imaginative sweet trolley. *No dogs.*

Credit Access, Amex, Diners, Visa

EDINBURGH

Handsel's Wine Bar

22 Stafford Street
Town plan A3 *Lothian*
031-225 5521
P street parking

Open 10am–10.30pm

Closed Sun, 25 & 26 Dec & 1 wk
Jan

Ham & avocado salad £3.30
Breast of woodpigeon in juniper
sauce £4.30   Lemon sole with
mussels £4.80   Strawberry
mousse £1.70   🍴 🐾

★ Andrew Radford's daily-changing menus show off
his undeniable talents to the full at this stylish wine
bar on the ground floor of a sumptuously restored
Georgian house. Using only the finest produce
available, he creates such memorable dishes as a
truly splendid seafood soup served with garlic and
parsley bread, bacon-wrapped breast of chicken with
a lovely, light nutmeg sauce, lemon sole with smoked
salmon, leek and saffron butter sauce, and freshly
baked croissant with smoked bacon and farmhouse
Brie. Superb sweets (orange chocolate roulade,
Amaretto ice cream with blackcurrant coulis), fine
local cheeses and excellent wines by the glass for the
perfect end to a magnificent meal. *No dogs.* ★

Credit Access, Amex, Diners, Visa

EDINBURGH

Helios Fountain

7 Grassmarket
Town plan C3 *Lothian*
031-229 7884
P meter parking

Open 10–6 (til 8 in Aug)
Closed Sun, 1 & 2 Jan & 25 & 26 Dec

Pasta in wine & cream sauce £2.60   Red
dragon pie £2.10   🐾

The Fountain is a vegetarian wholefood
café at the back of a book, toy and craft
shop. Most of the fresh food is made from
organically or bio-dynamically grown ingredients. Cooking standards are high and
dishes imaginatively conceived, like the
leek and mushroom croustade or pasta and
vegetable loaf. Delicious cakes too: vegan
carob or banana and yoghurt cake, for
example. You can sample both herb and
traditional teas as well as a good coffee.
Unlicensed. No smoking.

Credit Access, Amex, Visa

EDINBURGH

Hendersons Salad Table

94 Hanover Street
Town plan C2 *Lothian*
031-225 2131
P street parking

Open 8am–10.45pm, Sun 9am–9pm
Closed Sun (except during Festival) &
Bank Hols

Stuffed aubergines £2.20   Fruit salad
with soured cream & ginger £1.25   🍴

There is live music nightly at this popular,
counter-service vegetarian restaurant
which caters for vegans too. Try the
savoury snacks like the felafels, black-eyed
bean burgers and nut rissoles. The inventive salads include one of cashew, banana,
cucumber and soured cream. There are
lunchtime and evening hot dishes: vegetable curry, courgette and mushroom flan
with thick wholemeal pastry, and sweets
like dried fruits and carrot cake. *Non-
smoking area. No dogs.*

Credit Access, Amex, Diners, Visa   **LVs**

G. K. Chesterton
1874–1936

Tea, though an oriental
Is a gentleman at least;
Cocoa is a cad and coward,
Cocoa is a vulgar beast.
The Song of Right and Wrong

R. H. Barham
1788–1845

'Tis not her coldness, father,
That chills my labouring breast;
It's that confounded cucumber
I've ate and can't digest.
'The Confession'

Oscar Mendelsohn

Breathes there a man with nose so dead
Who never to himself has said:
'One pickled onion, one shallot,
Would raise this dish to what it's not'?
'Pickled Onions', in *A Salute to Onions* (1966)

Anonymous

I eat my peas with honey,
I've done it all my life.
It makes the peas taste funny
But it keeps them on the knife!
Manners

EDINBURGH   *Kalpna*

2 St Patrick Square
Town plan E4 *Lothian*
031-667 9890
P   street parking

Open   12–2 & 5.30–11

Closed   Sun, 1 & 2 Jan & 25 & 26 Dec

Samosa £1.25   Kachoris £1.25
Dosa masala £3   Kalpna thali £5.50

★ The simply furnished Kalpna, its walls hung with Indian art, has long been a favourite with students. The quality of the cooking sets this vegetarian restaurant apart. Starters include dishes like kachoris (a stuffed lentil pasty) and dosa masala (a crisp rice pancake with vegetable filling). Among the main courses are a mushroom curry with a wonderfully fragrant light sauce and baingan bharta (crushed roasted aubergines in yoghurt, with nuts, onions and fresh coriander). There are traditional set meals, or thalis, which are an ideal introduction to this cuisine. The freshly baked chapatis are outstanding; the rice is light and aromatic. Delicious desserts too. *No smoking. No dogs.* ★

Credit   Access, Visa

EDINBURGH   *Laigh Kitchen*

117a Hanover Street
Town plan C2 *Lothian*
031-225 1552
P   street parking

Open   8.30–4

Closed   Sun & Bank Hols

Quiche & salad £2.25   Stovies £2
Tuna bake £2.25   Hazelnut meringue cake £1.10

★ The Spicers have run their delightful, slightly Bohemian basement kitchen for twelve years now, and their regular clientele keep coming back for more. The stone flagged floor is strewn with rugs, the furniture is rustic and there is a roaring trade in their over-the-counter food. Freshly made doughnuts are the latest hit. There are also oatcakes, faultless scones, an indulgent whisky-soaked fruit cake, and an excellent flavoured hazelnut meringue gâteau. Lunchtime brings hearty broths, a dozen or so highly original salads, quiche and baked potatoes. In winter additional lunchtime specials like kedgeree, risotto or cauliflower cheese put in an appearance. *Minimum lunchtime charge £1.50. Unlicensed. Non-smoking area.* ★

EDINBURGH   *Lune Town*

38 William Street
Town plan A3 *Lothian*
031-220 1688
P meter parking

Open 12-2.30 & 6-12 (Sat, Sun from 4)
Closed 3 days Feb

Mandarin crispy duck £8   Scallops in
cashew nuts £4.30

Aromatic duck served with wafer-thin
pancakes and delicious plum sauce is one
of the tempting specialities at this popular
little ground-floor and basement Cantonese restaurant. Other delights include
exemplary wun tun soup (crystal clear and
fragrant), excellent dim sum, appetising
main courses such as baked crab in ginger
sauce, plus superlative Singapore-style rice
noodles. Ingredients are first rate, seasoning subtle and accurate. *Minimum charge
£6.50. No dogs.*

Credit Access, Amex, Diners, Visa

EDINBURGH   *Sunflower Country Kitchen*

4 South Charlotte Street
Town plan B3 *Lothian*
031-220 1700
P meter parking

Open 8-7
Closed Sun (except during festival),
1 & 2 Jan & 25 & 26 Dec

Wholewheat lasagne £2.25   Nut burger
& ratatouille £2.70

Those with a concern for healthy eating
can relax at this spacious wholefood
cafeteria where organic, low-fat, sugar-
free produce is used and the calorie count
is listed alongside most dishes. Excellent
salads, soups, filled rolls and quiches
precede hot lunchtime dishes like cheesy
baked potatoes, chicken risotto and bean
and tomato casserole. To finish, perhaps
carrot cake or fresh fruit sundae. *Non-
smoking area. No dogs.*

LVs

EDINBURGH   *Waterfront Wine Bar*

1c Dock Place, Leith
Town plan E1 *Lothian*
031-554 7427
P street parking

Open 11am-11pm (Fri & Sat till 1am)
Closed Sun, 1 & 2 Jan & 25 & 26 Dec

Smoked mackerel mousse £1.90   Spiced
lamb in almond sauce £3.70   🅢

Once the waiting room for the Aberdeen
packet, this lively, bustling wine bar is
kept snug and warm in winter and has a
conservatory and terrace for summer
snacking. Blackboards list well-chosen
wines and the day's appetising selection –
perhaps chicken and almond soup or garlic
mushrooms, followed by beef carbonnade,
smoked haddock pie or herrings in oatmeal
with mustard sauce. Creamy desserts or
cheese and oatcakes to finish. *No children
under five. No dogs.*

FALKIRK   *The Coffee Cabin*

Cockburn Street
MAP 2 C4 *Central*
Falkirk (0324) 25757
P Howgate car park

Open 9-5
Closed Sun, Bank Hols & 3 days Xmas
& New Year

Cheese & tomato pizza 95p   Chicken
curry & baked potato £1.30

Mouth-watering home-made cakes are on
display in Fiona Marshall's tiny café.
Among the delights are paradise cake, fruit
slices, meringues, chocolate or carrot
cakes, scones and an original aubergine
loaf. The menu also offers wholesome
savoury snacks and light meals: jacket
potatoes with a range of fillings, toasted
sandwiches, things on toast and filled rolls
or salads. For desserts choose from items
like fruit crumble or strawberries and
cream in season. *Unlicensed. No dogs.*

LVs

FALKLAND   *Kind Kyttock's Kitchen*

Cross Wynd
MAP 2 C4 *Fife*
Falkland (0337) 57477
P street parking

Open 10.30–5.30
Closed 25 Dec–31 Jan

Oatcake platter £2.20   Cheese
& pineapple salad £3.20 🍵

Bert Dalrymple's traditional home baking
is a real treat at the delightful little tea
shop he runs with wife Liz. Choose from
Scots pancakes and scones served with
cream and lovely home-made jam, clootie
dumplings and moist gingerbread – all
delicious with an excellent brew. Savoury
snacks (also available all day) include
Scotch broth, omelettes, filled jacket potatoes, salads, oatcakes served with cheese
and an apple, or toasted sandwiches. *Non-
smoking room upstairs. No dogs.*

GLASGOW   *Belfry*

652 Argyle Street
Town plan A3 *Strathclyde*
041-221 0630
P own car park

Open 12–2.30 & 6–10
Closed Sat lunch, all Sun & Bank Hols

Mushroom, brandy & chive terrine £2.85
Poached suprême of chicken with
avocado £7.25

In the basement of a former Victorian pub,
this atmospheric wine bar with its decor of
stained glass and carved Gothic woodwork
offers imaginative eating in impressive
surroundings. Stuffed cucumber with
creamy apple and celery salad could be
followed by a trio of steamed fish with
white wine and sherry vinegar butter, steak
with peppercorn sauce or a simple grilled
chop. Indulge yourself with hot banana
fritters and raspberry syrup to finish. *No
dogs.*

Credit Access, Amex, Diners, Visa

GLASGOW   *Café Gandolfi*

64 Albion Street
Town plan E4 *Strathclyde*
041-552 6813
P Ingram Street car park ♿

Open 9.30am–11.30pm
Closed Sun & Bank Hols

Salade niçoise £3.40   Gravad lax with
dill & mustard sauce £4.50 🍴

Young professionals favour this informal
café-restaurant in the restored warehouse
area of the city, but there is still something
for everyone at any time of the day. Choose
from soups, pastrami or wholemeal bread,
gravad lax with dill and mustard sauce or
a hot special such as tagliatelle or vegetable
lasagne. Hot croissants are available early
on, and sweet things include profiteroles,
fruit tarts, ice creams and sorbets. *No
dogs.*

GLASGOW   *Joe's Garage*

52 Bank Street
Town plan A2 *Strathclyde*
041-339 5407
P street parking

Open noon–midnight
Closed 1 Jan & 25 & 26 Dec

Burger Wellington £3.95   Chicken
enchiladas £4.75 🍷

This lively diner with a decor that includes
a petrol pump and old US licence plates
serves a range of dishes – potato skins
with various fillings, burgers, pasta, eggs
Benedict, meat loaf, salads, and a selection
of Mexican dishes such as enchiladas,
seafood tostada, chilli con carne and
tortillas. Sweets include ice creams, blueberry pie and pancakes. Sunday brunch is
a family affair.

Credit Access, Amex, Diners, Visa

GLASGOW   *De Quincey's/Brahms & Liszt*

71 Renfield Street
Town plan C3 *Strathclyde*
041-333 0633
P street parking

Open 12-2.30
Closed Sun & Bank Hols

Chicken mille-feuille £3.60   Pâté
£1.40 ℮

The self-service restaurant and wine bar
are on the ground and lower floor of a
substantial Victorian corner building. At
lunchtime there is a cold buffet with salads
and an appetising selection ranging from
pâté, cheese and honey-roast ham to
chicken mille-feuille or salmon en croûte.
There are also hot dishes like beef and
burgundy pie or pork and ginger casserole
and rich sweets such as cheesecake and
fruit flans. *No children. No dogs.*

Credit Access, Amex, Diners, Visa

GLASGOW   *Smith's*

47 West Nile Street
Town plan C3 *Strathclyde*
041-221 4677
P NCP in Gordon Street

Open 12-3
Closed Sun & Bank Hols

Prawn crêpes £1.80   Pâté £1.25

With the city's stock exchange just around
the corner, this wine bar is a haven for
businessmen at lunchtimes, although a
younger clientele takes over in the evenings. Polished mahogany and dark green
leather blend well, and the blackboard
menu lists ham & roast beef, as well as
cold, curried chicken, pies and quiches to
accompany a range of freshly made salads,
as well as prawn crêpes, home-made pâté
or lentil soup. Chocolate fudge cake for
afters. *No dogs.*

LVs

GLASGOW   *Ubiquitous Chip*

12 Ashton Lane, off Byres Road
Town plan A1 *Strathclyde*
041-334 5007
P Ashton Lane car park &

Open 12-2.30
Closed Sun, 1 Jan & 25 Dec

Vegan bean soup 60p   Chicken casserole
with brown rice £3 🐾

The focal point here is the charming
covered courtyard garden full of exotic
shrubs and climbing plants which can be
seen from both the main restaurant and
the first-floor lunch bar, where healthy
snacks are provided. Terrines, pâtés,
wholewheat flans, cold meats and salads
or chicken casserole with brown rice are
the main choices, followed by bread pudding. Despite the name, there is not a fried
potato to be seen! Full restaurant menu
also available. *No dogs.*

Credit Access, Amex, Diners, Visa

GLASGOW   *Upstairs Café*

11 Royal Exchange Square
Town plan C4 *Strathclyde*
041-221 3000
P NCP in Mitchell Street

Open 9.30-5.30
Closed Sun & Bank Hols

Smoked salmon bagel with cream cheese
£3.75   Croissant filled with chicken &
avocado £2.95 ℮

This stylish and chic café, decorated in
sophisticated greys and blacks, with elaborately draped curtains and a brass railed
gallery, has a wide ranging menu available
throughout the day. There are bagels with
smoked salmon and cream cheese, club
sandwiches and croissants generously
stuffed with a good mixed lettuce salad.
Pâtisserie include profiteroles with hot
chocolate sauce and caramel shortcake.
There are quality teas as well. *Non-
smoking area. No dogs.*

Credit Access, Amex, Diners, Visa **LVs**

GLASGOW   *Warehouse Café*

61 Glassford Street
Town plan D4 *Strathclyde*
041-552 4181
P Albion Street car park

Open 10–6
Closed Sun & Bank Hols

Pasta & tuna salad £2.75   Filled jacket
potato £2.40   🍵 🍵

On the third floor of a clothes store is this simple café serving interesting food. Starters include home-made soup, pâté and deep-fried Brie. Main courses have a New York flavour: smoked salmon bagels and chicken, bacon, lettuce and tomato on wholemeal bread. Weekly changing specials might be tagliatelle Neapolitan or chicken and pimento crêpe. To follow, apple and banana crumble or caramel shortbread. Espresso coffee and speciality teas. *Non-smoking area. No dogs.*

Credit Access, Amex, Diners, Visa

GLENSCORRODALE   *Glenscorrodale Farm Tearoom*

Isle of Arran
MAP 2 B5 *Strathclyde*
Sliddery (077 087) 241
P street parking

Open 11.30–4 & 7.30–9
Closed Tues & end Sept–May

Home-made soup 60p   Crofter's cheese
platter £1.60   🍵

This simple tea room is not the easiest of places to find, being part of a remote sheep farm about five miles west of Lamlash. It is run by Helen Driver who provides some simple but appetising home cooking. Scones, oatcakes and malt loaf appear in the mornings, followed by soup, filled rolls and fruit pie at lunchtime. For the more elaborate evening meals, like chicken Kiev and venison in red wine, be sure to book. *Unlicensed, bring your own, no corkage. No dogs.*

HARDGATE   *Elle Coffee Shop*

35 Glasgow Road
MAP 2 B5 *Strathclyde*
Duntocher (0389) 76335
P shopping precinct car park

Open 9.30–4.15
Closed Sun, Wed & Bank Hols

Soup & toast £1.55   Chocolate
banana flan 75p

Jennifer Macrae's friendly little coffee shop at the back of a dress shop is a haven in which to rest tired feet and satisfy hunger pangs. As well as favourites like soup, open sandwiches, salads and filled jacket potatoes, there are home-made pizzas and quiches, plus a daily lunchtime special such as steak pie. Good fresh baking from the trolley might include moist fruit bread, iced sponges, shortbread and caramel or mint slices. *Unlicensed. No dogs.*

HELENSBURGH   *Original Famous Coffee House*

102a West Princes Street
MAP 2 B4 *Strathclyde*
Helensburgh (0436) 2005
P street parking

Open 9–5.30
Closed Sun in winter, 1 & 2 Jan &
25 & 26 Dec

Cheese & bacon quiche £1.95   Hot
cherry tart 85p   🍵

Hungry shoppers head for this convivial town-centre coffee house where everything on the tempting menu is available throughout opening hours. Danish open sandwiches make popular gap-fillers (try succulent turkey garnished with orange and prune), or the really ravenous could choose hot soup plus spicy bean hotpot, pork and apple pie or lasagne. On the sweet side, the choice includes scones, chocolate-topped biscuits and luscious ices. *Unlicensed.*

INCHTURE — *Inchture Milk Bar*

Nr Dundee
MAP 2 C4 *Tayside*
Inchture (0828) 86283
P own car park

Open 9–6
Closed 25 Dec & all Jan

Home-made soup 45p   Roast beef
salad £2.75   🍵

Kathleen McLeish's magic way with pastry has been delighting customers to this simple café on the A85 for over 16 years. Try her splendid fruit pies (apricot, black-currant, cherry and apple), or choose the equally delicious scones, shortbread and chocolate cakes on offer. Savoury alternatives range from cooked breakfasts to soup, filled baps, and ham, pâté and chicken salads. Everything is available all day. *Unlicensed. No dogs.*

INVERNESS — *Brookes Wine Bar*

75 Castle Street
MAP 1 C2 *Highland*
Inverness (0463) 225662
P Castle Street car park

Open 11.30–3 & 5–11 (Sat
11.30am–11.45pm)

Closed Mon (Oct–Easter), Sun &
local hols in winter

Smoked salmon mousse £2.75
Stir-fried vegetable filled pancakes
£3.95   Fresh mussels £4.25
Boned & stuffed guinea fowl
£6.95

★ Splendid snacks are complemented by a fine selection of wines by the glass and bottle at this sophisticated wine bar opposite the castle. A daily-changing cold display offers treats like whole smoked trout, poached salmon and a marvellous meatloaf en croûte – all delicious with imaginative salads such as mushroom and fresh basil. There's always a choice of soups (try subtle celery and carrot), plus a couple of exemplary quiches and hot specials like tasty lamb and aubergine casserole. Round off your meal with gooey treacle flan, frangipane tart or fresh fruit roulade. More elaborate evening dishes can include guinea fowl in bitter orange sauce or coq au vin. *Non-smoking area. No dogs.* ★

ISLE OF GIGHA — *Gigha Hotel*

MAP 2 B5 *Strathclyde*
Gigha (058 35) 254
P own car park

Open 10–4

Ploughman's lunch £2   Buffet
lunch £5   🍵

You will find Scottish baking here as traditional as the welcome that greets you. In this idyllic setting lunchtime snacks are served in the bar and a cold buffet is offered in the lounge or on the terrace overlooking the Gigha Sound. Brown bread sandwiches, soup, ploughman's, cold meat salads and a daily hot dish are available at lunchtime. Shortbread and a slice of rich fruit cake will be accompanied by a refreshing cup of tea in the afternoon.

Credit Access, Visa

KENTALLEN OF APPIN   *Holly Tree*

MAP 1 B3 *Highland*
Duror (063 174) 292
P own car park &

Open 8.30–5
Closed mid Nov–beg. Mar

Scallops in garlic butter £6
Afternoon tea £2.50 &

The picture windows in this old railway station building provide spectacular views over Loch Linnhe. Morning coffee and tea are served in the bar area, and breakfast starts the day in the restaurant. At lunchtime, choose from soup, ploughman's and sandwiches or a hot special such as lamb casserole or trout baked with paprika and white wine. Teatime brings scones and home-made jam and a range of cakes. Traditional Sunday lunch. *Non-smoking area. No dogs.*

Credit Access, Visa

KILCHRENAN   *Taychreggan Hotel*

By Taynuilt
MAP 2 B4 *Strathclyde*
Kilchrenan (086 63) 211
P own car park

Open 12–2.15
Closed mid Oct–Easter

Ploughman's lunch £2   Home-made
hamburger & salad £2.15 &

Winding narrow roads bring visitors to this 400-year-old inn beside Loch Awe. Sit in the comfortable cocktail bar and admire the splendid view while tucking into some simple but appetising snacks. As well as home-made soup or pâté, succulent burgers, quiche and well-filled sandwiches, look out for locally-made giant sausages, assorted meat or fish platters and colourful salads based on honey-roast ham, prawns and fresh salmon. Garden and patio.

Credit Access, Amex, Diners, Visa

KILFINAN   *N·E·W ENTRY*   *Kilfinan Hotel*

Nr Tighnabruaich
MAP 2 B5 *Strathclyde*
Kilfinan (070 082) 201
P own car park &

Open 12–9, winter 12–2.30 & 5–9

Lentil soup 90p   Steak & stout pie
£3.20

A crackling log fire adds to the cosy atmosphere of this attractive restaurant in a former coaching inn. The short set menu and small à la carte selection change daily, making use of local produce – as in smoked venison with horseradish or seafood terrine with piquant tomato coulis. There are straightforward grills too, plus more elaborately sauced main dishes and tempting sweets like strawberry shortbread. Tables outside in summer.

Credit Access, Amex, Diners, Visa

KINCRAIG   *Boathouse Restaurant*

By Kingussie
MAP 1 C3 *Highland*
Kincraig (054 04) 272
P own car park

Open 10–9 (26 Dec–31 Mar from 12)
Closed 1 Nov–25 Dec

Seafood lasagne £6.50   Cheese & ham
toastie £1.50 &

Balcony seats at this log cabin above a stone boathouse command ringside views of Loch Insh and its windsurfers and skiers. At lunchtime, snack on pâté, ham or smoked mackerel, or tuck into soup, steak and kidney pie, seafood lasagne, a pizza, burger or filled jacket potato. High tea brings fruit cake and carrot cake, shortbread and toasted sandwiches, while from 6pm there's a more elaborate three-course menu. Children's menu. *Non-smoking area. No dogs.*

KINLOCHBERVIE   *Kinlochbervie Hotel*

By Lairg
MAP 1 B1 *Highland*
Kinlochbervie (097 182) 275
P own car park

Open 12–1.45 (Sun from 12.30)
& 2–5.30

Home-made soup 90p   Macaroni cheese
£1.25   🅑

This modern hotel on the remote Sutherland coast offers a commendable bar lunch.
Geraldine Gregory, proprietor, heads the
list of home-made specialities with macaroni cheese (using delicious Scottish Cheddar), nourishing broth, home-smoked ham,
smoked salmon sandwiches, salad and
beefburgers. Afternoon teas are served
daily and desserts include brandy mousse
and hazelnut slice. Essential to book
November to Easter. *Only residents'*
children in lounge bar. No dogs.

KYLE OF LOCHALSH   *N·E·W ENTRY*   *Highland Designworks*

Plockton Road
MAP 1 B3 *Highland*
Kyle (0599) 4388
P own car park

Open 10–9.30, winter 11–9 (Tues &
Wed till 4)
Closed 25, 26 Dec & all Jan

Herring in oatmeal £2.50   Poppy seed
cake 60p   🅑   🍵

Find this converted village school on the
Plockton road, half a mile from Kyle.
Young owner, architect Fiona Begg, is a
dab hand in the kitchen, and her self-
service counter displays nourishing soups,
pizzas and quiches, hot dishes like vegetable curry and herrings in oatmeal, and
wholesome cakes and scones. After 6pm,
there's waitress service for a short vegetarian menu, but it is still possible to have
just a coffee and a cake if required.
Unlicensed. No smoking. No dogs.

LAMLASH   *Carraig Mhor*

Isle of Arran
MAP 2 B5 *Strathclyde*
Lamlash (077 06) 453
P car park opposite

Open 10.30–11.45, 12.15–2 & 7–9.30
Closed Sun, Mon & 2 wks Nov

Quiche & salad £2.95   Chicken, ham
& mushroom omelette with French fries
& salad £3.45   🅑

This lovely pebbledash cottage on the
seafront with views of Holy Island is a
wonderful setting in which to enjoy the
home-made food. There are scones or
shortbread for morning coffee, and a
satisfying lunchtime selection of quiche,
prawn salad, smoked mackerel, ploughman's, or stuffed peppers, supplemented
by daily specials. Rhubarb crumble and
fruit meringues to follow. The evening
menu offers pork espagnole or fresh local
seafood. Check before you go as it closes
early when quiet. *No dogs.*

LARGS   *Green Shutter Tea Room*

28 Bath Street
MAP 2 B5 *Strathclyde*
Largs (0475) 672252
P Promenade car park

Open 10–6
Closed mid Oct–mid Mar

Fresh breaded haddock & chips £3.55
Quiche & salad £2.40   🍵

The Murdochs are new owners at this
popular seafront tea room where fine views
across the Clyde estuary accompany simple
home-made snacks. Freshly baked cakes
and biscuits including iced sponges, mincemeat slices, meringues and shortbread,
make a tempting display. Tasty savouries
available all day range from open sandwiches, jacket potatoes and salads to
vegetable soup and gammon steak. Fruit
tart for afters. Children's menu. *Minimum*
charge £1.50 12.30–2 & 4.30–6. Unli-
censed.

MILNGAVIE   *Famous Coffee House*

**Findlay Clark Garden Centre,
Boclair Road
MAP 2 B5** *Strathclyde*
Balmore (0360) 20700
P garden centre car park &

Open 10–5.30
Closed 1 Jan & 25 & 26 Dec

Original Italian lasagne £2.75   Pork &
apple pie £2.25 🍵

Tucked away in the corner of a large
garden centre is this comfortable and very
popular coffee shop. There's a central
display of gâteaux and fruit pies and
savoury items like the generous open
'Danwich' creations. There are daily hot
dishes which may include a choice of home-
made soups, spicy bean hotpot and
quiches. Scones, hot croissants, Danish
pastries, meringues and a selection of ice
cream dishes are available for the sweet-
toothed. Children's portions. *No dogs.*

MOFFAT   *N·E·W ENTRY*   *Rachel's Pantry*

**The High Street
MAP 2 C5** *Dumfries & Galloway*
Moffat (0683) 21010
P street parking

Open 10–5.30 (Fri & Sat in summer till
9) & Sun 11–6
Closed Oct–Mar

Tagliatelle & salad £2.20   Strawberry
cheesecake 90p 🍵

Rachel's Pantry is set in one of the oldest
houses in town and is a pleasant little café
where Alison Minto produces a range of
enjoyable food from her tiny kitchen:
gâteaux and scones, lovely cheesecakes,
quiches and, in summer, pâtés and colourful tasty salads. Simpler snacks are filled
rolls like ham or egg mayonnaise, but the
most popular is bacon. On summer Sundays there's a roast lunch. Afternoon
brings scones, cream cakes and a good pot
of tea. *No smoking. No dogs.*

NEW ABBEY   *Abbey Cottage*

**By Dumfries
MAP 2 C6** *Dumfries & Galloway*
Dunscore (038 782) 361
P Abbey car park &

Open 10–5
Closed Oct–Easter & weekdays Easter–
Spring Bank Hol

Ploughman's lunch £2.15   Home-made
soup & granary bread 65p

Inside the white-painted Abbey Cottage, a
craft shop shares space alongside the
coffee shop. Owners Mrs McKie and Mrs
Doyle work hard to prepare their unpretentious all-day offerings. Try a satisfying
soup with granary bread; beef and egg
mayonnaise salads or a Galloway country
pâté. Good quality tea or coffee accompanies scones, fruit loaf and a pleasing
selection of home-baked cakes. *Unlicensed. No smoking. No dogs.*

NEWCASTLETON   *Copshaw Kitchen*

**4 North Hermitage Street
MAP 2 C6** *Borders*
Liddlesdale (054 121) 250
P own car park &

Open 9–6.30 (Sun from 10 & Nov–Mar
till 5.30)
Closed Tues, 26 Dec & all Jan

Lasagne £2.45   Local sirloin steak £5

Splendid Scottish ladies welcome you after
your lovely scenic drive to Jean Elliot's
charming little tea room – it's well worth
the detour. Soup, possibly delicious thick
celery, comes with barley fadge – a Scottish
wholemeal bread. Other snacks might
include chicken liver pâté, sausage rolls or
pies with good light pastry and well
flavoured vegetables. All day there are
teacakes, rock buns, shortbreads and
cream cakes, and more elaborate restaurant meals in the evening. *Non-smoking
area. No dogs.*

Samuel Butler
1835–1902

The hen is only an egg's way of making another egg.
Life and Habit

Jonathan Swift
1667–1745

Fish should swim thrice: first it should swim in the sea . . .
then it should swim in butter, and at last, sirrah, it
should swim in good claret.
Polite Conversation

William Shakespeare
1564–1616

. . . who can . . . cloy the hungry edge of appetite
By bare imagination of a feast?
Or wallow naked in December snow
By thinking on fantastic summer's heat?
Richard II

Alexander Pope
1688–1744

Fame is at best an unperforming cheat;
But 'tis substantial happiness to eat.
Mr D'Urfey's Last Play

PEEBLES   *Kailzie Gardens Restaurant*

Kailzie
MAP 2 C5 *Borders*
Peebles (0721) 22807
P own car park

Open 11–5
Closed Oct–1 Apr

Quiche & salad £1.95   Apple tart 65p

Grace Innes is the new owner at this charmingly cottage restaurant, housed in converted stables in Kailzie Gardens beside the river Tweed. Her simple but appetising day-long selection of snacks ranges from home-made soup or chicken liver terrine to hot quiche served with new potatoes, smoked haddock and salad platters featuring chicken, gammon, tuna, prawns or Brie. Freshly baked cakes, scones and fruit tarts provide a sweet touch. *No dogs.*

PEEBLES   *Sunflower Coffee Shop*

4 Bridgegate
MAP 2 C5 *Borders*
Peebles (0721) 22420
P Edinburgh Road car park

Open 10–5.30
Closed Sun & Xmas–New Year

Broccoli & tomato quiche £2.65   Apple
pancake £1.75 🍵

A popular spot for vegetarian lunches and tasty snacks throughout the day, this friendly little place, tucked away behind the High Street, is part craft shop, part coffee shop. From midday you can enjoy such appetising hot dishes as cauliflower soup followed by a salad pancake with cheese sauce or potato-topped vegetable pie. At other times, tuck into toasted sandwiches, salads and baked potatoes, plus tempting sweets like carrot cake and chocolate brownies. *Non-smoking area.*

Prices given are as at the time of our research
and thus may change.

PITLOCHRY   *Luggie Restaurant*

Rie-Achen Road
MAP 1 C3 *Tayside*
Pitlochry (0796) 2085
P own car park

Open 9.30–5 & 6–9.30
Closed mid Nov–early Mar

Chicken pie & salad £3   Fresh Scottish
salmon £5.85 🥨

Once a dairy, this long beamed barn now houses an enormously popular self-service restaurant. Tempting cakes, gâteaux, scones and cheesecakes are available throughout the day, while at lunchtime there are crisp salads to enjoy with cold meats and fresh salmon, plus a daily hot meat pie. The more elaborate evening menu includes appetising roasts (venison with redcurrant jelly) and grills. *No dogs.*

Credit Access, Amex, Diners, Visa

ST ANDREWS   *Brambles*

5 College Street
MAP 2 C4 *Fife*
St Andrews (0334) 75380
P North Street

Open 10–4.30

Closed Sun, Mon, Bank Hols, 2 wks Sept & 2 wks Xmas

Caribbean vegetable savoury £1.90   Cashew nut roast with chestnut stuffing 80p   Mexican tostadas with nachos sauce £1.40 Carrot & pineapple cake 35p

★ For visitors to the ancient university town of St Andrews, this is a splendid stopping point while you gather strength for the next excursion. This little eating house is justly popular with tourists, townsfolk and students alike for Jean Hamilton's imaginative and tasty dishes are drawn from eating traditions all over the world. Try Greek spinach pie with crisp wholemeal pastry, or Jarlsberg courgette. There are simple filled baps or jacket potatoes and excellent puddings and home-baked cakes and biscuits. Attention to detail counts here, right down to the bramble-decorated pottery mugs. Various teas are offered. *Minimum lunchtime charge £1. No dogs.* ★

ST FILLANS   *N·E·W ENTRY*   *Four Seasons Hotel, Tarkon Bar*

Nr Crieff
MAP 2 C4 *Tayside*
St Fillans (076 485) 333
P own car park

Open 12.30–2 & 7–9.30
Closed Jan & Feb

Hot mushrooms in herb vinaigrette £1.95
Haggis, neeps and tatties £2.45

The Scott family have brought all their enthusiasm to their idyllic loch-side hotel with its terrace and picture windows overlooking quite memorable scenery. The menu is simple but tempting, with tossed smoked chicken and sweet corn salad, hot mushrooms with herb vinaigrette, smoked salmon on wholemeal toast with a herby butter, Highland game pie with succulent venison and classic haggis, neeps and tatties. Delicious desserts range from strawberry pavlova to chocolate marquise.

Credit Access, Amex, Diners, Visa

SELKIRK   *Philipburn House Hotel*

Linglie Road
MAP 2 C5 *Borders*
Selkirk (0750) 20747
P own car park &

Open 12–2.30 & 6–10

Rösti with egg, bacon & raclettes £4.50
Home-made fishcakes £2.50

Jill Hill's quick bite menu has something for everyone at this attractive pine-panelled bar in a friendly hotel on the A707. Traditionalists will enjoy favourites like soup, pâté, ploughman's and shepherd's pie, while for the more adventurous there's a lavish croque-madame with ham and prawns, hot croissants filled with bacon and Brie, or Loch Fyne herrings in sweet pickle. Apple strudel or rich sachertorte to finish. *No smoking. No dogs.*

Credit Access, Amex, Diners, Visa

STRANRAER   *L'Apéritif*

London Road
MAP 2 B6 *Dumfries & Galloway*
Stranraer (0776) 2991
P own car park

Open 12–2 & 5.30–9
Closed Sun & mid Jan–mid Feb

Cannelloni £3   Home-made steak pie
£3.25 🄴

Budget eaters should head for the downstairs lounge of this cheerful, family-run
Italian restaurant (more elaborate evening
meals are served upstairs). Lunchtime
choices include pasta and freshly made
pizzas, but you can also stay nearer home
with salads, fish and chips, steak pie,
omelettes, or a tasty home-made burger
topped with onions in a spicy sauce. Eclairs,
meringues, fruit salad, or delicious apple
pie for afters. *No dogs.*

STRATHCARRON   *Carron Restaurant*

Cam-Allt
MAP 1 B2 *Highland*
Lochcarron (052 02) 488
P own parking

Open 10.30–9
Closed Sun & mid Oct–Easter

Salmon quiche £2.75   Trout with salad
& jacket potato £5.30 🄴

Next to a craft shop, with views out over
Loch Carron, is this pleasant, modern
restaurant where Rob Teago and his family
will serve you sweet and savoury food all
day. Home-made cakes and pastries accompany coffee or tea, and savouries include
toasted sandwiches, quiches, baked potatoes and salads. Steaks, trout and venison
are cooked on the chargrill. Start with
onion soup, and finish with apple pie or
choose from the cake selection. *No dogs.*

Credit Access, Amex, Visa

STROMNESS   *N·E·W ENTRY*   *Hamnavoe Restaurant*

35 Graham Place
MAP 1 C1 *Orkney*
Orkney (0856) 850606
P Pumpwell car park &

Open 12–3
Closed Mon (Oct–Mar) & Tues

Open crab sandwich £2.50   Grilled fillet
of plaice with parsley & lemon butter
£3.25 🄴

Go down an alley off the High Street to
enjoy lunch at this attractive little restaurant where everything is prepared with flair
and care. Try the tasty cream of courgette
soup, tender, chunky beef stroganoff with
real sour cream or the cold seafood platter.
There might be rhubarb cheesecake with a
good biscuit base or a meringue surprise
among the afters. More elaborate evening
meals. *No dogs.*

Credit Access, Visa

TARBET   *Tigh-na-Mara Seafood Restaurant*

Scourie, By Lairg
MAP 1 B1 *Highland*
Scourie (0971) 2151
P parking nearby

Open 12–2.30 & 5.30–8
Closed Sun (except July & Aug) & early
Oct–Easter

Plaice with cream & cheese sauce £6
Mussels in garlic butter £2.50 🄴

This remote hamlet has two attractions: a
boat to the Hana Island bird reserve, and
this little restaurant offering locally-
caught seafood. Starters include home-
made broth, melon and avocado salad, but
the main attraction is the fresh seafood;
crab, halibut, locally farmed salmon,
smoked salmon and Mallaig smoked mackerel, all served with crisp salad or new
potatoes. There are a few desserts like fruit
crumble. *Unlicensed. No dogs.*

TAYNUILT *Shore Cottage*

Nr Oban
MAP 2 B4 *Strathclyde*
Taynuilt (086 62) 654
P own car park

Open 9.30–6

Closed Wed & end Oct–wk before Easter

Leek & potato soup with brown bread 65p   Wholemeal scone with home-made jam 30p   Filled rolls 60p   Walnut cake 30p

★ In her pretty whitewashed cottage on the shores of Loch Etive, Lilly McNaught continues to delight her customers with her excellent baking. Everything but everything is home-made, from her irresistible scones to the jam that fills them. Sit at blue check tablecloths and drink refreshing loose-leaf tea from fine white bone china tea cups while you decide what to eat. For a savoury bite choose from crisp salads, warming soups (the leek and potato or the split-pea broth is particularly good), filled rolls or sandwiches and snacks on toast. For the sweet tooth there is a choice of sponges (coffee, chocolate or lemon), or millionaire's shortbread, and it would be criminal not to try Lilly's sensational fruit slice. *Unlicensed. No smoking. No dogs.* ★

Our inspectors never book in the name of Egon Ronay's Guides.

They disclose their identity only if they are considering an establishment for inclusion in the next edition of the Guide.

ULLAPOOL *Ceilidh Place*

West Argyll Street
MAP 1 B2 *Highland*
Ullapool (0854) 2103
P own car park

Open 10am–10pm

Vegetarian haggis £2.25   Carrot & lemon soup 75p

Poetry recitals and live music are regular features at this delightfully informal plant-filled restaurant. Much of the homely and wholesome food offered is based on Scottish recipes, with choices as varied as vegetable lasagne, seafood pasta, freshly caught fish and a good variety of salads. Toothsome sweet items include fruity dumplings, date and walnut slice and various gâteaux, and on Sundays, a full traditional afternoon tea is served. Terrace. *Non-smoking area.*

Credit Access, Amex, Diners, Visa

WHITEHOUSE   *Old School Tearoom*

Nr Tarbert
MAP 2 B5 *Strathclyde*
Whitehouse (088 073) 215
P   own car park

Open 10.30–6

Closed Tues & mid Oct–mid Mar

Gourmet's delight £2.85   Salmon mousse £2.50   Lemon meringue pie 80p   Scone with jam & butter 40p

★ New owners, the Graingers, maintain high standards at this spotless tea room. Look out for the cake trolley where you will find a wickedly indulgent cream-filled Victoria sponge, coffee and chocolate gâteaux, shortbread, fresh cream meringues, fruit and nut loaf, coconut macaroons and a lovely, moist lemon meringue pie. Savoury dishes are available all day: home-made soup, both open and ordinary sandwiches, a smoked ham platter, smoked salmon, salads and a ploughman's lunch. In addition there are hot specials at lunchtime which might be ham and egg or cheese and onion pie, both served with fresh salad. *Unlicensed. No smoking. No dogs.* ★

WALES

ABERAERON
Hive on the Quay

Cadwgan Place
MAP 7 B3 *Dyfed*
Aberaeron (0545) 570445
P street parking

Open 10.30–5, July–end Aug
10–9

Closed end Sept–Spring Bank
Hol

Vegetable strudel £4   Buckwheat
pancakes £2.75   Salmon trout £5
Plum & cinnamon pie £1.50

★ The Holgates are charming and dedicated hosts at
this delightful café and restaurant with a conservatory
overlooking the harbour. Throughout the day
visitors can enjoy tea or coffee with delicious cakes
like honey spice and Madeira or ginger, plus excellent
sandwiches and super honey ice cream. Lunchtime
brings a cold buffet featuring lots of salads to
accompany quiche, local mackerel, pâté or honey-
baked ham, while on summer evenings there's a set
dinner with waitress service. A typical meal might
start with carrot and orange soup or fresh crab dip
with crudités, then move on to sweet Welsh lamb pie
or rabbit and bacon hot pot, with delicious puddings
and good local cheeses to finish. ★

ABERYSTWYTH
Connexion

19 Bridge Street
MAP 7 B2 *Dyfed*
Aberystwyth (0970) 615350
P street parking

Open 10.30–4 & 6.30–10.30
Closed Sun (except lunch in summer)

Portuguese chicken £6   Beef casserole
served with tagliatelle verde £5.50

The wide ranging menu at this intimate,
informal bistro, decorated with local artists' work, has something for everyone,
from pasta and salads to paella, stuffed
aubergines, local lobster and steaks. Vegetarians are well catered for and there is
a separate children's menu with meals at
half price. Lovely rich apple tart baked
with cinnamon and brown sugar for pud.
No dogs.

Credit Access, Visa

BETHESDA
N·E·W
ENTRY
Mountain Kitchen

Snowdonia National Park Lodge,
Ty'n y Maes
MAP 7 B2 *Gwynedd*
Bethesda (0248) 600548
P own car park

Open 12.30–2.30 & 7.30–9

Broccoli & Swiss cheese quiche £1.60
Mountain burger £4.10

You don't have to be on a diet to enjoy
lunch at this friendly little restaurant, part
of the Snowdonia National Park Health
Lodge. Soup, sandwiches and jacket potatoes make tasty light snacks, and there are
more substantial dishes too, like braised
Welsh lamb in red wine. Wonderful sweets
(the chocolate soufflé is heavenly) and
local cheese served with home-made walnut bread end your meal in style. Booking
is advisable at all times. *No dogs.*

Credit Access, Amex, Diners, Visa

CAERNARFON

Bakestone

26 Hole-in-the-Wall Street
MAP 7 B2 *Gwynedd*
Caernarfon (0286) 5846
P street parking

Open 12.30–2.30 &
6.30–8.30

Closed Thurs lunch & all Sun &
Mon, Bank Hol Mon lunch, 2 wks
Oct & 2 wks Jan

Home sweetcure herrings £2.10
Bakestone galette £4.40 Fresh
lemon tartlets £1.60 Lemon &
sugar crêpe £1.80

★ Wonderful flavours and textures set the tastebuds
tingling at this tiny, informal restaurant opposite the
castle entrance. Everything is prepared to order with
flair and imagination, from superb orange and
coriander baked prawn tails to marvellous main
courses such as succulent chicken suprême with
rosemary sauce, grilled sea bass or Welsh lamb and
kidney pie – all accompanied by crisply delicious
vegetables. Savoury crêpes are a deservedly popular
alternative (try the splendid Bakestone galette with
fresh spinach, bacon, melted Swiss cheese and a
coddled egg), while splendid sweets like beautifully
light lemon chiffon pie end the meal on a suitably
high note. *Minimum lunchtime charge £2.50,
evenings £6. No dogs.* ★

CARDIFF

Armless Dragon

97 Wyverne Road, Cathays
Town plan D1 *South Glamorgan*
Cardiff (0222) 382357
P street parking

Open 12–2.15
Closed Sat, Sun, Bank Hols & 1 wk
Xmas

Crab soup £2.50 Laverballs
& mushrooms £2.80

Just-a-biters can opt for a single lunchtime
course at this cheerful restaurant in a quiet
residential area north of the city centre.
Fish is a speciality, with choices ranging
from creamy crab soup to brill, hake and
halibut served with a variety of spicy
sauces. Meat dishes might include rabbit
in mustard and onion sauce or guinea fowl
with blackberries, and there are temptingly
rich desserts to finish. More elaborate
evening meals. *No dogs.*

Credit Access, Amex, Diners, Visa

CARDIFF

La Brasserie

60 St Mary Street
Town plan D3 *South Glamorgan*
Cardiff (0222) 372164
P NCP in Wood Street

Open 12–3 & 7–12.15
Closed Sun

Suckling pig £6.95 Fillet steak £6.45

A superb collection of Armagnacs dating
back to 1903, together with some 100
different French wines, are a great attraction at this popular wine bar. The menu is
French influenced with choices ranging
from dressed crab and mussels to seasonal
duck and game, lamb brochette and eve-
nings-only specials like roast suckling pig.
Salads and jacket potatoes accompany
your meal which is finished off with cheese.
No dogs.

Credit Access, Amex, Diners, Visa

CARDIFF   *Champers*

61 St Mary Street
Town plan D3 *South Glamorgan*
Cardiff (0222) 373363
P NCP in Wood Street

Open 12–3 & 7–12.15
Closed Sun lunch

Spare ribs £3.75   Fillet steak £6.45

The menu is biased towards meat eaters at this Spanish-style wine bar with sawdust-strewn floors, one of three similar restaurants (see also La Brasserie and Le Monde). Kebabs, burgers, chops and steaks are all expertly chargrilled and accompanied by delicious baked potatoes and help-yourself salads. Langoustines and shrimps feature among the fish options. Cheese platter to finish, and a fine selection of vintage ports, champagnes and Spanish wines. *No dogs.*

Credit Access, Amex, Diners, Visa

CARDIFF   *Le Monde*

61 St Mary Street
Town plan D3 *South Glamorgan*
Cardiff (0222) 387376
P NCP in Wood Street

Open 12–3 & 7–12.15
Closed Sun

Crab salad £4.95   Sea bass in rock salt £6.95

Chic black and chrome decorate the walls of this Art Deco-style restaurant. There are a few meat dishes on offer (maybe noisettes of lamb), but fish is the speciality. Choose your main course – sea bass, halibut, red mullet, salmon, langoustines – from a display and it will be prepared to order and served with good French fries and a selection of salads. Starters include whitebait and mussels, and there's cheese to round off your meal. *No dogs.*

Credit Access, Amex, Diners, Visa

CARDIFF   *Riverside*

44 Tudor Street
Town plan C3 *South Glamorgan*
Cardiff (0222) 372163
P street parking

Open noon–midnight

Dim sum from £2   Chinese roast duck £3.90

Welsh and Chinese locals alike flock to this hugely popular, elegantly decorated Cantonese restaurant in Cardiff's Chinese quarter. Although the extensive main menu is not expensive, it's the excellent dim sum selection that scores highest on quality and value. Choose from succulent prawns wrapped in rice paper, roast pork or chicken dumplings, crispy spring rolls and spare ribs in black bean sauce – all freshly cooked to order. *No dogs.*

Credit Access, Amex, Visa

CARDIFF   *Sage*

Wellfield Court, off Wellfield Road, Roath
Town plan E1 *South Glamorgan*
Cardiff (0222) 481223
P street parking

Open 9–5
Closed Sun, Bank Hols & 1 wk Xmas

Pumpkin pie 85p   Aduki bean pie £2.50

Tucked away in a little shopping mall, this simple vegetarian restaurant is run with friendly efficiency by a delightful mother and daughter team. Hot lunchtime dishes range from lentil and cumin soup to nut loaf and brown rice salad with soya dressing, while other wholesome choices always include a vegan and lacto-vegetarian special such as millet and vegetable gratinée. To finish, try tempting carob and orange cake. *Non-smoking area. No dogs.*

Ogden Nash
1902–71

By undraped nymphs
I am not wooed;
I'd rather painters painted food . . .
'The Clean Platter' in *The Face is Familiar* (1954)

———————

C. Herman Senn

Oh, I am a festive chafing dish,
I foam, and froth, and bubble,
I sing the song of meat and fish,
And save a deal of trouble.
Chafing Dish and Casserole Cookery (1908)

———————

Jonathan Swift
1667–1745

Promises and pie-crust are made to be broken.
Polite Conversation

———————

'Saki' (H. H. Munro)
1870–1916

I believe that I once considerably scandalised her
by declaring that clear soup was a more important
factor in life than a clear conscience.
The Blind Spot

CARMARTHEN   *Waverley Restaurant*

23 Lammas Street
MAP 7 B3 *Dyfed*
Carmarthen (0267) 236521
P   street parking

Open 9–4 (Thurs till 2)
Closed Sun & Bank Hols

Vegetarian lasagne with salad £2   Fresh
strawberry cheesecake £1

An airy and informal cafeteria-style restaurant at the rear of a wholefood shop on
one of the main shopping streets. Arrive
early to taste the hot food as soon as it
leaves the ovens – vegetarian moussaka,
lasagne and Scotch eggs, nutburgers and
hot fruit crumble – or choose one of the
day's four quiches with salads and baked
potatoes. Finish with cheesecake, apple
and ginger meringue or one of the selection
of cakes and scones. *No smoking. No
dogs.*

CHEPSTOW   *Willow Tree*

'The Back', Chepstow River Bank
MAP 7 C3 *Gwent*
Chepstow (029 12) 6665
P   riverbank &

Open 11–5
Closed Sun & Mon eves & all 25 & 26
Dec

Tagliatelle Waldorf £2.10   Rack of lamb
with honey & orange sauce £7.95   🍵
🍵

Jeremy Hector's super little 16th-century
cottage restaurant has a conservatory-
style tea room and a cosy, antique-furnished room where just-a-biters can enjoy
his fare. As well as delectable cakes and
scones, there are lunchtime blackboard
specials ranging from soup and garlicky
prawns to peppered beef in red wine, pork
tenderloin with plum sauce and an exemplary chocolate St. Emilion. More elaborate
evening meals. *No dogs.*

Credit Access, Visa

COWBRIDGE   *Off The Beeton Track*

1 Town Hall Square
MAP 7 C4 *South Glamorgan*
Cowbridge (044 63) 3599
P   Town Square car park

Open 10–2.30 & 7.30–10
Closed Sun eve, all Mon & Bank Hols

Cream of celery soup £1.80   Smoked
salmon parcels £3.50   🍵 🍵

Set back from the town square in its own
little courtyard where tables are put out
in summer, this pleasant stonebuilt
restaurant offers good eating throughout
the day. Pop in for coffee and shortcake in
the morning, or light lunches and suppers
featuring creamy soups, salads and nicely
sauced pasta, plus more substantial offerings such as hotpot or home-made meat
pie. Simple sweets and a fine cheeseboard.
Traditional roasts for Sunday lunch.
No dogs.

Credit Access, Amex, Visa

EGLWYSFACH   *Ty'n-y-Cwm Tea Rooms*

Artists' Valley, Nr Machynlleth
MAP 7 B2 *Dyfed*
Glandyfi (065 474) 278
P   own car park

Open 10.30–5.30 (Tues from 2)
Closed mid Nov–Easter

Chocolate fudge cake £1.25   Scone &
cream 75p   🍵

The café in Artists' Valley is the haunt of
walkers and painters, all of whom enjoy
the good, simple food and pretty garden at
this charming chalet by a stream. Follow
the narrow road through Forestry Com-
mission land for a couple of miles to reach
it. There are snacks like quiche, salads and
sandwiches and enjoyable sweet things:
Welsh cakes, gingerbread, scones with
jam and cream and the traditional Welsh
speciality cake, bara brith. *Unlicensed. No
smoking.*

HAY-ON-WYE   *The Granary*

Broad Street
MAP 7 C3 *Powys*
Hay-on-Wye (0497) 820790
P street parking

Open 10–5.30 (July & Aug till 9)
Closed 25 & 26 Dec

Steak & kidney pie £3.95   Nut roast &
salad £3.50   🍵   🐾

The cake and sweets buffet groans all day
long with the weight of home-baked
offerings, like the ever-popular yoghurt
and fresh fruit cheesecake. There is an urn
of hot home-made soup and daily-changing
hot specials. These might include lamb and
spinach curry, baked potatoes, spaghetti
bolognese, a ploughman's lunch and ratatouille. Everything is available all day long.
There is an overspill of customers on to
pavement tables in the summer.

Credit Access, Visa

HAY-ON-WYE   *Lion's Corner House*

6 Market Street
MAP 7 C3 *Powys*
Hay-on-Wye (0497) 820175
P Town centre parking

Open 11–2 & 7–9.30 (till 9 Mon & till
10 Sat)
Closed Sun (except before Bank Hols)
& Mon & Tues Jan & Feb

Deep fried Brie with herb mayonnaise
£1.95   Grilled pork with fennel &
caraway seed sauce £4.25   🍵

Owner Colin Thomson took the name with
him when he moved premises, even though
this site is not actually on a corner. The
cooking is careful and effective, with a
good variety of dishes on offer: fresh fish,
vegetable and nut roast, beef lasagne and
spinach pancake at lunchtime to more
elaborate evening choices. Kick off with
garlic snails or deep-fried whitebait and
finish with maple syrup tart, coffee fudge
pie or lemon soufflé. *Non-smoking area.*
No dogs.

Credit Access, Amex, Diners, Visa

LLANBERIS   <small>N·E·W
ENTRY</small>   *Y Bistro Bach*

43 High Street
MAP 7 B2 *Gwynedd*
Llanberis (0286) 871278
P street parking ♿

Open 12.30–9.30 (Oct–Easter
7.30pm–9.30pm only)
Closed Sun (except those preceding
Bank Hol Mons), 3 wks Jan–Feb & 1 wk
Xmas

Venison sausages served with fresh pasta
£3.25   Snowdon pudding £1.90   🍵

At the rear of their town-centre restaurant,
and with its own entrance, is this new
bistro-style venture for the Roberts. A
simple menu based on that of the restaurant, but with some interesting additions,
lists the freshly prepared and wonderfully
flavoured dishes. Select from local cockles
in a cream sauce with savoury crumble
topping, meaty venison sausages, leeks
wrapped in ham, smoked Finnan haddock
or delicious thinly sliced roast beef. *No*
smoking. No dogs.

Credit Access, Visa

LLANRHAEADR   *The Lodge*

Nr Denbigh
MAP 7 C2 *Clwyd*
Llanynys (074 578) 370
P own car park

Open 10–5, Mar–Aug 9–5.30
Closed Sun & Bank Hols

Ham & leek supreme £1.35   Cheesy
tortilla £1.50   🐾

The Dykins family's neat little coffee bar
shares premises with their stylish ladies
fashion shop on the A525. Customers can
take a break from trying on dresses over a
good cup of tea and delicious home-made
scones and cakes, or pop in at lunchtime
for a ploughman's salad or omelette.
Tempting fruit pies, Bakewell tarts, flapjacks, lemon meringue pie or nostalgic
knickerbocker glory to follow. *No dogs.*

Credit Access, Visa

LLANRWST   *Tu-Hwnt-i'r-Bont*

MAP 7 B2 *Gwynedd*
Llanrwst (0492) 640138
P own car park

Open 10.30–5.30
Closed Mon (except Bank Hols) & 1st
Sun in Oct–Tues before Easter

Ploughman's with Welsh Cheddar £2.15
Welsh tea with scones & jam £1.30   ℮
🍵

In this tiny ivy-clad cottage standing in its
own grounds on the river bank, the Holt
family run their charming little café. You
can watch Derek Holt making the scones
and filling the soft, floury baps. There's
cheese or pâté ploughman's and salads at
lunchtime. Afternoon tea includes cake or
bara brith and there are toasted teacakes,
home-baked cakes, sponges and sodas and
home-made jam. The tea in individual pots
is a treat. *Non-smoking area.*

MACHYNLLETH   *Centre for Alternative Technology*

Pantperthog
MAP 7 B2 *Powys*
Machynlleth (0654) 2400
P own car park

Open 10–2.30 & 3–5
Closed 25 & 26 Dec

Leek & mushroom croustade £2.60
Trifle 85p

Three miles north of Machynlleth, just off
the A487, this fascinating complex (admis-
sion £2.30) looks after the inner man with
some healthy, appetising snacks served in
both its vegetarian restaurant and coffee
house. Filled rolls, salads, hearty soups
(split pea, carrot and orange) and flavoursome cakes provide light bites, while more
substantial offerings include mushroom
quiche, nut roast and a daily vegan special
like sweet and sour vegetables with tofu.
Unlicensed. No smoking. No dogs.

---

*We publish annually
so make sure you use the current edition.*

MACHYNLLETH   *Quarry Shop*

13 Maengwyn Street
MAP 7 B2 *Powys*
Machynlleth (0654) 2624
P street parking

Open 9–4.30 (till 5 in summer)
Closed Sun (except in summer) & 25
& 26 Dec

Leek & sweetcorn soup 70p   Cashew nut
risotto & salad £2.10

Part of a vegetarian wholefood shop run
by the same cooperative responsible for
the Centre for Alternative Technology,
this simple, pine-furnished restaurant offers wholesome snacks based on organically grown produce. At lunchtime a vegan
soup (perhaps French onion) precedes
hearty main dishes such as red bean
bourguignon, pizzas, quiches and colourful, imaginative salads. Lovely vegan cakes
too (try lemon spice or chocolate malt),
plus moist banana bread and trifle. *Unlicensed. No smoking. No dogs.*

NEWPORT   *Cnapan*

East Street
MAP 7 A3 *Dyfed*
Newport (0239) 820575
P street parking

Open 10.30–5
Closed Tues & Nov–Easter (except Sun lunch & Fri & Sat eves)

Crab & laverbread flan £3.50   Plum & almond crumble £1.10   ℰ

In a lovely listed Georgian house complete with pretty garden and five letting rooms, this delightfully homely restaurant is run with charm and style by the Lloyds and Coopers. Traditional baking accompanies morning coffee and afternoon tea, or for a hearty lunch try a local-cheese platter, an oat-based flan or a bumper pizza. Round things off with a raspberry and macaroon slice or an apple and mincemeat flan. More elaborate evening meals. *Non-smoking area. No dogs.*

Credit Access, Visa

RHYD-Y-CLAFDY   *Tu Hwnt i'r Afon*

Llanbedrog
MAP 7 A2 *Gwynedd*
Llanbedrog (0758) 740929
P own car park

Open 12–3 & 7–9.30
Closed Sun in winter

Crayfish in garlic £6.50   Chargrilled leg of lamb £5   ℰ

Dating back to the 14th century, these converted farm buildings are steeped in history. The floor is black Welsh brick, the refectory tables are black too, but all is brightened with fresh flowers, fruit and gleaming copperware, and in summer there are tables outside. The printed menu and specials board offer choices like mussels in garlic, vegetarian lasagne, chicken stuffed with cheese and mushrooms, fresh lobster salad, genuinely home-made pizzas and a selection of local Welsh cheeses. *No dogs.*

SWANSEA   *La Braseria*

28 Wind Street
MAP 7 B3 *West Glamorgan*
Swansea (0792) 469683
P car park opposite

Open 11–2.30 & 7–12
Closed Sun lunch & 25 Dec

Spare ribs £2.75   Sea bass in rock salt £6.95   ℰ

Heavy oak timbers, a sawdust-strewn floor and candles at night create an atmospheric setting for simple but satisfying eating at this spacious restaurant. Charcoal grills are the speciality, the choice ranging from fillet steak to wonderfully flavoursome sardines and melt-in-the-mouth salmon, all served with a jacket potato and mixed salad. No sweets, but a good selection of cheeses and some 40 different Spanish wines. *No dogs.*

Credit Access, Amex, Diners, Visa

WOLF'S CASTLE   *Wolfscastle Country Hotel*

Haverfordwest
MAP 7 A3 *Dyfed*
Treffgarne (043 787) 225
P own car park

Open 12–2

Sautéed mushrooms with garlic & cream £2.50   Savoury meat rissoles £2.95   ℰ

A country hotel with an interesting mix of hungry lunchtime customers in its welcoming bar. Excellent light snacks range from creamy soup, ploughman's and salads based on cold, cooked meats, quiche and locally-smoked trout to baked potatoes with tasty fillings like prawn mayonnaise or cottage cheese and pineapple. For the heartier appetite, there's beef casserole and smoked haddock roulade, with tempting sweets like hot lemon pie or sticky toffee pudding to finish.

Credit Access, Amex, Visa

G. K. Chesterton
1874–1936

Tea, though an oriental
Is a gentleman at least;
Cocoa is a cad and coward,
Cocoa is a vulgar beast.
The Song of Right and Wrong

R. H. Barham
1788–1845

'Tis not her coldness, father,
That chills my labouring breast;
It's that confounded cucumber
I've ate and can't digest.
'The Confession'

Oscar Mendelsohn

Breathes there a man with nose so dead
Who never to himself has said:
'One pickled onion, one shallot,
Would raise this dish to what it's not'?
'Pickled Onions', in *A Salute to Onions* (1966)

Anonymous

I eat my peas with honey,
I've done it all my life.
It makes the peas taste funny
But it keeps them on the knife!
Manners

CHANNEL ISLANDS

ST ANNE — *Gossip*

6 Victoria Street
MAP 8 D3 *Alderney*
Alderney (048 182) 3485
P street parking

Open 9.30–4.30 (9–5 in summer) & 7–9.30, Sun 10.30–12.30 & 7–9.30
Closed 1 Jan, Good Fri & 25 & 26 Dec

Filled jacket potato 90p   Pizza £1.80

A popular meeting place with locals and tourists alike, this convivial coffee shop on the cobbled main street offers simple, satisfying snacks throughout the day. Plain or toasted sandwiches, soup, salads and jacket potatoes are favourite light bites, while on the sweet side there are scones, flapjacks and a delicious chocolate gâteau. A pizzeria operation takes over in the evening in summer. *Unlicensed (bring your own). No dogs.*

ST PETER PORT — *Flying Dutchman Hotel*

Ruette Braye
MAP 8 C3 *Guernsey*
Guernsey (0481) 23787
P own car park

Open 12–2 & 6–10
Closed Sun, 25 & 26 Dec, last wk Jan & all Feb

Brill meunière £7.50   Mushroom crêpe £2.50

Delightfully jovial hosts the Deutchmanns offer a varied menu including specialities such as gravad lax and a perfectly cooked bratwurst with authentic sauerkraut. Filled crêpes, croque-monsieur, crab toast and Danish open sandwiches provide alternative choices. Son Bjorn has inherited his father's pâtisserie skills – a sublime Princess gâteau (filled with custard and topped with marzipan) and *real* Black Forest gâteau should not be missed. *No dogs.*

Credit Amex, Visa

Any person using our name to obtain free hospitality is a fraud.

Proprietors, please inform Egon Ronay's Guides and the police.

GOREY VILLAGE   *Jersey Pottery Restaurant*

MAP 8 D3 *Jersey*
Jersey (0534) 51119
P own car park   &

Open 9–5.30

Closed Sat & Sun, Bank Hols
& 10 days Xmas

Avocado with prawns £3.95
Parma ham & melon £3.95
Whole lobster £13.95
Strawberries & cream £1.95

★ On sunny days eat in the delightful garden of this enormously popular restaurant and adjoining working pottery. Superb seafood is the speciality here, including huge, colourful salads featuring lobster, dressed crab, prawns and smoked salmon, plus an over-flowing plateau de fruits de mer. There are also tempting starters like tomatoes with mozzarella or fresh asparagus, as well as cold meats and filled rolls. Finish in style with delicious home-made pastries or succulent strawberries in season – served with lashings of thick Jersey cream. Service is friendly and efficient and the whole place is spotlessly kept. Children's portions. Patio and terrace. *No dogs.* ★

Credit Access, Amex, Diners, Visa

---

*We welcome bona fide recommendations or complaints
on the tear-out pages at the back of the book
for readers' comments.*

*They are followed up by our professional team,
but do complain to the management on the spot.*

ST BRELADE'S BAY   *Hotel L'Horizon, Beech Lounge*

St Brelade
MAP 8 D3 *Jersey*
Jersey (0534) 43101
P own car park   &

Open 4–5.30

Jersey cream tea £2.40   Fresh salmon
sandwich £3.65

The quiet and elegant surroundings make a relaxing setting for a sumptuous afternoon tea served with style. There is a set tea of scones and Jersey cream, or you can indulge in the more lavish Jersey strawberry tea. Various well-filled sandwiches are on offer with a wide variety of scrumptious pastries, cakes and fruit tarts. There is an extensive choice of teas, all to be enjoyed on a sunny terrace with lovely views. Children's portions. *No dogs.*

Credit Access, Amex, Diners, Visa

ST SAVIOUR   *Longueville Manor Hotel*

MAP 8 D3 *Jersey*
Jersey (0534) 25501
P   own car park

Open 12.30–5

Seasonal terrine £5   Full
afternooon tea £5.50   Smoked
chicken & king prawn salad £6.50
Seafood platter (for 2) £37.00

The elegant lounges and bar of this famous hotel
create an ideal setting for a delicious light lunch or
afternoon tea. Sit by the pool or in the garden in fine
weather and enjoy a menu that is short, but
★   imaginative, using fresh salads and local seafood –   ★
well flavoured and perfectly presented. Fresh fruit
desserts and sorbets follow, but everyone should try
the gorgeous Eton Mess – layers of crushed meringue
and strawberries with thick Jersey cream. The set
afternoon tea is a traditional affair of finger sandwiches, scones and cream and fresh pastries. *No
dogs.*

Credit Access, Amex, Diners, Visa

SARK   *Stocks Buffet*

MAP 8 D3 *Sark*
Sark (0481 83) 2001

Open 10–8.30
Closed Oct–Easter

Seafood provençale £3.95   The Crock
Pot £3.95

The pace of life on Sark is just right for
allowing time to sit on the informal terrace
at Stocks Hotel and enjoy some eminently
capable baking and cooking. Throughout
the day cakes and pastries, both lavish and
plain, are served. At lunchtime more
savoury dishes appear, either as quick
bites, or as fare for healthy appetites, like
chilli, vegetarian pasta, quiche, or local
crab or lobster. Afternooon tea offers
scones and cream. Children's menu.

Credit Amex

ISLE OF MAN

BALLASALLA — La Rosette

Main Road
MAP 3 A3 *Isle of Man*
Castleton (0624) 822940
P street parking

Open 12–3

Closed Sun, Mon, Bank Hols &
last 2 wks Jan

Grilled stuffed mushrooms £3.85
Crêpe farci aux crevettes et
champignons £4.95 Quiche
lorraine £3.50 Smoked salmon
sandwich £3.95 ℮

★ Bob Phillips offers a fine choice of French-inspired dishes at the delightful little restaurant he runs with his charming wife Rosa. Dependably excellent standards of cooking characterise his quarterly-changing menus, and prime ingredients are enhanced by delicious sauces and fresh herbs. Grilled stuffed mushrooms, smoked salmon with prawns and coquilles St Jacques are typically elegant snacks or starters, while more substantial offerings might include tender beef in sweet and sour sauce, grilled fresh fish and hot quiche salad. Finish with a tempting sweet like kiwi fruit cake or ground almond and treacle tart. More formal evening meals available. *No dogs.* ★

Credit Access, Visa

DOUGLAS — L'Expérience

Summerhill
MAP 3 A3 *Isle of Man*
Douglas (0624) 23103
P street parking

Open 12–2 & 7–11
Closed Sun & Tues (except lunch in summer), 1 Jan & 25 & 26 Dec

Prawn omelette £3.30 Croque-
monsieur £1.20 ℮

Piping hot onion soup under a crust of melted cheese, a French ploughman's (with Brie), super croques and a platter of salami and garlic sausage are typically delicious Gallic snacks served at this friendly, informal seafront restaurant. There's always a daily special (usually a casserole), plus three-egg omelettes, juicy steaks and more elaborate evening meals. Simple sweets and French cheeses to finish. Patio. *No dogs.*

Credit Access, Diners, Visa **LVs**

RAMSEY   *Harbour Bistro*

East Street
MAP 3 A3 *Isle of Man*
Ramsey (0624) 814182
P street parking   ♻

Open 12.15–2.30 & 6.30–10.30
Closed Sun, Good Fri, 3 days Xmas &
3 wks Jan

Fisherman's pie £6.35   Grilled duck
£8.85

You can enjoy a full meal or a snack at this
informal bistro by the harbour. The choices
range from sole and plaice, cooked in a
number of ways, to the famous Manx
queenies lightly cooked and full of natural
flavour; from giant prawns to salmon
cooked in a puff pastry shell with a creamy
prawn sauce. Meat eaters can opt for
steaks, chicken or duck as an alternative.
Pleasant sweets to finish. Book. *No dogs.*

Credit Access, Visa

BATH

Town plan opposite

Population 84,000

The Romans settled in Bath because of the waters and built baths used for therapy and recreation. In the 18th century spa treatment reached the peak of fashion and Bath was greatly enlarged at this time. Being wholly built within the space of a century, all its buildings are of the same classic, elegant style. Its Georgian character and charm remained unchanged until very recently. Yet Bath has become the centre of much environmental controversy: should the face of Bath be gradually eroded to develop it as a 20th-century commercial city, or should it be enshrined for ever as a masterpiece of urban architecture?

Annual Events
Bath Festival (music and drama) *May–June*
Royal Bath and West Show

Sights Outside City
Cheddar Gorge, Wookey Hole Caves, Wells Cathedral, Glastonbury Abbey, Longleat House and Safari Park, Castle Combe Village, Lacock Abbey and Village, Stourhead House and gardens, Avebury Circles, Corsham Court

Tourist Information Centre
Abbey Church Yard
Telephone Enquiries Bath 462831

Fiat Dealer
MTR Services Bath
Locksbrook Road
Bath
Avon BA1 2PW
Tel. Bath 428000

1 Abbey *15th c* B4
2 American Museum at Claverton Manor *2¼ miles, life in the New World from 17th c to 1860* C3
3 Artsite B4
4 Assembly Rooms *Finely restored Georgian suite, also houses world-famous Museum of Costume* A2
5 Bath Industrial Heritage Centre A2
6 Bath Spa Station B5
7 Botanical Gardens in Victoria Park A2
8 The Circus, Royal Crescent and Lansdown Crescent *superb examples of Georgian town-planning* A1 & A2
9 Guildhall Banqueting Room *fine Adam-style room* B3
10 Herschel House A3
11 Holburne of Menstrie Museum *paintings, silver, objects d'art* C2
12 Huntingdon Centre B2
13 Lansdown Race-course A1
14 Museum of Bookbinding B4
15 National Museum of Photography B3
16 Postal Museum B3
17 Pulteney Bridge *Adam bridge lined with shops* B3
18 Pump Room and Roman Baths *the heart of Bath, includes Britain's finest Roman remains* B4
19 Sally Lunn's House *oldest House in Bath* B4
20 Sham Castle *18th-c folly and viewpoint* C2
21 Theatre Royal A3
22 Tourist Information Centre B4
23 University C3
24 Victoria Art Gallery *works by mainly West Country Artists; glass; Delft; horology* B3

Bath F I A T

CHIPPENHAM 13miles

A4

• Recommended
  Establishments

CHIPPENHAM 13miles

WARMINSTER 17miles

BRISTOL 13miles

WELLS 21miles

EXETER 80miles

LONDON ROAD

LONDON ROAD

Cleveland Bridge

River Avon

BATHWICK STREET

JULIAN ROAD

CIRCUS MEWS

BENNETT STREET

BROCK ST

THE CIRCUS

ROYAL AVENUE

GEORGE ST

GAY

A4 CHARLOTTE QUEEN ST SQ

CHARLES ST

NEW KING STREET

A3118

JAMES STREET WEST

MONMOUTH STREET

WESTGATE STREET

GREEN PARK ROAD

A36 LOWER BRISTOL ROAD

CORN STREET

River Avon

A367 WELLS ROAD

HOLLOWAY

CALTON GARDENS

CALTON ROAD

PARAGON

WALCOT STREET

BROAD ST

Moon & Sixpence

Rossiters

Number Five

Bath Puppet Theatre

LAURA PLACE

GRAND PARADE

HIGH ST

PIERREPONT ST

MANVERS ST

Canary

The Walrus & the Carpenter

Theatre Vaults

Tarts Restaurant

SOUTH PARADE

NORTH PARADE ROAD

Bus Sta

DORCHESTER ST

Churchill Bridge

CLAVERTON STREET

ROSSITER RD

PULTENEY ROAD

SYDNEY PL

A36

WIDCOMBE HILL

PRIOR PARK ROAD

0   220   440 yards
0   200   400 metres

© 1988 Egon Ronay's Guides

BIRMINGHAM

Town plan opposite

Population 1,007,600

Birmingham is the centre of one of Britain's most dynamic regions. It achieved industrial fame as a result of a fine tradition of craftsmanship. Today the city is noted for its production of motor cars, electrical equipment, machine tools and plastics. It has a splendid tradition in metal ware, including gold and silver work. Birmingham sponsored the £20m plus National Exhibition Centre at Bickenhill, just nine miles south-east of the city. This exhibition centre is Britain's first ever purpose-designed centre and ranks among the most modern in the world.

Sights Outside City
Airport, Coughton Court, Black Country Museum, Ragley Hall, Packwood House, Warwick Castle, West Midland Safari Park, Arbury Hall, Charlecote Park, Stratford-upon-Avon

Information Office
Birmingham Convention & Visitor Bureau, Ticket Shop & Tourist Information Centre, City Arcade, Birmingham B2 4TX
Telephone 021–643 2514

Fiat Dealers
Colmore Depot Ltd
35 Sutton New Road
Erdington, Birmingham B23 6TD
Tel. Birmingham 377 6533

Colmore Depot Ltd
979 Stratford Road
Hall Green, Birmingham B28 8BG
Tel. Birmingham 778 2323

Marston Green Garage
32 Station Road, Marston Green
B37 7AX
Tel. Birmingham 779 5140

1 Alexandra Theatre **C3**
2 Aston Hall *Jacobean masterpiece open to public* **D1**
3 Baskerville House **B2**
4 Botanical Gardens **A3**
5 Bull Ring Shopping Centre *rotunda, multi-level shopping centre and market* **C/D3**
6 Cannon Hill Park **C3**
7 Central Libraries **B2**
8 Council House **B2**
9 Hall of Memory **B2**
10 Hippodrome Theatre **C3**
11 Lickey Hills *500 beautiful acres with views from Beacon Hill of ten counties* **C3**
12 Midland Red Bus Station **C3**
13 Museum and Art Gallery *from Veronese to Picasso via Hogarth and Constable* **B2**
14 Museum of Science and Industry *a link with the Industrial Revolution* **B1**
15 Repertory Theatre **A/B2**
16 New Street Station **C3**
17 Post Office Tower **B1**
18 St Chad's Cathedral *first English Roman Catholic Cathedral since Reformation* **C1**
19 St Philip's Cathedral *18th-c Palladian with later Burne-Jones windows* **C2**
20 Tourist Information Centre **C2**
21 Town Hall *meeting place and home of Symphony Orchestra* **B2**
22 University of Aston **D1**
23 University of Birmingham **C3**

Birmingham

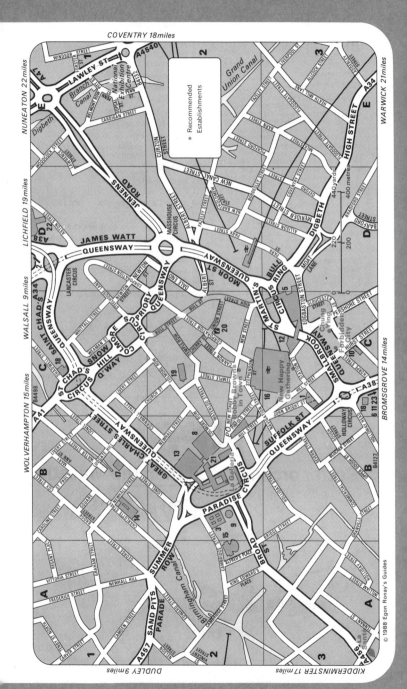

Recommended Establishments

© 1988 Egon Ronay's Guides

FIAT GUIDE TO SIGHTS

BRIGHTON

Town plan opposite

Population 153,700

Brighton is Regency squares and terraces, the maze of art and junk shops called the Lanes, the beach and piers, the conferences and entertainments, the milling crowds in Brighton, and the quiet lawns of Hove, a day out for Londoners, a holiday and retirement centre, a commuter's town and a university town. The person most responsible for all this was George IV, who made it the vogue and commissioned his unique palace, the Royal Pavilion.

Annual Events
Brighton Festival *May*
Glyndebourne *May–August*
London to Brighton veteran car run *Nov*

Sights Outside Town
Arundel Castle, Petworth House, Bluebell Railway

Information Centres
Marlborough House, Old Steine and Sea-front opp. West Street
Telephone Brighton 23755

Fiat Dealers
Tilleys (Sussex) Ltd
100 Lewes Road
Brighton BN2 3QA
Telephone Brighton 603244
Map reference **1E**

Tilleys (Sussex) Ltd
2 Church Road
Hove BN3 2FL
Telephone Brighton 738949
Map reference **2A**

1 Aquarium and Dolphinarium **D3**
2 Booth Bird Museum *British birds in natural surroundings* **B1**
3 Brighton & Hove Albion F.C. **A1**
4 Brighton Conference & Exhibition Centre **C3**
5 Churchill Square **C3**
6 County Cricket Ground **A2**
7 Devil's Dyke *4 miles, Sussex beauty spot* **B1**
8 Information Centres **C3**
9 The Lanes *network of old fisherman's cottages, now world centre for antiques* **C3**
10 Marina **E3**
11 Museum & Art Gallery **C/D3**
12 Palace Pier **D3**
13 Preston Park and Preston Manor *18th c* **C1**
14 Race-course **E1**
15 Rottingdean *2¼ miles, toy museum* **E3**
16 Royal Pavilion *Regency exhibition, art gallery and museum* **C/D3**
17 Station **C2**
18 Sussex University *4 miles* **E1**
19 Theatre Royal **C3**
20 Volks Railway *first electric railway, on seafront* **D3**

TIPO.
Better orchestrated than the Maestro.

To see how the Tipo beats the Maestro, contact your local Fiat Dealer. See pages 84–87

Brighton

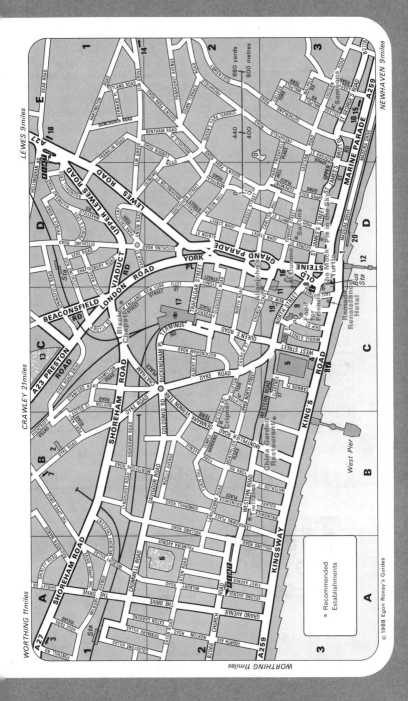

BRISTOL

Town plan opposite

Population 391,500

The Birthplace of America–the Cabots sailed from here to discover Newfoundland in 1497. This and later voyages brought Bristol prosperity, largely in sugar, tobacco, rum and the slave trade. Architecture surviving the 1940 war damage ranges over the 13th-century Lord Mayor's Chapel, St Mary Redcliffe Church, England's oldest working theatre (Theatre-Royal–now completely renovated), and Clifton's Georgian terraces.

Annual Events
Powerboat Grand Prix *June*
Senior Citizens' Day *June*
World Wine Fair *July*
Bristol Harbour Regatta & Rally of Boats *July*
International Balloon Fiesta *August*
Bristol Maritime Carnival *August*
Bristol Flower Show *August/September*
Christmas Illuminated Water Carnival *December*

Sights Outside City
Severn Bridge, Berkeley Castle, Wells Cathedral, Cheddar Gorge, Severn Wildfowl Trust, Castle Combe Village, Bath

Tourist Information Centre
Colston House, Colston Street
Telephone Bristol 293891

Fiat Dealers
Autotrend Ltd
724–726 Fishponds Road
Bristol BS16 3UE
Tel. Bristol 659491

Bawns Ltd
168–176 Coronation Road
Bristol BS3 1RG
Tel. Bristol 631101

1 Airport *6 miles* A3
2 Arnolfini (Arts Centre) C3
3 Ashton Court Estate *beautiful parklands* A1
4 Blaise Castle House Folk Museum *Henbury* A1
5 Bristol Industrial Museum C3
6 Bristol Cathedral *dates from 12th c* B3
7 Bristol Tapestry and Permanent Planning Exhibition D1
8 Cabot Tower *Brandon Hill, built 1897* A2
9 Central Library B3
10 Chatterton House *Chatterton's birthplace* D3
11 Christmas Steps *antique shops* C1
12 City Museum & Art Gallery *fine & applied arts* B1
13 Clifton suspension bridge A1
14 Colston Hall concert hall B2
15 Council House B2
16 Entertainment Centre B2
17 The Exploratory Hands-on-Science Centre A1
18 Georgian House *late 18th-c showpiece* B2
19 Harveys Wine Museum B2
20 Hippodrome B2
21 John Wesley Chapel *first Methodist Chapel* D1
22 Little Theatre C2
23 Lord Mayor's Chapel *13th c* B2
24 Nails and the Exchange C2
25 National Lifeboat Museum C3
26 Norman Arch B3
27 Observatory, Clifton Down A1
28 Red Lodge *late 16th-c showpiece* B2
29 Royal York Crescent *Regency* A2
30 St Mary Redcliffe Church *dates from 13th c* D3
31 St Nicholas Church Museum C2
32 St Peter and St Paul *R.C. Cathedral* A1
33 S.S. 'Great Britain' *Great Britain Dock* A3
34 Temple Meads Station E3
35 Theatre Royal *home of the Bristol Old Vic* C2
36 Tourist Information Centre B2
37 Zoo *including flowers and rare trees* A1

Bristol F I A T

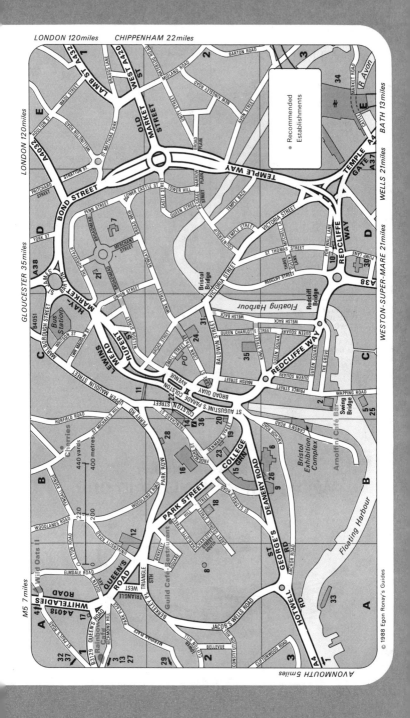

CANTERBURY

Town plan opposite

Population 36,290

The Metropolitan City of the English Church (since 602), where St Augustine preached (597), and Archbishop Thomas à Becket was martyred in the Cathedral (1170). Canterbury was successfully settled by the Belgae, the Romans, the Saxons and the Normans. It has been a town of pilgrim-tourists since 1008 and the Cathedral, medieval buildings and archives well repay a lingering visit. It is strong in literary association through Chaucer and Marlowe.

Sights Outside City
Bodiam Castle, Chilham, Dover Castle, Herne Bay, Leeds Castle, Lympne Castle, Reculver Towers, Rye and Winchelsea, Walmer Castle, Whitstable Castle and Grounds

Information Office
34 St Margaret's Street
CT1 2TG
Telephone Canterbury 766567
Leisure Line 67744

Fiat Dealer
Martin Walter Ltd
41 St George's Place
Canterbury
Kent CT1 1UR
Tel. Canterbury 763800
Map reference **3D**

1 Blackfriars _13th-c Friary_ C1
2 Cathedral _11th–15th c_ D2
3 Christchurch Gate and Buttermarket **C2**
4 Conquest House **C1**
5 Dane John Garden _a memorial to Marlowe_ C3
6 East Station **B3**
7 Greyfriars _first Franciscan settlement_ B2
8 The Marlowe Theatre **C1**
9 Martyrs' Memorial _to Bloody Mary's victims_ B3
10 Norman Castle _large Norman keep_ B3
11 Norman Staircase _very fine roofed steps_ and King's School _originally Priory hostel_ D1
12 Queen Elizabeth's Guest Chamber **C2**
13 Roman Pavement and hypocaust **C2**
14 Royal Museum **C2**
15 St Augustine's Abbey _layered monastic remains_ D2
16 St Dunstan's church _contains head of Sir Thomas More_ A1
17 St George's Tower **D2**
18 St Martin's Church _oldest in use_ E2
19 St Peter's Church _Anglo-Saxon_ C2
20 St Peter's Street _typical medieval street_ C2
21 St Thomas's (Eastbridge Hospital) _collection of 12th-c–17th-c buildings, beautiful Norman crypt_ C2
22 Sir John Boys's House _ancient lopsided house_ C1
23 The Weavers _16th-c weavers' houses_ C2
24 Tower House **B2**
25 University and Gulbenkian Theatre A1
26 West Station **B1**
27 Westgate Gardens **B2**
28 Westgate Tower _arms and armour museum_ B1

Canterbury F/I/A/T

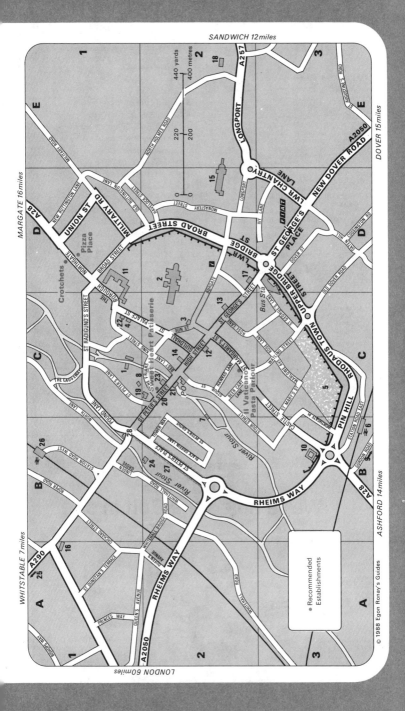

© 1988 Egon Ronay's Guides

● Recommended Establishments

CARDIFF

Town plan opposite

Population 284,400

Though it enshrines Welsh culture and history, Cardiff is both modern and cosmopolitan. Its population was less than 2,000 at the beginning of the 19th century, when its port developed with export of coal from the near-by mines. No British city is more compact in its many offerings to visitors, everything dominated by the comprehensive City Centre and the lovingly restored Castle. It is a matter of choice whether Welsh tradition, commerce or sport matter most to the visitor, though certainly the last attracts the most visitors *en masse*, especially to Cardiff Arms Park. Though Cardiff is an ideal base for touring South Wales, a short visit offers more than enough to remain within the city limits.

Annual Events
Cardiff Festival *July/August*
Festival of Music *November–December*
Horticultural Show *September*
Llandaff Festival *June*
Lord Mayor's Parade *August*
Military Tattoo *August* (every other year)

Information Office
Public Relations Officer
City Hall, Cardiff
Telephone Cardiff 822000

Wales Tourist Board
Brunel House
2 Fitzalan Road, Cardiff

Fiat Dealer
T. S. Grimshaw Ltd
Fiat House
329 Cowbridge Road East
Cardiff CF5 1JD
Tel. Cardiff 395322
Map reference **2A**

Yapp's Garages Ltd
Fidlas Road
Llanishen
Cardiff CF4 5YW
Tel. Cardiff 751323

1 Bute Park **C1/2**
2 Cardiff Castle *fairy-tale magnificence bequeathed by the Bute family* **C2**
3 Civic Centre **C1/2, D1/2**
4 General Station **C/D3**
5 Llandaff Cathedral **A1**
6 National Museum of Wales **D1**
7 National Sports Centre for Wales **B1**
8 New Theatre, Park Place **D2**
9 Queen Street Station **E2**
10 St David's Centre **D2**
11 St David's Hall **D3**
12 St John's Church, St John Square **D2**
13 Sherman Theatre **D1**
14 Tourist Information Office **D3**
15 Wales National Ice Rink **D3**
16 Welsh Industrial and Maritime Museum, Bute Street **D3**
17 Wood Street Bus Station **C3**

Cardiff FIAT

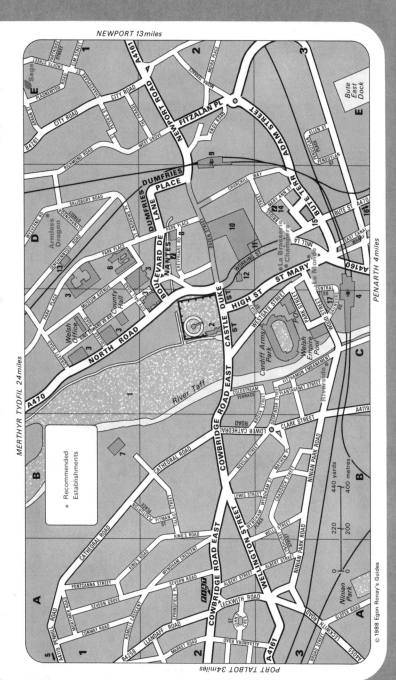

Cardiff map — © 1988 Egon Ronay's Guides

- Recommended Establishments

F I A T Edinburgh

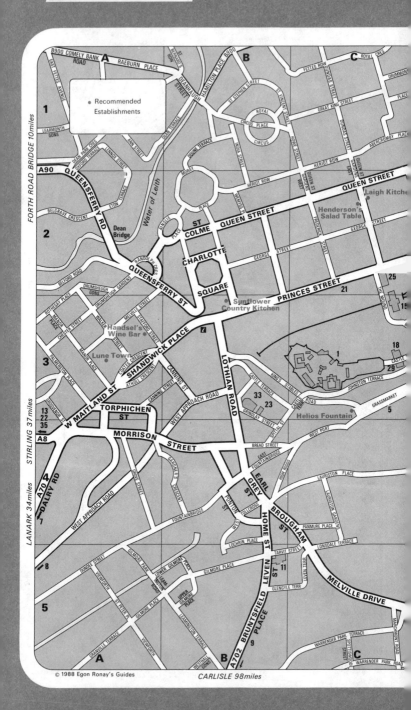

• Recommended Establishments

Laigh Kitchen

Henderson's Salad Table

Sunflower Country Kitchen

Handsel's Wine Bar

Lune Town

Helios Fountain

Dean Bridge

© 1988 Egon Ronay's Guides

CARLISLE 98miles

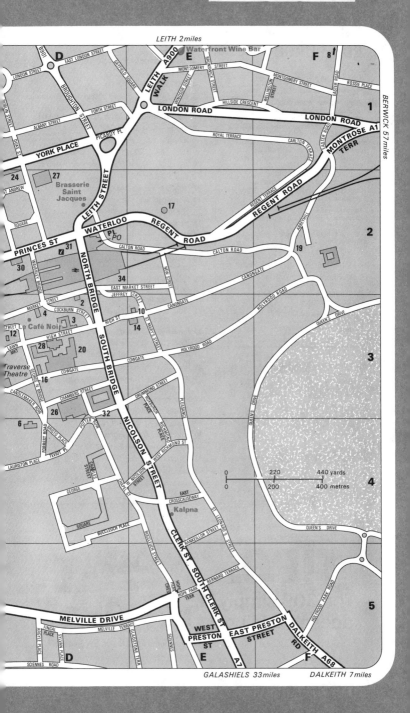

EDINBURGH

Town plan on preceding page

Population 444,741

Edinburgh was founded about a thousand years ago on the Rock which dominates the city. The narrow Old Town, with its one main street (the Royal Mile stretching from the Castle to Holyroodhouse) is the city of John Knox and Mary Queen of Scots. Its Royal Charter was granted by Robert the Bruce in 1329. The gracious New Town is a magnificent example of 18th-century town planning. Today Edinburgh is a centre of festival and pageantry, culture and conferences.

Annual Events
Edinburgh Festival *13th August–2nd September*
Festival Fringe *13th August–2nd September*
Military Tattoo *11th August–2nd September*
Royal Highland Show *18th–21st June*

Sights Outside City
Cramond Village, Duddingston Village, Forth Bridge, Lauriston Castle, Craigmillar Castle

Tourist Information Centre
Waverley Market
3 Princes Street EH2 2QP
Telephone 031–557 2727

Fiat Dealers
Hamilton Bros. (Edinburgh) Ltd
162 St Johns Road
Corstorphine
Edinburgh EH12 8AZ
Tel. 031–334 6248

Croall & Croall
Glenogle Road
Edinburgh EH3 5HW
Telephone 031–556 6404

1 Castle **C3**
2 City Art Centre **D3**
3 City Chambers **D3**
4 Festival Booking Office **D3**
5 Grassmarket *picturesque old buildings and antique shops* **C3**
6 Greyfriars Kirk *and Greyfriars Bobby statue* **D4**
7 Heart of Midlothian F.C. **A4**
8 Hibernian F.C. *Easter Road Park* **F1**
9 Hillend *dry ski centre open all year* **B5**
10 John Knox's House *1490, timber galleries* **D/E3**
11 King's Theatre **B5**
12 Lady Stair's House *1692, literary museum* **D3**
13 Murrayfield Rugby Ground **A4**
14 Museum of Childhood **E3**
15 National Gallery *try 'Sound Guide'* **C3**
16 National Library **D3**
17 Nelson's Monument *viewpoint* **E2**
18 Outlook Tower *Camera obscura and Scottish life exhibition* **C3**
19 Palace of Holyroodhouse and Arthur's Seat and the Park **F2**
20 Parliament House and Law Courts **D3**
21 Princes Street *shopping and gardens, bandstand, floral clock, war memorials* **B3/C2/D2**
22 Royal Highland Showground **A3**
23 Royal Lyceum Theatre **B3**
24 Royal Museum of Scotland **D2**
25 Royal Scottish Academy **C2**
26 Royal Scottish Museum *largest museum of science and art in U.K.* **D3**
27 St Andrew Square Bus Station **D2**
28 St Giles' Cathedral **D3**
29 Scotch Whisky Heritage Centre **C3**
30 Scott Monument *viewpoint* **D2**
31 Tourist Information Centre **D2**
32 University of Edinburgh **D3**
33 Usher Hall **B3**
34 Waverley Station **D2**
35 Zoo **A3**

GLASGOW

Town plan overleaf

Population 755,429

Prime factors in Glasgow's history were
the River Clyde and the Industrial
Revolution (helped by the Lowland
genius for shipbuilding and engineering).
Glasgow is the home of Scottish Opera,
Scottish Ballet and the Scottish National
Orchestra. The city has a fine collection
of museums, most notably that at
Kelvingrove and the Burrell Gallery.
Famous for learning (two universities),
sport (soccer), shops, and art galleries,
the city boasts over seventy parks and the
Scottish Exhibition and Conference
Centre.

Annual Events
Mayfest, Paisley Festival *May*
Jazz Festival *June/July*
Horse Show and Country Fair *July*

Sights Outside City
Paisley Abbey, Forth and Clyde Canal at
Kirkintilloch, Clyde Muirshiel Park at
Lochwinnoch, Weavers Cottage
(Kilbarchan)

Tourist Information Offices
35/39 St Vincent Place, Glasgow G1
2ER. Open June–Sept Mon–Sat 9am–
9pm Sun 10am–6pm. Open Oct–May
Mon–Sat 9am–6pm Sun Closed
Telephone 041–227 4880.
Telex 779504
Town Hall, Abbey Close, Paisley
PA1 1JS. Open June–Sept Mon–Fri
9am–6pm, Sat 9am–5pm, Oct–May
Mon–Fri 9am–5pm
Telephone 041–889 0711

Glasgow Airport
Open Mon–Sun 9am–9pm
Telephone 041-848 4440

Fiat Dealers
Peat Road Motors (Jordanhill) Ltd
120 Whittingehame Drive
Jordanhill, Glasgow GL12 0YJ
Tel. Glasgow 357 1939

Ritchie's
393 Shields Road Glasgow G41 1NZ
Tel. Glasgow 429 5611

1 Airport **A5**

2 Art Gallery and Museum *paintings, ceramics, silver, costumes, etc.* **A2**

3 The Barrows *weekend street market* **F5**

4 Botanic Gardens **A1**

5 Briggait **D5**

6 Burrell Gallery *paintings, stained glass, tapestries, ceramics* **C5**

7 Central Station **C4**

8 Citizens' Theatre **D5**

9 City Chambers *fine loggia* **D3**

10 City Hall **E4**

11 Clyde Tunnel **A4**

12 Glasgow Cathedral *impressive Gothic* **F3**

13 Glasgow Cross *1626 Tolbooth Steeple* **E5**

14 Glasgow Green *city's oldest riverside park* **F5**

15 Glasgow Zoo **F5**

16 Haggs Castle *fun for the children* **C5**

17 Hunterian Museum & Art Gallery (Glasgow University) *early books, archaeology* **A2**

18 King's Theatre **A2**

19 Mitchell Library and Theatre **A2**

20 Museum of Transport *comprehensive collection. Also engineering, shipbuilding* **A2**

21 People's Palace *local history* **F5**

22 Pollok House *Spanish paintings, English furniture, rare silver, in Adam building amid parkland* **C5**

23 Queen Street Station **D3**

24 Scottish Exhibition and Conference Centre **A4**

25 Tenement House **B1**

26 Theatre Royal **C2**

27 Tourist Information Centre **C3**

Currie of Shettleston
85–89 Amulree Street
Glasgow G32 7UN
Tel. 041–778 1295

FIAT Glasgow

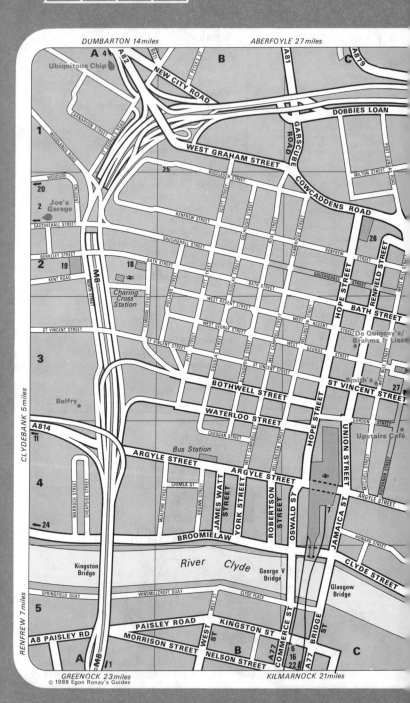

DUMBARTON 14 miles   ABERFOYLE 27 miles

A4 · A82 · B81 · ST PETER'S ST · A81 · A879 · C · A879

Ubiquitous Chip

NEW CITY ROAD

DOBBIES LOAN

CANNARVON STREET · WOODLANDS ROAD · ST GEORGE'S ROAD · GARSCUBE ROAD · PORT DUNDAS ROAD

WEST GRAHAM STREET

COWCADDENS ROAD

MILTON STREET

1

WOODSIDE CRESCENT

WOODSIDE

20

25 · BUCCLEUCH STREET · SCOTT STREET · ROSE STREET · CAMBRIDGE STREET

26

Joe's Garage

2

SAUCHIEHALL STREET

RENFREW STREET

DALHOUSIE STREET

RENFREW · STREET · RENFIELD STREET · WEST NILE STREET

BERKELEY STREET

2

19

18

BATH STREET

SAUCHIEHALL STREET

SAUCHIEHALL · STREET

KENT ROAD

NORTH STREET

M8

ELMBANK STREET

HOLLAND STREET

PITT STREET · DOUGLAS STREET · WEST CAMPBELL STREET

BATH STREET

HOPE STREET · BATH STREET

Charing Cross Station

WEST REGENT STREET

ST VINCENT STREET

WEST GEORGE STREET

WELLINGTON STREET · WEST REGENT · STREET

De Quincey's/ Brahms & Liszt

3

ST VINCENT STREET

ST VINCENT STREET

WEST · GEORGE · STREET

Smith's

ST VINCENT STREET

27

Belfry

BOTHWELL STREET

HOPE STREET

GORDON · STREET · WEST NILE STREET

A814

11

WATERLOO STREET

Upstairs Café

CADOGAN STREET

UNION STREET

MITCHELL STREET · BUCHANAN STREET

4

WARRICH STREET

CHEAPSIDE STREET

Bus Station

ARGYLE STREET

WEST CAMPBELL STREET · WELLINGTON STREET

ARGYLE STREET

ARGYLE STREET

CRIMEA ST

7

MCALPINE STREET

BROWN STREET

JAMES WATT STREET

YORK STREET

ROBERTSON STREET

OSWALD ST

JAMAICA ST

HOWARD STREET

24

BROOMIELAW

CLYDE STREET

Kingston Bridge

River Clyde

George V Bridge

Glasgow Bridge

SPRINGFIELD QUAY

WINDMILLCROFT QUAY

CLYDE PLACE

WEST ST

BRIDGE ST

5

PAISLEY ROAD

KINGSTON ST

COMMERCE ST

A8 PAISLEY RD

MORRISON STREET

WEST ST

NELSON STREET

A77

A77

6 16 22

BRIDGE ST

A

M8

1

B

C

GREENOCK 23 miles   KILMARNOCK 21 miles
© 1988 Egon Ronay's Guides

CLYDEBANK 5 miles · RENFREW 7 miles

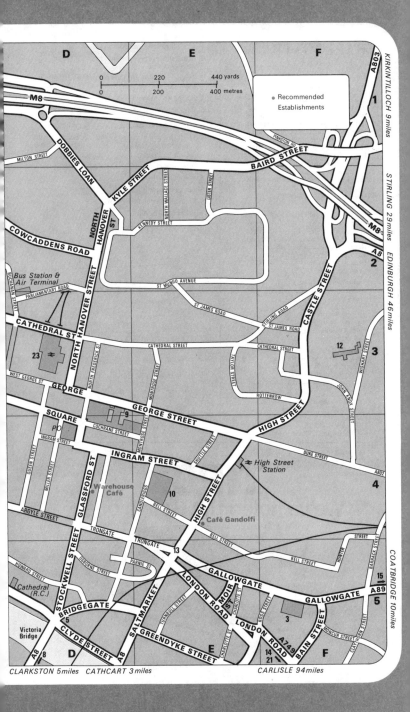

HARROGATE

Town plan opposite

Population 67,000

The Tewit Well in Harrogate was found to have healing properties in 1571 and the town developed into a spa resort as further chalbyeate and sulphur springs were discovered. Its popularity in the Victorian era is reflected in its architecture. The Royal Baths Assembly Rooms, formerly the main hydro-therapy centre, now houses traditional Turkish baths and modern sauna and solarium facilities. As well as being a historically famous spa resort, Harrogate is now a cosmopolitan conference venue.

Annual Events
International Youth Music Festival *15th-22nd April*
Spring Flower Show *23rd-25th April*
Great Yorkshire Show *14th-16th July*
Harrogate International Festival (music and drama) *29th July-12th August*
Great Autumn Flower Show *18th-19th September*

Sights Outside Town
Fountains Abbey
Ripley Castle
Newby Hall
Knaresborough
Ripon
Pateley Bridge
Brimham Rocks

Tourist Information Office
Royal Baths Assembly Rooms
Crescent Road HG1 2RR
Telephone Harrogate 525666

Fiat Dealer
Croft & Blackburn Ltd
Leeds Road
Pannal
Harrogate HG3 1EP
Tel. Harrogate 879236

1 Art Gallery and Public Library **C3**
2 Conference Centre *incorporating a 2000-seat auditorium* **B1**
3 Exhibition Centre *six halls comprising 10,000 square metres* **B2**
4 Harrogate Theatre **B2**
5 Royal Baths Assembly Rooms *originally a hydro-therapy centre, now housing the Tourist Information Centre and Turkish baths* **B2**
6 Royal Hall *when opened in 1903, an entertainment venue for those taking the waters, now a theatre* **B2**
7 Royal Pump Room Museum *containing local historical material* **B2**
8 St John's Well **E2**
9 Sun Colonnade **A2/3**
10 Tourist Information Office **B2**
11 Valley Gardens **A2**

TIPO.
We've holed the Golf in one.

To see how the Tipo beats the Golf, contact your local Fiat Dealer. See pages 84–87

Harrogate F I A T

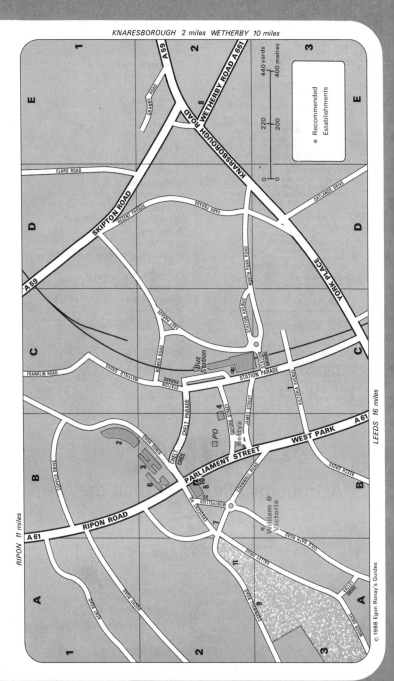

KNARESBOROUGH 2 miles WETHERBY 10 miles

RIPON 11 miles

LEEDS 16 miles

440 yards
400 metres
220
200
0

● Recommended
  Establishments

A 59
GRANBY ROAD
KNARESBOROUGH ROAD
WETHERBY ROAD A 661
CLARO ROAD
SKIPTON ROAD
REGENT PARADE
PARK PARADE
OATLANDS DRIVE
A 59
NORTH PARK ROAD
YORK PLACE
EAST PARADE
STATION AVENUE
FRANKLIN ROAD
MAYFIELD GROVE
BOWER ROAD
STATION PARADE
Bus Station
STATION BRIDGE
STATION PARADE
VICTORIA AVENUE
CHELT. PARADE
JAMES STREET
OXFORD STREET
PO
Bettys
KING'S ROAD
CHELT. CRES.
PARLIAMENT STREET
WEST PARK
A 61
BEECH GROVE
CRESCENT RD
MONTPELLIER RD
CORNWALL ROAD
RIPON ROAD
A 61
William & Victoria
COLD BATH ROAD
VALLEY DRIVE
CORNWALL ROAD
VALLEY DRIVE
MOOR DRIVE

© 1988 Egon Ronay's Guides

LEEDS

Town plan opposite

Population 748,000

Originally Loidis, a Celtic settlement, it was given its industrial send-off by a 13th-century community of monks, who practised the crafts that made the town great–notably cloth-spinning and coal-mining but the big leap came between 1775 (population 17,000) and 1831 (population 123,000).

It has taken gargantuan efforts to eliminate the excesses of unplanned industrial and population growth, but its post-war housing and roads record and industrial mix are making Leeds a prouder city. Today it can boast as much of its University and Poly, its shopping areas, parks and new estates as it has always done of its choir, cricket, rugby league, soccer and fish and chips.

Yet it is as true today as when Henry VIII's Librarian first stated it, that 'the town stondith most by clothing'.

Information Centre
19 Wellington Street
Leeds LS1 4DE
Telephone Leeds 462453/4

Fiat Dealers
JCT 600
Spence Lane
Leeds LS12 1AG
Tel. Leeds 431843

Whitehead & Hinch Ltd
South Bradgate Lane
Horsforth, Leeds LS18 4AG
Tel. Horsforth 585056

1 Adel Church *St John the Baptist 12th c* **B1**
2 Airport *Yeadon 8 miles* **B1**
3 Central Library **C2**
4 City Art Gallery **C2**
5 City Museum **C2**
6 City Station **B/C3**
7 City Varieties *'Good Old Days'* **C2**
8 Civil Theatre **C2**
9 Grand Theatre **C2**
10 International Pool **A2**
11 Kirkstall Abbey *12th c* **A2**
12 Kirkstall Abbey House Folk Museum **A2**
13 Leeds Industrial Museum **A2**
14 Leeds Parish Church **D3**
15 Leeds United F.C. *Elland Road* **C3**
16 Middleton Colliery Railway *1785, oldest in world* **C3**
17 Playhouse **B1**
18 Queen's Hall *Exhibitions* (Leeds Exhibition Centre) **C3**
19 Roman Catholic Cathedral **C2**
20 Roundhay Park **E1**
21 Rugby League and Cricket *Headingley* **B1**
22 Temple Newsam House *15th c and Park, home of Darnley, husband of Mary Queen of Scots; outstanding furniture collection* **E2**
23 Tourist Information Centre **B3**
24 University **A/B1**

TIPO.
Astronomically better than the Astra.

To see how the Tipo beats the Astra, contact your local Fiat Dealer. See pages 84–87

Leeds FIAT

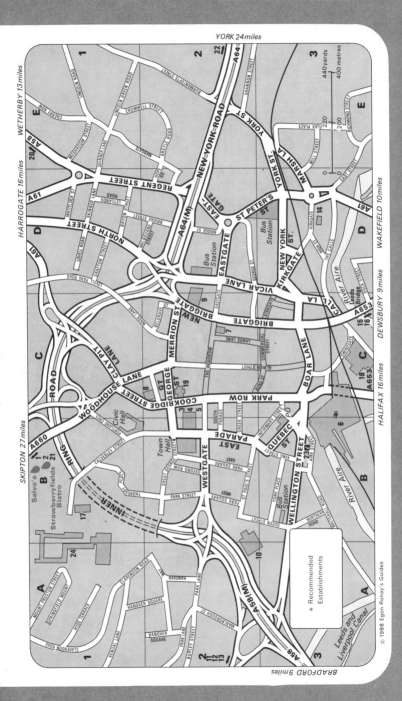

F I A T Liverpool

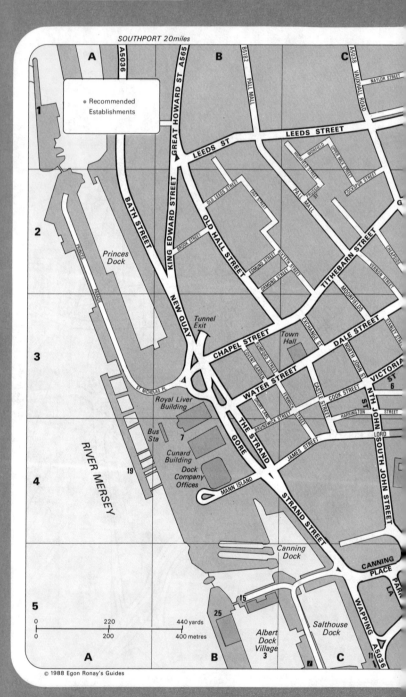

SOUTHPORT 20miles

A | B | C

Recommended Establishments

RIVER MERSEY

Princes Dock

Tunnel Exit

Town Hall

Royal Liver Building

Bus Sta

Cunard Building

Dock Company Offices

Mann Island

Canning Dock

Albert Dock Village

Salthouse Dock

CANNING PLACE

LEEDS STREET
LEEDS ST
GREAT HOWARD ST A465
KING EDWARD STREET
BATH STREET
NEW QUAY
OLD HALL STREET
CHAPEL STREET
WATER STREET
THE STRAND
GORE
STRAND STREET
DALE STREET
TITHEBARN STREET
PALL MALL
VAUXHALL ROAD
NAYLOR STREET
NORTH JOHN ST
SOUTH JOHN STREET
JAMES STREET
WAPPING A5036

0   220   440 yards
0   200   400 metres

© 1988 Egon Ronay's Guides

LIVERPOOL

Town plan on preceding page

Population 509,981

Since King John granted its Charter in 1207, Liverpool has taken increasing advantage of its sheltered Merseyside position to become England's leading Atlantic port and an industrial magnet, while the Arts are as vigorously pursued as football. The Royal Liverpool Philharmonic Orchestra, the Walker Art Gallery, the University's music-making, and the city's five theatres are at least as important to it as pop.

Annual Events
Grand National at Aintree *April*
City of Liverpool Parade *May*
Mersey River Festival *June*
Orange Day Parade *July*
Beatle Convention *August*

Sights Outside City
Aintree, Hoylake, Chester, New Brighton, Southport

Information Office
Lime Street
Liverpool 1
Telephone 051–709 3631

Fiat Dealers
Stanley Motors Ltd
243 East Prescot Road
Liverpool L14 5NA
Tel. Liverpool 228 9151

Crosby Park Garage Ltd
2 Coronation Road, Crosby
Liverpool L23 3BJ
Tel. Liverpool 924 9101

Lambert Autos Ltd
Custom House
Brunswick Business Park
Liverpool L3 4BJ
Tel. Liverpool 708 8224

1 Aintree Race-course **E1**

2 Airport **D5**

3 Albert Dock, *Shopping, business, conference centre* **B5**

4 Anglican Cathedral *20th-c Gothic, complete after 75 years* **F5**

5 Birkenhead Tunnel Entrance **D2**

6 Cavern Walks *site of Beatles' Cavern Club* **C3**

7 Cunard Building, Dock Board office and Royal Liver Building *waterfront landmarks* **B4**

8 Empire Theatre **E2**

9 Everton Football Club **E1**

10 Everyman Theatre **F4**

11 Festival Gardens and Otterspool Promenade **C5**

12 Library and Museum *Hornby library has outstanding prints and first editions. Museum houses aquarium, ivories, jewellery, birds, shipping gallery* **E2**

13 Lime Street Station **E/F3**

14 Liverpool Football Club **E1**

15 Maritime Museum **B4/5**

16 Museum of Labour History **E2**

17 Neptune Theatre **D4**

18 Philharmonic Hall **F5**

19 Pier Head **A4**

20 Playhouse Theatre **D3**

21 Roman Catholic Cathedral *space-age architecture* **F4**

22 Royal Court Theatre **E3**

23 St George's Hall *former Assize Courts and Concert Hall* **E3**

24 Speke Hall *Elizabethan house with beautiful gardens on the Mersey* **D5**

25 Tate Gallery Liverpool **B5**

26 Tourist Information Centre **E3**

27 Walker Art Gallery *England's largest collection outside London* **E2**

OXFORD

Town plan overleaf

Population 114,200

Despite the encroachment of industry, Oxford remains incomparable–except with Cambridge–as a centre of learning for 800 years, interrupted only by the disturbance of the Civil War siege in the 1640s. No city has more to offer the sightseer in its own architectural glories and the beauty of its surroundings–the Thames Valley, the Cotswolds and so much besides.

Annual Events
St Giles Fair *September*
Eights Week (5th week of University term)
Sheriff's Races *summer*

Sights Outside City
Blenheim Palace
Burford Village
Dorchester-on-Thames
Chipping Campden
Cogges Farm Museum
Cotswold Wild Life Park
Sulgrave Park
Waddesdon Manor

Information Centre
St Aldate's, Oxford OX1 1DY
Telephone Oxford 726871
Accommodation 726871
Guided Walking Tours 726871

Fiat Dealer
J. D. Barclay Ltd
Barclay House
Botley Road
Oxford OX2 0HQ
Tel. Oxford 722444

1　Apollo Theatre **C3**
2　Ashmolean Museum *art and archaeology treasures* **C2/3**
3　Bate Collection of Historical Musical Instruments **D5**
4　Botanic Garden *one of the oldest in the country* **E4**
5　Carfax Tower *viewpoint open in summer* **D4**
6　Christ Church Meadow **E5**
7　Coach Park **B4**
8　Divinity School *15th-c fine vaulted ceiling* **D3**
9　Folly Bridge **D5**
10　Martyrs' Memorial **C3**
11　Museum of History of Science **D3**
12　Museum of Oxford **D4**
13　Oxford Ice Rink **B5**
14　Oxford Information Centre **D4**
15　Oxford Story **D3**
16　Pitt Rivers Museum of Ethnology **D1**
17　Playhouse **C3**
18　Sheldonian Theatre *Wren building for conferment of degrees* **D3**
19　Station **A3**
20　Town Hall **D4**
21　University Museum **D1**
22　University Parks **D/E1**

$\boxed{F}\boxed{I}\boxed{A}\boxed{T}$ Oxford

STRATFORD-
UPON-AVON 40miles BANBURY 23m

A4144   A4165

A   B   C

1

Castle Mill Stream

St. Anne's College

Green College

WOODSTOCK ROAD

BANBURY ROAD

Somerville College

Browns

River Thames

Oxford Canal

2

Regents Pk College

ST. GILES ST.

Pusey House

Ruskin College

St. Cross College

2

Worcester College

BEAUMONT ST.   10

Randolph Hotel Lounge   17

Station   19

Bus Sta.   1

3

HYTHE BRIDGE ST.

Nuffield College

GEORGE   ST. MICHAEL'S

Munchy Munchy

SWINDON 29miles

A420   BOTLEY   ROAD   PARK   END   STREET

WORCESTER ST.

NEW   ROAD

St. Peter's College

HOLLYBUSH ROW

ST. THOMAS STREET

Caf M.O.M.

OSNEY LANE

PARADISE   STREET

CASTLE   STREET

OLD GREYFRIARS ST.

4

WEST STREET   BRIDGE STREET   EAST STREET   MILL STREET

SOUTH   STREET

OXPENS   ROAD

7

13

THAMES   SPEEDWE
ST.

River Isis

Mill Stream

TRINITY

5

• Recommended
  Establishments

River Thames   FRIARS WHARF

River Isis

A   B   C

© 1988 Egon Ronay's Guides

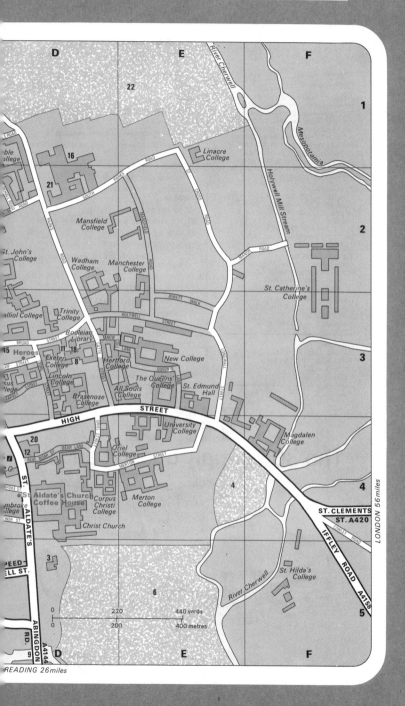

D   E   F

1

River Cherwell

Mesopotamia

22

16

Linacre College

21

SOUTH PARKS ROAD

MANSFIELD ROAD

ST CROSS ROAD

Holywell Mill Stream

Mansfield College

2

MANOR ROAD

St. Catherine's College

St. John's College

Wadham College

Manchester College

Trinity College

JOWETT WALK

HOLYWELL STREET

Balliol College

Bodleian Library

BROAD STREET

NEW COLLEGE LANE

QUEEN'S LANE

LONGWALL STREET

3

15 Heroes

11 18

8

Exeter College

Hertford College

New College

Lincoln College

esus lege

Brasenose College

All Souls College

The Queen's College

St. Edmund Hall

HIGH STREET

University College

Magdalen College

20

BEAR LANE

ORIEL STREET

Oriel College

MERTON STREET

12

BLUE BOAR ST.

4

LONDON 56 miles

ST. ALDATE'S

St. Aldate's Church Coffee House

mbroke lege

Corpus Christi College

Merton College

ST. CLEMENTS ST. A420

COWLEY ROAD

SPEED LL ST.

3

Christ Church

6

River Cherwell

St. Hilda's College

IFFLEY ROAD A4158

0   220   440 yards

0   200   400 metres

5

ABINGDON RD. A4144

9

D   E   F

READING 26 miles

FIAT GUIDE TO SIGHTS

YORK

Town plan opposite

Population 99,910

A northern bastion and trading town from Roman times, in the 8th century York became a religious and learning centre, although the present university is twenty-four years old. York's medieval wealth came from wool and monasteries, its modern prosperity from the advent of the railway, chocolate factories and tourists. Architectural gems blend the Middle Ages, pre-Reformation churches and the 18th century.

Annual Events
York Races *10th–12th May, 10th & 11th June, 8th & 9th July, 16th–18th & 31st August, 1st September, 5th, 6th & 8th October*
York Early Music Festival *July*
Historic Vehicle Rally, *Knavesmine, 11th September*

Sights Outside City
Castle Howard, Fountains Abbey, Ripley Castle, Harewood House, Knaresborough, Newby Hall (Boroughbridge), Kirkham Priory

Information Centre
De Grey Rooms, Exhibition Square, York YO1 2HB
Telephone York 621756

Fiat Dealer
Piccadilly Auto Centre Ltd
84 Piccadilly, York YO1 1NX
Tel. York 34321
Map reference **3C**

1 Art Gallery *English and European* **B1**
2 Castle Folk Museum *unique reconstruction of period street and interiors* **C3**
3 Clifford's Tower *13th-c keep* **C2/3**
4 Fairfax House *former gentleman's residence* **C2**
5 Guildhall and Mansion House **C2**
6 Impressions Gallery of Photography **C2**
7 Jorvik Viking Centre **C2**
8 King's Manor *home of monks and kings* **B1**
9 Merchant's Adventurers' Hall *timbered medieval Guild Hall* **C2**
10 Merchant's Taylor's Hall *14th-c tailors' livery* **C1**
11 Minister *chief glory of York* **C1**
12 National Railway Museum *Britain's chief collection* **A1/2**
13 Racecourse **A3**
14 Railriders World *model railway exhibition* **B2**
15 Regimental Museum **C2**
16 St Mary's Abbey *ruins* **B1**
17 Shambles *derived from 'Fleshammels' meaning 'street butchers'* **C2**
18 Station **A/B2**
19 Theatre Royal **B/C1**
20 Tourist Information Centre **C1**
21 Treasurer's House *mainly 17th-c valuable furniture and pictures* **C1**
22 University *modern architectural interest* **E3**
23 Waxwork Museum **C2**
24 York Story *exhibition of York's history and architecture* **C2**
25 Yorkshire Museum *archaeology, natural history* **B1**

TIPO.
The 309 simply doesn't add up.

To see how the Tipo beats the 309, contact your local Fiat Dealer. See pages 84–87

York F I A T

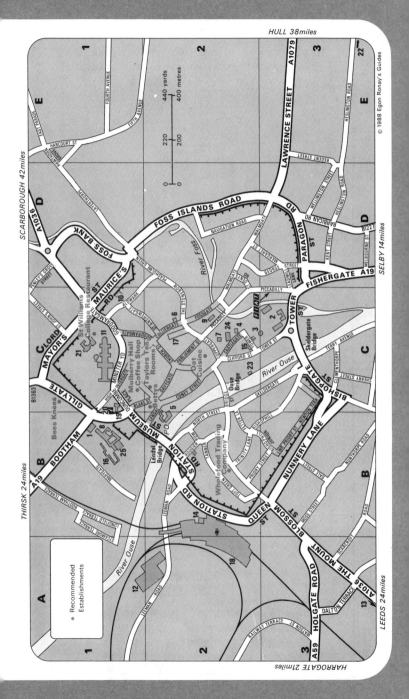

HULL 38miles

SCARBOROUGH 42miles

THIRSK 24miles

SELBY 14miles

FISHERGATE A19

LEEDS 24miles

HARROGATE 21miles

© 1988 Egon Ronay's Guides

Recommended
Establishments

Owen Meredith
1831–91

He may live without love – what is passion but pining?
But where is the man who can live without dining?
Lucile

Bennett Cerf

Good manners: The noise you don't make when you're
eating soup.
Laughing Stock (1945)

Marie Dressler

If ants are such busy workers, how come they find time
to go to all the picnics?
Cited by Cowan in *The Wit of Women*

P. B. Shelley
1792–1822

Though we eat little flesh and drink no wine,
Yet let's be merry: we'll have tea and toast:
Custards for supper, and an endless host
of syllabubs and jellies and mince pies,
And other such lady-like luxuries.
Letter to Maria Gisborne

AN·OFFER·FOR·ANSWERS
A DISCOUNT ON THE NEXT GUIDE
(For UK Residents only)

Readers' answers to questionnaires included in the Guide prove invaluable to us in planning future editions, either through their reactions to the contents of the current Guide, or through the tastes and inclinations indicated. Please send this tear-out page to us *after you have used the Guide for some time*, addressing the envelope to:

**Egon Ronay's Just a Bite Guide
City Wall House, Basing View, Basingstoke, Hampshire RG21 2AP**

As a token of thanks for your help, we will enable respondents resident in the UK to obtain the 1990 Guide post free from us at a 33⅓% discount off the retail price. We will send you an order form before publication, and answering the questionnaire imposes no obligation to purchase. All answers will be treated in confidence.

**This offer closes 30 June 1989 and is limited to
addresses within the United Kingdom.**

Please *print* your name and address here if you would like us to send you a pre-publication order form for the 1990 Guide.

Name

Address

Postcode

Please tick

1. Are you

male?		Under 21?		31–45?	
female?		21–30?		46–65?	
				over 65?	

2. Your occupation

3. Do you have any children?   Yes ☐   No ☐

4. Do you have any previous editions of this Guide?

1986 ☐   1987 ☐   1988 ☐

5. Do you refer to this Guide

four times a week?	☐	once a week?	☐
three times a week?	☐	once a fortnight?	☐
twice a week?	☐	once a month?	☐

6. How many people, apart from yourself, are likely to consult this Guide (including those in your home and place of work)?

7. Do you have our Hotel & Restaurant Guide?

1987 ☐   1988 ☐   1989 ☐

8. Do you have our Pub Guide?

1987 ☐   1988 ☐   1989 ☐

9. How many times have you travelled overseas in the past year?

10. How many nights have you spent in hotels during the past year?

11. Do you occupy more than one home? Yes [ ] No [ ]
Do you own the house you live in? Yes [ ] No [ ]

12. Your car
type _____ year _____

13. What is your daily newspaper?

14. Which of the following credit cards do you use?
Access [ ] Diners [ ]
American Express [ ] Visa [ ]

15. What fields would you like us to survey or what improvements do you suggest?

....
....
....
....
....
....
....
....
....
....
....
....
....
....
....
....
....
....
....
....
....
....

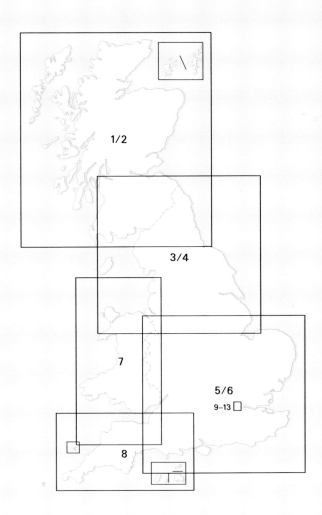

·MAP·SECTION·

1/2

3/4

7

5/6

9–13

8

Key to Maps

M1	Motorways	
A5	Primary Routes	● Wimborne Minster — Location of Guide Establishment
A50	Selected 'A' Roads	
——	County Boundaries	

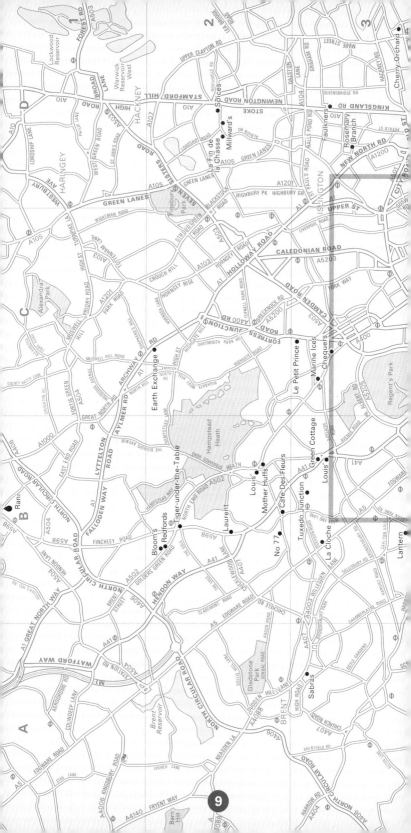

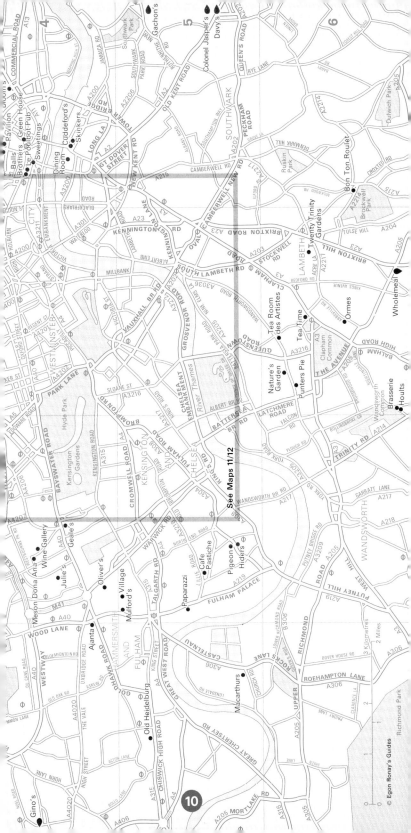

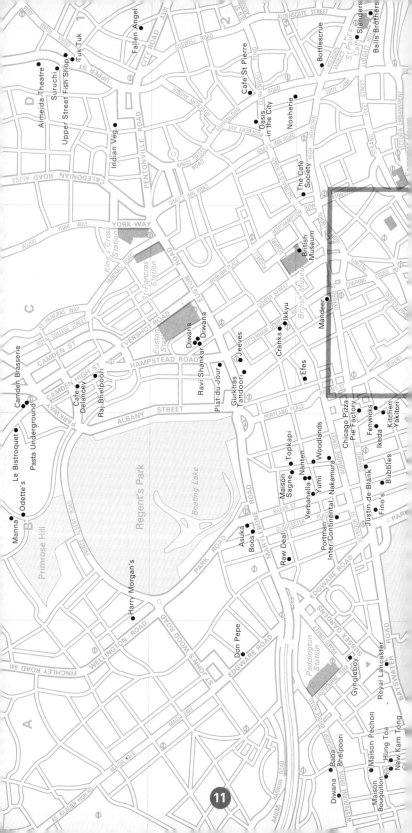

Meson Don Felipe

Methuselah's

Wilkins Natural Foods

Tapster

Carriages

L'Autre

Goring Tiles

Aspava
Athenaeum
Inn on the Park
Hard Rock
Inter-Continental

Ebury

Hyde Park
Sheraton Park Tower
Hyatt Carlton Tower

L'Express

Justin de Blank
at General
Trading Company

Chicago Rib
Shack

Maxie's
Le Metro

Harrods

Grill St Quentin

La Brasserie
Draycott's
Fifty-One Fifty-One
Charco's

Pasta Connection

Wine
Gallery

Daquise

Tui

Victoria & Albert Museum

Wine Gallery

Muffin Man

Lou Pescadou

Villa Estense

12

READER'S·COMMENTS

Please use this sheet for recommendations. *Not* restaurants offering full meals but establishments *of the type in this Guide* which serve food of **really outstanding quality**.

Your complaints about any of the Guide's entries will be treated seriously and passed on to our inspectorate, but we would like to remind you always to take up your complaint with the management at the time.

Please post to: **JUST A BITE GUIDE 1989**
Egon Ronay's Guides, City Wall House, Basing View, Basingstoke, Hampshire RG21 2AP

Name and address of establishment

Your recommendation or complaint

NB We regret that owing to the enormous volume of readers' communications received each year, we will be unable to acknowledge these forms but they will certainly be seriously considered.

NAME OF SENDER
(in block letters)

ADDRESS OF SENDER
(in block letters)

READER'S·COMMENTS

Please use this sheet for recommendations. *Not* restaurants offering full meals but
establishments *of the type in this Guide* which serve food of **really outstanding
quality**.

Your complaints about any of the Guide's entries will be treated seriously and
passed on to our inspectorate, but we would like to remind you always to take up
your complaint with the management at the time.

Please post to: **JUST A BITE GUIDE 1989**
**Egon Ronay's Guides, City Wall House, Basing View, Basingstoke, Hampshire
RG21 2AP**

NB We regret that owing to the enormous volume of readers' communications received each year, we will be unable to acknowledge these forms but they will certainly be seriously considered.

Name and address of establishment

Your recommendation or complaint

PG TIPS
JUST A BITE GUIDE

NAME OF SENDER
(in block letters)

ADDRESS OF SENDER
(in block letters)